# Web Programming

## Second Edition

# *Web Programming*

## *Building Internet Applications*

### Second Edition

**Chris Bates**
*Sheffield Hallam University*

**JOHN WILEY & SONS, LTD**

***Other Wiley Editorial Offices***

John Wiley & Sons Inc., 111 River Street, Hoboken, NJ 07030, USA

Jossey-Bass, 989 Market Street, San Francisco, CA 94103-1741, USA

Wiley-VCH Verlag GmbH, Boschstr. 12, D-69469 Weinheim, Germany

John Wiley & Sons Australia Ltd, 33 Park Road, Milton, Queensland 4064, Australia

John Wiley & Sons (Asia) Pte Ltd, 2 Clementi Loop #02-01, Jin Xing Distripark, Singapore
129809

John Wiley & Sons (Canada) Ltd, 22 Worcester Road, Etobicoke, Ontario M9W 1L1

***Library of Congress Data***

Bates, Chris (Chris D)
Web programming: building Internet applications/Chris Bates.
    p. cm.
Includes bibliographical references and index.
    ISBN 0 470 84371 3
    1.  Internet programming  2. Web sites – Design.   I. Title.

    QA176. 625. B38 2002
005.2′76 – dc21

                                    2001057382

***British Library Cataloguing in Publication Data***

A catalogue record for this book is available from the British Library

ISBN 0 470 84371 3

Produced from LaTeX files supplied by the author
Printed and bound in Great Britain by Biddles Ltd, Guildford and King's Lynn
This book is printed on acid-free paper responsibly manufactured from sustainable forestry,
in which at least two trees are planted for each one used for paper production.

# Contents

# *Preface to the Second Edition*

Since I wrote the first edition of this book much has changed on the Web, yet much has stayed the same. The Web is a fast moving medium. Content appears, may be widely use and disseminated further then suddenly disappears without trace. Web surfers have no way of guaranteeing that a site they visit today will be available tomorrow. Despite this tendency towards change many Web sites stay *in situ* for years on end, growing and evolving but always there.

A textbook isn't like a Web site. OK, that's obvious since textbooks are physical entities rather than *virtual* collections of data, but that's not what I mean. Rather I mean that books exist in a different timescale to the Web. They change much more slowly. The pace at which books change is dictated by the speed at which authors can create or amend their content, the schedules of printers or the marketing and distribution strategies of publishers. For readers and casual browsers, Web sites are often transitory. How many of us visit Web sites regularly? Those we revisit tend to be news sites where the content has a naturally short lifespan. We keep textbooks around for many years, referring back to them for new information or to refresh our memories.

A textbook about the Web must try in some way to exist in both of these timescales. On the one hand, its content has to be sufficiently accurate and useful to stand the test of time, on the other it has to keep up with the pace of change on the Web. This is a book about technologies, those which are used to create and publish Web sites. Fortunately, both for authors and readers, these change much more slowly than the content of the Web but they do change. That's why *Web Programming...* is now in its second edition. It's not that there was anything wrong with the first edition, it's just that things have moved on and the book needs to keep up.

So what's changed in the book? Well, first of all let me point out that I haven't removed anything. Everything from the first edition remains good and accurate. I have amended one or two of the sample programs for clarity and I've altered the structure slightly to emphasize important things such as the CGI.pm Perl module. What I've mostly done is to add things which I think matter. These include more JavaScript. Two years ago when I wrote the first edition the role and future of JavaScript on the Web looked insecure. Now I see it everywhere so I've given a much fuller treatment to it. Secondly I've taken a look at some interesting Perl modules which can be used to create images on the fly plus a module called HTML::Mason which massively simplifies the building of large, complex sites. Finally I've added a whole new language: PHP. This language lets developers create complex dynamic content yet its a very user-friendly and accessible language. PHP use is growing at an incredible rate and I hope I've done the language, and its developers, justice here.

The technologies of programming languages and protocols which I describe in this book tend to change through evolution not revolution. That is they alter gradually as new ideas are developed but they are almost always *backwards compatible*. A fundamental tenet of life on the Web is that if you develop a site today it will still be usable in the future regardless of how the Web changes. That might be a fundamental idea, it's also a forlorn hope. Sadly, many Web sites are developed using proprietary formats or software such as Quicktime, Flash or GIF images. These are developed by software manufacturers to do neat, useful or just plain interesting things and are often supported by browser *plug-ins*[1] What happens if in five or ten years the manufacturer has gone out of business along with all information about the data formats they created? In such cases Web sites using their ideas may continue to work but this cannot be guaranteed.

What's the alternative to proprietary software formats? The answer is Free Software[2] or *open source*. Here all information about the data structure or program including source code are openly available for anyone who wants them. The Web is based around Free Software from the networking protocols used to send data around, through HTML which is used to format Web pages to languages such as Perl and PHP which are used to create dynamic content. If there's one thing that the Web has demonstrated it is the power of openly sharing ideas. In this book I've tried to concentrate on teaching open source technologies. Sure, I digress from my principles to briefly look at Microsoft's Active Server Pages and Sun Microsystem's Java programming language. These are both important in their own right but you'll see when you read about them that they don't really give us much that we can't get elsewhere for Free.

---

[1] Pieces of software which extend the functionality of a Web browser.
[2] For information about Free Software take a look at http://www.fsf.org

## Contacting the Author

I would be delighted to hear from readers of this book. It's my first attempt. Or maybe it's now my second since there's so much additional material in this new edition. Whichever is the case, I hope it won't be the last, and I'm sure there are things that I can improve in the future. Anyone who teaches will tell you that education is a dialogue in which teacher can learn from pupil just as pupil learns from teacher. Not everything in this book will make sense; you may have problems with exercises or with changing technologies and standards. I'd be happy to discuss those things with you.

I have a Web site which contains material related to this book at:

```
http://www.shu.ac.uk/schools/cms/teaching/crb/index.html
```

which I use mostly as a way of communicating with my students. More information, exercises and errata will appear there too.

If you want to send me e-mail I'll try to respond as quickly and accurately as I can. My email address is:

```
c.d.bates@shu.ac.uk
```

CHRIS BATES

*Sheffield, UK*

# *Preface*

This book is about implementing Web sites. Take a quick look at the contents and you'll see chapters which discuss HTML 4.0, XHTML, Dynamic HTML, JavaScript, Perl, CGI scripting, PHP and more. Now look around the computing shelves of any bookshop and you'll see they're groaning under their load. Most of that load seems to be made of books which cover those same topics. The difference is that I cover them all – other authors tend to look at one subject in the tiniest detail. If you need to learn about building some Dynamic HTML then you could easily find yourself buying three or four expensive books and only using a few chapters from each.

Some people will object to the title. Dedicated Computer Scientists will contend that some of the technologies I've included aren't programming languages at all. It's undoubtedly true that HTML and XML are simply markup languages. They can't be used for any of the things that *real* programming languages can such as controlling devices or building complex systems. That's perfectly true and a point well taken... but in the real world most people think of HTML development as being in some way programming. The real world is dirty and awkward, academic theories don't always apply. Being pragmatic, potential readers will be looking for a book about Web development on the shelves under *programming*, and that's just where this one will be.

This book grew out of my experience teaching Web development at Sheffield Hallam University in the UK. My students needed a good practical book which taught them how to do the programming but left the theory to other classes. They wanted something which they could use in the laboratory over a whole semester but which didn't contain too much material that they would never use. In a series of lab classes the only information that the students wanted had to be *relevant*: they didn't have the time to work out what was important and what wasn't.

Looking at the available texts it was clear that no single volume met the needs of lecturers and students alike. Those which tried, tended to rush past the difficult subjects such as introductory Perl while laboring over easier topics such as introductory HTML. The only answer was to create a custom-made booklet which would meet my needs and those of my students, so I started writing. After a while the booklet had grown far beyond my initial vision and was turning into a book, and it kept on growing. The Web has so many important technologies which colleagues, academic reviewers and others insisted *had* to be covered. Usually I agreed wholeheartedly and where I didn't agree I was probably too open to persuasion.

This book is the result. It's a practical, hands-on sort of book which will help you to get the job done. It's suitable for use in many teaching and training situations but will also work as a teach-yourself manual. It probably won't, on its own, turn you into the world's greatest Web developer but it will certainly give you the best possible start. I hope you enjoy learning about (and using) this stuff as much as I've enjoyed writing about it.

## The Intended Audience

Let's consider the intended audience for a moment: a mixture of students and professional developers. The book is ideally suited as support to a series of practical laboratory classes at either undergraduate level or on Masters courses for non-specialists. Developers who suddenly find that they have to implement an interactive Web site using technologies which are new to them will find much in this book that is useful. A third audience is composed of those who already know a little about developing Web sites but aren't totally confident in what they're doing. Some of this group will have done a lot of HTML using WYSIWYG environments such as Dreamweaver or FrontPage and now want to understand what is happening *behind the scenes*; others will have no Web coding experience and want to start.

I assume that readers have a certain level of technical ability. A background which includes a bit of programming and some knowledge of networks and file systems would help with some of the content but neither is essential. I've tried, though, to be gentle. Each idea is introduced and explained and there are examples throughout the text that you can try out on your own.

I'll be honest right away and say that programming the Web is hard; learning about it requires patience and dedication but can be infinitely rewarding.

## Pedagogy

Pedagogy is the theory and practice of teaching. It's a word which we often use when we talk about the *way* that we teach. I've tried to incorporate a teaching method into this book.

My personal approach to teaching computer science is to give practical skills first with the theory following on behind. I don't think that students can really understand a subject unless they have tried to *do* it.

There's a lot of theory in this book but there's a lot more doing. I hope that when you have tried some of the pieces of code or worked through the exercises you'll start to ask *why* the Web works as it does. You can then go to some of the resources I've listed at the end of the book, which include just as much detail as you can handle. Once you start to really work through this book and implement the ideas within it you may notice that it's not a comprehensive resource. Each of the technologies that I discuss has been the subject of any number of thousand-page tomes. These give you absolutely all of the detail on the workings of each technology but they often lack context. In this book I've given enough detail to build all but the most complex e-commerce site. To coin a phrase, 80 per cent of programmers use just 20 per cent of the facilities in their chosen system. I've concentrated on the 20 per cent that you'll actually find a use for.

Throughout the book you'll find exercises and questions. Some involve programming and some involve thinking. Many of the thought exercises relate directly to facts taken from the text but others are more abstract. You'll be expected to wonder about the why and how of the Web. I haven't supplied any answers to the exercises. Those which involve writing code can often be answered in a variety of ways: there are no perfect programs. The thought exercises often don't *have* answers. Which leaves the factual questions. The answers to these are to be found in the text preceding the question. Giving sample answers would be like rewriting the book in ultra-brief form. If you can't answer a question that's probably a sign that you should go back and read the chapter again (and again) so that it makes sense.

Finally, some of the examples I give are simple and some are trivial. What you'll soon notice is that many apparently very complex Web sites use just these simple ideas. You'll gain more practical skills from fully understanding simple examples than from partial understanding of overly complex systems.

## Typography

I have used a number of different typefaces[3] throughout this book. Each has a particular meaning. I've also structured some parts of the book, especially definitions of code, to clarify the meaning of the content. It's important that you understand what I've done, otherwise you may end up writing code that doesn't work.

First all code is written in a `monospaced Courier` font. This is done to distinguish it from the descriptive text within the book. Here's an example of some HTML code:

---

[3]You may also see these called founts or fonts.

```
<html>
   <head>
      <title>A Minimal HTML document</title>
   </head>

   <body>
      <h2>Some text...</h2>
      <p>A sample paragraph showing formatting and
      followed by a line across the screen.
      <hr>
   </body>
</html>
```

Notice that it is clearly different from normal text. Code samples like this can be used directly in functioning programs.

Second definitions of terms appear as **bold monospaced Courier**. Again, these stand out from the text but the use of **bold** text indicates that they are *not* functional code. You cannot type the definitions straight into a program and expect them to work. Here's a definition of a typical HTML tag followed by an explanation:

**<ol [type=1|a|A|I|i] [start=n] [compact]>...</ol>**
An ordered list has a number instead of a bullet in front of each list item.

- HTML tags are all surrounded by angled brackets (< and >). Where you see these brackets used in HTML they are part of the code and must be reproduced in your programs.

- Tags which, in the jargon, *close* HTML elements always include a slash (/).

- Many HTML tags and programming constructs, have optional attributes. Because these are optional you can *choose* to use one of them if you so desire. Throughout this book these optional attributes are listed inside square brackets ( [ ] ). The square brackets are not part of the HTML code and *must* be omitted from your pages.

- Optional items in lists are always separated by short vertical lines ( | ). These lines are not part of the HTML code and *must* be omitted from your programs.

- Many of the HTML tag and style definitions include an ellipsis (...). These are used to indicate places where you should add your own text. For instance <h1>...</h1> might become <h1>A HEADING</h1> in your page.

- The letter n is used to indicate a place where you must enter a numerical value, usually in the definitions of HTML elements which have variable size, and programming functions which require parameters.

If you are unsure about the use of any of these elements try these two things.

- Look at the sample programs throughout the book and see how I've used the tags and attributes. This should give you some pointers about what you can, and cannot, do inside your HTML.

- Write some code, load it up in a browser if it's HTML or run it from the command-line if it's Perl, and see what happens. During the testing and development process, especially with HTML, very little can go seriously wrong so try things out. It won't hurt. Honestly!

## A Lesson

Everyone says that writing a book is difficult. It really is. When you write a programming book you have to check the words, the code, the images, and the diagrams. Changes have unforeseen effects. Altering a code sample leads to changes throughout the explanatory text and possibly a new screen shot. It is sometimes difficult to track what's going on. In a way I've been lucky because I haven't had to cram my writing into weekends, evenings and early mornings. I've also been able to write on many working days; after all it's part of my job as an academic.

About six weeks before the manuscript was due at the publishers I had a lot still to do on it. Then all of the parts for our new kitchen arrived and I was going to fit them myself. I now had to balance writing and teaching with joinery, plumbing, and tiling. The kitchen took longer to fit than I originally hoped but didn't interfere too much with my writing. What I learnt was that when there's lots to do, an awful lot can be done. But I wouldn't do it this way again. If I ever fit another kitchen I'll make sure I'm not writing a book at the same time!

# Acknowledgments

I am not arrogant enough to believe that this is the definitive book in its area. I *am* arrogant enough to believe that it's quite good. It's actually a whole lot better than it might have been thanks to a number of colleagues and students who passed comment on earlier iterations. I'm particularly grateful to Peter Scott for looking through the Perl, CGI, and Active Server Pages chapters and to Hugh Lafferty for his comments on the XML chapter. The Web development course on which I teach is run by Samir Al Khayatt. Samir has been a driving force for simple examples and clear explanations in my writing, for which I am, again, grateful.

Before publishers decide to publish a book they put it out to review. Anonymous academics and trainers throughout the world read an early draft and came back with literally hundreds of useful suggestions. I must particularly thank Dr. David Marshall of Cardiff University for his kind and perspicacious words. Gaynor Redvers-Mutton of John Wiley & Sons has done a great job as editor - without her the booklet would never have grown into a book. Also at Wiley Robert Hambrook has proved to be an excellent production editor on this second edition and Linda Bristow has performed valiantly as copy-editor and chief spotter of typing mistakes and other unexpected erors.

## Saving the best 'til last

Although writing a book is an essentially solitary occupation, normal life continues unabated. I'm really fortunate that my wife Julie and our daughters, Sophie and Faye, are willing to live with a writer. They let me chase strange syntax errors until 3 a.m. or spend sunny Sunday afternoons reading specification documents instead of going for a walk in the park. Their support and love has been as central to the creation of the second edition as it was to the first. It can't be said too often: Julie, Sophie and Faye I love you all.

C. D. B.

# 1
# *Introduction*

This book is an introduction to some of the basic technologies for creating and processing content on Internet Web sites. It is not meant to be a comprehensive guide to any of the areas covered, there are plenty of those available if you need them, but it should provide enough information for the majority of readers. If you find that you want more information, better tutorials or the comprehensive coverage that so many authors favor nowadays, you are directed to the computing shelves of your nearest bookshop. I have attempted to introduce a number of technologies which when combined make an interesting and user-friendly Web site. Hopefully throughout the text there are enough examples to get you started with each of them.

If you are thinking about creating a Web site then you are probably planning to use a lot of text and some images to make it lively, and possibly a sound clip or two. What about building a dynamic and interactive multimedia extravaganza? Sounds intimidating, doesn't it? Fortunately the Web now has a technology called *dynamic HTML* to help you out. It won't reduce the development workload or effort but because DHTML is increasingly being supported by popular browsers you can create leading-edge Web sites without needing to use things like plug-ins or Java applets. For those who are interested in going beyond static text I'll introduce DHTML and demonstrate simple but effective applications using a simple programming language called JavaScript.

The Web is no longer just a way of presenting information on a computer screen. Being realistic, it hasn't been for a number of years now. Many commercial sites include some way of getting information from a browser and back to their server. The usual way of doing this is by writing small programs called scripts which run on the server. The process uses a protocol called the Common Gateway Interface or *CGI* for short. Does this book cater for CGI developers? You bet it does, but to be realistic if you're going to develop any sort of CGI script then you *have* to understand at least something about programming. It's not *so* complicated that it has to be left to the people with computer science degrees and years of experience in the internals of complex programming languages like C++ or ADA, but it *is* complicated. Having said all of that, with a little bit of patience, plenty of hard work, and some thought, many people can write effective server-side scripts.

CGI scripts can be written in almost any programming language. I've chosen to use a language called Perl. It's probably not the easiest programming language but people from many different backgrounds pick it up quickly enough if they get the right support. The important thing about Perl is that it is perfectly suited to CGI scripting, although it has lots of other uses too.

Those of you interested in CGI scripting should be able to cope with the HTML and JavaScript in the book. Even if you're new to the field you can soon learn what you need to know. But you may want to add more to your site: collecting data about users, creating tailored Web pages, or accessing databases and file systems. Some of these are relatively trivial tasks, as you'll see later, others are at the complicated end of the programming spectrum. If you're keen to learn and willing to work through the examples and exercises even the hardest of these scripts should not prove too difficult.

I also look at a few technologies that are creating large waves in the Web industry. First, Microsoft is making inroads into the Web server market with two products: Personal Web Server and Internet Information Server. IIS supports a technology called Active Server Pages which lets developers include scripts in their Web pages. These scripts are processed by the server to add dynamism and complexity to a Web site.

The second important technology that I can't ignore is something called XML (Extensible Markup Language).[1] This is like HTML after a trip to the gym,[2] it's a way of formatting almost any data so that many applications can handle it. And, fortuitously it just happens that Microsoft's Web browser Internet Explorer 5 is one of those applications. With XML, data from spreadsheets, reports, databases, or even applications like CAD packages can be displayed on Web sites. It can be amended and stored in a variety of ways.The computer industry has been looking out for something like XML for a long time. In this book I'll give you a taste of what it is and how it can be used and show you a few scripts that let you add the power of XML to your Web site.

Thirdly, there's PHP. This is a free, open-source solution which works a little like Active Server Pages. PHP works with any Web server but can be optimized to run with Apache using an extension to that server. The interesting thing about PHP is that its growth has happened almost unnoticed by the wider computing community. It's rarely mentioned in the media, yet it's used by millions of sites around the World. PHP is an underground phenomenon which just can't be ignored.

If you go into any technical bookshop you'll see shelves full to overflowing with books about developing for the World Wide Web. You can learn to develop HTML using any

---

[1]For much more information on creating and using XML see Chapter 14.
[2]OK, not really, although the analogy will do for now.

number of graphical tools, create dynamic pages using code libraries supplied on the CD-ROM that is inevitably inserted into the back of the book, and even use the primitive CGI scripts they include. Why did I bother to write a guide to topics which are so comprehensively covered in these hundreds of books from all of the main publishing houses? And why should you read this rather than use free sources of information such as Web sites?

Many reasons leap to my mind:

- Web sites have a tendency to be inaccurate, incomplete or to disappear just as quickly as they appear;

- published books are either too large and provide much irrelevant information or too brief to be useful;

- perhaps most importantly I have been able to closely couple the reading material, exercises, and self-study questions and focus them all on what I regard as important for beginners.

When I sat down to write this book it seemed an impossible task, partially because the book was going to try to cover a variety of complex topics, and attempt to put information across in a sensible and friendly manner. As I write this introduction I have finished most of the content and the whole experience has been relatively painless. That is undoubtedly because I knew the topic areas well before I started writing, but it's also because I've not let myself get bogged down in too much detail. You'll find some pretty fearsome code in the sections on Perl, PHP and CGI, especially if you're a novice programmer, but compared to the intricacies of the code shown in many dedicated Perl programming books it is actually quite pleasant and user-friendly.

Chapter 18 gives you the chance to implement a large system based around an imaginary problem. You can cherry-pick the parts that you choose to do: for instance you may not have access to CGI and database facilities. Whichever part(s) you try should give you a feel for what Web development is all about today. And before anyone asks, no, I don't have a sample solution. There are as many correct (and good) Web sites for any customer as there are developers building those sites.

One more thought, don't dive straight into the most complex parts. Each of the main chapters has some exercises to help you *learn*. Once you've done the learning you'll be able to apply your new knowledge, but not before. That's obvious when someone says it, but take a look around the Web. It's a mess of broken links, bad coding, and sites that are permanently *under construction*. It's better to know what you're doing, take your time over it and produce an exemplary Web site than to rush in and create something quick but dirty. Surveys suggest that Web sites, especially commercial ones, have just one chance to attract surfers. Make the most of that chance and you'll get repeat visits. If you are building business sites then repeat visits equal repeat sales. Customer loyalty starts from that first ever download.

## 1.1 HTML, XML, AND THE WORLD WIDE WEB

What is HTML and what is it for? First of all, the acronym HTML means *Hypertext Markup Language*. HTML is a method of describing the format of documents which allows them to be viewed on computer screens. HTML documents are displayed by Web browsers, programs which can navigate across networks and display a wide variety of types of information. HTML pages can be developed to be simple text or to be complex multimedia extravaganzas containing sound, moving images, virtual reality, and Java applets. Most Internet Web pages lie somewhere along that continuum, being mostly text but with a few images to add interest and variety.

The Internet is a global phenomenon which can provide documents from servers across the world to browser clients which can be in any location. If documents are to be readily exchanged across such a vast and complex network, some sort of global protocol is required which allows that information to be viewed anywhere.

The global publishing format of the Internet is HTML. It allows authors to use not only text but also to format that text with headings, lists, and tables, and to include still images, video, and sound within the text. Readers can access pages of information from anywhere in the world at the click of a mouse-button. Information can be downloaded to the reader's own PC or workstation, printed out or e-mailed on to others. HTML pages can also be used for entering data and as the front-end for commercial transactions.

It's probably also worth briefly mentioning what HTML isn't. It's not a programming language – you can't write an HTML program and expect anything to happen. It's not a data description language – the HTML that you write won't tell anyone anything about the structure of your data, although XML will add those capabilities should you choose to use them. Finally HTML isn't really very complicated – although the creators of WYSIWYG authoring tools would like you to think that it is.

> Note:
> Using HTML forces a separation between content and formatting. You can readily change how your pages will look without having to change what they say.

## 1.1.1 A Little Bit of History

The idea of hypertext and hyperlinked documents has been around for a while. In order to be practical it required the implementation of a number of technologies which began to come together in the 1980s, an early example being the HyperCard information management system from Apple. HTML itself was developed by Tim Berners-Lee when he worked at CERN, the European center for particle physics. The phenomenal success of HTML as a format was due to the Mosaic browser developed at NCSA, the US super-computing center, and the simplicity of the language itself.

Mosaic was the result of a US government funded research project and was distributed free of charge. Much of the functionality that we now see in the Netscape Navigator browser in particular, has evolved directly from the early Mosaic browser so that, although Mosaic itself is no longer in development, its influence lives on.

HTML is an application of something called SGML, the Standardized General Markup Language. SGML grew from a number of pieces of work, notably Charles Goldfarb, Edward Mosher and Raymond Lorie at IBM who created a General Markup Language in the late 1960s. In 1978 The American National Standards Institute (ANSI) set up a committee to investigate text processing languages. Charles Goldfarb joined that committee and lead a project to extend GML. In 1980 the first draft of SGML was released and after a series of reviews and revisions became a standard in 1985.

The use of SGML was given impetus by the US Department of Defense. By the early 1970s the DoD was already being swamped by electronic documentation. Their problem arose not from the volume of data, but from the variety of mutually incompatible data formats. SGML was a suitable solution for their problem – and for many others over the years.

Many people mistakenly believe that the Internet and World Wide Web are the same thing. In fact the Internet has been growing for a long time and supports a number of TCP/IP based protocols. Standards exist for sending e-mail (SMTP), Usenet news (NNTP), and file transfer (FTP), alongside a variety of indexing and searching mechanisms such as Gopher and Archie.[3] The 1990s has seen explosive growth in the use of networked computing and the Internet, based in large part upon the growth of homepages on the Web. These homepages are attractive to authors and readers because they are written in HTML and can be formatted in a wide variety of appealing ways.

To be successful the Web depends on Web page authors and browser vendors sharing the same conventions for HTML. Commercial vendors such as Netscape (e.g. frames) and Microsoft (e.g. banners) have attempted to develop proprietary tags so that certain text formatting can only be seen on their browser. Such developments are both unwelcome and unlikely to succeed against the libertarian and anarchic framework of the Web. Where a development is seen to be both popular and widely useful, such as Netscape's frame tag or some of Microsoft's Dynamic HTML developments, it will be accepted into a revision of the HTML standard. Where tags are either too system specific or lack technical merit they tend to fall into disuse. There is little point developing a Web site using fancy formats which visitors cannot see with their browser.

HTML standards[4] are created by a group of interested organizations and individuals called W3C. There have now been three official HTML standards: version 2.0 was released in 1994 and remains the baseline for backwards compatibility and should be supported by all browsers and authoring tools; version 3.2 was released in 1996 with many useful

---

[3]Now both *very* obsolete.
[4]W3C calls these standards *recommendations*.

additions; version 4.0 was ratified towards the end of 1997 and slightly amended in late 1999. Although many books have been published based around the HTML 3.0 specification this version was never officially released by W3C. When you create your new documents try to stick to using HTML 4.0 – all of the major browsers will soon support it and relatively few Web surfers use the older versions of browsers.

> Note:
> The HTML 4.0 specification document from W3C says:
>
> > ...HTML documents should work well across different browsers and platforms. Achieving interoperability lowers costs to content providers since they must develop only one version of a document. If the effort is not made, there is much greater risk that the Web will devolve into a proprietary world of incompatible formats, which will ultimately reduce the Web's commercial potential for all participants.

HTML has been developed so that a wide variety of client systems should be able to use information from the Web: PCs and workstations with graphics displays of varying resolution and color depths; cellular telephones; handheld devices; devices for speech for output and input; computers with high or low bandwidth; and cable-television systems. Authors, especially those developing commercial Web sites need to be aware of all these. Excluding anyone from using a site means excluding customers – fancy Web pages are very nice but surely counter-productive if they lead to a smaller growth in the customer base than might have been expected. Having said that, there's no excuse for ignoring the standards. If authors had not implemented the new tags as they were ratified by W3C we wouldn't have tables and forms, or stylesheets, or a myriad of other useful formats. The whole Web surfing experience would surely be poorer for these omissions.

## 1.1.2 XML: The Future of the Web

HTML has, literally, changed the way that we look at and present information. There is now a clear distinction between content and format and new rules for designing and laying-out content are evolving. It is now clear that images, still or moving, and sound can become part of the reader's experience and yet HTML is unsatisfactory in a number of ways:

- advanced Web sites which rely upon the latest tags or use scripting and programming languages to animate the Web page are unusable by many people with disabilities,

- the Web remains largely the preserve of people using the English alphabet. More support is required for different character sets and for different approaches to document preparation,

- many types of content cannot be expressed in conventional alphabets. Most mathematics and much hard science and engineering require different notations. These need to be processed in different ways to conventional text and often cannot be included in HTML documents except as inline images.

Fortunately the limitations of HTML have been widely recognized and are being solved. The most important of the solutions is XML, *Extensible Markup Language* which is a grammer[5] for creating other markup languages. The power of XML comes from allowing Web designers to specify their own tags to meet their own needs. A site developer who uses a unique data type or wants to express a particular idea in a Web page can create their own specification and use it in on the Web.

Here's a quick example showing how XML includes lots of information which is lost when HTML is used:

**HTML**

```
<h1>Car</h1>
<h2>Make</h2>
<p>Ford Mustang
<h2>Seats</h2>
<p>5
<h2>Top Speed</h2>
<p>70 m.p.h.
```

**XML**

```
<h1>Car</h1>
<make>Ford Mustang</make>
<seats>5</seats>
<speed units="mph">70</speed>
```

Browsers have recently started to appear which support XML. Microsoft lead the field here with Internet Explorer, which is in version 5 as I write. This has good support for XML and in fact its parser is available for use by other applications. XML may soon become a ubiquitous data format on the PC desktop.

The W3C consortium has already specified a markup language which can be used to express and format mathematical expressions, and other markup grammars are available for multimedia and for describing chemical structures. Combining these markup languages with stylesheets and scripting provides a powerful set of tools, especially for developers inside large organizations. Much complex data can now be presented inside Web pages for consumption either internally or for use by those outside the organization.

HTML is also changing. A new standard has just been agreed called XHTML. This brings together the strict rules applied to XML markup and conventional HTML tags. Section 3.5 provides a brief guide to converting your HTML 4 Web page into XHTML. This is important because the intention is that all browsers and servers will move to supporting XHTML. HTML is not compliant with the XHTML standard in a number of ways but with care it *can* be.

### 1.1.3 Hypertext

As the name suggests, hypertext is more than simply text. Text is two-dimensional and linear; it flows from one place to another. The meaning that we extract from text is often multi-dimensional, with the words that we read able to trigger associations or set us off

---

[5] A set of rules.

on tangential thoughts. Many novelists, poets, and playwrights have tried to place the multiple dimensions of meaning directly into the text. Whether authors such as Thomas Pynchon or William S.Burroughs succeed as they de-construct the novels they write, while writing them, is a matter of debate. What is obvious is that their techniques cannot usefully be applied to non-fiction material where clarity of meaning and intent is so important.

Factual material is definitely non-linear and seeks to break out of its two constraining dimensions. Factual material can break boundaries and make new connections for readers: some of you will have read the previous paragraph and wondered what I was writing about and why I was bothering; others will be intrigued by the references to Pynchon and Burroughs and will want to seek out more information; while anyone who has read and enjoyed *Gravity's Rainbow* or *Junkie* may be inspired to read those works instead of this!

Hypertext lets the author add diversions and dead-ends into a piece of work. If this were a hypertext document I would have been able to include links to pieces about Pynchon or theories of writing. Anyone inspired to go down one of those diversions could easily have done so. This is a technical document and there will be many occasions on which I will want to explain terms and ideas in more detail but to do so would break the narrative flow. If I include such explanations they will be footnotes to the main page, which may reduce their significance. In a hypertext document I would be able to divert interested readers towards peripheral, yet important, information.

Conventional academic or technical writing includes a bibliography so that the keener reader knows where to look for more information. A hypertext document can include a link directly to those sources. In effect such links can be used to include many documents within one framework.

The final benefit of hypertext is that it lets the author create links within a document. Often when reading technical books meanings, ideas, and links occur to the reader. To follow up such ideas the reader has to search back through the whole book to find the information needed to complete a thought. With the modern computer textbook weighing in at around the 800 page mark, looking for a single paragraph becomes nearly impossible, even if a good index has been included.

> Rule of Thumb:
> When done well, hypertext is a powerful aid to presenting, finding and using information. When done badly it can obscure meaning, mask content, and make documents unusable.

### 1.1.4 Styles versus Formatting

Anyone who has used a WYSIWYG[6] word processor for any significant document preparation has at some point formatted text. When many people use a word processor they

---

[6]What You See Is What You Get: screen content is formatted as exactly as possible to the printed version.

re-enter the formatting information each time that they use it. This is time-consuming and can easily lead to inconsistencies, especially in large documents. A much more effective way of formatting text is to use styles. A style is a set of formatting commands which can be applied to any text. For instance the style of a paragraph in a word processor might be:

- font: 10 point Arial,
- text fully justified,
- indent left 2cm,
- line-spacing 1.5 lines,
- 12 point space after paragraph.

By highlighting text and applying a style to it I can easily use lots of formatting information at the same time. If I decide that I prefer a Times New Roman font to the Arial, I can alter the entire text of the document simply by changing the way that the style is set up. This will work without affecting the formatting of other elements such as headings or footnotes.

HTML presents text in a very different way. The page author simply specifies which style should be used for a piece of text but has no control over how that text will actually appear. This approach to formatting has been used for quite a number of years on text-processing systems such as UNIX groff, nroff, TeX, and LaTeX. Sections of the document are surrounded by macro commands which specify what style is required but not how that style should look. The actual styles are formatted separately in *macro* packages. This allows a certain degree of flexibility in the formatting of the text as the same document can be made to look radically different simply by using a different macro package. This approach particularly appeals to scientists, who may submit a paper to a number of conferences or journals knowing that they can easily format it to suit the style of whichever one accepts their work for publication.

In fact, this book was prepared using LaTeX and I made very few creative efforts to format the text. I relied upon the pre-existing sets of formatting commands that came with the LaTeX distributions I use. I simply decide that something is a paragraph and the system will try its best to typeset a beautiful paragraph for me.

Some of the more highly configurable browsers actually allow the reader of the document to change the way that the different styles look. Thus, formatting is controlled more by the reader than the author. Later we will examine stylesheets, a method by which authors can provide absolute formatting information.

It is important that users can define how text styles are presented by their browser because of the accessibility issues that I've already, briefly, mentioned. Many people who use computers to view documents have visual problems of different types. It is important that they can adjust the look of text so that they can actually read it. Sometimes even those who do not have such impairments will want to reconfigure a style for their own reasons, they may find the default style lacking in æsthetic pleasure or, more commonly, the background, colors and images make a particular configuration unusable.

> Rule of Thumb:
> Formatting is best achieved through the use of styles. Where absolute format-
> ting, such as choosing individual fonts within the text, is used, authors should be
> careful about readability and æsthetics.

### 1.1.5 Relative Positioning

The HTML approach to styles is carried over into the positioning of material on the screen. As each object is placed on the screen it is placed relative to items already placed or to any containers such as frames or tables which might be holding the item. The WYSIWYG approach places objects in an absolute position on the page, within reasonable constraints. HTML browsers cannot know the structure of the whole document in advance. HTML documents arrive in pieces, separately, across the network and those pieces can only be placed once they and surrounding sections have arrived. A word processor has the whole of the document available before it starts to place items onto the page.

An additional problem for HTML browsers is that the position an item can take on the screen depends upon the area available to the browser. A browser may be using the whole screen or only a small part of it. The location of items depends upon the area available for viewing.

> Rule of Thumb:
> Whenever possible use relative rather than absolute positioning. Let the viewing
> software perform the page layout: it's designed to do just that and is likely to be
> better at it than you.

### 1.1.6 HTML Authoring Tools

There are many tools available to help in the creation of HTML documents. Some of these are useful to all authors, especially tools which create image maps, identify the hexadecimal values of colors or combine individual GIFs into moving images. There is another category of tool which I regard as less helpful. These are the programs which are used to write actual HTML. These tend to operate exactly like typical PC word processors. The user enters text and then selects a style to apply to that text. Tools usually let the author add hyperlinks and images by entering data in popup boxes.

The more sophisticated authoring programs provide preview facilities which purport to show how the finished page will look. Unfortunately HTML is not a WYSIWYG system, it can't be for the reasons outlined on page 10. Therefore the best that automated tools can provide is a sort of What You See Is What You *Might* Get. The tools must make assumptions about what you are trying to achieve.

Of course software developers are always trying to improve their products. HTML authoring tools are no exception. Tools such as FrontPage from Microsoft and Dreamweaver from Macromedia bear little relation to the editors of even a couple of years ago. They include good support for scripting languages such as JavaScript, and have libraries of scripts than can be used *straight out of the box*. In many circumstances, such as when creating the typical Web *homepage*, an authoring tool is more than adequate. However, there are a number of good reasons for learning all about HTML even if you mostly use a tool.

For straightforward Web sites an authoring tool will usually provide acceptable HTML, but not always. These tools can only be as good as their developers and can make mistakes. The question then arises of how the code can be corrected: the tools can't be used to correct the broken code because it was the tool which broke the HTML in the first place. You can leave the code as it is – large areas of the Internet are littered with broken HTML. If you understand HTML then you have the knowledge to examine the code and correct any mistakes that the tool made. Of course this leaves the problem of what happens when your corrected version of the code is loaded back into your WYSIWYG editor. The code may be rejected, flagged up as incorrect, or automatically adjusted back into the broken format that the editor expects. Frankly the process is fraught with potential pitfalls.

If you try to write more complex Web sites, possibly using frames or tables to format the site, then an automated tool is not usually going to be of any use. Your apparently simple desire to use a different format is likely to fall outside of the parameters that the editor finds acceptable. Don't despair though: as this book shows, HTML is fairly simple and you can build complex sites quite easily with a bit of practice.

For anyone who is going to build a truly dynamic Web site there is no alternative to writing HTML by hand. Dynamic sites use CGI scripts or Active Server Pages to actually build the pages on the server. These are then sent to the browser and may be unique for every user on every visit to the site. On static sites the pages are simply stored on a server and always look the same. You might wonder what the point of building pages dynamically is. Well, it gives users a more *personal* experience. You might build a large site in which users can choose to see only links to topics that interest them; your site might be commercial, with order forms, or you might have so much data that creating static pages is impractical. In all of these cases writing scripts which run on the server is your only option.

### 1.1.7 MIME Types and Multimedia Content

In the early days of HTML the content of Web pages was simply text based. Support for the viewing of still images began to be incorporated in one of the early versions of the Mosaic browser and since 1993 there has been development in moving the Web towards a fully multimedia environment. Web pages can now contain any of the following (incomplete) list:

- text that is formatted, colored, and structured
- still images in any graphics format

- sound
  - typically as WAV or AU files
  - MIDI files
  - CD quality audio stored in MPEG compressed format
- moving images
- animated GIFs
  - QuickTime movies made using Apple technology
  - MPEG compressed video
  - Shockwave movies created using Director from Macromedia
- files for download using file transfer protocol
- Java applets

How, then, does the browser recognize the type of data it is receiving, and having recognized it how does it process the data correctly? The answer is MIME.

### 1.1.7.1 *Multipurpose Internet Mail Extensions*

The solution to recognizing and handling file types is not Web specific; in fact, Web browsers use a technology which was around for a number of years before HTTP [7] was designed. In the 1980s scientists at Carnegie-Mellon University in the USA recognized that e-mail users wanted to share more than plain text files. File sharing had always been done via FTP with the sender uploading the file onto an FTP site and then e-mailing the IP address of that server to the recipients. They would use FTP to download the file from the FTP server. This was not an ideal solution as it relied upon both sender and receiver having sufficient computer knowledge to cope with command-line FTP.

MIME simplifies the process. The formatted file is attached to the e-mail and when the server transmits the message it also sends information about the type of the attached file. The receiving software uses this type information to handle the attachment. For instance if the attachment was compressed using GNU-zip, the mail program would launch GNU-zip to uncompress the message.

Web browsers do exactly the same thing. When they get a MIME-compliant file they decode the MIME information and use it either to process the file themselves or to launch an external application to process the data for them.

### 1.1.7.2 *Helper Applications*

The actual Web browser can process only a limited range of data types. It can display images in GIF, JPG, PNG, or XBM formats, cannot process sound, and has no compression utilities. Therefore to process almost any multimedia data the browser needs some help. This is provided by helper applications and plug-ins. Helper applications are ordinary programs such as PKZIP or the Microsoft Windows media player which the browser can call upon for help.

---

[7]Hypertext Transfer Protocol

Plug-ins are small applications which handle specific data types and which may either run as stand-alone applications or embedded within the browser. Generally when a software house devises a new multimedia type for the Web it will sell the authoring tool but give away the viewer for free. This is done for good commercial reasons: the easiest way to get authors to use the format is to make viewing the data easy for readers. Similarly once authors adopt a format it is important that readers can quickly, and cheaply, acquire the means to view their pages.

The free viewer model was developed by Adobe with their Portable Document Format tools Acrobat, the authoring tool, and Acrobat Reader, the viewer. Although authors must pay to buy tools to create PDF documents anyone can download the document viewer free of charge. In fact the Adobe PDF viewer is given away on the cover disks of many computer magazines.

Plug-ins are available for all of the popular data types such as QuickTime and Shockwave. Some data types which require plug-ins are international standards. An example of this is the MPEG series which specify compression for video and audio. A range of freeware, shareware, and try-before-you-buy tools are available from Internet sites for creating, editing, and using MPEG data. The ready availability of such tools has led to the increasing popularity of these formats, especially MP3, which is being used on many Internet sites to supply CD quality music from a variety of sources.

## 1.2 EXERCISES

1. Briefly outline the early history of the World Wide Web.

2. Can you think of three advantages to using a common data format such as XML? What about some disadvantages?

3. What are the main Internet application protocols?

4. What is the role of the W3C?

5. List some reasons for using hypertext when creating technical documentation.

6. Why are organizations such as W3C so keen to emphasize the separation of data and its formatting?

7. Compare and contrast relative and absolute positioning of content.

8. While HTML authoring tools may aid the beginner they can create more problems than they solve. Why are such tools almost inevitably obsolete as soon as they appear?

9. What is MIME?

10. Assess the validity of the following statement:

    Within 50 years the era of the printed word will be over. On-line presentation, multi-media data, virtual reality worlds, and as yet undreamt of new technologies will have too many advantages. The printed book cannot survive.

# 2
# *Hypertext Markup Language*

## 2.1  BASIC HTML

HTML is pretty straightforward when you consider the powerful and complex applications that it can be used to build. The basic principle when using HTML is that you take some content, usually a mixture of text and images, and then apply formatting information to it. The Web browser uses that formatting information to correctly process the content. The processing may take the form of display on the screen, sending it to a printer or reading the page to a visually impaired user. That's just like word processing really, the big difference being that we can directly edit the formatting information *in situ*. In a word processor the formatting information is done through special control codes which are not legible to, or suitable for editing by, humans. Web documents may contain hyperlinks to other documents. Again these are entered as simple plain text. All of the complex processing is performed by the browser once it has downloaded the Web page. In this chapter I'll show you how to write HTML to create well-structured Web pages.

The most primitive Web pages contain just text, possibly with a few hyperlinks. You'll still see sites around the Web which are formatted just as pages were in the mid 1990s. These sites are often trying to impart information and their developers regard presentation as a secondary attribute. I think of such markup as basic HTML – the sort of thing that we were writing before the Web became interactive and multimedia. I'll describe some of the more visual parts of HTML later but let's start off by learning about the simplest types of Web page.

## 2.1.1 Tags

Any formatted text document is composed of a set of elements such as paragraphs, headings, and lists. Each element has to be surrounded by control information which tells the presentation or printing software when to switch on a piece of formatting and when to switch it off. In HTML formatting is specified by using *tags*. A tag is a format name surrounded by angle brackets. End tags which switch a format off also contain a forward slash. For instance, the following example sets the text to the style H1 and switches that style off before processing any more of the document:

```
<h1>Text in an H1 style</h1>[1]
```

A number of points should be noted about HTML tags:

- tags are delimited by angled brackets: <h1>;

- they are not case sensitive: <HEAD>, <head>, and <hEaD> are equivalents;

- styles must be switched off by an end tag. There are a few exceptions to this rule[2], their differences will be noted in their descriptions;

- some characters have to be replaced in the text by *escape sequences*. If < was not *escaped* the software would attempt to process anything that followed it as part of a tag. Therefore if you want to include such a character in your code you must replace it with the escape sequence. There is more on all of this in Section 2.3;

- white space, tabs, and newlines are ignored by the browser, they can be used to make the HTML source more readable without affecting the way that the page is displayed. Actually they're not ignored, but multiple white spaces are replaced by a single space while newlines and tabs are treated as spaces;

- if a browser doesn't understand a tag it will usually ignore it.

## 2.1.2 Structure of an HTML Document

All HTML documents follow the same basic structure. They have a head which contains control information used by the browser and server and a large body. The body contains the content that displays on the screen and tags which control how that content is formatted by the browser. The basic document is:

```
<html>
    <head>
        <title>A Minimal HTML document</title>
    </head>

    <body>
```

---

[1]See the preface details of typefaces used in this book, and their meanings.
[2]End tags became compulsory with the creation of XHTML, see Section 3.5 for more information.

```
    <h1>The Largest Heading</h1>
    <p>A sample paragraph showing formatting and
    followed by a line across the screen.</p>
    <hr>
  </body>
</html>
```

Despite its simplicity, this document needs a little explaining for novices. The entire document is surrounded by `<html>...</html>` which tell the software that it is now processing HTML. Most Web browsers can display a number of types of content. At the very least they are able to display plain text and HTML. If the page were not enclosed in `html` tags the page might be displayed as plain text with both content and formatting information on display. Web browsers are very tolerant pieces of software, if you omitted these the browser would start to read the file and when it came across something like HTML tags it would switch into HTML mode. Magically your badly formed page would display as you intended.

> Rule of Thumb:
> Although current versions of Web browsing software are tolerant of errors, future versions are not guaranteed to behave in the same way. If you want the pages you create to be viewed in the future make sure that you format your content according to the W3C recommendations.

The Web page has `<head>...</head>` and `<body>...</body>` sections. All of these tags are compulsory in all HTML documents that you write because of their central role in structuring the page.

### 2.1.2.1  *Commenting Your Pages*

Programmers are always encouraged to document their code through the use of *comments*. A programmer might create a working program today, see it used for months or years and then have to make changes to it. Many programming languages are fairly cryptic and if the program is complex even the original author can struggle to understand what the code is meant to do. Programming languages include a mechanism called the comment that lets developers write plain text inside their code files. This plain text is used to describe what the program does and, sometimes, how it works. It's a good idea to add comments to your HTML files. Possibly they are not needed when you're writing simple pages but they certainly are when you start to introduce some of the advanced ideas shown in this book such as JavaScript, styles and multiple layers.

Comments in HTML documents are the same as those used by SGML. Comment tags start `<!` and end with `>`. Each comment can contain as many lines of text as you like. If the comment runs over a number of lines, each must start and end with `--` and must not contain `--` within its body. Here's an example:

```
<! -- this is a comment --
-- which is continued --
```

```
-- here -- >


<! ---- >
```

Comments can be placed in either the head or body of your documents, although it seems sensible to use them as near to the feature you're describing as possible. Good practice in programming is to use comments to describe *what* the code does rather than *how* it works. A programmer might modify the way that the code performs at a later date but they will still want the same outcome from it.

Here's one idea that you can use even as a novice HTML developer. In the head of your documents include some simple *version control* information. Software developers often place some comments which give:

- the name of the application,

- a description of the purpose of the code in the file,

- the name of the author,

- the original creation date,

- a version number,

- copyright information.

I would advise you to get into the habit of doing the same thing in your Web pages. I suggest placing this information into the head section simply because it is about the file and is not intended to be displayed within the browser. Here's an example:

```
<html>
   <head>
      <title>Bill Smiggins Inc.</title>

      <!-- Version Information --
      -- File: index.html --
      -- Author: Chris Bates --
      -- Creation: March 17th, 2001 --
      -- Description: This is the introductory page on the --
      -- new corporate Web site. The layout by Chris Bates --
      -- Copyright: All material on this page is copyright --
      -- Bill Smiggins Inc. For more information see --
      -- document BS_copy03v2.Doc --
      -->

   </head>
   <body>
      <h1>Bill Smiggins Inc.</h1>
      <h2>About our Company...</h2>
```

```
      <p>This Web site provides clients, customers,
      interested parties and our staff with all of the
      information that they could want on our products,
      services, success and failures.</p>
   </body>
</html>
```

### 2.1.3   The Document Head

This is a brief introduction to the document head. More detail is given in Section 3.4. The document head holds control information to be used by browsers and servers. When you're just starting to write Web pages you really don't need to know what that information is, or how it is used. Actually many people never use any of the head tags except for `title` which is mandatory. As you browse the Web take a look at the source code of a few pages. You're more than likely going to find that where control information is provided it was placed there by a WYSIWYG editor without the author knowing!

The only tag that most authors insert in their head sections is the title.

**`<title>...</title>`**
    All HTML documents have just one title which is displayed at the top of the browser window. The title is also used as the name in bookmark files and on search engines.

To see the effect of the `title` tag look at the example of a simple Web page in Section 2.1.2.


## 2.2   THE DOCUMENT BODY

I'm going to concentrate on the most commonly used, or useful, tags here. There are other tags and plenty of sources of information describing how to use them. If you need more detail I'd advise you to go to those sources.

### 2.2.1   Blocks

In HTML, documents are structured as blocks of text, each of which can be formatted independently. A block has no meaning outside of a particular document. When you format some text as, for instance, an h2 heading, you are simply telling the browser what combination of font and color it should apply to the text. You are *not* defining something which can be used in searching or in creating indices. This is radically different to using a word processor. In that application when you describe something as a level two heading you are saying something about its role within the document. Word processors use information about things such as heading levels in their tools for outlining and the creation of tables of contents. When you read Section 3.5 you'll discover that this is gradually changing as the

HTML recommendation evolves into something which has wider applicability than simple Web page formatting.

The two major blocks of text in HTML documents are the paragraph and the heading. Almost all text and images in your documents will be part of either a heading or a paragraph. The exceptions are lists and tables which we'll consider later.

```
<p [align="left"|"center"|"right"]>...</p>
```
Most text is part of a paragraph of information. Every paragraph has to be explicitly tagged within the source of the document. Each paragraph can be aligned on the screen either to the left (the default option which does not need specifying), the right, or centered. Like so many things in computing, HTML tags are English words or are derived from variants of them. However, notice the spelling of *center*, HTML uses standard American spellings rather than the British alternative. Fortunately for non-English speakers, HTML has been designed to support content written in many languages and which uses many different font types. Chapter 15 takes a look at how you can *internationalize* the content of your pages.

HTML processors ignore all white space in your source documents except for spacing between words. This means that tabs, newlines, and paragraphs are not formatted as you would expect: in fact any of these that are encountered in your source code get converted into a single space character. Any spaces that you place between words will also get converted into a single space in the displayed document. To display more than one whitespace you have to use an *escape sequence*. These are described in Section 2.3, for now it is enough to know that wherever you want to place more than a single whitespace character you should use the sequence  .

If you align a paragraph either to the right or in the center of the screen always specify that the next paragraph is aligned to the left. Not all browsers automatically return to the default value.

```
<h1 [align="left"|"center"|"right"]>...</h1>
<h2 [align="left"|"center"|"right"]>...</h2>
<h3 [align="left"|"center"|"right"]>...</h3>
```
These three are the different levels of heading that are commonly used. In fact HTML has six levels of headings but these three should be enough for most purposes. As with paragraphs they can, optionally, be moved horizontally across the screen although this should be done with care. Most readers will expect headings either in the center or on the left of the screen and putting them to the right may be confusing. All headings require an end tag.

The largest heading is <h1> which should be used for main titles. Often these will be the same as the title of the document as given in the <head> section of the page. Use <h2> and <h3> for subsections of the document. If you find that you need more levels of heading it may be a good idea to restructure your Web site into more, smaller, pages rather than present a cluttered monolithic site.

HTML elements often have *attributes*. These are items which affect the way that the element operates but are not, strictly, part of its content. The heading tags can be aligned on the screen to the left, to the right or in the center of a line. In this case each heading tag has an attribute called `align` which can be set to `left`, `center`, or `right`. In this case the attribute is optional; if it is left out the browser will, by default, align all items to the left.

```
<hr [align="left"|"center"|"right"] [size="n"] [noshade]
[width="nn%"] >
```

This places a horizontal line across the screen. These lines are used to break up the page and give it a little structure. However they should be used sparingly as too many lines waste valuable screen *real-estate* and detract from the content.

The options determine how the rule will be displayed. It can be aligned but by default is centered on the screen. The `size` option specifies the thickness of the rule in pixels, `noshade` draws the rule as a single thick line rather than giving it the default three-dimensional appearance. The width of the line is best given as a percentage of the available screen size. This means that if the browser window is resized the rule will resize in a logical manner. The percentage length should be placed inside quotes like this: `<hr width="50%">`. The `<hr>` tag does not require an end tag.

---

Rule of Thumb:
In Western languages, text looks best if you left align it. If you try to center everything on the screen the effect is slightly unnerving. You should try to make the visitor's experience of your Web site as pleasant as you can – that way they may come back again.

---

## 2.2.2   The Basic Web Page – A Worked Example

Throughout the book I'm going to show you lots of working code. This code is *not* meant to be the greatest, most optimal code you'll ever see. It is meant to demonstrate the ideas and principles which I'm describing. Where appropriate I've included a screenshot of the output which the code produces. As you look through the book you'll see screenshots which are taken under both Microsoft Windows and GNU/Linux operating systems[3] but I would like to encourage you to enter the code and see for yourself that it works. This will give you good practice at structuring your code and it'll give you the opportunity to play around by altering, removing and adding items to see what effect that has.

---

[3]Sorry, I don't have access to an Apple Macintosh but all of the code complies with the relevant standards and so should work on that system too.

> Note:
> Almost none of the code in this book is in any way dangerous to your system. In fact I would be very surprised if there's anything in here which will damage any system. You might find that some things such as the JavaScript can crash your Web browser if you type them in wrongly, but it can easily be restarted. Don't be afraid, play around, it's the only way you'll find out what works.

The following code is a typical example of the sort of thing you'll find scattered through the book. Usually I won't introduce them, their function and purpose should be clear from the context in which they appear. This example should be used as the basis of your first Web page.

```html
<html>
    <head>
        <title>Bill Smiggins Inc.</title>
    </head>
    <body>
        <h1>Bill Smiggins Inc.</h1>
        <h2>About our Company...</h2>
        <p>This Web site provides clients, customers,
        interested parties and our staff with all of the
        information that they could want on our products,
        services, success and failures.</p>
        <hr>
        <h3>Products</h3>
        <p align="center">We are probably the largest
        supplier of custom widgets, thingummybobs, and bits
        and pieces in North America.</p>
        <hr width="50%">
    </body>
</html>
```

## 2.3  TEXT

The text on an HTML page can be altered in a number of ways: the actual font used can be changed to attempt to force the browser to use a specific font and the look of the text can be changed for emphasis. XHTML requires the use of stylesheets for formatting and deprecates[4] the tags in this section. They are included here both for backwards compati-

---

[4]They are no longer part of the standard and ought not to be used.

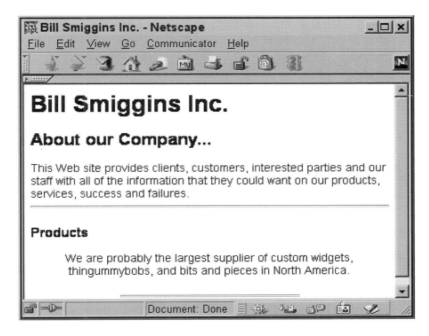

**Figure 2.1** The Basic Web Page

bility and because many HTML editing tools still use them so chances are that you'll come across these at some point.

`<basefont size="n">`

Lets you specify a minimum font size for basic text but not for headings. The size argument takes an integer from 1 to 7.

`<font size="[+|-]n" color="#rrggbb">`

Sets the font size relative to either the default value or to any size set by `<basefont>`. Absolute font sizes can be forced by using an integer from 1 to 7; relative font sizes are set by using +/- 1 to 7.

The color of the text is set with the `color` argument. This takes a hex value which represents the amounts of red, green, and blue in the chosen color. The easiest way to discover these hex values is to use a piece of software: several *color choosers* are available for free download from sites around the Internet. For more information on using colors see Section 2.8.

The following code sample and Figure 2.2 show what this looks like in practice:

```
<html>
    <head>
        <title>Changing Font Sizes</title>
    </head>
    <body>
```

```
        <h1>Changing Font Sizes</h1>
        <basefont size="3">
        <p>Here is some text in size three
        <p>And here is some <font size="7">larger</font>
            <font size="+3">t</font>
            <font size="+2">e</font>
            <font size="+1">x</font>
            <font size="-1">t</font>
            </basefont>
    </body>
</html>
```

***Figure 2.2*** Changing Font Sizes

```
<b>...</b>
<i>...</i>
<strong>...</strong>
<tt>...</tt>
<sub>...</sub>
<sup>...</sup>
```

Altering the appearance of text can subtly change its meaning. If text is in a bold typeface then it is often read with added emphasis. When you are writing Web pages which present information you'll need to use standard typographical methods of changing the appearance of text.

These should all be used with care as they can make the text unreadable. For instance you may want to emphasize something such as a warning or a special offer on a commercial site. The best way to do that is often by using color; using something such as bold font may make the text difficult to read which in turn may cause visitors to pass on, ignoring your message. On the other hand browsers on platforms such as mobile phones or PDAs, or browsers which are used by the disabled may not be able to display your colors. These browsers depend upon the standard text formatting commands, as shown here, to change the way that they display content.

The bold and italic tags should be self-explanatory. The `<strong>` tag is used as a form of emphasis, usually rendered as a bold-faced font. The browser will choose an alternative if bold is not available. Therefore use `<b>` when you want a bold-face and `<strong>` to ensure the text is always emphasized. The `<tt>` tag lets text be rendered using a monospaced font to simulate typewriter output which can be useful if you want to include program code, for instance, on a Web page. Finally `<sub>` renders text as a subscript, `<sup>` as superscript. These can be useful when rendering mathematics[5], for instance, or symbols such as @ or ©.

```
<html>
    <head>
        <title>Font Variations</title>
    </head>
    <body>
        <h1>Font Variations</h1>
        <p>We can use <b>simple</b> tags to <i>change</i> the
        appearance of <strong>text</strong> within <tt>Web
        pages</tt>. Even super<sup>script</sup> and sub<sub>
        scripts</sub> are <em>supported</em></p>
    </body>
</html>
```

**`<br>`**

Forces a line break within a passage of text where a paragraph is not desirable. On complex pages it is sometimes useful to put a `<br>` before and after tables, lists, or `<hr>` as this simplifies rendering for the browser.

**`<pre>...</pre>`**

Sometimes you will want to include ready-formatted text on a Web page, for instance program code, recipes, or poetry. Inside a `<pre>` tag the text is only wrapped when the source has a line break and tabs or multiple white spaces are not converted to a single space.

**`&amp; &lt; &gt; &quot;   &copy;`**

These are character escape sequences which are required if you want to display characters that HTML uses as control sequences. When HTML finds a character such as < in the text of a page, it treats it as an instruction. Therefore you cannot display such a character simply by using it in your page. Instead you must use one of the alternatives shown here. All of these replacement sequences start with an ampersand, &, and are terminated with a semicolon.

---

[5] Although browsers are now starting to provide support for the MathML maths markup language.

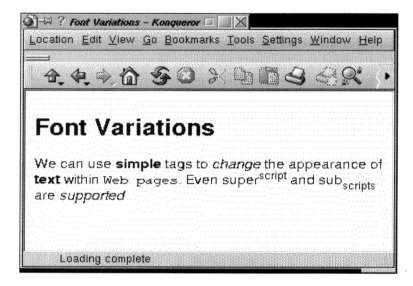

**Figure 2.3**    Font Variations

Although double quotes usually display normally, this behaviour is not guaranteed, it is safer to use &quot; which always behaves correctly. If you want to force a white space where one would not be used by default you should use  . Figure 2.4 shows the effect of these sequences. Unlike the rest of HTML 4 but in common with XHTML these escape sequences are case-sensitive. A fuller list of escape sequences is given in Appendix C.

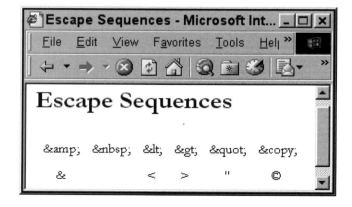

**Figure 2.4**    Escape Sequences

> Rule of Thumb:
> Make your text easy to read by judicious use of different font styles. Remember that you will have to use text formatting to try to convey ideas such as humour or irony. Even simple font styling can make a lot of difference to the way that large blocks of text read on the screen. Reading from a screen is not like reading from a page so make it simple for your visitors.

### 2.3.1 Text Formatting – A Worked Example

```html
<html>
   <head>
      <title>Bill Smiggins Inc</title>
   </head>
   <body>
      <h3>Placing Orders</h3>
      <p> You can place <strong>orders</strong> via our
      <font color="#121212"> Web site</font> or by using the
      <font size="+2">telephone</font> if you <i>must</i>.
      Call in person for orders &lt; 50 dollars.<br> <i>&quot;
      We are always ready to help &quot;</i></p>

      <h3>Our Address</h3>
      <pre>
         Unit 5,
         Tax Havens Industrial Estate,
         Enterprise City, USA
      </pre>
   </body>
</html>
```

## 2.4 HYPERLINKS

The power and flexibility of HTML comes from the simple method it uses to link documents together. The importance of the hypertext concept was introduced in Section 1.1.3, if you skipped by the introduction you might want to go back and read that now. A single tag is used for all types of links. Links should be used freely within documents where they either add to the understanding of the work or can be used to reduce download times. It is better to have many links to medium sized documents containing about a screenful of information rather than forcing readers to download a single massive document. When

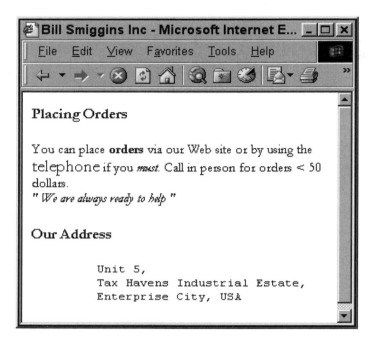

**Figure 2.5** Formatted Text

structuring a Web site always consider that most users will be accessing your site via 56 Kbps modems rather than their own ISDN or T1 link. If a page takes a long time to download these users will go elsewhere for their information or business.

`<a href="address">...</a>`

The link tag has three sections: the address of the referenced document, a piece of text to display as the link, and the closing tag. The link text can be formatted using any of the text formatting options. Hypertext references, the `href` part of the tag, can be: links to documents or services at other Internet sites; links to documents within the same Web site, or links to a specific part of either the current page or another page. For example:

`<a href="pagetwo.html">Next Page</a>`

Links to another page in the same directory. The browser displays Next Page on the screen and highlights it so that readers know it is a hyperlink. Usually this highlighting takes the form of displaying the link in blue text and underlining it.

`<a href="http://www.somesite.co.uk/index.html">Some Site</a>`

Links to another Web site. This time Some Site is displayed and highlighted.

A sample hyperlink is shown in Figure 2.6.

**Figure 2.6**  Hyperlinks

### 2.4.1   Relative Paths

Whenever possible relative, rather than absolute, paths should be used in hypertext links. If you want to know more about the terms relative and absolute you should consult any good reference on the UNIX operating system for a full explanation. This is a simplified guide for the timid. This description of paths uses Figure 2.7 as a template.

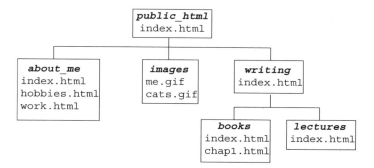

**Figure 2.7**  Sample Site Map

Basically an absolute path gives the full system path of a file. For instance a specific file on a UNIX system could be referenced as:

`/home/chris/public_html/writing/index.html`

but if I were already looking at the `/home/chris/public_html` directory, that reference might become:

`./writing/index.html`

The current directory is indicated by the single dot at the start of the path. HTML uses the UNIX style of forward slashes as separators in directory paths. If I wanted to access an image in directory`/home/chris/public_html/images` from the `writing` directory I would use:

`../images/cats.gif}`

The pair of dots at the start of the path is used to indicate that a file is in the parent directory of the current one, i.e. the one *above* it in the directory tree and hence the directory which contains it. Complex paths can be created so that, for instance, a link can be created between `index.html` in the `lectures` directory and `work.html` in `about_me`, like this:

`../../about_me/work.html`

Why go to all of this trouble? Well, if you developed your Web site on your home PC you might store all files on your C drive. At first sight it would seem sensible to give the full path of each file in every link:

`c:\My Documents\webpage\inxx.html`

That's fine on the local machine but what about when you transfer your Web site over to the server? The files will be placed in a totally different directory. The server may not even *have* a C drive![6] None of your carefully constructed links will work. Using relative paths means that the Web site can be moved from computer to computer and it will still all work perfectly.

> Note:
> All file paths in HTML use a forward slash. You might be used to using backslashes in your operating system, take a little care to get it right in your Web pages. If you don't, your site simply won't be usable.

### 2.4.2 Uniform Resource Locators

Web browsers can be used to access several different services across the Internet. So that the browser knows how to process the incoming data, each service type is identified by a different URL. The commonest services that you might link to are FTP, Usenet news, and other HTML pages. All use the same format of:

`type://host.domain/path/file`

where `type` can be FTP, news or HTTP. You are unlikely to want to connect to Internet services such as Gopher, WAIS, or Archie which are now falling into disuse. A fuller description of URLs is given in Chapter 17.

### 2.4.3 Linking to Specific Sections

Linking to a specific section of a document is a straightforward process but if you have many links they can become confusing. Therefore it is a good idea to liberally sprinkle comments around these definitions so that you can maintain the code. A link has an address component and a target.

---

[6]Your PC may not have one either, but the same principle applies to all directory structures.

```
<a href="#target">...</a>
```

The start of the link simply requires an address to which the browser should jump. The address is prefixed by # and has to be given a name that is unique for that document.

```
<a name="target">...</a>
```

The target of the jump requires just the target name.

```
<a href="./nextpage.html#target">...</a>
```

This type of link is used to go to a specific section of another document.

Here is an example of linking to sections of a document. In the file `car.html` we might have this text:

```
As well as the <a href="./engines.html#engine"> engine </a>, cars
have <a href="#wheels"> wheels </a> ...
```

The targets would be formatted as follows:

in cars.html:

```
<a name="#wheels"> Wheels </a> are quite important
to cars.
```

in engines.html:

```
<a name="#engine"> Noisy, oily things</a> under the
<a href="./car.html#hood"> hood</a>.
```

> Rules of Thumb:
> Whenever possible use relative rather than absolute links. If you move a Web site to a different server or a new directory you won't have to change all of the links that you have made. Use hyperlinks to structure your site into a number of small/medium sized packets of related information. Minimize download times wherever possible.

## 2.4.4 Linking to Other Pages – A Worked Example

The file containing the start of the link contains

```
<html>
   <head>
      <title>Bill Smiggins Inc</title>
   </head>
   <body>
      <h3>Linking to Another Page</h3>
      <p>Bill Smiggins is, of course a multi-national business.
      We even have overseas offices, well, <em>an</eM overseas
      office. If you are nearer to <i>that</i> Web server please
      <a href="www.smiggins.co.uk/index.html">click here</a>.
```

```
        </p>
        <hr>
    </body>
</html>
```

The file which is the target of the link contains nothing special. All of the work is done at the start.

```
<html>
    <head>
        <title>Bill Smiggins Inc</title>
    </head>
    <body>
        <h1>Bill Smiggins Inc</h1>
        <h2>Overseas Branch</h2>
        <p>Welcome to the British Web server
        <hr width="50%">
        <h2>About our Company...</h2>
        <p> This Web site provides clients, customers, interested
        parties and our staff with all of the information that
        they could want on our products, services, success and
        failures.</p>
        <hr>
        <h3>Products</h3>
        <p align="center">We are probably the largest supplier of
        custom widgets, thingummybobs, and bits and pieces in North
        America and here in the European Union.</p>
        <hr width="50%">
    </body>
</html>
```

This shows that the link from the first page leads us to a second page. This second page may even be on a different server. The hypertext sorts it out for us.

## 2.5   ADDING MORE FORMATTING

That's the basics out of the way. Now it's time to learn how to add color and life to a Web page. We'll start by formatting data in the simplest way: the list. We'll then start to add color and multimedia objects such as sound, applets, and animations. Finally in this chapter I'll show you how to add forms to your Web site which you can use to acquire data from users.

**Figure 2.8** Linked Web pages

## 2.6 LISTS

One of the most effective ways of structuring a Web site or its contents is to use lists. Lists may be for something as simple as supplying a piece of information or for providing a straightforward index to the site, but could become highly complex. As an example, a commercial Web site may use pictures of its products instead of text in hyperlinks. These can be built as nested lists to provide an interesting graphical interface to the site.

HTML provides three types of list: the basic bulleted list, a numbered list, and a definition list. Each has a different use but generally the definition list is the most flexible of the three as it easily incorporates images and paragraphs of text while keeping an obvious structure.

> Note:
> Lists can be easily embedded within other lists to provide complex yet readable structures.

`<li>...</li>`

The ordered and unordered lists are each made up of sets of list items. Elements of a list may be formatted with any of the usual text formatting tags and may be images or hyperlinks. Strictly the closing tag is not part of HTML. It is, though, required under the rules of XHTML. I've included it here because whilst using it does no harm since browsers which do not support XHTML will simply ignore it, not using it will cause problems in the future.

`<ul [type="disc"|"square"|"circle"] [compact]>...</ul>`

The basic unordered list has a bullet in front of each list item. Everything between the tags must be encapsulated within `<li>...</li>` tags. More recent browsers support different types of bullet which can be specified by the `type` attribute. If you want to minimize the amount of space that a list uses then add the compact attribute.

`<ol [type="1"|"a"|"A"|"I"|"i"] [start="n"] [compact]>...</ol>`

An ordered list has a number instead of a bullet in front of each list item. Different numbering schemes can be specified depending upon preference. A list can number from any value that you desire: the starting value is given by the `start` attribute. As with the unordered list all items in an ordered list must be enclosed within `<li>...</li>` tags.

`<dl [compact]>...</dl>`

Definition lists are different to the previous types in that they do not use list items to contain their members. Elements within a definition list are either items being defined or their definitions.

`<dt>...[</dt>]`

Definition terms mark items whose definition will be provided by the next data definition. They can be formatted using any regular text formatting. The closing tag is optional as it is assumed once a `<dd>` tag is reached.

`<dd>...[</dd>]`

Definitions of terms are enclosed within these tags. The definition can include any text or block formatting elements. The text of a definition is usually rendered indented and on the line below the preceding item. Hence `<dd>` can be used outside a definition list to provide conventionally indented text, although this is not guaranteed to work in all browsers.

---

Rule of Thumb:

Lists provide a simple formatting option which can be used in many situations. They are easily understood and should be used instead of complex image maps on sites which require fast access and navigation.

### 2.6.1 Lists – A Worked Example

The basic unordered list and the numbered list are fairly intuitive to anyone who has used a word processor. Almost everyone will, at some point, have created a list of items or the outline of an essay or report using them. What about the definition list, though? That's not quite so easy to understand. The following code shows all three lists in action, hopefully you'll see from its structure that the definition list is actually a very powerful construct with many applications.

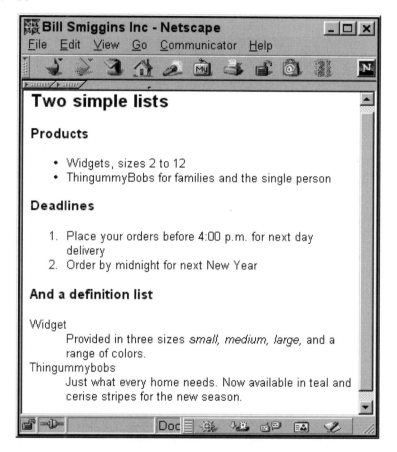

**Figure 2.9** Lists

```
<html>
   <head>
      <title>Bill Smiggins Inc</title>
   </head>
   <body>
   <h2>Two simple lists</h2>
```

```
<h3>Products</h3>
<ul>
   <li>Widgets, sizes 2 to 12</li>
   <li>ThingummyBobs for families and the single
   person</li>
</ul>

<h3>Deadlines</h3>
<ol>
   <li>Place your orders before 4:00 p.m. for next
   day delivery</li>
   <li>Order by midnight for next New Year</li>
</ol>

<h3>And a definition list</h3>
<dl>
   <dt>Widget</dt>
      <dd>Provided in three sizes <i>small, medium,
      large</i>, and a range of colors.</dd>
   <dt>Thingummybobs</dt>
      <dd>Just what every home needs. Now available in
      teal and cerise stripes for the new season.</dd>
</dl>
</body>
</html>
```

## 2.7 TABLES

The table is one of the most useful HTML constructs. You'll find tables all over the Internet. Often you don't even know that the page you're looking at is awash with tables; instead it just appears to be a very well structured site.

Tables have two uses: structuring pieces of information and structuring the whole Web page. If you want that professional look it is worth finding out how to use tables. Many of the best designed sites on the Internet are based around tables. Alternatively you can structure a page using frames or images. I'll look at using frames in Section 3.2 and talk about the advantages and disadvantages of each approach in Section 15.2.

So tables are a good thing, but what are they? Well, a table is a grid of information such as you might have seen in a ledger or spreadsheet. Unlike a table from a spreadsheet the data items in an HTML table do not need to have any kind of relationship. Unlike data in spreadsheets, you can put things in a table simply because you want to. If a table simplifies layout or formatting and you feel that you need one on your page then you can use one.

The only consideration that you must think about is processing – most browsers struggle to process complex tables. The browsers are not optimized for tables and where tables are deeply nested on a page the browser may have difficulty displaying the page. Web browsers have a *layout engine* which arranges the pieces before the Web page is displayed. Where the page is difficult to lay out there will be a noticeable delay before your content appears. This problem is made worse by the use of images within tables, especially where the size attributes of the image have not been set. Therefore use tables freely but keep them as simple as possible.

Figure 2.10 shows how simple a table can be. The code which created it is pretty simple too:

```
<html>
   <head>
      <title>A Simple Table</title>
   </head>
   <body>
      <h2>A Simple Table</h2>
      <table border="1">
      <tr>
         <th>Left Column</th>
         <th>Right Column</th>
      </tr>
      <tr>
         <td>A little bit of data</td>
         <td>Rather more data in this cell which will
         wrap around...</td>
      </tr>
      </table>
   </body>
</html>
```

**<table [align="center"|"left"|"right"] [border [="n"]]**
**[cellpadding="n"] [width="nn%"] [cellspacing="n"]> ...</table>**
Everything between these two tags will be part of the table. These attributes control the formatting of the table as a whole, not that of the items in each cell. Tables can be aligned on the screen like most other items, usually they are centered for impact and clarity. A table can have a border, which includes a border between the cells. If the border attribute is not set the table has no border. When the border attribute is set but a valid value is not given, a single pixel wide default border is drawn. For wider borders you must give a positive integer value.

***Figure 2.10*** A Simple Table

Cellpadding, in pixels, determines how much space there is between the contents of a cell and its border; cellspacing sets the amount of white space between cells. The width attribute sets the amount of the screen that the table will use. This is best given as a percentage so that if the browser is resized the table will continue to make sense.

---

Rule of Thumb:

Tables can, if used carefully, provide the best way of structuring a Web page. If you are using a table to format the whole page it is best to avoid using a border and to play around with cellpadding and cellspacing to see what effects you can achieve.

---

`<tr [align="left"|"center"|"right"]`
`[valign="top"|"center"|"bottom"]> ...</tr>`

Each row of the table has to be delimited by these tags. The row can be aligned horizontally and vertically within the table if you want. Although the `</tr>` tag is strictly optional since it is obvious when rows end you should always use it. If you are creating a complex table which has other tables nested within it these may be rendered incorrectly if all rows are not explicitly closed.

`<th [align="left"|"center"|"right"]`
`[valign="top"|"center"|"bottom"]`
`[nowrap] [colspan="n"] [rowspan="n"]>...</th>`

These are table cells which are to be used for headings. Typically a table header will be rendered in emphasized text such as `<strong>`.

The contents of the cell can be aligned vertically and horizontally within their row; these attributes override any that were set for the row. If nowrap is set, the contents of the cell will not be automatically wrapped as the table is formatted for the screen. To prevent long lines messing the look of your tables use `<br>` to force text wrapping.

The `colspan` and `rowspan` attributes allow individual cells to be larger than a one by one grid. It is often useful to have a heading which spans more than one column, for instance if you are nesting headings, in which case you should use `colspan`. Similarly some data cells may need to be more than one cell deep and `rowspan` should be used.

```
<td [align="left"|"center"|"right"]
[valign="top"|"center"|"bottom"] [nowrap] [colspan=n]
[rowspan=n]>...</td>
```
The basic data cells. For explanations of the options see `<th>`.

---

Rule of Thumb:

Be very careful when counting columns and rows for the `colspan` and `rowspan` attributes. Get it wrong and your table will look a little weird. Spanning columns and rows gives your tables a very slick look and is very useful when the table is being used to format the page.

---

### 2.7.1  A Table of Data - A Worked Example

```html
<html>
    <head>
        <title>Bill Smiggins Inc - catalog</title>
    </head>
    <body>
    <h3>Product Lists</h3>
        <table border="1" align="center">
        <tr>
            <th colspan="3" align="center"> Products</th>
        </tr>
        <tr>
            <th><i>Name</i></th>
            <th><i>Description</i></th>
            <th><i>Cost</i></th>
        </tr>
        <tr>
            <th>Widgets</th>
            <td>For families and the single person,<br>
            available in three sizes: <i>small, medium, and
            large, </i><br> and a range of colors.</td>
            <td>12 dollars each, <br>delivery 50 dollars per
            mile.</td>
        </tr>
        <tr>
```

```
            <th>ThingummyBobs</th>
            <td>Just what every home needs.<br> Now available
            in teal and cerise stripes for the new season.<br>In
            sizes 2 to 12.</td>
            <td>34 dollars per dozen.</td>
        </tr>
    </table>
    </body>
</html>
```

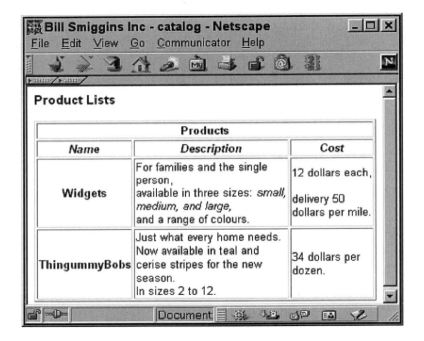

**Figure 2.11**  Data in Tables

## 2.7.2  Advanced Table Elements

**`<caption>string</caption>`**

This optional element is used to provide a string which describes the contents of the table. If used it *must* immediately follow the `table` element.

**`<thead>...</thead>`**

**`<tfoot>...<tfoot>`**

**`<tbody>...<tbody>`**

The rows in a table *can* be grouped into one of three divisions. This grouping is optional. The idea is that browsers will be able to scroll the `tbody` section of the table without moving either the thead or tfoot sections. When long tables extend over more than one page the information in thead and tfoot can be automatically replicated on each page.

**<colgroup [span="n"] [width="n"]>...</colgroup>**

Columns within a table can be logically grouped together. Each group of columns can be assigned a default width which will apply to all columns which do not set one of their own. The span indicates the number of columns in the group.

**col [span="n"] [width="n"]>...</col>**

The attributes of individual columns are set using the col element. The span and width attributes work in the same way as for the colgroup element.

**Figure 2.12** A Comprehensive Table

The following code shows a table which, whilst admittedly uninteresting in itself, shows how to use all of the table elements. The result is shown in Figure 2.12.

```
<html>
    <head>
      <title>A Comprehensive Table</title>
    </head>
    <body>
      <h1>A Comprehensive Table</h1>
      <table align="center" width="75%" border="1">
        <caption>Comprehensive Table</caption>
        <colgroup width="30%" span="2">
        </colgroup>
        <colgroup span="3">
```

```
      </colgroup>
      <thead>
        <tr><td colspan="5">The Table Header</td></tr>
      </thead>
      <tbody>
        <tr>
          <td>First</td>
          <td>Second</td>
          <td>Third</td>
          <td>Fourth</td>
          <td>Fifth</td>
        </tr>
        <tr>
          <td>First</td>
          <td>Second</td>
          <td>Third</td>
          <td>Fourth</td>
          <td>Fifth</td>
        </tr>
      </tbody>
      <tfoot>
        <tr><td colspan="5">The Table Footer</td></tr>
      </tfoot>
    </table>
  </body>
</html>
```

## 2.8  USING COLOR AND IMAGES

Why are some Web pages attractive and pleasant to use while others are just a visual turn-off? It's simply that some page authors make good use of colors and images on their Web sites while others think that either more is better or that images get in the way. The reason that people enjoy surfing the Web is that it is a mixed medium with text, images, and multimedia content.

Color is essential to the Web experience; it brings pages alive and takes them beyond the mundane. Color is also dangerous and must be used carefully. Some cautionary examples leap to mind: those Web sites that would like to be *dangerous* and so use red text on a black background which does not make for a pleasurable reading experience; and sites using white text on a dark background which sometimes print out as blank pages.

Color can be used in a number of places on a Web page: the background can be colored, individual elements can be altered, and links which are already colored can have their colors adjusted.

To change the colors of links or of the page background hexadecimal values are placed in the `<body>` tag[7]:

```
<body bgcolor="#nnnnnn" text="#nnnnnn" link="#nnnnnn"
vlink="#nnnnnn" alink="#nnnnnn">
```

The `vlink` attribute sets the color of links visited recently, `alink` the color of a currently active link. The six figure hexadecimal values must be enclosed in double quotes and preceded by a hash (#).

The colors of page elements can be altered by using the color modifier. For instance, to change the color of an individual heading you could use:

```
<h2 color="#ababab">My Heading</h2>
```

and within a table the table headers could be colored by:

```
<th bgcolor="#ababab">
```

---

**Rule of Thumb:**
Color is important to the Web experience but must be used wisely. Generally subdued autumnal or pastel colors work best. Do not choose a set of colors that are too close together: many people set their monitors to view only 256 or 16,000 colors. Your site may look nice on your flashy 32 million color set-up but become ugly and monochrome on your visitor's display.

---

## 2.9 IMAGES

Images are the second aspect of a pleasant Web experience. The problems with images are legion if they are not used wisely. First, experienced, or impatient, Web surfers often switch image loading off by default, on their browsers. If your site relies on an image to get important information across these people may never see it. Second, loading images is a slow process and if you use too many, or your images are too large, the download times can easily become intolerable.

Browsers display a limited range of image types. You can only guarantee that GIF and JPG will be displayed everywhere, although more and more browsers are now able to display the PNG format, which is intended as a free replacement for the copyrighted GIF format. If you want high quality, good compression, and lots of colors use JPG, for instance

---

[7] Again this was deprecated in HTML 4.0

when displaying photographs. Generally, though GIFs are more common as they tend to be smaller files – and can be animated.

```
<body background="URL">...</body>
```
Sets the background of your page to use the given image. Images are tiled (repeated) to fill the available space by default. If you want to use a single image across the width of a page make it 1281 pixels wide then it cannot be tiled horizontally. This is a useful technique if you have an image with a differently colored left edge and want a classy looking page. Background images tend to work best in pale greys and browns but if they are too complex they may hide the text.

```
<img src="URL"|"name" height="n" width="n" [alt="string"]
[align="top"|"center"|"bottom"] [usemap="URL"]>
```
Displays an inline image, that is an image which appears in the body of the text rather than on a page of its own or in a spawned viewer program. The height and width of the image, in pixels, tell the browser how much space to allocate to an image when displaying a page. Some browsers also use these to shrink/stretch images to fit but generally it is safest to use the correct sizes for the image.

> Note:
> It is a good idea to provide a piece of text that will be displayed if the image is not loaded, the `alt` attribute is used for this purpose. Text and speech based browsers will handle this `alt` text to aid users understand the structure of your pages.

By default any text which follows an image will be aligned alongside its bottom edge. You can alter this so that the first line of text displays alongside the center or top of the image. Once the text wraps it will continue below the image. If you want to be sure that a block of text is shown next to an image you must use a table. To display an image without text, make it into a paragraph:

```
<p align="center"><img src="./mygif.gif" alt="Myself"></p>
```

This is one case in which it is important to end the paragraph properly. The `usemap` attribute is used in image mapping which is explained below.

```
<a href="URL">text message</a>
<a href="URL"><img src="filename"></a>
```
Images can also be viewed on pages of their own. The first example uses an ordinary hypertext link but the URL should point to the image file, giving its name and type, e.g. mypic.gif or mypic.jpg. In the second case we are using an image as the link to another image. This can be useful if you want to display a page of thumbnail images and allow the reader to choose which ones to view full-size. This is one way of speeding up the loading times of graphically intensive sites.

Image maps are probably the most complex, yet most visually satisfying, method of navigating around a Web site. An image map is a large picture which has areas that the reader can click with a mouse. Each clickable area provides a hypertext link. The image map has two parts: the image and a map.

`<img src="URL" usemap="URL">`

Tells the browser to display the source image and to map the second URL, the image map, onto it.

`<area shape="circle"|"rect"|"poly"|"default"`
`href="URL" coords="string" alt="string">`

creates a clickable area on an image map. The `alt` text in this case is displayed by the browser as an indicator for the reader of where the link goes. If you do not supply an `alt`, your image map is invalid and may not be displayed. The meaning of `href` should be clear: it is the destination of the link. The clickable area can have one of four shapes. Each shape is defined by coordinates, pairs of integers which give locations on the image in pixels:

- The default location does not require coordinates and is used to indicate what happens if the user clicks outside of the mapped areas. Each image map can have only one default.

- A `rect` has four coordinates which are paired. The first pair defines the top left corner and the second pair the bottom right corner of the area.

- A `circle` is defined by its center and its radius. The center is given by a pair of values, the radius by a single value. Therefore this requires just *three* values in the coordinate string.

- A `polygon` is made from a set of coordinates with the last pair listed being joined to the first to complete the shape.

An example image map with the mapping in the same file as the image link might look like this:

```
<img src="./mappic.gif" usemap="#main_map"
    height=30 width=50>

<a name="#main_map">
<map name="main_map">
<area shape="rect" href="./images/img1.jpg"
    alt="Image One" coords="0,0,25,25">
<area shape="rect" href="./page1.html"
    alt="Page One" coords="26,26,50,50">
<area shape=default href="./page32.html"
    alt="Page 32">
</map>
</a>
```

> Rule of Thumb:
> Image maps load slowly and are terrible if you get them wrong. It is very easy
> to send readers to the wrong location. Many sites achieve the same effect more
> simply by making a complex image from a set of smaller, simpler ones. Each
> smaller image then acts as its own hyperlink. If you do this, switch the borders
> off on your images.

### 2.9.1   Images – A Worked Example

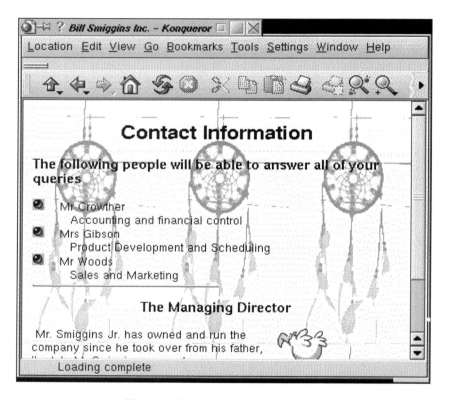

**Figure 2.13**   Using Colors and Images

```
<html>
   <head>
      <title>Bill Smiggins Inc.</title>
   </head>

   <body bgcolor="#000000" background="./Dream.gif"
   text="#000000">
```

```
<h1 align="center">Contact Information</h1>
<h3>The following people will be able to answer all
of your queries</h3>

<dl>
    <dt><img src="./bullet.gif" alt="bullet">   
    Mr Crowther</dt>
    <dd>Accounting and financial control</dd>
    <dt><img src="./bullet.gif" alt="bullet">   
    Mrs Gibson</dt>
    <dd>Product Development and Scheduling</dd>
    <dt><img src="./bullet.gif" alt="bullet">   
    Mr Woods</dt>
    <dd>Sales and Marketing</dd>
</dl>
<hr width="50%">

<h3 align="center">The Managing Director</h3>

<img align="right" src="./boss.gif"
        textalign="top" alt="The Boss">
Mr. Smiggins Jr. has owned and run the company since he
took over from his father, the late Mr Smiggins, several
years ago.
    </body>
</html>
```

## 2.10 EXERCISES

### Basic HTML

1. What are HTML tags? How do the tags that switch a format on differ from those which switch it off?

2. Which tags and sections must *all* HTML documents contain?

3. How is a comment shown in HTML?

4. What is the difference between `<title>...</title>` and `<h1>...</h1>`?

5. Create an empty HTML file containing just the head and body sections with no content. Store this in your new directory as `template.html`. You can use this as the basis of all your pages. As you learn more about file headers you can easily update this template file.

6. Try putting a `title` and an `h1` level header into an HTML file.  Save the file as `test.html` remembering to use the `.html` extension.  Now try to open the file inside your favourite Web browser. If you can't do that using the `open` command of the `file` menu read the documentation that came with your browser.

## Formatting

1. How can page content be formatted horizontally across the screen?

2. Why does the browser ignore white space and newline characters in the source text for your page?

3. List the formatting options that are provided for plain text. How can the font size be changed using basic HTML rather than a stylesheet?

4. Discuss the differences between relative and absolute paths in hyperlinks.

5. When should you use relative hyperlinks, and when are absolute hyperlinks needed?

6. A hyperlink can be used to move around within a single page rather than to load another page. How is this done?

7. Open your `test.html` file from the previous section inside an editor.  Add some paragraphs of text and `h2` and `h3` headers. Open the file in your browser to check how it looks. Pretty dull isn't it? Well that was how everything on the Web looked back in the early 1990s!

8. Try changing the font size for individual page elements. What effect do the emphasis tags have?

9. Now try changing the colors of some of those page elements.  Use the chart in appendix A to help.  Try using both hexadecimal values and the proper names of the colors.

10. Create a second page called `test2.html` in the same directory as `test.html`. Try to make a hyperlink in each one so that you can swap backwards and forwards between the two files.

11. Add a link from one of your files to a site you've used on the Web. Go on-line and test this link.

12. This final exercise is for anyone who is still confused about absolute and relative hyperlinks.  Edit `test.html` and `test2.html` so that the links between them are like this:
```
<a href="c:/mypages/test.html">link text</a>
<a href="c:/mypages/test2.html">link text</a>
```

Try the links again in your Web browser. Now move the files to a temporary directory. Don't copy them, make sure they are moved. Open the files in their new location in your browser and try the links. They shouldn't work if you done everything correctly.

Now edit the files so that the links are relative like this:

```
<a href="./test.html">link text</a>
<a href="./test2.html">link text</a>
```

Try that in your browser. The links should now work again. Copy the two files back into your working directory and test them once more from this, their original location.

## Colors and Images

1. The Web started out as a text-only medium. Now many sites are unusable if you can't see their images. How has the increased use of images affected different groups of Web users?

2. Think about the colors that you see on Web sites. Which combinations of colors work well together, and which are unpleasant and make sites difficult to read?

3. Modify some of the pages that you've created so far so that they have colored text and backgrounds. Play around with the colors until you get a set that looks good. (Appendix A should help.)

4. What are the most commonly encountered image types on the Web? How does the browser cope if it cannot handle an image type itself?

5. Use an image as the background to a Web page. If you don't have any suitable ones in the cache of your browser then do a Web search. Many sites give away copyright free images that anyone can use. Again, try a number of different combinations of image and text formatting. What combinations are generally successful?

6. Place some images on a page. There are a number of ways of getting a good layout but the easiest effects are achieved by using a table. Try to create a pleasing effect.

7. Once you've got a page that looks good use one of the images as the starting point for a hyperlink.

8. Rather than placing large images on a page, the preferred technique is to use thumbnails by setting the `height` and `width` parameters to something like 100 pixels by 100 pixels. Each thumbnail image is also a link to a full-sized version of the image. Create an image gallery using this technique.

9. What sorts of multimedia object can be hosted within a Web page? How does the HTML 4 standard support all multimedia types, even those not yet developed?

## Lists and Tables

1. Create a simple HTML page which demonstrates the use of the three types of list. Try adding a definition list which uses unordered lists to define terms.

2. What advantages do tables have over other methods of presenting data? Are there likely to be any difficulties if you use large tables and embed tables inside tables?

3. Add a table to your Web page. Try different formatting options – how does the table look if it doesn't have a border, for instance?

4. Nest a second table inside the first as one of the rows.

# 3
# *More HTML*

Soon you'll be ready to try your hands at system independent design and scripting. Not yet, though. Before you get to the complicated ideas, I'm going to look at a few things which aren't basic HTML and aren't always needed but which can be important on some sites. HTML ideas never get complicated enough to be called *advanced* so this chapter is more of a miscellany of topics which don't fit elsewhere.

After working through the material in Chapter 2, you have enough material to put together a pretty interesting Web site. My personal opinion has always been that the content of a site matters most, followed by its usability, which leaves the overall design trailing at the back of the pack. Other people disagree, many professional Web *designers* place their emphasis on image and interactivity. In Chapter 15, I discuss a range of issues and ideas which are important when designing a site. This chapter looks at some things which can be used to introduce some elusive interactivity to your Web pages.

Interactive elements within Web pages range from fancy graphics through animation created using Macromedia's Flash and Shockwave technologies to streamed data, virtual worlds and JavaScript elements. A large section of this book looks at JavaScript which has many applications on the Web. In this chapter I'll look at how you can use other types of multimedia data inside a Web page.

If you're building a complicated site then you have to provide users with some form of navigation aid to help them find their way around. You don't want potential customers taking their business elsewhere simply because they can't find what they want on your site. I'm going to show you two ways of helping. The first uses a *frameset* to display more than one page at a time. Framesets are sometimes controversial, many Web designers seem to really hate them, but they're also very useful. The alternative navigation aid uses simple hyperlinks to let users orient themselves within a site.

This chapter concludes with a discussion of XHTML, the latest recommendation from the W3C. This formulates HTML using the rules of XML.

## 3.1 MULTIMEDIA OBJECTS

One of the biggest attractions of the Web must be the amount of multimedia data that can be presented from *within* simple text documents. You may have heard commentators over the years talking about the growing together of all types of media, well on the Web that has started to happen. This isn't a universal truth, very many Web sites use only text and graphics, yet are still capable of providing effective and informative experiences to visitors. There was a trend in the late 1990's towards sites which were very interactive and heavily laden with graphics and sounds. These tended to be unpopular with visitors due to the long download times which they required and the lack of substance they provided after the wait. The trend now is towards judicious use of multimedia to *enhance* not replace textual content.

Multimedia is an all-encompassing term which can mean radically different things to different people. On the Web it is generally used to mean sound and image data, although it is probably best used to define any data which is not plain text or simple images. This can encompass everything from a JavaScript roll-over button to a fully populated three-dimensional world, taking in all types of Java applet along the way. There are good reasons for minimising your use of multimedia data, which are covered in Chapter 15. For now let's ignore the negative and look at how you can include something a little more dynamic in your pages.

If you want to include external objects in your Web site you have a couple of choices. Images can simply be embedded in the text as shown in Section 2.9 and they will display normally because the browser understands how to process them itself. Of course I'm assuming here that you are using an image type that your visitors can handle. Some data types, for instance MIDI sound or MPEG encoded movies, may be beyond the capabilities of some Web browsers.

Typically Web site developers have included complex data items as hyperlinks and left the browser to *spawn* an external application to handle the data. This may involve running an application outside the browser as happens with players for streamed data in Real audio and Real video formats. Other applications may be opened embedded inside the browser. Figure 3.1 shows Microsoft's PowerPoint presentation application opened inside Internet Explorer 5 and displaying one of my lectures. The differentiation between these approaches depends upon the configuration of the browser and the type of data. If you are listening to a radio broadcast over the Web using Real Player,you probably want to be able to continue surfing at the same time. Tying up a whole browser window would be a waste of screen space and system resources so you often get something like Figure 3.2 instead. However, sometimes the Real Player *can* be embedded inside a browser window. Figure 3.3 shows this being done.

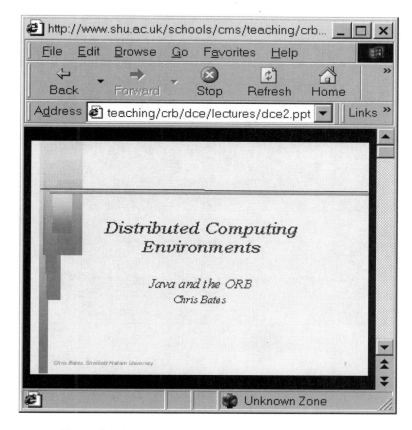

**Figure 3.1**  Microsoft PowerPoint Inside Internet Explorer

**Figure 3.2**  Separate Real Player

## 3.1.1  Including Objects

HTML 4 has an `object` tag which is used to embed multimedia objects directly into the page. It seems likely that in some future version of HTML the `img` tag will be fully replaced by `object` and, for sites that will be visited only by surfers using HTML 4 compatible browsers it may be safely replaced now.

**Figure 3.3** Embedded Real Player

```
<object classid="URL" data="URL" [codebase="URL"]
type="string" [standby="string"] height="n" width="n"
[title="string"]>...</object>
```
Each object requires a classid which identifies the URL of the object. The codebase parameter is optional. It identifies the directory which contains the object but if it is not supplied, the full URL can be placed in the classid parameter. If classid has only a file name, the object is assumed to be in the same directory as the HTML page.

When an object needs command-line parameters these can be passed in through the param tag, which is defined below.

The type parameter is used to specify the MIME type of the object. This information can then be used by the browser to launch pre-set helper applications. For many data types no helper will have been established and in these cases the type tag is redundant. Most objects must have their height and width defined so that the browser can allocate screen space to them. Finally the standby parameter is used to display alternative text while the object itself is being downloaded from the server.

```
<param name="string" value="string" type="string"
valuetype=["ref"|"object"|"data"]>
```
Each parameter needs a name which corresponds to the name that the object expects to receive. The value parameter specifies the value that will be passed into the object. However, the value passed does not have to be numerical or textual. valuetype is used to tell the browser the format of each parameter, which can be an actual piece

of data (`data`), the URL of a piece of data (`ref`) or another object (`object`). If the `valuetype` is set to `ref` then the browser needs the MIME type of the data. This is set through the `type` parameter.

The following example shows how an arbitrary script object might be embedded within a page.

```html
<html>
   <head>
      <title>An Embedded Object</title>
   </head>
   <body>
      <h1>An Embedded Object</h1>
      <p>The next paragraph contains an object and
      some parameters</p>
      <object height="50" width="250"
         classid="http://www.smiggins.com/objects/greet.py">
         <param name="greetee" value="Bill Smiggins"
            valuetype="data">
      </object>
   </body>
</html>
```

### 3.1.2   Applets

Before HTML 4 Java applets[1] had to be treated separately via the `applet` tag, but that is no longer part of the HTML standard and its role has been subsumed into `object`. For backwards compatibility it may be necessary to retain use of `applet` in the short term. You'll also see this tag used very widely if you ever use any Java programming texts and, hence, I'll discuss it briefly here. Whilst `applet` was a Java-specific tag, `object` supports all non-native data and hence presents the possibility that in future applets themselves may be written in languages such as Visual Basic, JavaScript or even C++. I have seen a plug-in which embedded applets written in the TCL scripting language inside Web pages[2].

```
<applet code="classfile" [name="string"] width="n"
height="n" [codebase="URL"]>
```
The browser needs to understand a number of things about the Java applet before it can be run. Firstly it needs to know where to get the file from, this information is optionally supplied by the `codebase` parameter. If no `codebase` is given the applet is assumed to come from the same directory as the HTML page. Java applets are compiled into an interpretable form called classfiles. Each applet has a classfile from

---

[1]Literally a small application with limited functionality and running under strict security conditions.
[2]See `http://www.scriptics.com` for more details.

which it is initiated, the name of which *must* be given to the browser so that the applet can be executed. Applets can optionally be given unique names to identify them on the page through the name parameter. This means that the applet can be referred to by other objects, applets, and scripts executing on the same page.

Some, but not all, applets require command-line parameters. These are passed to it by the parameter object and work in exactly the same way as for the HTML 4 object tag.

Finally the browser needs to know how much space it should allocate to the interface of the applet. This is done by the height and width parameters.

Here are two code samples showing the use of the applet tag to include some Java, and then the same thing rewritten to use object. Figure 3.4 demonstrates the running Java applet.

```
<html>
    <head>
        <title>A Simple Applet</title>
    </head>
    <body>
        <p>Here is the SimpleAWTApplet</p>
        <p align="center">
            <applet code="SimpleAWTApplet.class"
                width="200"
                height="50">
            </applet>
        </p>
    </body>
</html>

<html>
    <head>
        <title>A Simple Applet</title>
    </head>
    <body>
        <p>Here is the SimpleAWTApplet</p>
        <p align="center">
            <object code="SimpleAWTApplet.class"
                width="200"
                height="50">
            </object>
        </p>
    </body>
</html>
```

**Figure 3.4** A Java Applet

## 3.2 FRAMES

If you want a complex page structure but don't feel confident using a table to create it, you could use frames. Originally an extension of HTML from Netscape, frames are now supported in most browsers and are part of the HTML 4 specification. Frames provide a pleasing interface which makes your Web site easy to navigate but there are a number of problems if you use them. These problems are covered in Section 15.2. If you're unsure about what frames actually *are* then skip ahead and look at Figure 3.5. When we talk about *frames* what we are really referring to is a *frameset* which is a special type of Web page. The frameset page contains a set of references to HTML files, each of which is displayed inside a separate *frame*. All of the pages within a frameset are displayed inside the same browser window and can actually be made to appear to be a single page.

Because frame-based sites display more than one page at the same time, they can be complex to set up. Once the layout is established, frame-based sites can require less maintenance than alternative approaches. This is simply because the index is usually in one frame with page content displayed in another. If new pages are added to the site, their details are only added to the index. Non-frame sites tend to place an index on every page so that as new pages are added, or removed, all of the existing content needs editing.

A frame-based page is actually made from a set of documents, each displayed in its own frame. Each subdocument can have its own scrollbars and can be loaded, reloaded, and printed as if it were occupying the whole screen. Frames can be rather confusing and only really make sense when you see them in action. First I'll define the tags that are needed then present some examples.

```
<frameset [cols="%,%"] [rows="%,%"]>...</frameset>
```

This tag determines how the screen will be divided between the various frames that you're using. You can have as many frames either vertically or horizontally as you want. Each has to be allocated a percentage of the screen. You can also nest framesets so that individual rows or columns can themselves be broken up into frames.

> Rule of Thumb:
> If you use several frames you will be occupying screen real-estate with information-free furniture such as scrollbars. Most people will be using a PC monitor set to 800 by 600 pixels and will not be happy to see too much of that stuff when really it's your content they are after. Use frames sparingly.

```
<frame [name="name"] src="filename"
[scrolling="yes"|"auto"|"no"] [frameborder="0"|"1"]>
```
The src attribute works like an image source or a hyperlink address. It should point to a valid HTML file or image which can be displayed within the frame. It is a good idea to name your frames, as we shall see in the examples. If you know that you won't want a scrollbar on a frame then you can force the browser not to use one, similarly you don't have to have borders on every frame – setting the frameborder attribute to 0 stops it being displayed.

```
<a href="source" target="n">
```
To ensure that pages display in the *correct* frame we need to extend the basic address tag. We need to add the target attribute, which takes the name of the frame that we are going to use to display the information.

### 3.2.1 Frames – A Worked Example

You've already seen the two pages being displayed. The file company.html was used in Section 2.1 and the file orders.html in Section 2.3.1. Figure 3.5 shows what this frameset looks like in Netscape Navigator.

```
<html>
   <head>
      <title>Bill Smiggins Ltd</title>
   </head>
   <frameset rows="25%,50%">
      <frame name="A" src="./company.html">
      <frame name="B" src="./orders.html" scrolling="no">
   </frameset>
</html>
```

## 3.3 FORMS – TOWARD INTERACTIVITY

**Figure 3.5**  Using Simple Frames

Forms are used to add an element of interactivity to a Web site. They are usually used to let the reader send information back to the server but can also be used to simplify navigation on complex Web sites. As with my discussion of frames I'll outline the elements of the form first, describe how they work, and then give examples.

First a word of warning. If you use fill-out forms then you will usually need to have programs running on the server which can process the information that you get sent. I'll be covering the Perl language later in this book before discussing CGI scripting. Forms can be written so that email is used to transfer data from the Web browser to the email account of the sites owner or administrator. Clearly this is unreliable since it only works if visitors to the site have their browser set up to handle email. If your site runs on a server which doesn't support CGI scripting this alternative may be better than not collecting data from visitors. I'll show you how to configure your forms and your browser for email operation in Section 3.3.2.

If you want to use forms, check with the system administrator of your server that you're allowed to run CGI scripts, and if you are find out which languages they allow.

CGI scripting raises issues of technical support and security which many internet service providers (ISP) would rather not address. Clearly, forms and scripts are important for commercial Web sites so look around before selecting your ISP.

**<form action="URL" method="post"|"get">...</form>**

All forms are encapsulated like this. A form can contain virtually all other markup tags but cannot be nested within another form. The `action` attribute specifies the name, and location, of a CGI script that will be used to process the data.

Data can be sent in one of two ways: `post` or `get`. A fuller discussion of this can be found in Chapter 9. Basically you should use `get` to retrieve information from a server and `post` to send information *to* a server. The choice of approach is made by the `method` attribute. When `get` is used, the data is included as part of the URL. The `post` method encodes the data within the body of the message. `Post` can be used to send far larger amounts of data, and is far more secure, than `get`. `Post` is also capable of sending a wide variety of character sets but `get` can only return ASCII data. If you expect to get data written in non-English languages then use `post`.

**<input type="text"|"password"|"checkbox"|"radio"|"password"| "submit"|"reset"|"button"|"image" name="string" [value="string"] [checked] [size="n"] [maxlength="n"] [src="URL"] [align="top"|"bottom"|"middle"|"left"|"right"]>**

The chances are that if you want to get data from visitors then you are going to use some variant of an input *widget*[3]. Several types of input widget such as text fields, radio buttons, and check boxes exist. You'll be used to these widgets from other applications which you have used such as word processors, Web browsers or email clients. I'm going to give some more details of the widgets so that you are clear about their use in an HTML form:

- `text` creates an input device up to `size` characters long and is able to accept up to `maxlength` characters as input. If `value` is set, that string will be used as the default text. These fields support only a single line of text, if you need a to accept a larger amount of text then use a `textarea`.
- `password` works exactly like `text` but the input is not displayed to the screen. Instead each character is replaced by * (an asterisk). The password is not encoded but is sent to the server as plain text and hence provides very little real security but is a useful way of tracking your users.
- `radio` creates a radio button. These are always grouped: buttons within a group should have the same name but different values. The CGI script differentiates them by name + value.
- `checkbox` produces a simple checkbox. It will be returned to the server as name=on if checked at submission.

---

[3]The components in graphical toolkits which are to build the interfaces to programs are often called widgets.

- `submit` creates a button which displays the `value` attribute as its text. It is used to send the data to the server.
- `reset` also creates a button but this one is used to clear the form.
- `image` can be used to place a picture on the page instead of a button. This is a simple way of brightening an otherwise dull form. Use the `align` attribute to control the positioning of the image.

**`<select name="string">...</select>`**

It is often very useful to have a list of items from which the user can choose. The tag encloses a set of options and, when sent to the server, the name of the particular select tag and the name of the chosen option are returned.

**`<option value="string" [selected]>...</option>`**

The `select` statement will have several options from which the user can choose. The values will be displayed as the user moves through the list and the chosen one returned to the server. If an option has `selected` set it will be the value chosen initially when the form appears.

**`<textarea name="string" rows="n" cols="n">...</textarea>`**

creates a free format plain text area into which the user can enter anything they like. The area will be sized at `rows` by `cols` but will support automatic scrolling.

### 3.3.1  Forms – A Worked Example

```
<html>
   <head>
      <title>Bill Smiggins Inc</title>
   </head>
   <body>
      <h2 align="center">Visitor Feedback</h2>
      <hr width="65%">

      <form action="http://www.smiggins.com/cgi-bin/guest.cgi"
      method="post">
         <p align="left">Your Name: <input type="text"
         maxlength="32" size="16">

         <p align="left">Your E-mail Address:
         <input type="text" maxlength="32" size="16">

         <p align="left">Select Your Location:
            <select name="country" size="1">
               <option value="United States" selected>
               United States
```

```
                <option value="Mexico">Mexico
                <option value="Canada">Canada
                <option value="Brazil">Brazil
            </select>

        <p>Comments:
        <br><textarea name="comments" rows="5" cols="35">
        </textarea>
        <p align="center"><input type="submit"
        name="feedback" value="Submit Details">
    </form>
    <hr width="65%">
    </body>
</html>
```

***Figure 3.6*** Getting Information via a Form

### 3.3.2 Getting Form Data Through Email

Getting form data sent to your email requires two configuration steps. Firstly a small change is needed to the script, secondly the Web browser needs to be configured to support email. I should include a word of warning here: I've written many Web pages, forms and scripts, and I've used a wide variety of browsers[4] but I've only ever tested this particular idea using Netscape Navigator. Systems such as Internet Explorer which use an external email client probably won't handle this process too comfortably.

If you are only writing a script and don't ever intend to actually use the facility yourself then you won't need to perform the browser configuration. It makes sense to test your form so that you know exactly what it will email back to you. A final pointer, the data which you get through the email will be converted so that characters such as spaces and ampersands are *escaped* into HTTP format.

***3.3.2.1 Configuring Your Script*** The script needs minimal changes. The data is going to be emailed rather than sent as part of a URL which obviously means that the post method *must* be used. The question then is, how do you force the browser to use its email client? That is done through the action attribute of the form tag. The action is written as mailto: followed directly by an email address. Notice the colon there, you need to use this as a separator between the mailto and your email address. The form tag in the earlier example would change to:

```
<form action="mailto:c.d.bates@shu.ac"
    method="post">
```

If you're going to try this for yourself then change the email address there to your own.

***3.3.2.2 Configuring Netscape*** I'm going to describe how you can get Netscape to transmit form data inside email messages. If you don't use Internet Explorer, I can't help configure your browser to send data through email sinced it uses external email programs such as Outlook. I'm sure that the same process can be made to work but you'll need to read your user manual for details. As for other browsers, there are simply so many available... and they each seem to work in their own way. A variation on the following Netscape 4.7 procedure should work for most circumstances. If you don't know the details of your email account which the following procedure requires, look in the configuration or preferences dialogue of your email client.

- From the Edit menu choose the Preferences option,
- select the Mail and Newsgroups item by clicking on the small triangle,
- choose the Identity item and enter your email address and name in the appropriate boxes,

---

[4]Netscape version 2 onwards, Mozilla, Internet Explorer since version 4, Opera 3 and 4, Lynx and Konqueror.

- choose the `Mailservers` item next,
- if you want to read email using Netscape then add the mail server address which your ISP uses,
- add the name of the SMTP server which your ISP uses, this is the machine which you send email to from your PC and which then relays your email across the Internet,
- enter the log-on name which you use with your ISP,
- select `OK` to save the changes.

## 3.4   THE HTML DOCUMENT HEAD IN DETAIL

I introduced the document head in Section 2.1.3. The head is a very important part of any HTML page: it contains lots of control information that is needed by browsers and servers. Actually, having said that you *could*, and many people *do*, write HTML pages with nothing more complex than a title in the head section. If you want to use scripts or stylesheets, or provide information to search engines, then the simple head section is not appropriate: you need to use some of the tags that are discussed here.

### 3.4.1   Document Type Declarations

Before the initial `<html>` tag the type of the document should be specified so that SGML tools can understand it. Remember that HTML is a subset of SGML and should be capable of being processed by any SGML tools. The document type declaration for basic HTML is:

```
<! doctype html public "-//w3c//dtd html 4.0//en"
     "http://www.w3.org/TR/PR-html4.0/loose.dtd" >
```

If a version of HTML other than 4.0 is used the version number in the doctype declaration should be changed. Languages other than English are specified by changing the en as appropriate.

I'll be describing document type declarations in more detail in Section 14.2. Although that discussion focuses on XML, the same principles and ideas apply to HTML. The W3C has created the following DTDs for HTML:

1. loose,
2. strict
3. transitional
4. frameset.

DTDs list the rules which must be obeyed if a document is going to conform to the HTML recommendation. Each has a different use but generally you should try to create pages which are as compliant as possible. The easiest way of finding how compliant your pages are is to use a *validator*. W3C provide one at their Web site which is fast and fairly straightforward. Current Web browsers are tolerant of poorly written, and even severely broken, HTML but that behaviour cannot be guaranteed in future. Complying with the recommendations is arduous but not too difficult, you ought to get into the habit of including DTDs and checking your pages as soon as possible.

### 3.4.2 Control Information

The head of the document contains control information to be used by servers and browsers. It contains the title of the document which will be displayed at the top of the browser and, optionally, a list of keywords, a description of the document, any files to be linked into the document, and information about how the document was prepared.

```
<! doctype html public "-//w3c//dtd html 4.0//en"
    "http://www.w3.org/TR/PR-html4.0/loose.dtd">
<html>
    <head>
    <base href="http://www.smiggins.com">
    <link rel="Stylesheet" href="./test.css" type="text/css"
        media="screen">
    <meta name="author" content="Chris Bates" >
    <meta http-equiv="expires" content="Wed, 05 Dec 2001
        23:29:05 GMT">
    <meta name="description" content="On-Line Catalogue
        for Bill Smiggins Inc.">
    <title>Bill Smiggins Inc. On-line Catalogue</title>
    </head>
    <body>
    </body>
</html>
```

**`<title>...</title>`**
All HTML documents have just one title which is displayed at the top of the browser window. The title is also used as the name in bookmark files and on search engines. The HTML recommendation makes clear that valid HTML documents *must* have a `title`. This should provide meaningful information since you have no way of knowing how your page will actually be accessed. Something like *Bill Smiggins Inc. On-line Catalogue* has far more meaning and is far more useful than *Index* for instance. The `title` element has to be made available to users by whatever device they are using.

**`<base href="URI">`**
This tag is used to enforce relative links. Linking between pages and documents will be explained in detail in the body section. This tag is optional.

**`<link rel="type" href="URI" type="string" media="string">`**
The link tag is used to allow other documents to be linked to, or included in, the cur-

rent document. This tag has not commonly been used but it is important and useful when using stylesheets. I will be discussing this in more detail in Chapter 4. This tag is optional.

```
<meta name|http-equiv="string" content="string">
```

Any information which describes the whole document should be included using one of these two alternatives. There are many possible meta tags, in fact you can create as many of your own as you need to adequately describe your document. You should use the `name` attribute for meta-data which you are defining. Meta tags can take a URI as a parameter, usually this will be inside the `content` attribute.

The `http-equiv` attribute is used to define meta-data which is intended to be part of an HTTP response message. Such messages are defined as part of the HTTP specification so you can't simply invent your own.

The first two meta tags in the Bill Smiggins example indicate the author of the document, which is useful for version control, and an expiry date which tells the browser to reload from the server rather than using a cached version of the page after the specified date and time.

The third meta tag in the example gives a description of the document to be used by Web search and indexing engines. If it is not used they will include the first few lines of the actual document in their catalogue. It is possible to force a Web engine to see only the main page of your site in which case such descriptions become essential. This tag is optional. You can also define a set of keywords which will be used by indexing systems, robots and crawlers as they gather information.

## 3.5   XHTML – AN EVOLUTIONARY MARKUP

Most HTML authors are yet to make the move from writing HTML 3.2 to writing compliant HTML 4. The W3C has moved even faster and authors must now play catch-up with a target that is getting further away. It's important that you write pages which adhere to the standards and which are based around the latest standards that are available. Current Web browser technology is very forgiving. Major browsers such as Internet Explorer have been designed to display pages which contain invalid HTML. In fact you can get Explorer and Netscape Navigator to show pages which struggle to be identified as HTML at all. These pieces of software are a credit to their developers. Unfortunately, because they are so forgiving, Web developers have had little incentive to write compliant pages. That is all changing.

The big buzz in the on-line industry at the moment is not some new tag or a new scripting technology. Many of the big players are getting very excited indeed about the possibility of delivering on-line content to a range of new devices but predominantly to mobile telephones. A state-of-the-art Dynamic HTML page may look good on a PC screen, it may perform scripted miracles with a fast processor but it won't work on these next-generation devices. Instead it's likely that we'll see two parallel versions of the Web running side-by-side. The existing computer-based Web undoubtedly meets the needs of many users but it has severe limitations for Web surfers using mobile devices to access content.

When a manufacturer creates a new type of device such as the Web-enabled phone they can choose to make it compatible with existing practice or to push developers toward best-practice. A protocol called Wireless Application Protocol (WAP) has already been created to control content delivery to mobile browsers. These new systems will require compliant HTML. Devices with limited processing capabilities must be able to understand a document and ignore those parts which they cannot handle. Next generation developers cannot expect that the client-side software will cover up their limitations.

> Note:
> The W3C has produced a recommendation which expresses HTML as an XML application. XHTML 1.0 was formally released on 26th January, 2000 and should become the new standard which Web authors use. Fortunately the move from HTML 4 to XHTML does not appear to be particularly arduous. If you are writing well-formulated HTML then you are already most of the way to XHTML compliance.

## 3.5.1 The XHTML Document

XHTML[5] is an application of XML. Therefore all XHTML documents must be capable of being generated by XML editors and of being parsed by XML parsers. You may be worried that your browser will be unable to support XHTML pages. In fact the more recent versions of both Explorer and Navigator should have few problems handling compliant XHTML. I have already discussed the support that Internet Explorer version 5 provides for XML; because XHTML *is* XML, Explorer will handle it very well.

> Note:
> The following discussion requires familiarity with XML terminology. If you are unfamiliar with XML ideas, please read Chapter 14 before this section.

### 3.5.1.1 *Control Data*
The actual tags that are used to markup XHTML documents have not changed from HTML 4. What has changed is how those tags are used. I'll examine the changes in the next section. First, though, I'll look at the control information which you must place into your Web pages as you move toward XHTML.

---

[5]The XHTML recommendation can be downloaded from:
`http://www.w3.org/TR/2000/REC-xhtml1-20000126`

*Using An XML Declaration*   Not all XML documents start with an XML declaration. The declaration tells applications that they are handling XML and which particular version of the standard has been used in the markup. The application is then able to make informed decisions about how it handles the markup. For instance it may choose to bypass tags which it does not understand, or it may choose to flag them as errors. In XML, parser applications which validate documents are supposed to stop when they encounter an erroneous tag and may display an error. Other types of application are supposed to render all tags that they can and display the content of tags which they are unable to render. Where they encounter attributes which they don't understand, those attributes should be ignored. Clearly, knowing what your application is dealing with is important. Hence the use of the XML declaration. Start your XHTML documents with the following statement:

```
<?xml version="1.0" encoding="UTF-8">
```

This statement makes it clear to the application that it is handling XML and tells it how the characters within the document were encoded.

### The New Document Type Definitions

XML documents must have Document Type Definitions (DTDs). These are used by validating parsers to check that the markup has been used correctly. DTDs are available for versions of HTML but have rarely been used by authors. Some of the HTML editing tools automatically include an appropriate DTD in the document but few authors pay much attention to their presence. XHTML documents have to have a DTD.

All XHTML DTDs take the same format:[6]

```
<!DOCTYPE html
    PUBLIC "-//W3C//DTD XHTML 1.0 Transitional//EN"
    "DTD/xhtml1-transitional.dtd">
```

There are three different DTDs to choose from. Replace `transitional` from the example with the one you want to use:

- `transitional` should be used in pages which include some presentational markup such as `<font>` tags. These documents will be accessible to browsers which don't understand stylesheets for instance.

- `strict` is used when you want your document to be fully compliant with the standard. All presentational control is done through the use of cascading stylesheets.

- `frameset` lets you partition the screen into a number of separate frames.

### The Expanded HTML Tag

The top-level node of an XHTML document *must* be an `<html>` node. In previous versions of HTML this tag was used to carry control information about formatting and events such as `onLoad`. It now holds information about the page itself.

---

[6]The declaration can be placed on a single line in your documents.

```
<html xmlns="http://www.w3c.org/1999/xhtml"
  xml:lang="en" lang="en">
```

The `html` tag declares the namespace for the document through the `xmlns` attribute. The valid namespace for XHTML 1.0 is as shown above. The language of the document is also declared inside the `html` tag. The `xml:lang` attribute takes precedence over any other language declarations.

### 3.5.1.2 *XHTML Tags*    Although the tags remain the same as in HTML 4, the ways in which they may be used have been tightened up considerably.

- Nested tags must be terminated in the reverse of the order in which they were declared. You will no longer be able to have overlapping tags. The following example shows incorrect code followed by the correct version:

```
<tr><td>Some <b>Data</td></b></tr>
<tr><td>Some <b>Data</b></td></tr>
```

- XML is case-sensitive. All XHTML tags and attributes *must* be in lower-case.

- All tags which have, or may have, content must have end tags. Again I'll show some incorrect code and then the correct version:

```
<p>
<p>Here's a paragraph of text

<p></p>
<p>Here's a paragraph of text</p>
```

- Empty elements, tags which do not contain content, must either have end tags or be terminated properly. A space should be placed before the terminating slash. This example shows valid alternatives:

```
<hr></hr> <hr />
```

- All attribute values must be placed inside quotes. This applies equally to numerical and textual arguments:

```
<hr width="50%"></hr>
<p align="center">Content</p>
<table rows="3">
```

- Scripts and styles must be *wrapped* so that they are not parsed as markup. Even inside `<script>...</script>` tags the characters < and & will be treated as part of the XHTML markup. To avoid this, scripts and styles are declared as containing #PC-DATA. The script element is included like this:

```
<script>
  <![CDATA[
```

```
        // your script goes here
    ]]>
</script>
```

- Some HTML elements have had a `name` attribute with which they could be uniquely identified by scripts. This has been particularly important for forms and for elements such as `div` which have been manipulated through scripting. In XHTML 1.0 the `name` attribute has been deprecated to be replaced by `id`. According to the recommendation document the `name` attribute will be removed from a future version of XHTML altogether. This is because XML has attributes only of type `id`.

### 3.5.2  An Example

The following document, which is admittedly trivial, demonstrates the structure of an XHTML document. Notice that all tags are closed including the *empty* ones. Because this document is also an XML document it starts with the XML version identifier. Whilst not all XML documents *require* this, it is advisable to use it in XHTML so that you can show which character encoding you are using. Typically you will use UTF-8, occasionally UTF-16. Apart from that, this document looks and feels like XHTML and should display nicely in your browser.

```
<?xml version="1.0" encoding="UTF-8">
<!DOCTYPE html
    PUBLIC "-//W3C//DTD XHTML 1.0 Transitional//EN"
    "DTD/xhtml1-transitional.dtd">

<html xmlns="http://www.w3c.org/1999/xhtml"
    xml:lang="en" lang="en">

    <head>
        <title>Sample XHTML Document</title>
    </head>
    <body>
        <h1>Sample XHTML Document</h1>
        <hr/>
        <p>This very basic document is an XHTML
        document</p>
        <ul>
            <li>It has an xml version identifier</li>
            <li>It has a valid DTD</li>
            <li>All tags are closed</li>
        </ul>
        <hr/>
```

```
    </body>
</html>
```

## 3.6  EXERCISES

### Framesets

1. Try using a simple frameset to display two pages at the same time. Split the screen first horizontally, then vertically. Which do you prefer?

2. Now try having a single screen with up to five frames, some horizontal and some vertical. Does that work from either a design or development perspective?

### HTML Forms

1. What is the role of the HTML form?

2. Outline the relationship between HTML forms and CGI scripts. Can form data be processed if there is no related script?

3. Create an HTML form with all possible elements onboard. That's a bit messy, so try a simple form such as might be used for a guestbook. Format the form so that it looks OK on the screen. Use a table to format the form.

### The Document Head

1. What is a document type declaration and why is it needed?

2. What sorts of meta-information can be placed in the **head** of a document?

3. Add some meta information such as keyword lists to one of your pages. Does this have any effect upon the way that the browser handles the page?

### XHTML

- Why has W3C developed the XHTML specification?

- Take an HTML 4 page that you have developed, possibly one of those from this book, and rewrite it so that it conforms to the XHTML recommendation.

- Search the Web for an XML validator. Does your XHTML page pass the validation process?

# 4
# *Cascading Stylesheets*

## 4.1  INTRODUCTION

One of the most important aspects of HTML is the capability to separate presentation and content. This is a sort of holy grail for anyone who is interested in publication. Often desktop publishing software, rather than a word processor, is used to lay out documents yet a word processor will have been used to create the content. The layout of documents includes positioning on the page and the choice of fonts, colors, borders, backgrounds and so on.

Formatting content for traditional publishing is a complicated procedure but is well understood and many aspects are now capable of complete automation. The Web presents a somewhat different proposition because the author or designer of a Web page has no way of knowing how it will be accessed. The page may be viewed on a television screen, a computer screen or mobile phone, any of which may show images, text, tables or a mixture of them all. Straightforward HTML does not have the facilities that are needed to cope with this diversity, but stylesheets provide them.

A style is simply a set of formatting instructions that can be applied to a piece of text. There are three mechanisms by which we can apply styles to our HTML documents:

- the style can be defined within the basic HTML tag,
- styles can be defined in the `<head>` section and applied to the whole document,
- styles can be defined in external files called stylesheets which can then be used in any document by including the stylesheet via a URI.

In this book I'll concentrate on the third technique as it seems to me that it is the most flexible. If you are interested in using the other techniques the simple examples I give should be enough to get you started. Comprehensive lists and definitions of the properties and values which you can use in creating styles are beyond the scope of this book. They can easily be found with a quick Web search, as can details of which browsers support which styles.

Not all browsers support stylesheets and many which do cannot yet process them fully. This does not matter too much as browsers are designed to ignore any HTML tags or attributes that they do not understand. When someone with an older browser views your pages the content will be formatted as if you had not used stylesheets. This means that you have to be careful about how you apply styles and how much you depend upon them. You may come up with a radical design which looks excellent on your system, but when viewed without the styles it might look terribly mundane.

Styles can be *cascaded*. This means that formats override any which were defined or included earlier in the document. For instance you may include an external stylesheet which redefines the h1 tag, then write an h1 style in the head of your page before finally redefining h1 in the body of your page. The browser will use the last of these definitions when showing the content. Furthermore you can define a style which is applied to all instances of an HTML element, for instance, so that all h1 headings are changed, or you can alter the appearance of specific h1 elements, leaving the others unchanged.

---

Rule of Thumb:

More browsers are including support for style sheets. Styles can be used to provide complex formatting which previously had to be *kludged* using images. Therefore move to using styles now, but make sure that your pages are browser-friendly.

---

## 4.2 USING STYLES: SIMPLE EXAMPLES

Unfortunately you can't really learn about stylesheets in a gradual or incremental fashion. You need to use a resource such as the list of tags in this book and then dive straight in. The following examples are just about as simple as the use of styles can get.

*Changing h1*   In this first example the `<h1>` tag is redefined. The text is colored in red, centered on the screen and has a thin border placed around it. Figure 4.1 shows the effect that this produces in the Konqueror browser.

```
<html>
   <head>
      <title>Simple Stylesheet</title>
      <style>
      <!--
         h1{
            color: red;
```

**Figure 4.1**   Changing h1

```
        border: thin groove;
        text-align: center;
      }
    -->
    </style>
  </head>
  <body>
    <h1>Simple Stylesheet</h1>
  </body>
</html>
```

Notice that I'm declaring the style in the head of the document using the style tag. I place the actual style definition inside an HTML comment so that it will be ignored by browsers which don't support styles. The declaration has the name of the element which is being changed and then a definition which is placed inside braces. The attributes which are being changed are placed in a list with each term separated by a semi-colon. I usually place each attribute on a new line so that the definition is easier to read and maintain. Each definition is made from the attribute and a list of values which are separated by a colon. You might expect the values to be surrounded by double quotes in the same way that the attributes of HTML tags are. Don't do this: it isn't needed and, actually, the browser won't be able to handle the code if you include them. There are, as ever, exceptions to this. If you use a hexadecimal value to declare a color or if you use a font name which includes spaces then you can use either single quotes or quotation marks around it.

*Changing More Styles*   This example goes slightly further by altering both h1 and a paragraph. The paragraph is moved slightly to the right by giving it a left margin, has a colored background and a ridged border. The resulting Web page is shown in Figure 4.2.

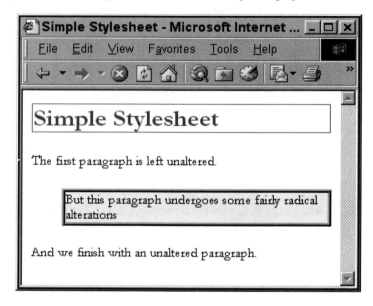

**Figure 4.2**   Declaring Styles Inline and in The Head

```
<html>
   <head>
      <title>Simple Stylesheet</title>
      <style>
      <!--
         h1{
            color: red;
            border: thin groove;
         }
      -->
      </style>
   </head>
   <body>
      <h1>Simple Stylesheet</h1>
      <p>The first paragraph is left unaltered.</p>
      <p style="margin-left: 10%; border: ridge;
         background: #ffffcc">
      But this paragraph undergoes some fairly radical
      alterations.</p>
```

```
      <p>And we finish with an unaltered paragraph.</p>
   </body>
</html>
```

The syntax of the style definition changes when it is done inside an HTML tag. The definition becomes an *attribute*, named style, of the tag. The description of the style is passed as the value of the attribute and so must follow an equals sign. The definition is placed inside quotation marks but otherwise uses the same syntax that we saw a moment ago.

Redefining elements as I've done with the paragraph in the example is unsatisfactory. There is no separation between the processing of an element and the definition of that element. Remember the markup should be logical; any physical changes (i.e. new formats) should appear outside of that markup.

*A Slightly More Complex Example*   This second example of styles builds upon the first. This time two classes are declared. There's much more on the use of classes in Section 4.3.3 and in Section 4.6.1. Notice this time that whole blocks of text can be moved around the screen. Here an entire paragraph is moved to the right of another, and hence acts as a sort of label. This code produces a page like that shown in Figure 4.3.

```
<html>
   <head>
      <title>Simple Stylesheet</title>
      <style>
        h1 {
           color: red;
           border: thin groove;
        }
        h2 {
           color: green;
           margin-left: 60%
        }
        .myid {
           text-align: right;
           color: purple;
        }
        .myid2 {
           align: right
        }
      </style>

   </head>
   <body>
```

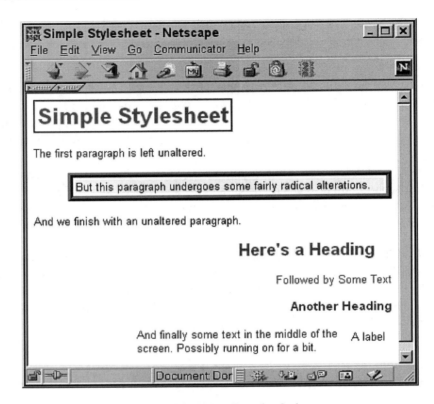

***Figure 4.3***   Using Complex Styles

```
<h1>Simple Stylesheet</h1>
<p>The first paragraph is left unaltered.
<p style="margin-left: 10%; border: ridge;
   background: #ffffcc">
But this paragraph undergoes some fairly radical
alterations.</p>
<p>And we have an unaltered paragraph.</p>
<h2>Here's a Heading</h2>

<p class="myid">Followed by Some Text</p>
<h3 class="myid">Another Heading</h3>

<p class="myid2">A label</p>
<p style="margin-left: 30%; color: blue">
And finally some text in the middle of the screen.
Possibly running on for a bit.</p>
```

```
    </body>
</html>
```

## 4.3 DEFINING YOUR OWN STYLES

Styles are defined by simple rules. A style can contain as many rules as you want and, as with processing HTML, if something doesn't make sense it will be ignored.

### 4.3.1 Cascading Styles

Conventionally styles are cascaded. This means that you do not have to use just a single set of styles inside a document – you can import as many stylesheets as you like. This is useful if you define a set of organizational styles that can be modified by each department. The only difficulty with importing multiple stylesheets is that they cascade. This means that the first is overridden by the second, the second by the third, and so on. Of course the overriding only happens if a later stylesheet contains a definition of a style that is already defined. You can also override styles by defining styles within the body of the page as I showed in Section 4.2.

### 4.3.2 Rules

A style rule has two parts: a selector and a set of declarations. The selector is used to create a link between the rule and the HTML tag. The declaration has two parts: a property and a value. Selectors can be placed into classes so that a tag can be formatted in a variety of ways. Declarations must be separated using colons and terminated using semicolons.

`selector {property:  value; property:  value ...}`

This form is used for all style declarations in stylesheets. The declaration has three items: the property, a colon, and the value. If you miss the colon or fail to put the semicolon between declarations the style cannot be processed. Rules do not have to be formatted as I've shown – as with HTML you can lay the text out however you like. The rule will be more readable if you put each declaration on its own line. This is an example of a simple rule, followed by a more complex one:

```
body {
    background-color: #eebd2;
}

h1 {
    color: #eeebd2;
    background-color: #d8a29b;
    font-family: "Book Antiqua", Times, serif;
```

```
        border: thin groove #9baab2;
}
```

The detail of these style attributes will be discussed in Section 4.4.

### 4.3.3   Classes

The method shown above applies the same style to all examples of a given tag. That is fine
if you want every paragraph equally indented or every level one heading in the same font.
If you only want to apply a style to some paragraphs, for instance, you have to use classes:

**selector.classname {property:   value; property:   value}**

**<selector class=classname>**

These examples show how classes should be used. In the stylesheet itself the rule is
slightly modified by giving the style a unique name which is appended to the selector
using a dot. In the HTML document when you want to use a named style the tag is
extended by including class= and the unique name.

```
h1.fred {
    color: #eeebd2;
    background-color: #d8a29b;
    font-family: "Book Antiqua", Times, serif;
    border: thin groove #9baab2;
}
```

```
<h1 class="fred">A Simple Heading</h1>
```

The benefit of classes is that they can provide a lot of variety. They are especially good
if you want to redefine the paragraph style so that your introductions look different from
your content.

#### 4.3.3.1   *Anonymous Classes*   Sometimes you want to apply a piece of formatting
to many different elements within a page but not necessarily to the entire page. You could
redefine every element in a stylesheet to make it use your formatting, and then redefine
individual elements back to their defaults as you needed to. This is a rather awkward
approach and would inevitably lead to a lot of duplication of effort. Cascading stylesheets
provides a way of defining styles within reusable classes. The following code and Figure
4.4 show how this works.

```
<html>
    <head>
        <title>Anonymous Classes</title>
        <style>
        <!--
            .fred {
```

**Figure 4.4**   Using Classes of Style

```
        color: #eeebd2;
        background-color: #d8a29b;
        font-family: "Book Antiqua", Times, serif;
        border: thin groove #9baab2;
      }
    -->
    </style>
  </head>
  <body>
    <h1 class="fred">A Simple Heading</h1>
    <p class="fred">Applying the style fred to a
       paragraph of text</p>
  </body>
</html>
```

### 4.3.4   Including Stylesheets

I've already mentioned how to include stylesheets in Section 3.4. The following, adapted for your local needs, must be included in the <head> of your HTML page:

**<link rel="StyleSheet" href="url" type="text/css" media="screen">**
  The href is a hyperlink to your stylesheet, rel tells the browser what type of link you are using. It is likely that in the future there will be many types of relationship available. You have to tell the browser what type of document you are including, the type

statement gives the relevant MIME type. Finally it is useful, although not compulsory, to tell the browser how the document will be used. HTML specifies a variety of ways of using a document, including screen viewing, printing, and as presentations. Use the `media` attribute to describe the type of use.

This example shows how to include your organizational stylesheet:

```
<link rel="StyleSheet"
href="http://www.smiggins.co.uk/mainstyles.css"
type="text/css" media="screen">
[<style type="text/css">]
<!- @import url(url); - ></style>
```

These lines are both needed if you intend to use more than one stylesheet. The first sheet is included as if it were the only one; any further stylesheets have to be imported. Notice that the `@import` is enclosed within a comment so that it can be easily ignored by older browsers.

```
<link rel="StyleSheet"
href="http://www.smiggins.co.uk/mainstyles.css"
type="text/css" media="screen">
<style type="text/css">
  <! -- @import
     url("http://www.smiggins.com/style.css")
  -- >
</style>
```

## 4.4 PROPERTIES AND VALUES IN STYLES

A number of properties of the text can be altered. These can be grouped together. I'll list the properties in useful groups and give some of the options that you can alter. The best way of discovering how styles work is to play around with some of these properties. Try giving absurd values to elements and see what happens.

> Rule of Thumb:
> Don't change too many options. You're trying to present information, not give a lesson in typography and colors. Be careful, as ever, and make sure that your key changes are available to your target audience. Don't rely too heavily on styles yet – within a year or two they may be everywhere but at the moment Web surfers have to wait for the next revision of their browsers.

In the following descriptions of the properties I won't give examples; there is a large and fairly comprehensive example later in this section.

### 4.4.1 Fonts

`font-family:  <family name> [<generic family>]`

Fonts are identified by giving the name of a specific font. Many Microsoft Windows and Apple systems have similar sets of TrueType fonts. Unfortunately UNIX systems use Type 1 and PostScript fonts. Therefore it is unlikely that a reader on one of those computers will have access to the fonts from your PC. The TrueType fonts look better than Type 1 fonts and the user-base of Web surfers with access to true type is far greater.

You should try to use TrueType fonts in your Web pages but provide an option for users who don't have these fonts. This can be done in two ways. First, you may specify as many fonts as you like for each style in the hope that most people will have at least one of them. Second, you can specify a default generic font which all browsers on all systems can handle. Five generic fonts are specified: *serif (times)*, *sans-serif (arial)*, *cursive*, *fantasy*, *monospaced (courier)*. Font names which include whitespace should be placed in quotes. Generally a list of fonts is provided, the browser will try to use each in turn until it finds one that it recognises:[1]

```
p {
   font-family: "Bookman Old Style",
      "Times New Roman", Times, serif;
}
```

`font-style:  normal|italic|oblique`

Fairly straightforward. Oblique fonts are slanted, italic do not have to be.

`font-weight:  normal|bold|bolder|lighter|100|200|`
`300|400|500|600|700|800|900`

The weight of any font can be altered. The first four options are relative while the numbered values give absolute weights. Not all fonts support all possible weights and you may want to be careful using absolute weights.

`font-size:  [small|medium|large] | [smaller|larger] |`
`<length>|<percentage>`

As well as changing the weight you can alter the size. Again, a choice of relative sizes is possible. Font lengths should be given in appropriate units such as pt. A discussion of units is given in Section 4.4.5. Absolute sizes include small, large, and so on, while relative sizes are larger or smaller.

## 4.4.2  Backgrounds and Colors

`color:  <value>`

`background-color:  <value>|transparent`

`background-image:  URL|none`

The color of any attribute can be changed. Values should be given as hexadecimal values. Backgrounds for the whole page or individual elements can have their color set

---

[1]The line break here is simply so that the code fits onto the page.

from the stylesheet. Elements can also have transparent backgrounds. Instead of a color an image can be used, identified by its URL. If you set the `background-color` you should set the `background-image` to none.

### 4.4.3  Text

`text-decoration:` `none`|`underline`|`overline`|`line-through`
> Any piece of text can be decorated. If you want to remove the underlining on links try this:

```
A:link, A:visited, A:active{text-decoration:  none}
```

`text-transformation:` `none`|`capitalize`|`uppercase`|`lowercase`
> Allows you to set the case of text. This can be useful if you can't be sure that text will be entered appropriately. For instance if you are listing countries by their initials create a capitalized style.

`text-align:` `left`|`right`|`center`|`justify`
> One of the most useful text styles. Allows you to fully justify text in paragraphs, which many people like. By default HTML uses ragged right margins.

`text-indentation:` `length`|`percentage`
> Before stylesheets were devised text could not be indented on the left side. Many people like their text indented, as this paragraph is, and would use small transparent GIFs to achieve it. Using the style is much better, as it downloads along with the text and it is flexible. Use a percentage and the amount of space will scale nicely if the browser window is resized.

### 4.4.4  Boxes

Many items can be encased in boxes. This can give some very good effects although care needs to be taken. If the boxes become overwhelming or are used too much they can start to look rather odd.

`margin:` `length`|`percentage`|`auto` `{1,4}`
`border-width:` `thin`|`thick`|`medium`|`length` `{1,4}`
`padding:` `length`|`percentage` `{1,4}`
> Any of the margins of a box can be changed. This time it may often be better to specify an absolute length – if you use a percentage the margins may become overly crowded when the window is resized. You can specify 1, 2, or 4 margin values. If you specify 4 they are applied in the order: top, right, bottom, and left. Specify just one value and it is applied to all four margins. Specify two values and the first will be applied to top and bottom, the second to left and right margins. As with margins you can specify the amount of white space within an element. Padding and border width are applied in the same way as margins.

```
border-color:    value {1,4}
border-style:    none|dotted|dashed|solid|double|groove|
ridge {1,4}
```

This sets the color of the border around the element. Up to four different colors can be specified. They are applied to the borders in the same order as margins. Each edge of the border can have a different style.

```
width:    length|percentage|auto
height:   length|auto
```

Any block-level element can be given a specific width or height. As with so many items it is better to specify the width as percentages to allow for resizing of the browser window. The height must be specified as an absolute size.

### 4.4.5   Units and URLs

***4.4.5.1   Lengths***   These can be either absolute or relative. A relative length can be either positive or negative, which is indicated by preceding the value with an optional + or −.

Relative units that can be used are:

- em: the height of the font for this element
- ex: the height of the letter "x" in the current font
- px: pixels

Allowable absolute units are:

- in: size in inches
- cm: size in centimeters
- mm: size in millimeters
- pt: points where 1 pt equals 1/72 inch
- pc: picas where 1 pc = 12 pt

***4.4.5.2   URLs***   URLs can be used in stylesheets just as they can in HTML documents. The format of the URL reference is:

```
url(location)
```

URLs can optionally be quoted and may be either absolute or relative. If a URL is partial it is considered to be relative to the location of the stylesheet source, not the HTML document source.

## 4.5   STYLESHEETS – A WORKED EXAMPLE

### 4.5.1   The stylesheet

```
body {
    background-color: "#eeebd2";
```

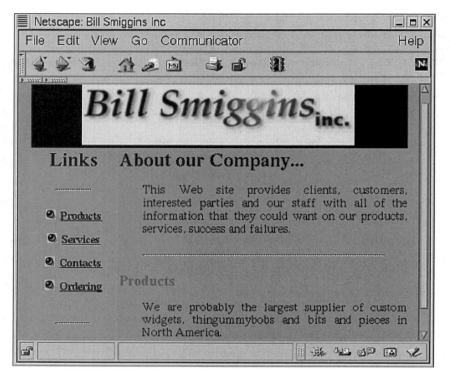

**Figure 4.5**  Formatting Using Stylesheets

```
   margin: 5px 5px 5px 5px;
}

h1 {
   color: "#eeebd2";
   background-color: "#d8a29b";
   font-family: "Book Antiqua", Times, serif;
   border: thin groove #9baab2;
}

h2 {
   color: "#8b007c";
   font-family: "Book Antiqua", Times, serif;
   border: thin groove "#8b007c";
}

h3 {
   font-family: "Book Antiqua", Times, serif;
```

```
      color: "#8b007c";
}

em {
   font-weight: bold;
   font-style: italic;
}

hr {
   margin-right: 10%;
   margin-left: 10%;
}

p.link {
   color: "#8b007c";
   text-align: center;
   font-family: "Lucida Casual", Times, serif;
   font-weight: bold;
   font-size: 10pt;
   margin-left: 0%;
}

p {
   font-family: "Bookman Old Style", Times, serif;
   margin-left: 10%;
   text-align: justify;
}

strong {
   font-family: Arial, sans-serif;
   font-size: 12pt;
   color: red
}

th {
   background-color: "#b2a474";
   align: center;
   color: #8b007c
}

table {
```

```
      padding: 2pt 2pt 2pt 2pt;
}


td.firstcol {
   background-color: "#00acac";
   font-weight: bold;
   text-align: center;
}


table.main {
   padding: 0px 0px 0px 0px;
}
```

### 4.5.2  The HTML Page

```
<html>
   <head>
      <title>Bill Smiggins Inc</title>
      <link rel="StyleSheet" href="./test.css" type="text/css"
         media="screen">
   </head>
   <body bgcolor="#ffffff" text="#362e00">
   <! -- start of the table -->

   <table class="main">
      <tr>
         <! -- first of all the logo >
         <td colspan="2" align="center" bgcolor="#000000">
         <img src="./logo.gif"> </td>
      </tr>
      <tr>
         <td  bgcolor="#7cb98b" width="20%" valign="top">
         <! -- and then the links -->

         <h2 align="center">Links</h2>
         <hr width="50%">

         <h3>
         <p class=link><img src="./bullet.gif"> 
         <a href="./products.html">Products</a></p>

         <p class=link><img src="./bullet.gif"> 
```

```
          <a href="./products.html">Services</a></p>

          <p class=link><img src="./bullet.gif"> 
          <a href="./products.html">Contacts</a></p>

          <p class=link><img src="./bullet.gif"> 
          <a href="./products.html">Ordering</a></p>

          <br><hr width="50%"><br>
          </h3>

          </td>
          <td width="70%">
          <! -- and finally the information -->

          <h2>About our Company...</h2>
          <p>This Web site provides clients, customers,
          interested parties and our staff with all of the
          information that they could want on our products,
          services, success and failures.</p>

          <hr>
          <h3>Products</h3>
          <p align="center"> We are probably the largest
          supplier of custom widgets, thingummybobs and bits
          and pieces in North America.</p>

          <hr width="50%">
          </td>
      </tr>
   </table>

   </body>
</html>
```

## 4.6  FORMATTING BLOCKS OF INFORMATION

To conclude this discussion of stylesheets I'm going to re-emphasize a couple of points and mention something new. It's important that you're clear about classes and how they work and that you understand two new ideas: divisions and spans. All of these affect the way that the page is laid out by the browser, but you also need to have a grasp of layers. I haven't mentioned these before because they can be a little confusing. However, when I start to look at using JavaScript to create dynamic HTML pages I'll be using layers (and divisions) quite a lot. In this section you'll learn how to use layers to perform interesting textual effects as a prelude to using them to manipulate images and text together.

### 4.6.1 Classes

The discussion of stylesheets and the comprehensive example in Section 4.5.1 showed how to use classes. This is a reminder of why they are used, and what they're used for. Styles can be used to change the appearance of individual elements but often you'll want to change the way that every instance of an element appears. This is easily done through the stylesheet, but what if you only want to alter *some* elements? In that case the most effective thing you can do is use a class.

A class is a definition of a set of styles which can be applied as you choose: if you don't want the styles then you don't have to use them. Classes can be applied to a single type of element, or may be *anonymous* and hence applicable to any element. The following code shows the difference between the two types:

```
h1 {
   color: red;
   border: thin groove;
   }
h2.some {
   color: green;
   margin-left: 60%;
   }
.anyelement {
   text-align: right;
   color: purple;
   }
```

The style defined for h1 applies to all h1 elements in the document. The h2 style is only applied when it is explicitly called:

```
<h2 class="some">...</h2>
```

The .anyelement style can be applied wherever it is needed:

```
<h2 class=anyelement>...</h2>
<p class=anyelement>...</p>
```

Notice that an h2 element is formatted using a class in that second example. Even though the h2 is already declared in predefined format *and* modified by an explicit h2 style, we can still apply a class of style to it.

It's probably a good idea to move to using stylesheets and classes as quickly as possible. Version 4 of HTML clearly and strongly requires a separation of formatting and content. If you want to make the background of your page red and use white text you might do this with:

```
<body bgcolor="red" text="white">
```

Doing this places formatting information about colors in with the text of the document. Browsers will continue to happily handle such statements but only for backwards compatibility. The preferred alternative would be to do this:

```
<html>
   <head>
      <title>Changing the body</title>
      <style>
      <!--
         body {
            color: white;
            background-color: red;
         }
      -->
      </style>
   </head>
   <body>
      <h1>A New Page</h1>
   </body>
</html>
```

And, of course, the benefit of this system is that you can change the formatting of parts of your text without having to work though the document making lots of small changes.

## 4.6.2 Divisions

An element in an HTML document is either a block element or an inline element. A block would be something like a paragraph, while an inline might be something like text, a figure or an individual character that is part of a block. Each of these can be manipulated separately.

First I'll look at changing the appearance of block elements. This is really very simple. Rather than applying the formatting to the element itself, a <div>...</div> pair of tags are wrapped around the element. Any formatting that needs adding is placed inside the div tag thus:

```
<div class="anyelement">
   <p>...</p>
   <h2>...</h2>
```

```
<p>...</p>
<hr>
</div>
```

This doesn't immediately offer much that isn't already available from the other HTML tags. But a division is now a logical part of the document and we can start to treat divisions as individual items. I'll show how this can be used to create interesting effects in Section 4.7, and how it is used when writing Dynamic HTML in Chapter 7.

### 4.6.3 Spans

The HTML standard no longer supports the idea of modifying individual items in place. This is to remove problems that can arise with the indiscriminate use of colors and `<font>...</font>` tags. It is no longer regarded as acceptable to modify these items from within the body of the document. That does not mean that they *can't* be altered; in fact the reverse is true.

A simple and efficient model has been devised based around the span tag. Spans are used as follows:

```
<p><span class="anyelement">The</span> span tag
```

Whilst that is no easier to code than using font attributes directly, it will make sense when the page is accessed through any type of medium. Whether viewed on a browser such as Internet Explorer, accessed from a text-only browser like Lynx or though a browser devised for the visually handicapped, that span tag can be rendered in some meaningful way.

```
<div [id="..."] [class="..."|style="..."]>...</div>
<span [id="..."] [class="..."|style="..."]>...</span>
```
The div and span tags have identical parameters but the effects of those parameters are altered by the context in which they are used. Each can have an id so that it can be identified by other elements on the page. This is not generally useful on a static page of text but it is useful in the context of Dynamic HTML as will be shown in Chapter 7. Styles are applied to span and div through either the class or style parameters. A set of styles can be defined within the tag and applied though style while a pre-defined class is applied through class. As with any use of styles these tags can, of course, be cascaded.

---

Rule of Thumb:
This cannot be overstated. Whenever possible use browser-independent tags. Make your site accessible to more browsers and you increase your potential revenue streams.

---

## 4.7 LAYERS

The page layout that a browser creates results from layering text and images on top of each other. This lets Web designers use images as the backgrounds of their pages and then place further images and text over them. By extending the idea slightly we can place text items and images on top of each other in multiple layers. This isn't especially impressive on a static Web page but, as I'll show in Chapter 7, it lets the Dynamic HTML developer create some very interesting effects.

Netscape has extended the HTML standard by adding a `layer` tag which you may see discussed in books, magazines and on their Web site. The `layer` tag is browser-specific and its use leads to confusion with the more general idea of layers. Frankly it would be better if everyone forgot[2] about that particular tag so I'm not going to consider it in this book. Instead I'll explain a platform-independent alternative that will work in the major browsers and should work in other browsers that comply with the standard.

When I discussed the `div` tag in Section 4.6.2 I deliberately ignored some of its most powerful attributes so that I could explain them in the context of layers.

**`z-index:  n`**

>The browser maintains a stack of layers of content. The background image is placed first, with text and images on top of it. For each `div` that you use you can determine where in that stack it will appear by setting the `z-index` parameter.
>
>The lowest layer, appearing on top of the background, has a `z-index` of 1. There isn't a functional upper limit to the value that you can assign to `z-index`. However, if you number your layers sequentially as you move up the stack you are unlikely to place more than about 20 layers before the screen becomes unmanageable.
>
>Many layers can have the same `z-index` value if you want to place them at the same level. This is useful in many situations: for instance you may have layers containing images placed around the screen which you want your text to appear over (or under!), or you may use some of the techniques I'll demonstrate using Dynamic HTML to make content appear and disappear.

**`position:  absolute|relative`**

>Divisions have to be placed on the screen so that their top left corner starts at pixel 0,0 They can be given specific locations, but the placement of that layer may be either `absolute` (a fixed point on the screen) or `relative` to the placement of other content. This is optional and defaults to absolute.

**`left:  n`**

**`top:  n`**

>The location of the division in pixels. You locate divisions around the screen by speci-

---

[2]A number of ugly browser-specific "extensions" to HTML have appeared and died over the years. Netscape's `blink` and Microsoft's `banner` were particular abominations.

fying the position of their top-left corner. Usually this is given relative to the origin of the screen, but it may also be relative to items that you've already placed.

These parameters are optional and both default to `0,0`.

`width:  n`
`height:  n`
The size of the division in pixels. Defaults to the amount of space needed to display the content of the division.

### 4.7.0.1  *Layers – A Worked Example*    Now you know what layers *are* you probably want to know what they look like. The result is shown in Figure 4.6.

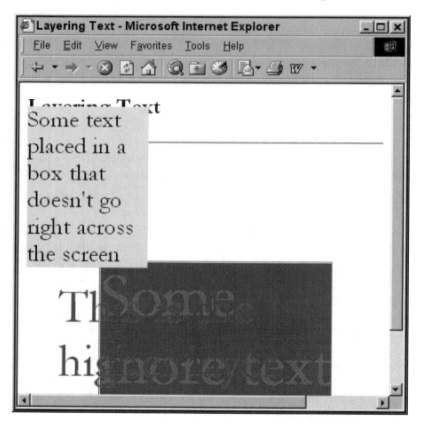

**Figure 4.6**   Using Layers to Format Pages

```
<html>
   <head>
      <title>Layering Text</title>
   </head>
   <body>
```

```
    <h1>Layering Text</h1>

    <div style="z-index: 2; left: 50px; top: 250px;
    position: absolute; color: red; text: white;
    font-size: 36pt; border: thin-groove;">
        <p>This is the higher layer</p>
    </div>

    <div style="z-index: 1; left: 100px; top: 225px;
    position: absolute; font-size: 46pt; color: magenta;
    background-color: green; border: thin groove">
        <p>Some more text</p>
    </div>

    <div style="z-index: 4; left: 10; top: 30px; width: 150px;
    position: absolute; background-color: yellow;
    color: black; font-size: 18pt;">
        <p>Some text placed in a box that doesn't go right
        across the screen
    </div>

    <div style="position: absolute; top: 300px; left: 500px;
    width: 25; background-color: #aeae00; color: blue;
    font-size: 16pt; font-style: italic; z-index: 2">
        <p>And in the bottom right corner...
    </div>

    <hr>
    </body>
</html>
```

## 4.8 EXERCISES

### Styles

1. What do Web designers mean when they talk about a *style*?

2. Although stylesheets have been a W3C recommendation for a while now, many browsers do not yet support them fully. How should a browser behave if it encounters formatting that it cannot handle?

3. Describe the different ways that styles can be added to a page.

4. What are the benefits of using styles compared with placing formatting directly into the text of the Web page?

5. What is a stylesheet class?

6. Create a stylesheet for your Web site. You will probably make a few mistakes, even if only in typing. How does *your* browser react to these errors?

7. What happens if you specify a font that is unavailable?

## Formatting blocks of content

1. HTML has two commands which are used to apply formatting to elements within the page. Compare and contrast the use of `<div>` and `<span>`.

2. In one of your pages include a number of `div` elements. How does the browser handle these? If you have access to more than one type of browser compare the effects that the same commands can create.

3. What is a layer? How are they described within HTML code?

4. Alter the page that you created using `<div>` so that each division acts as a layer and is moved vertically relative to other layers.

5. Try using *absolute* and *relative* positioning. What effect do they give both with and without the use of layers?

# 5
# *An Introduction to JavaScript*

Static Web pages are fine: they are useful and can be entertaining or informative. What they are not is part of a truly interactive multimedia experience. Nothing moves about, pages don't respond to the reader's actions and pages can't be dynamically tailored to suit a user's needs. The static Web page is essentially just a different way of presenting information that could equally easily have been published in a book.

From a developer's point of view a Web page can be equally frustrating. As an example consider the humble Web form. Users enter data and submit it to the server, where a CGI script is used to verify and validate that data. The whole process of passing data across the network before it can be checked is slow. How much more interactive could a site be if data were checked by the browser and any error messages originated locally? Users are always more likely to return to a fast site than a slow one, and of course return visitors are important to all businesses. The interactive Web site becomes more like an application than a book, which changes the whole Web experience.

A number of technologies have been developed that enable the creation of Web applications rather than static Web pages. The Java programming language is probably the best known such technology. It is a fully-fledged development language which is much nearer to C++ than it is to HTML. It's complex and requires a good deal of skill when building even simple applications. The benefit of Java is that developers can place Java applets (small programs) inside HTML pages. Java is slow and such applets can take a long time to download and initiate. In fact many Web surfers switch the Java functionality off in their browser because of the overhead of using it.

Few programming languages other than Java have been adapted for use in client-side Web applications. The venerable Tcl/Tk from Scriptics Inc. and Visual Basic from Microsoft are probably the best known but neither is very widely used for these browser applications. In fact most programming on the client side is done in a language called ECMA Script.

You may never have heard of ECMA Script but you will almost certainly have heard of JavaScript (from Netscape) and JScript (from Microsoft).

ECMA Script is an international standard which was developed retrospectively and based around version 1.1 of JavaScript. The language was specified by the European Computer Manufacturers Association in a document called ECMA-262 and later ratified by the International Organisation for Standards (ISO). Further versions of the standard have been released and adopted by browser developers: Netscape 6 and Mozilla both implement edition 3 as version 1.5 of JavaScript. Broadly speaking the language is well implemented by Netscape and Microsoft in their browsers but each company has chosen to extend the language and to implement different Document Object Models (DOM).

The differences in DOM implementation from the two big players mean that most scripts work in one browser or the other but rarely in both. Most developers code for either Netscape Navigator or Microsoft Internet Explorer. I'll try to show some code that will work with both, but I'll also demonstrate the differences between the two environments and show how to code for each of them.

You *can* program successful JavaScript sites without understanding the underlying mechanisms, generally, though, if you want to develop sites which work across platforms and devices you'll need to understand the DOM. Scripts can only manipulate objects on the page because of the Document Object Model. This was developed by the World Wide Web Consortium (W3C) but neither of the big two yet adheres fully to it.

## 5.1 WHAT IS DYNAMIC HTML?

Dynamic HTML is a combination of content formatted using HTML, cascading stylesheets, a scripting language, and the DOM. Usually the scripting language is ECMA Script compliant although it doesn't have to be. By combining all of the technologies from W3C developers can create interesting and interactive Web sites which continue to download quickly and which have relatively low hardware requirements. Many multimedia plug-ins need modern high specification PCs and are unusable by the disabled or through non-traditional hardware. For instance, a page based around a fancy plug-in cannot be used via a mobile telephone but a DHTML page can.

> Rule Of Thumb:
> The DHTML aspects of the page should be the icing on the cake rather than the cake itself.

You may have been left wondering what ECMA Script is. It's really a standard rather than a real thing: it's the standard for languages which manipulate the document object model and is actually based upon Netscape's JavaScript version 1.1. Given that JScript from Microsoft is equivalent to JavaScript, and that both of them are ECMA Script compliant in many ways, either can be used to develop standard Dynamic HTML pages.

## 5.2   JAVASCRIPT

I'm going to refer to JavaScript throughout the next few sections. Much of what I'll have to say is appropriate to programmers who are working with JScript because the two languages are meant to be implementations of the same thing.

JavaScript originates from a language called LiveScript. The idea was to find a language which could be used to provide client-side in-browser applications but which was not as complicated as Java. Although in the original concept there was a certain overlap between the roles of Java and JavaScript, the actual implementations are radically divergent. The only similarity between the two languages is in their names. Having good programming skills in Java will make the learning of JavaScript relatively simple. Having good JavaScript skills will not help you to learn Java.

JavaScript is a fairly simple language which is only suitable for fairly simple tasks. The language is best suited to tasks which run for a short time and is most commonly used to manipulate the pieces of the document object model. Many developers experience problems when they try to build Web pages which have embedded JavaScript and which must run on both of the major browsers. Often these problems are more closely related to the implementations of the DOM than to the implementations of the language.

The version of JavaScript that was used as the basis of the ECMA Script standard was 1.1. Therefore everything that is written using JavaScript 1.1 should comply with the standard.

### 5.2.1   How Easy is Programming in JavaScript?

A few companies have added JavaScript capabilities to their graphical HTML editors. They supply a library of common code that you can adapt and use in your own pages. Most people who use the language won't have access to such a tool, and most of those who *do* will eventually find the tool quite limited. That's because the tool can only ever do what its designer envisaged.

A language is far more flexible than any tool and hence it is likely that sooner or later you will want to write code that your tool doesn't support. In addition, and as I said when I introduced HTML, if you don't understand the detail of how your code works then you can't fix it when it goes wrong. It is inevitable that at some point your code will fail. Hopefully that happens during the development process, but not always and the Web is full of seriously broken code. You will want to debug and repair your code, and as browsers change and requirements get more sophisticated you will also want to upgrade and add new code. To do that you need to be able to program.

So how easy is programming in JavaScript? Well most experienced software developers will tell you that writing scripts isn't really like programming. Programs tend to be large pieces of code, possibly a number of modules which combine together to make a full application. Scripts are small pieces of code which accomplish a single, relatively simple, task. I don't agree with this view. If you're a novice but can write some JavaScript to control a rollover effect on a Web page, then you should be as pleased with your efforts as a programmer with thirty years experience who writes part of a word processor. Programming is simply making a computer do what you want, when you want it to.

Of course there are differences between full-scale programs and small pieces of JavaScript. Programs tend to be compiled while scripts are interpreted. That simply means that if you've written a script, another program called an interpreter takes that script code and works through it, carrying out the instructions that are contained in the script. When a program is compiled it is converted into *binary code*, a series of 0s and 1s. These can be run directly by the operating system of the computer.

Compiled programs are hardware and operating system specific and have to be compiled separately for every platform on which they will execute. Because it is the text of the script which will be run by the interpreter, any script can be run on any system that contains a suitable interpreter. I can write JavaScript code on a PC that is running Linux then place it on my Web site. Users on any system, whether Linux, Windows 2000, Apple MacOS or anything else – can use that script if their browser contains a suitable JavaScript interpreter.

So JavaScript is nicely platform independent and can be run everywhere. And using it isn't like writing a program in, say, C or Pascal or C++. In fact JavaScript has been designed to run through browsers and can actually do very little. If you have never programmed, then learning it may initially seem a bit daunting but very quickly you'll feel comfortable.

## 5.2.2   Borrowing Code

One of the many good things about the Web is that there's an awful lot of code out there. All the JavaScript that your browser encounters is freely available to you. It all gets stored in the cache of your machine and you can look at it at your leisure. That doesn't mean that you can steal that code. Far from it. Everything you download has a copyright, even when it doesn't have an explicit copyright notice. Most Web developers won't mind you taking a look at their code to see how they implement things. In fact most programmers, whatever the type of system they build, started like that – most of us still use other people's code samples when we learn a new language. Those samples might come from a Web site or a textbook but they are an invaluable learning aid wherever they are from.

Any book can only give a few ideas. Hopefully the code samples that I'll show you will cover a wide range and yet are generic enough to be used in many applications. If they aren't suitable for you then look around for anything that will help.

---

Warning:
Borrowing ideas is fine. Borrowing code is **NOT**. It is copyright theft unless the original author specifically states otherwise.

---

### 5.2.3 Benefits of JavaScript

JavaScript has a number of big benefits to anyone who wants to make their Web site dynamic:

- it is widely supported in Web browsers;
- it gives easy access to the document objects and can manipulate most of them;
- JavaScript can give interesting animations without the long download times associated with many multimedia data types;
- Web surfers don't need a special plug-in to use your scripts;
- JavaScript is relatively secure – JavaScript can neither read from your local hard drive nor write to it, and you can't get a virus infection directly from JavaScript.

### 5.2.4 Problems with JavaScript

Although JavaScript looks like it should be a win-win for both developers and users, it isn't always:

- most scripts rely upon manipulating the elements of the DOM. Support for a standard set of objects currently doesn't exist and access to objects differs from browser to browser;
- if your script doesn't work then your page is useless;
- because of the problems of broken scripts many Web surfers disable JavaScript support in their browser;
- scripts can run slowly and complex scripts can take a long time to start up.

### 5.2.5 Do I Have to Use JavaScript?

There are many alternative solutions to the problem of making Web sites interactive and dynamic. Some of these rely upon complex multimedia data, while others are script based. Some of the scripting solutions which might be considered as competitors to JavaScript are listed below along with some comments.

Always remember that your Web pages don't *have* to provide a total interactive experience. If you want to provide content and information rather than entertainment then you are probably best advised to keep it simple and stick mostly to text and static images.

**`Perl`**
> A complex language that is commonly used for server-side CGI scripting. Perl is available for client-side work through a subset called Perlscript which can also be used when writing Active Server Pages. It isn't widely used in client-side applications although that situation may change. Due to its text manipulating nature it is probably better fitted to remaining on the server.

**VBScript**

> Widely used but, unfortunately, platform specific. This language is only available under the Microsoft Windows operating system. It can be used to develop browser applications but they will only run inside Internet Explorer.

**Python**

> A little known language that is making inroads into the CGI writing area. A Web browser has been written in Python which can run Python applets. It's likely that Python will also move more towards client-side scripting.

**Tcl**

> This has been a popular choice for systems programming. The language itself has been widely criticised by proponents of other scripting languages but it is clearly effective in its own niche. A Tcl plug-in can be downloaded from the Internet and the demonstration programs show that this is in fact a worthy contender in many of the same application areas as Java.

**Java**

> This is not a scripting language[1] but it is used for many of the same things as JavaScript. It's very good at menus and data validation on the client but can be very slow. It is probably a better language for the development of proper networked applications than simple browser applets.

In summary, if you want to embed some interactivity within a Web page then you can use any combination of a number of scripting languages and multimedia packages. If you want to make the basic HTML of your page both dynamic and interactive then you currently have no choice but to use JavaScript.

## 5.3  JAVASCRIPT – THE BASICS

In many respects JavaScript code resembles C. I don't mean that programming in JavaScript is in anyway like programming in C, but if you look at a page of code in each language then the two will look fairly similar. The semantics[2] of the two languages are very different but the syntax[3] of a JavaScript program and of a simple C program are quite close. The syntax of a language is the set of tokens that comprise it. Many languages borrow from the set of tokens used in C simply because most programmers can read C and hence most programmers can read code written in other languages.

JavaScript can be run on some file and Web servers but the vast majority of users are developing front-ends for Web pages. That is the use that I am going to demonstrate. Many of the keywords and built-in functions of JavaScript are included in Appendix B. I'm

---

[1] Although it is *interpreted*. Actually it is compiled *and* interpreted.
[2] The meaning of the code.
[3] The symbols and construction.

not going to explain the whole language in intricate detail. Plenty of books and on-line resources are available which will do that. A list of keywords doesn't really help you to learn the language – a basic explanation of how it all works and some simple examples is a much more useful educational tool.

### 5.3.1    A Simple Script

The script that follows could hardly be easier. It's almost the JavaScript version of "Hello World!". It's a program that everyone can use to convince themselves that they really *could* learn to program. Read through the code first then I'll explain what's going on.

```html
<html>
    <head>
        <script language="javascript">
        <!--
        function popup(){
            var major = parseInt(navigator.appVersion);
            var minor = parseFloat(navigator.appVersion);
            var agent = navigator.userAgent.toLowerCase();
            document.write("<h1>Details in Popup</h1>");
            window.alert(agent + " " + major);
        }

        function farewell(){
            window.alert("Farewell and thanks for visiting");
        }
        //-->
        </script>
    </head>
    <body onLoad="popup()" onUnload="farewell()">
    </body>
</html>
```

JavaScript programs contain variables, objects, and functions. These will all be covered in detail soon. All that you ought to try to get to grips with now is the structure of a JavaScript program. The key points that you need to apply in all scripts are listed below.

- Each line of code is terminated by a semicolon.

- Blocks of code  must be surrounded by a pair of curly brackets. A block of code is a set of instructions that are to be executed together as a unit. This might be because they are optional and dependent upon a Boolean condition or because they are to be executed repeatedly.

- Functions have parameters which are passed inside parentheses.

- Variables are declared using the keyword `var`.

- Scripts require neither a `main` function nor an `exit` condition. These are major differences between scripts and *proper* programs. Execution of a script starts with the first line of code and runs until there is no more code.

## 5.3.2 JavaScript and the HTML Page

Having written some JavaScript you need to include it in an HTML page. You can't execute these scripts from a command line as the interpreter is part of the browser. The script is included in the Web page and run by the browser, usually as soon as the page has been loaded. The browser is able to debug the script and can display errors.

> Note:
> To get Netscape Navigator to show errors, type `javascript:` in the location box. A console will appear which will display the errors, although they may not be stunningly useful. Navigator doesn't display errors by default. Internet Explorer uses a different scheme. When it encounters a script error it opens a popup window with details of the error. A debugger for scripting language can be downloaded free of charge from the Microsoft Web site.

If you are only writing small scripts, or only use your scripts in a few pages, then the easiest scheme is to include the script code in the HTML file. The following example shows how this is done. It's important that you remember to use the HTML comments around the script code. If you don't do this then some browsers may try to display your JavaScript code as part of the page.

```
<html>
   <head>
      <title>A Sample JavaScript</title>
      <script language="javascript">
      <!--
         // the JavaScript code goes here...
      // -->
      </script>
   </head>
   <body>
      ...
   </body>
</html>
```

If you use a lot of scripts or your scripts are complex then including the code inside the Web page will make your source files difficult to read and debug. A better idea is to put your JavaScript code in a separate file and include that code in the `head` of the page as shown below. By convention, JavaScript programs are stored in files with the `.js` extension. In the following example notice that the script element must be terminated by an end tag, `</script>`.

```
<html>
    <head>
        <title>A Sample JavaScript</title>
        <script language="javascript" src="sample.js"></script>
    </head>
    <body>
        ...
    </body>
</html>
```

Finally, small pieces of code can be included inside the body of the Web page. Doing this may have side-effects, that is it can cause things to happen which you did not intend. Let's look at how the script is included first, then I'll consider possible side-effects.

```
<html>
    <head>
        <title>A Sample JavaScript</title>
    </head>
    <body>
        <script language="javascript">
        <!--
            alert("The page has loaded");
        //-->
        </script>
    </body>
</html>
```

### 5.3.2.1 *Side Effects*

Sometimes a piece of code is intended to do one thing but, when run, it does another. I'm sure that most of you will, at some time or another, have used a program which occasionally displays erratic behaviour. Often these problems are caused by *side-effects*. A piece of code may appear to be perfect in isolation but when used it has effects on programs which are already executing. Some programs even have unforeseen effects upon *themselves* as they run. Often these problems are caused because the programmer has made a trivial mistake such as incorrectly setting a value.

HTML pages with embedded JavaScript rarely exhibit serious flaws, but they can have side-effects. This is especially true if you place your scripts inside the body of the page. If you have a script at the top of the page then some HTML, the script may be executed before the body of the page has loaded. Similarly having the script at the foot of the page causes the reverse to be true: the script only executes after the text of the page has been loaded. These differences in when a script is run are caused because the browser is loading the page in order from the top and executing the scripts as it loads them. If your page relies upon a combination of scripts, text and images you might not be getting the result that you expect: the images will be downloaded a long time after the text and will be processed last by the browser. If the script and images rely upon each other then the page will not run properly.

Scripts which are loaded from separate files or placed in the head of the page do not exhibit this behavior because they need to be triggered by *events* which are controlled externally. The relationship between JavaScript and events is discussed in Section 6.5.

### 5.3.3 The Output

Take the code from Section 5.3.1 and save it in a file called `SimpleScript.html`. The script writes some text into the Web browser window and opens up an alert window which contains a message. The result of all of which is shown in Figure 5.1. It's easy and useful and, in fact, we're going to use the same idea in several of the scripts in Chapter 7.

**Figure 5.1** Opening an Alert Box

## 5.3.4 The Code Samples

I'm going to spend the rest of this chapter describing the features of the JavaScript language. You can't do a lot with this code in isolation or in small snippets but it's important that you understand the language before I introduce more complicated ideas and full programs. Wherever possible I've attempted to place code samples into simple Web pages to illustrate the text. If you really want to learn this language, type these code samples into your favorite text editor, save them as HTML files and view them in your Web browser.

Don't worry if you make mistakes and the scripts don't work straight out of the box. Debugging simple code is good practice for what comes later. Never believe anyone who tells you that they can program without making mistakes: we all have to track bugs through our work.

> **Note:**
> If you use Netscape, typing `javascript:` in the location bar brings up a console which displays error messages. Figure 5.2 shows this in action.

**Figure 5.2** The Netscape JavaScript Console

The scripts in this chapter are really very simple, in fact I guess you could almost call them *scriptlets*. Despite their simplicity, they all use a couple of the really neat features of the DOM. Browsers are able to open dialog boxes to display messages to the user and to get data from them. These dialogs are really easy to use from within JavaScript so rather than trying any fancy programming tricks or writing non-interactive scripts, I'm going to use them. Figure 5.3 shows the dialog boxes in action from within Netscape.

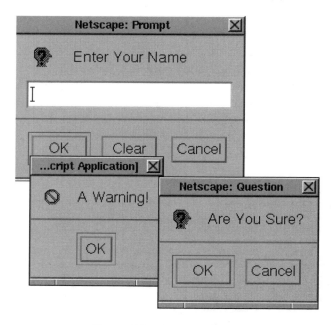

**Figure 5.3**   The Dialog Boxes

## 5.4   VARIABLES

Like any programming language, JavaScript has variables. These are data items that you can manipulate as the program runs. If you've never programmed before then you need to know a little something about variables. If you *have* done some programming then skim over this bit as I bring the beginners up to speed.

A variable is a named value that you use in your programs. Most people will have used variables without realizing it. If you remember something that looked like x = 5 being written at school, then you remember seeing a variable. That example is of a variable named x which is set to the value 5. In computing we call giving a value to a variable *assignment*. Variables in programs don't have fixed values, just as they didn't in basic algebra. Instead the variable name is used to track changing values as the program runs. If you are unsure about what I mean try finding the values of x and y after the following set of mathematical statements:

```
x = 0
y = 3
```

```
x = y + 4
y = x times x
```

At the end x equals 7 and y equals 49. If you didn't follow that, spend some time think-ing about what was happening before you read on.

## 5.4.1   Variable Names

There are strict rules governing how you name your variables in JavaScript:

- names must begin with a letter, digit, or the underscore (_);
- you cannot use spaces in names;
- names are case-sensitive, so that fred, FRED and frEd all refer to different variables;
- you cannot use a reserved word as a variable name. Reserved words are those words which are part of the JavaScript language. They are detailed in Appendix B.

Provided you obey the rules then anything goes when choosing variable names. It's al-ways better to make them meaningful. It's more than likely that once your code is running you'll want to start making improvements and changes. All programmers do that all of the time but we usually call it maintenance. You can call it tinkering if you like. Imagine tracking two variables through a program, one called visitor_name, the other called vn, both of which are the user name of a visitor to your Web site. Many simple and potentially disastrous mistakes are possible with the variable named vn. For instance you would be unlikely to write:

```
visitor_name = visitor_name + 45.32
```

but might accidentally write:

```
vn = vn + 45.32
```

which would be equally illogical within the context of your script.

## 5.4.2   Data Types

Programming languages usually have several different types of data. Commonly program-mers may use characters, integers (whole numbers), Booleans (logical values of true and false), strings (ordered sets of characters), reals (complex numbers), and many others be-sides. In keeping with its restricted ambitions, JavaScript has only four types of data:

**numeric**
> These are basic numbers. They can be integers such as 2, 22, and 2,222,000 or floating point values like 23.42, –56.01, and 2E45. You don't need to differentiate between them as you declare and use them – in fact, you can merrily change the type of data which a variable holds as the program runs. Ideally, of course, doing so will make sense in your program.

**strings**

These are collections of characters that are not numbers. The value of a string can even contain spaces and may be totally made from digits. All of the following are strings: "Chris", "Chris Bates", and "2345.432". How can the last one possibly be a string? Well why not. If it is never used in a mathematical expression the system has no way of knowing that it is a number. In JavaScript anything which isn't used in a mathematical expression is not a number, even if it looks like one.

When a value is assigned as a string to a variable name you must tell the JavaScript system what type of data it is now handling. To do this you put quotes around the value:

```
visitor_name = "Chris Bates"
visitor_name = 'Chris Bates'
visitor_name = "34.45"
```

If you are nesting strings one inside another you have to be careful about how you use quotes. The best approach is to use double quotes for the outer string and single quotes for all inner strings. Don't try to do more than one layer of nesting in this way because it won't work:

```
visitor_quote = "A quote inside 'a quote'";
```

If you simply have to use nested quotes then you can force the interpreter to do your bidding by placing a \ before the inner quotes. This momentarily switches off the default behavior:

```
visitor_quote = "A quote inside \"a quote\"";
```

**Boolean**

Boolean variables hold the values `true` and `false`. These are used a lot in programming to hold the result of conditional tests. You might want to know if a particular event has happened yet or if a value has been assigned. You will be seeing lots of Boolean values throughout the rest of this book.

**null**

This is used when you don't yet know something. A `null` value means one that has not yet been decided. It *does not* mean nil or zero and should not be used in that way – ever.

## 5.4.3 Creating Variables

Creating a variable couldn't be easier. You don't need to decide upon the type of data that the variable is going to hold when you declare it. That's completely different to languages such as Pascal and C++ . All that you need to do is use the keyword **var** before the variable name. You don't even have to give the variable a value – that can be done later. Finally, you can easily copy the value of one variable directly into another as you create it. Look at the following examples:

```
var first = 23;
var second = "Some words";
var third = second;
var first_boolean = true;
```

If you were to examine the value in `third` you would see that it contains the string `Some words`. That's not the exact same string as in the variable `second`, but is a copy of it.

When you have finished with a variable you don't have to delete it or set it to `null`. Just leave it there and the browser will automatically delete it for you when a different Web page is loaded.

One more thing about variables is that the use of the JavaScript keyword `var` is often optional. The interpreter knows just enough about scripts to understand that if it sees an unquoted string inside a script, it is dealing with a variable. Unfortunately the behavior that the variable displays may vary depending upon the way it's being used. Since we want our scripts to be consistent and to work as we intended when we wrote them, it's best to always use `var` before variable declarations.

### 5.4.3.1 *Using Variables in JavaScript*   The simplest way of finding how variables work is, perhaps not surprisingly, to actually use them. The following code prompts the user for their name and then writes that information into the browser window.

```
<html>
   <head>
      <title>A Sample JavaScript</title>
   </head>
   <body >
      <script language="javascript">
      <!--
            var visitor_name;
            visitor_name = prompt("Enter Your Name", "");
            document.writeln("<h1>Your name is</h1>");
            document.writeln("<h2>" + visitor_name + "</h2>");
            document.close();
      //-->
      </script>
   </body>
</html>
```

The input from the user is stored in a variable called `visitor_name`. Writing the text out to the browser window uses a method called `writeln` which is actually part of the document. The document is a special type of JavaScript object and is covered in some detail on Chapter 6. All that you need to know about it for the moment is that it enables you to write HTML formatted text into a browser window. Notice that I've placed that script into the body of the page. This simplifies the process of writing to the document. If the script had been placed inside the page head, an entire HTML page would have had to be written out. In the simple case, the script is run as soon as the page is loaded, if the code is in the head then the page must force execution of the script. The following code shows how this is done:

```html
<html>
   <head>
      <title>A Sample JavaScript</title>
      <script language="javascript">
      <!--
         function test() {
            var visitor_name;
            visitor_name = prompt("Enter Your Name", "");
            alert("Your name is " + visitor_name);
            document.writeln("<html><head>");
            document.writeln("<title>Sample</title>");
            document.writeln("</head><body>");
            document.writeln("<h1>Your name is</h1>");
            document.writeln("<h2>" + visitor_name + "</h2>");
            document.writeln("</body></html>");
            document.close();
         }
      //-->
      </script>
   </head>
   <body onLoad="test()">
   </body>
</html>
```

I'll show you how to create and use functions in Section 5.10, for now I'll stick to the simple model. In both of those examples the variable held string data which the user had entered, and then displayed that data. In JavaScript you can do an awful lot more with your data. The language has many builtin functions which you can use to simplify your coding tasks.

> **Rule:**
> One of the most important lessons that a programmer can learn is to stand on the shoulders of giants. Many simple and repetitious tasks have been programmed by others and are available for your use. JavaScript has a copious library of routines, instead of writing your own data manipulation routines, use the ones which are supplied. They're likely to be faster and more efficient than yours anyway.

I'm not going to describe all of the operations, functions and capabilities which JavaScript provides. Netscape have a reference guide which does just that and which is available in HTML and PDF formats. It's long; very long and I don't have the space to cover all of that material here. Instead I've picked selected highlights, those parts of the language which you'll use most often, and described them. In most cases I'll demonstrate some partial code which shows how the functions are used. Some functions are so interesting or useful that I'll devote more time and space to them and give complete examples. I would advise taking the smaller pieces of code and building them into your own test pages, and where I haven't provided an example, try writing your own. This is good practice and it'll give you a real feel for the language.

## 5.5 STRING MANIPULATION

Most of the data that you'll handle in your JavaScript is going to be text strings. Some of the most useful text manipulations involve *regular expressions*. These are an advanced topic which you'll need quite a lot of knowledge to really tackle. Consequently I've left a discussion of regular expressions until Section 6.2, by when you'll have seen, and hopefully written, quite a lot of JavaScript.

Even if we only think about relatively simple operations using strings, JavaScript has many which are very useful. Broadly speaking string manipulation involves either joining strings together, splitting them apart or searching through them. JavaScript has functions which perform all of those operations and much more.

### charAt(index)

This function returns the character which is at position `index` in the string. By repeatedly calling the function you can parse a whole string, which is quite useful if, for instance, you want to perform crude validation of data input. Here's an example:

```html
<html>
  <head>
    <title>A Sample JavaScript</title>
  </head>
  <body>
  <script language="javascript">
  <!--
```

```
        var you = prompt("Enter your name", "");
        var num = prompt("Enter a whole number", "");
        document.writeln("<h1>charAt</h1>");
        document.write("<p>The character at position ");
        document.writeln(num + " in your name is</p>");
        document.writeln("<h2>" + you.charAt(num) + "</h2>");
        document.close();
     //-->
     </script>
     </body>
</html>
```

Do you remember that I said that JavaScript doesn't have formal data types? You can change the type of data which a variable is holding as the program executes. This example gives you the opportunity to play around with that idea. Try entering a number as your name or a string as the position indicator. Rather than crash with some terrible error the program simply prints what it can into the browser and ignores data it can't handle. The same thing happens if you enter a number that's higher than the number of characters in your name – and also if you enter a negative number.

### concat("string"[, "string"[,..."string"]])

JavaScript has two ways that you can join strings together. The simplest is to use the + operator as I did in the last example. If you want to create a new string by joining two existing strings then + is slightly unsatisfactory. As an operation it is not *explicit* about what it's doing. Remember, JavaScript variables can change their data type so whilst the following code may leave the result holding a sensible value in some circumstances, in others it may not.

```
var you = prompt("Enter your name", "");
var yourage = prompt("Enter your age in months", "");
var result = you + yourage;
```

The solution is to use the concat() operator. This function is part of the string object and takes another string, or comma separated list of strings as its argument. Don't worry about the slightly strange syntax of the dot operator, that will be explained when I look at JavaScript objects.

```
var msg = "Thank You ";
document.writeln(msg.concat(you));
```

```
var you = prompt("Enter your name", "");
var yourage = prompt("Enter your age in months", "");
var result = you.concat(yourage);
var result = you.concat(yourage, "Thanks");
```

### indexOf("search"[, offset])

The string is searched for the string or quoted character in the first parameter. If the search is successful, the index of the start of the target string is returned. The indices in the original string, number from 0 to `string.length - 1`. If the search is unsuccessful the operation returns –1. By default the `indexOf()` function starts at index 0, however, an optional offset may be specified so that the search starts part way along the string.

The following example shows how this works:

```html
<html>
    <head>
        <title>Browser Agent</title>
    </head>
    <body>
        <script language="javascript">
        <!--
        // find the maker of the browser
        var agent = navigator.userAgent.toLowerCase();
        var result = agent.indexOf("microsoft");

        document.writeln("<h1>Your Browser is</h1>");
        document.writeln("<p>" + agent + "</p>");

        if(result == -1){
            document.write("<p>It was not made by ");
            document.writeln("Microsoft</p>");
        }
        else
            document.writeln("<p>It was made by Microsoft</p>");

        document.close();
        //-->
        </script>
    </body>
</html>
```

### lastIndexOf("search"[, offset])

This function does exactly the same thing as `indexOf()` but works its way backwards along the string. The offset works in exactly the same way as for `indexOf()`, but the default value is `string.length - 1`.

### length

Value which holds the number of characters in the string. Note that this is *not* a function and so you don't have to place parentheses when using it.

```
var agent = navigator.userAgent.toLowerCase();
var ll = agent.length;
```

**split(separator[, limit])**

Often we need to split a string apart into its constituent elements. The `split()` function breaks the string apart whenever it encounters the character passed in as the first parameter. The pieces of the string are stored in an *array*. `split()` has an optional second parameter which is an integer value indicating how many of the pieces are to be stored in the array.

Add the following code into the earlier example just before `document.close();` and see what happens.

```
var words = agent.split(" ");
for(var i = 0; i < words.length; i++)
    document.writeln("<p>" + words[i] + "</p>");
```

**substr(index[, length])**

This function returns a substring which starts at the character indicated by the index parameter. The substring continues either to the end of the string or for the number of characters indicated by the length parameter.

If the index is greater than the length of the string then nothing is returned. If it is negative then it is taken as the offset from the *end* of the string working backwards along its length. If a length of 0, or a negative number, is provided then no characters are returned.

```
piece = agent.substring(3, 17);
document.writeln("<p>" + piece + "</p>");
```

**substring(index1[, index2])**

Returns the set of characters which starts at *index1* and continues up to, but does not include, the character at *index2*. The following rules apply:

1. If *index1* is less than 0, it will be treated as 0.
2. If *index2* is greater than the length of the string, it is treated as the length of the string.
3. If the two index values are equal, an empty string is returned.
4. If *index2* is missing, all characters up to the end of the string are taken.
5. If *index1* is greater than *index2*, a runtime error occurs.

**toLowerCase()**

Converts all characters in the string to lower case.

**toUpperCase()**

Converts all characters in the string to upper case.

## 5.6 MATHEMATICAL FUNCTIONS

Mathematical functions and values are part of a builtin JavaScript object called Math. All functions and attributes used in complex mathematics must be accessed via this object. This is usually done by preceding the function name with the object name:

```
var area = Math.PI * (r * r);
var next = Math.ceil(area);
```

If a section of your code includes a lot of math operations the repetition of Math can become tedious. It can be replaced using the keyword with like this:

```
with(Math) {
    var area = PI * (r * r);
    var next = ceil(area);
}
```

The choice of construct is yours. Sometimes using Math. will add clarity to your code. At other times it will lead to confusion as the code will be needlessly crowded with the same construct.

**NaN**

This is a value which represents something which is not a number. That might sound slightly peculiar: why should a programming language need to indicate whether values are numbers? Because variables can hold different types of data in JavaScript, you need a way of knowing if a value is currently numeric so that your script can decide how to process it.

Many functions return numbers if they have completed successfully. Checking the return value against NaN gives a way of deciding if the function operated properly.

> Note:
> In all versions of JavaScript before 1.3 NaN was not a *top-level* object. This meant that it could not be accessed directly. Instead it had to be used through the Number object. If you want your code to work in browsers running older versions of JavaScript be sure to use Number.Nan.

**abs(value)**

Returns the absolute value the number passed into it.

**acos(value), asin(value), atan(value)**

These functions return the arccosine, arcsine and arctangent, respectively, of the value passed into them. All return values are in radians.

**atan2(value1, value2)**

Returns the arctangent, in radians, of the quotient[4] of the values passed into it.

---

[4]The result of dividing one by the other.

`ceil(value)`

Returns the smallest integer which is greater than, or equal to, the value passed in.

`cos(value)`, `sin(value)`, `tan(value)`

These return the cosine, sin and tangent, respectively, of the value passed in as an argument.

`floor(value)`

Returns the largest integer which is smaller than, or equal to, the number passed in.

`isNan(value)`

This function returns `true` if its argument is not a number and `false` if it is numeric.

`log(value)`

Returns the natural logarithm of its argument. If the argument is not a number or is a negative number then `NaN` will be returned.

`max(value1, value2)`

Returns the larger of its arguments.

`min(value1, value2)`

Returns the smaller of its arguments.

`parseFloat(string)`

This function parses a string, passed in as an argument, and returns it as a floating point number. The string is parsed from the start with the parser looking for the numbers 0 through 9, the signs + and −, decimal points and exponents[5] only. When any other character is encountered the parser stops and returns what it has already found. If the first character of the string does not belong to the valid set, `NaN` is returned.

`parseInt(string[, radix])`

The string is parsed and its value as an integer returned. Once an invalid character is encountered the parsing stops and the function returns what it has already found. If the first character of the string is invalid `NaN` is returned.

The function optionally takes a radix as its second argument, defaulting to base 10 if an alternative is not supplied. The set of valid characters depends upon the supplied radix:

- in base 2 only the characters 0 and 1 are permitted,
- in base 10 the digits 0 through 9 are permitted,
- in base 16 the characters 0 through 9 and the letters a, b, c, d, e and f, in lower or upper case, are allowed,
- if the string starts with `0x` the number is assumed to be hexadecimal (base 16).

`pow(value, power)`

Returns the result of raising *value* to *power*.

---

[5]The characters e and E.

`random()`

Returns a pseudorandom number between 0 and 1. The random number generator is seeded from the current time.

Creating a truly random number computationally is impossible. All random number generators create sequences of numbers which will eventually repeat themselves. The trick in writing such code is to create such a long sequence that it will not repeat during the expected runtime of the program. That way the sequence, and its effects, will appear random to the user.

`round(value)`

Returns the result of rounding its argument to the nearest integer.

`sqrt(value)`

Returns the square root of the value.

*Table 5.1*   JavaScript Numerical Constants

| Constant | Description |
|---|---|
| Math.E | Approximately 2.718. Euler's Constant, base of natural logarithms. |
| Math.LN2 | Log of 2. |
| Math.LN10 | Log of 10. |
| Math.PI | 3.14159. The ratio of the circumference of a circle to its diameter. |
| Math.SQRT1_2 | The square root of 1/2. |
| Math.SQRT_2 | The square root of 2. |

The code which follows is a template which you can use to try out the Math object and its functions.

```
<html>
  <head>
    <title>The Math Object</title>
  </head>
  <body>
    <script language="JavaScript1.2">
    <!--
    document.writeln("<h1>The Math Object</h1>");

    // Use this in all your tests
    var valueOne = prompt("Enter a number", "");

    // Use this if the function you're testing
```

```javascript
    // has two parameters.
    var valueTwo = 32.45;

    // Change the next line to test other functions
    var result = Math.floor(valueTwo);

    if(isNaN(result)) {
        document.write("<p>The value you gave was ");
        document.writeln("not a number</p>");
    }
    else {
        document.write("<p>The result was " + result);
        document.writeln("</p>");
    }
    document.close();
    //-->
    </script>
 </body>
</html>
```

## 5.7   STATEMENTS

Programs are composed of two things: data and code which manipulates that data. I have already shown how to define data items. Now I'm going to show you how to create usable code. Program instructions are grouped into units called statements. A statement is a fairly low-level thing: as you'll see, one statement won't do anything worthwhile on its own. We create programs from lots of statements.

**if ...else**

Whenever you want to test the truth of a condition before executing any more of your program, use this construct. This statement means that if some condition is true then do one thing, if the condition is false do another. Easy – and useful even in the simplest of scripts. You'll be using this one a lot. Here's a typical example:

```html
<html>
   <head>
      <title>Browser Sniffing</title>
   </head>
   <body>
      <script language="javascript">
      <!--
         var agent = navigator.userAgent.toLowerCase();
```

```
    document.writeln("<h1>Browser Sniffer</h1>");
    document.write("<p>");

    if(agent.indexOf("mozilla") != -1){
        document.write("Your browser is Netscape");
    } else {
        document.write("Your browser is Not Netscape");
    }
    document.writeln("</p>");
    document.close();
  //-->
  </script>
 </body>
</html>
```

Sometimes you might want to test for more than one possible condition at the same time. In that case you must *nest* your if . . . else statements like this:

```
if(agent.indexOf("mozilla") != -1){
  if(major <= 4){
    document.write("Your browser is Netscape");
  } else {
    document.write("Your browser is Mozilla");
  }
}
```

Notice how the brackets are placed to help make the nesting of the code a bit clearer. There are many ways of setting out your code; whichever you end up using, try to ensure that it clarifies the code for reading rather than making it easier to write.

### for(counter = 0; counter <= n; counter++)

Many operations need to be repeated a number of times. These go inside a for loop. By convention these start counting at 0 and terminate when the desired number of iterations[6] has been reached. The variable which holds the counter can be given any name you like. Often counters are called i or j. Those names are meaningless but traditional. If you are just starting to program I would encourage you to use names like count instead. They may take longer to type but at least they make sense.

```
<html>
  <head>
    <title>For Loops</title>
  </head>
  <body>
```

---

[6]Passes through the loop.

```
<script language="javascript">
<!--
    document.writeln("<h1>A For Loop</h1>");
    for(var count = 0; count < 12; count++) {
        // repeated statements go here
        document.write("<p>The counter is " + count);
        document.writeln("</p>");
    }
    document.close();
//-->
</script>
</body>
</html>
```

The syntax of the `for` loop can worry some people. The parentheses contain three statements which are separated by semicolons. The first one initializes the counter when the loop is first encountered. The second statement tells the program when the loop has finished. The third statement contains an operation that is performed to the counter at the end of each loop. In the example the counter is incremented (increased) by one.

### `while(boolean condition)`

Sometimes you don't know how many iterations are going to be needed. The loop may continue forever if an external event doesn't act upon it. Or you may be processing data and not know how much data you're going to get. In cases like these use the `while` loop:

```
<html>
    <head>
        <title>While Loops</title>
    </head>
    <body>
        <script language="javascript">
<!--
        document.writeln("<h1>While Loop</h1>");
        var done = false;
        var msg;

        while(done == false) {
            // Get a string from the user then display it
            msg = prompt("Enter a String");
            document.writeln("<p>" + msg + "</p>");

            // If the input was quit, QUIT, Quit
```

```
                // or any other variant then finish
                if(msg.toLowerCase() == "quit") {
                    document.writeln("<p>Thanks, Goodbye</p>");
                    done = true;

                } // if
            } // while

        document.close();
        //-->
        </script>
    </body>
</html>
```

Again, testing for logical conditions inside loops is something you will need to do quite often in your scripts.

## break

What happens if you want to be able to leap out of the middle of a loop? You can either create a construct based around a `while` loop with `if` statements embedded in it or use the `break` statement. Use `break` with care. Your loops should always be designed to run smoothly. If you `break` out of the middle of them you may put variables into unknown states. Compare these two loops and decide which you prefer.

```
var answer = 0;
var correct = 49;
var done = false;
var counter = 0;

while((done = false) && (counter < 3)) {
    // note that && means a logical 'and'
    answer = prompt("What is 7 times 7?", "0");
    if(answer = correct) {
        done = true;
    }
    else {
        counter++;
    }
}

for(counter = 0; counter < 3; counter++) {
    answer = prompt("What is 7 times 7?", "0");
    if(answer = correct) {
        break;
```

```
        }
    }
```

**eval()**

This is a very useful JavaScript builtin function. String versions of mathematical expressions can be passed into the function where they are evaluated and the result returned as an integer – great for bringing simple interactivity to a page. For instance:

```
eval("32 * 75674.21");
```

**switch**

Choosing between a number of alternatives can lead to awkward code if you only use `if...else` statements. Where you need to make a choice between more than two items you'll find the `switch` statement much easier to write and maintain. The complete `switch` looks like:

```
switch(expression) {
  case label:
      statement;
      [statement;]
      break;
  [case label:
      statement;
      [statement;]
      break;]
  [default:
      statement;]
}
```

A `switch` selects between a number of choices depending upon the value of the expression. The choices are identified by `case` statements, each has a `label` which equals one of the potential values of the expression. If none of the `cases` matches the expression, the optional `default` may be used instead.

Each `case` includes one or more statements and is terminated by a `break`. If you omit the `break` you'll get random, potentially harmful, behavior.

Here's an example of the `switch`:

```
<html>
    <head>
        <title>Using Switches</title>
    </head>
    <body onLoad="Switcher()">
    <script language="javascript">
    <!--
        function Switcher() {
```

```
var inp = prompt("Enter a number from 1 to 4", "");
var val = 0;
switch(Math.floor(eval(inp))){
    case 1:
        val = inp;
        break;
    case 2:
        val = inp;
        alert("Case 2");
        break;
    case 3:
        val = inp * inp;
        break;
    case 4:
        val = Math.sin(inp);
        break;
    default:
        alert("Only values from 1 to 4 are allowed");
}

document.writeln("<h1>Using Switches</h1>");
document.writeln("<h3>val is now " + val + "</h3>");
document.close();

        }
    //-->
    </script>
    </body>
</html>
```

The script prompts for an input, and stores it in a variable. To perform the selection, the script converts the input to an integer using a combination of `Math.floor()` and `eval()`. If an invalid input is encountered, the default behavior is triggered and an alert box is shown.

## 5.8  OPERATORS

JavaScript has two types of operator: those used in tests of logic and those used to affect variables. All should be fairly easy to understand and are shown in Table 5.2. If you look through the code in this book you'll see these operators used by both JavaScript and Perl. In fact most programming languages use these same constructs. Instead of giving lots of examples of the use of these operators here, I'm going to rely on your finding them as you work through the book and referring back to this table when you need more information. Generally, though, you'll be able to work out from the code what each operator is used for.

Although you can't subtract strings, you *can* add them. The process is called concatenation and joins the second string onto the end of the first:

```
var first = "A string is ";
var second = "added to the end";

// a new string which is the others added to each other
var third = first + second;

// change the value of first to be itself + second...
first += second; // honestly!
```

Table 5.2: JavaScript Operators

| Operator | Meaning |
| --- | --- |
| + | If the arguments are numbers then they are added together. If the arguments are strings then they are concatenated[7] and the result returned. |
| – | If supplied with two operands this subtracts one from the other. If supplied with a single operand it reverses its sign. |
| * | Multiplies two numbers together. |
| / | Divides the first number by the second. |
| % | Modulus Division returns the integer remainder from a division. |
| ! | Logical NOT returns false if the operand evaluates to true. Otherwise it returns true. |
| > | Greater than returns true if the left operand is greater than the right. |
| >= | Returns true if the left operand is greater than or equal to the right one. |
| < | Returns true if the left operand is less than the right. |
| == | Returns true if the two operands are equal. |
| <= | Returns true if the left operand is less than or equal to the right one. |
| != | Returns true if the two operands are not equal. |
| && | Logical AND returns true if both operands are true. Otherwise returns false. |
| \|\| | Logical OR returns true if one or both operands are true, otherwise returns false. |
| = | Assigns a value to a variable |
| += | Adds two numbers then assigns the result to the one on the left of the expression. |

---

[7]One is joined to the end of the other.

Table 5.2: JavaScript Operators

| Operator | Meaning |
|---|---|
| - = | Subtracts the term on the right from the term on the left, then assigns the result to the one on the left of the expression. |
| * = | Multiplies two values then assigns the result to the one on the left of the expression. |
| / = | Divides the term on the left by the term on the right and then assigns the result to the one on the left of the expression. |
| % = | Performs modulus division then assigns the result to the one on the left of the expression. |
| ++ | Auto-increment, increases the value of its (integer) argument by one. |
| -- | Auto-decrement, decreases the value of an integer by one. |

## 5.9  ARRAYS

An array is an ordered set of data elements which can be accessed through a single variable name. Conceptually an array is made up of a set of slots with each slot assigned to a single data element. You access the data elements either sequentially by reading from the start of the array, or by their *index*. The index is the position of the element in the array (with the first element being at position 0 and the last at (array length − 1)). Figure 5.4 visualizes what an array looks like.

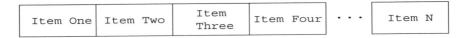

**Figure 5.4**   The Structure of an Array

In many programming languages arrays are contiguous areas of memory which means that the first array element is physically located next to the second, and so on. In JavaScript an array is slightly different because it is a special type of object and has functionality which is not normally available in other languages. Generally I've left discussion of JavaScript objects until Chapter 6, but arrays are so fundamental to programming that I'm making an exception in this case.

An array is a data store. Its sole function is to hold data until the script requires it. The data inside an array is *ordered*, because elements are added and accessed in a particular order, but is not *sorted*. There is no relationship between the way the data is held and any external meaning it has. For instance, if words are being added to the array they are not necessarily going to be stored in alphabetical order. The contents of the array may have a particular ordering as an artifact of the way that they were presented to the array but not as a result of being in an array. This point needs emphasising simply because many beginning programmers assume that the system can order data for them. Fortunately, as we'll see in Section 5.9.2, JavaScript has some rather neat features which overcome the limitations of the array format.

### 5.9.1 Basic Array Functions

Before I look at JavaScript arrays as objects, I'm going to show how they can be used as more *traditional* arrays. The basic operations that are performed on arrays are: creation, addition of elements, accessing individual elements, removing elements. I'll look at each of these in turn.

***5.9.1.1 Creating Arrays*** JavaScript arrays can be constructed in no fewer than three different ways. The easiest way is simply to declare a variable and pass it some elements in array format:

```
var days = ["Monday", "Tuesday", "Wednesday", "Thursday"];
```

That creates an array of four elements, each holding a text string. Notice that the array of elements is surrounded by *square* brackets. In most programming languages square brackets denote arrays and array operations. The second approach is to create an array object using the keyword new and a set of elements to store:

```
var days = new Array("Monday", "Tuesday", "Wednesday", "Thursday");
```

Using this construct, the contents of the array are surrounded by parentheses because they are parameters to the constructor of the Array object. Finally an empty array object which has space for a number of elements can be created:

```
var days = new Array(4);
```

JavaScript arrays can hold mixed data types as the following examples show:

```
var data = ["Monday", "Tuesday", 34, 76.34, "Wednesday"];
var data = new Array("Monday", 34, 76.34, "Wednesday");
```

***5.9.1.2 Adding Elements to an Array*** Array elements are accessed by their index. The index denotes the position of the element in the array and, as in for loops, these start from 0. Adding an element uses the square bracket syntax we saw a moment ago:

```
var days[3] = "Monday";
```

What happens if you want, or need, to add an item to an array which is already full? Many languages struggle with this problem but JavaScript has a really good solution: the interpreter simply extends the array and inserts the new item:

```
1. var data = ["Monday", "Tuesday", 34, 76.34, "Wednesday"];
2. data[5] = "Thursday";
3. data[23] = 48;
```

The code creates an array of four elements in line one. A new element is added at position 5 in line two. At line three an element is added to position 23. To do this the array is first expanded so that it is long enough and then the new element is added.

### 5.9.1.3 *Accessing Array Members*    The elements in the array are accessed through their index. The same access method is used to find elements and to change their value.

#### `length`

When accessing array elements you don't want to read beyond its end. Therefore you need to know how many elements have been stored. This is done through the `length` attribute. Remember that index numbers run from 0 to `length - 1`.

The following code shows how to read through all elements of an array:

```
<html>
   <head>
      <title>Looping Through an Array</title>
   </head>
   <body>
      <script language="javascript">
      <!--
         document.writeln("<h1>Looping Through an Array</h1>");
         document.write("<p>");

         var data = ["Monday", "Tuesday", 34, 76.34, "Wednesday"];
         var len = data.length;

         for(var count = 0; count < len; count++) {
            document.write(data[count] + ", ");
         }
         document.writeln("</p>");
         document.close();
      //-->
      </script>
   </body>
</html>
```

The result of running that code inside Konqueror is shown in Figure 5.5.

**Figure 5.5**  Looping Through an Array

### 5.9.1.4 *Searching an Array*

To search an array, simply read each element in turn and compare it with the value that you're looking for. Try the following code in the script you've just seen. This loops through the array, compares each element with a string, if the two elements are equal a message is printed out. To stop the search, I use the builtin `break` function which terminates the current loop. You can use `break` with `for` and `while` loops.

```
for(var count = 0; count < len; count++) {
  if(data[count] == "Tuesday"){
     document.write(data[count] + ", ");
     break;
  }
}
```

### 5.9.1.5 *Removing Array Members*

Removing elements from an array is quite straightforward. JavaScript doesn't provide a builtin function to do this for you. Given the rich set of facilities the language *has*, this is quite a surprising omission. To remove an element for yourself use the following procedure:

- read each element in the array,
- if the element is *not* the one you want to delete, copy it into a temporary array,
- if you want to delete the element then do nothing,
- increment the loop counter,
- repeat the process.

The next piece of code loops through an array and deletes a single item. The output it gives in Netscape is shown in Figure 5.6. I tried this code in Konqueror but the original array was not written to the screen until all of the script had executed. This is the sort of nasty feature which can easily bite JavaScript developers. Simply because your code works in one browser on one platform you have no guarantee that it will execute as you intend on every platform.

**Figure 5.6**   Removing an Array Element

```
<html>
   <head>
      <title>Removing an Array Element</title>
   </head>
   <body>
      <script language="javascript">
      <!--
      document.writeln("<h1>Removing an Array Element</h1>");

      var data = ["Monday", "Tuesday", 34, 76.34, "Wednesday"];

      // Show the original array
      document.write("<p>");
      var len = data.length;
      for(var count = 0; count < len; count++) {
         document.write(data[count] + ", ");
      }
```

```javascript
document.writeln("</p>");

// Ask the user what to remove
var rem = prompt("Which item shall I remove?", "");
var tmp = new Array(data.length - 1);
var count2 = 0;

// This loop searches for, and removes a single item
for(var count = 0; count < len; count++) {
    if(data[count] == rem) {
        // do nothing
    } else {
        tmp[count2] = data[count];
        count2++;
    }
}

data = tmp;

// Show the new Array
document.write("<p>");
var len = data.length;
for(var count = 0; count < len; count++) {
    document.write(data[count] + ", ");
}

document.writeln("</p>");
document.close();

//-->
</script>
</body>
</html>
```

Some of the code there is quite cryptic so I'll briefly explain the key features. The script includes a loop which writes out the contents of the array as an HTML paragraph. If you've done a bit of programming then you may think that this code should have been removed and placed in a *function* which could have been called twice. This is certainly the best way of writing a program but since I haven't covered functions yet, I've used a more straight-forward brute-force approach. The display code is basically the loop which you've now seen used a couple of times:

```
document.write("<p>");
var len = data.length;
for(var count = 0; count < len; count++) {
    document.write(data[count] + ", ");
}
document.writeln("</p>");
```

Removing an element from the array is slightly more complicated, although it is still based around a loop. The basic algorithm for the removal of an array element is:

- create an empty, temporary array,
- initialize separate counters for each array,
- read the next array element,
- compare the element with the target for removal,
- if the two elements do not match, copy the element from the original array into the temporary array,
- if the elements *do* match,
    - increment the counter on the original array,
    - copy all remaining elements from the original array into the temporary one,
- otherwise, if the original array has any remaining elements, return to the third step.

What's happening in the algorithm is that we are copying all of the data from our array into a temporary data structure *except* for the element which we want to remove. Each array needs its own counter because once an item has been removed the two arrays will be working on different items. Look at the following code and try to understand how it works:

```
var rem = prompt("Which item shall I remove?", "");
var tmp = new Array(data.length - 1);
var count2 = 0;

// This loop searches for, and removes a single item
for(var count = 0; count < len; count++) {
    if(data[count] == rem){
        // do nothing
    } else {
        tmp[count2] = data[count];
        count2++;
    }
}

data = tmp;
```

If the code is confusing you, simply insert some statements to print the values held by array counters and in the array elements as the loop progresses:

```
for(var count = 0; count < len; count++) {
    if(data[count] == rem){
        // do nothing
        document.write("Target found. data[count] = " + count);
        document.write(": " + data[count] + "<br>");
    } else {
        tmp[count2] = data[count];
        document.write("Copying. data[count] = " + count);
        document.write(": " + data[count] + "<br>");

        document.write("  tmp[count2] = " + count2);
        document.write(": " + tmp[count2] + "<br>");

        count2++;
    }
}
```

### 5.9.2   Object-based Array Functions

In JavaScript an array can act like an object[8]. Don't worry about the details of what objects are, or how they work, for now you don't need to know. What you *do* need to do is spend some time familiarizing yourself with the useful functions which follow. Each of the array functions is used in the same way. You must specify the name of the array which you want to operate on, followed by a dot, then the name of the function. Finally in parentheses you must specify any parameters in a comma separated list:

```
arrayname.function(parameter1, parameter2);
```

I'll give a few examples which should help ease you through the notation as I describe the functions.

#### concat(array2[, array3[, arrayN]])

A list of arrays is concatenated onto the end of the array and a new array returned. The original arrays are all unaltered by this process. If you are worried about the idea of a list of arrays, don't be. I simply mean that some arrays are specified in a particular order. If you are joining just two arrays, that's fine because in computing a list can, and often does, have just one item. Here's some code which concatenates three arrays:

```
<html>
    <head>
```

---

[8]Actually a JavaScript array *is* an object.

***Figure 5.7***   Concatenating Arrays

```
  <title>Concatenating Arrays</title>
</head>
<body>
  <script language="javascript">
  <!--
  document.writeln("<h1>Concatenating Arrays</h1>");

  var first = ["Monday", "Tuesday", 34, 76.34, "Wednesday"];
  var second = ["one", "two", "three", 76.9];
  var third = new Array("an", "object", "array");

  var result = first.concat(second, third);

  // Show the resulting array
  document.write("<p>");
  var len = result.length;
  for(var count = 0; count < len; count++) {
     document.write(result[count] + ", ");
  }
  document.writeln("</p>");
  document.close();
  //-->
  </script>
```

```
    </body>
</html>
```

The resulting output from the concatenation is shown in Figure 5.7.

**`join(string)`**

Sometimes it's useful to have all of the elements in array joined together as a string. For instance, in earlier examples I've been using a loop to display an array, if that process could be wrapped into a single function it would be cleaner and simpler. That's exactly what the `join` function does. It passes through the array creating a string of all elements. In the resulting string the elements are separated using the optional string parameter. If this is omitted the elements will be separated using a comma but if you want anything more complex, such as `", "`, then you'll have to specify it explicitly.

**`pop()`**

This function removes the last element from the array and in doing so reduces the number of elements in the array by one.

**`push(element1[, element2[, elementN]])`**

Adds a list of items onto the end of the array. The items are separated using commas in the parameter list.

**`reverse()`**

As the name suggests, this function swaps all of the elements in the array so that which was first is last, and vice versa.

**`shift()`**

Removes the first element of the array and in so doing shortens its length by one.

The following code and Figure 5.8 show those five functions in action:

*Figure 5.8* Array Operations

```
<html>
   <head>
      <title>Array Operations</title>
   </head>
   <body>
   <script language="javascript">
   <!--
      document.writeln("<h1>Array Functions</h1>");

      var first = ["Monday", "Tuesday", 34, 76.34, "Wednesday"];
      document.write("<p>");

      document.write(first.join(", "));
      document.write("<br>");

      first.pop();
      document.write(first.join(", "));
      document.write("<br>");

      first.push("one", "two", "three", 76.9);
      document.write(first.join(", "));
      document.write("<br>");

      first.reverse();
      document.write(first.join(", "));
      document.write("<br>");

      first.shift();
      first.shift();
      document.write(first.join(", "));

      document.writeln("</p>");
      document.close();
      //-->
      </script>
   </body>
</html>
```

## slice(start[, finish])

Sometimes you need to extract a range of elements from an array. The slice() function does exactly this. Two parameters are possible: the first element which you want to remove is specified in the first parameter, the last element you want is specified in the second one. If you only give a single parameter, all elements from the specified one to the end of the array are selected. Once the elements have been sliced they are returned as a new array. The original array is unaltered by this function.

**sort()**

The array is sorted into lexicographic, *dictionary*, order. Elements in the array which are not text are first converted to strings before the sort operation is performed. This means that, for instance, 732 will be placed before 80 in the sorted array.

You can optionally create a function which will control how the sort is performed. This function can be called as a parameter to the `sort` function. I'm not going to describe how this can be done, look in an advanced JavaScript book for details.

**splice(index, number[, element1[, element2[, elementN]]])**

If you need to alter an array by removing some elements and at the same time adding in new ones, then you'll need the `splice` function. This function is somewhat peculiar, read through the following explanation, then look at the example. Finally re-read the explanation which *should* be a bit more clear.

The `splice` function has two compulsory parameters and an unlimited number of optional ones. The first parameter indicates the position in the array at which the new elements will start. The second parameter indicates how many elements will be deleted from the original array. If you don't want to delete elements then set this to 0. Finally there is a list of elements which are to be inserted into the array. If you insert more elements than you remove then the array will grow longer. Figure 5.9 shows this in action.

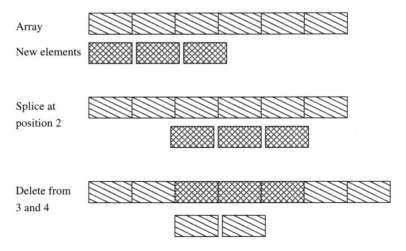

**Figure 5.9** Splicing Arrays

```
document.writeln("<p>");
data.splice(2, 0, "element one", "element two");
```

```
document.writeln(data.join(", ") + "<br>");
data.splice(3, 3, "element three", "element four");
document.writeln(data.join(", "));
document.writeln("</p>");
```

**unshift(element1[, element2[,elementN]])**

> Inserts a list of elements onto the front of the array. The list of new elements can have just one item.

Although this discussion of arrays has been long and rather involved, they are an important structure in JavaScript. When I start to show some dynamic HTML you'll see that everything revolves around the manipulation of arrays so it's important that you have a good understanding of how they work.

## 5.10 FUNCTIONS

A function is a piece of code that performs a specific task. These tasks are larger than those of a statement – almost every function is made up of a number of statements. By creating a function the same piece of code can be used repeatedly throughout the time that the program runs yet it only needs to be developed in one place. JavaScript has a lot of functions built into the language. You have already seen some of these and you'll meet more as we go along. A larger set of JavaScript 1.1 functions is shown in Appendix B.

Once you've created some functions you need to know how to use them. This is done by *calling* the function. When programmers talk about a function call they are talking about using the code in the function at another point in the program. Until the program *calls* a function, that code won't do anything. This can be useful as it means that you can partially develop your functions without affecting the rest of your program *provided you don't call them*.

### 5.10.1 Defining Functions

**function name(parameters)**

> Functions are defined using the function[9] keyword. The function name can be any combination of digits, letters, and underscore but cannot contain a space. That's the same rule as for variable naming. With function names it's even more important that you make them meaningful because you'll use them so often.
>
> A function is a block of code and so has to have its curly brackets:

```
function a_first_function() {
    // the code goes here
    }
```

---

[9]Surprise surprise!

## 5.10.2 Parameter Passing

Not every function accepts parameters. Not all values have to be passed as parameters. Remember global variables? Well they can be used by any function without having been passed in as parameters, which looks like a good idea but can get very messy when you are writing complex programs.

**Figure 5.10** Function Call 1

When a function receives a value as a parameter, that value is given a name and can be accessed using that name by the function. The names of parameters are taken from the function definition and are applied in the order in which parameters are passed in. Let's look at a simple function and see what all of that means. The function takes in three parameters – name, age, and shoe size – and displays them in a Web page:

```
function about_you(name, age, shoesize){
   document.write("<h1>All About You</h1>");
   document.write("<p><strong>Your Name is:
              </strong>" + name);
   document.write("<p><strong>You Are</strong>"
              + age + "Years Old");
   document.writeln("<p><strong>Your Shoe Size is:
              </strong>" + shoesize);
   document.close();
   }
```

That might be called like this as the page is loaded:

```
<html>
   <head>
```

```
        <title>About You</title>
    </head>
    <body onLoad="about_you('Chris', 34, 8)">

        <script language="javascript">
        <!--
        function about_you(name, age, shoesize){
            document.write("<h1>All About You</h1>");
            document.write("<p><strong>Your Name is:
                </strong> " + name);
            document.write("<p><strong>You Are</strong> " + age
                + " Years Old");
            document.writeln("<p><strong>Your Shoe Size is:
                </strong> " + shoesize);
            document.close();
        }
        //-->
        </script>
    </body>
</html>
```

or simply like this from within a more complex script:

```
about_you('Chris', 34, 9);
```

which would print out exactly as you might expect (it's shown in Figure 5.10). But what if the order of the parameters was messed up in the call? Well then you end up with strange output. That's not too important here but would be if you were going to use the numbers in some later mathematical function. Here's that error (shown in Figure 5.11):

```
about_you(9, "Chris", 34);
```

It's also OK not to pass any parameters in. You can also miss out a parameter altogether – but only the last one. If you want to miss out any other parameter then pass in an empty string (""). Here's an example with a missing parameter (see Figure 5.12):

```
about_you("Chris", "", 9);
```

### 5.10.3 Examining the Function Call

In JavaScript parameters are passed as arrays. Every function has two properties that can be used to find information about the parameters:

**function.arguments**
    This is the array of parameters that have been passed.

**Figure 5.11**    Function Call 2

**Figure 5.12**    Function Call 3

`function.arguments.length`

This is the number of parameters that have been passed into the function. You could easily use this to check that all parameters have been sent and to issue a warning if they haven't.

You might also write a function that can accept a variable list of parameters and use these two functions to control its operation.

### 5.10.4 Comments

JavaScript code, like code written in most programming languages, can be difficult to read. If you need to look back at your code to alter it you may struggle to remember what it is doing and how. This has always been a problem in software development. The solution is to find a way of adding *documentation* to your programs which describes them. This is done by placing comments throughout the program.

Comments are pieces of text which can be used by programmers as they read through the source but which are ignored by the interpreter or compiler. In JavaScript each line of comment is preceded by two slashes and continues from that point to the end of the line.

```
// this is a JavaScript comment
```

Unlike some other languages JavaScript doesn't have a way of commenting large blocks of text as a block. If you want a block comment then you have to comment each and every line.

### 5.10.5 Parsing

Why doesn't the JavaScript interpreter raise an error when strange parameters are being passed around? Well because JavaScript doesn't spend a lot of effort telling numbers from strings the interpreter doesn't need to bother. If you tried to pass a string into a Math function such as Math.sin() you'd get an error. Ordinarily though, the difference is not important *to the interpreter*. Of course the difference matters to the application so it's up to you as the developer to check that you are handling the correct data.

When a Web page is loaded, the browser will check through it looking for mistakes in the code. Most browsers don't mind errors in HTML code – in fact the browser manufacturers almost seem to encourage poor code. Browsers do care about errors in JavaScript programs but only certain types of error.

Any JavaScript in the head section is parsed[10] by the browser. If it finds any errors in your coding such as missing semicolons or inverted commas, or even mistyped builtin function names, then you'll get an error. However, the parser does not check the logic of your code. It checks that your code *could* run correctly but it doesn't check that it *will*. That's a job for you.

### 5.10.6 Returning Values

Hopefully you remember that any variables that you declare in a function are local to that function. You cannot get at their value outside the function unless you pass them around as parameters. Well that's not always convenient, so a mechanism is needed to return a value from a function. That mechanism is provided by the return statement.

---

[10]Read through and checked.

Although you can only pass a single value with `return` that value can be a JavaScript object which, as you'll see in Chapter 6, can be a complex data set.

```
var reset = my_func(32);

function my_func(number){
   var answer = sin(number);
   return answer;
   }
```

That simple example should be quite clear. A variable is set based upon the return value of a function. The `sin()` function is, of course, yet another of JavaScript's useful builtin functions.

### 5.10.7   Scoping Rules

Scoping is an important concept in programming. When you declare a variable you might naively expect that it can be used anywhere in your program but that is not actually the case. If every variable were available to every function then your code would get messy, you would make mistakes and find that your programs were actually quite inefficient. Programming languages usually impose rules, called *scoping*, which determine how a variable can be accessed. JavaScript is no exception. In JavaScript variables can be either *local* or *global*.

**global**

> Global scoping means that a variable is available to all parts of the program. Such variables are declared outside of any function and are usually used to hold static data that you won't alter once it's been created. A good use of a global variable might be to find the type of browser so that you can tailor your code to suit.

**local**

> Local variables are declared inside a function. They can only be used by that function. If you want the value associated with a local variable to be available to other functions then you must pass it as a *parameter*. How this is achieved is shown in Section 5.10.

The following code shows the difference between global and local variables:

```
<html>
   <head>
      <title>Variables, Functions and Scope</title>
   </head>
   <body>
      <script language="javascript">
      <!--
         var the_var = 32;
         var tmp = the_var;
```

```
        var tmp2 = setLocal(17);

        document.writeln("<h1>Scope</h1>");
        document.writeln("<p>The global is " + the_var);
        document.writeln("<br>tmp is " + tmp);
        document.writeln("<br>tmp2 is " + tmp2);
        document.writeln("</p>");
        document.close();

        function setLocal(num) {
            the_var = num;
            alert("tmp is: " + tmp);
            return(the_var);
        }
    //-->
    </script>
  </body>
</html>
```

In the script I declare three global variables. These are accessible from anywhere in the rest of the script. When a script is written in the body of the page it is parsed as it is loaded and global variable declarations are possible. If you want to declare your script in the head of the page then global variable declarations won't work. You'll have to create some sort of object to hold the values and initialize them when the script is loaded. I'll show you how to do that in Chapter 6.

In my example, the first line of the script assigns a value to the_var. This is copied into tmp in line 2 for storage. I'm going to attempt to manipulate the original and I want a copy so that I can display its starting value later. In line 3 I call a function, setLocal() with the value 17 as an argument and set the variable tmp2 based upon the return value from this function.

The setLocal() function has it's own variable called the_var which it sets to be equal to the argument it receives. In this case the_var is going to be set to 17. It might, therefore seem reasonable that since we declared a variable earlier called the_var, *it* now has a value of 17. After all the two variables have the same name so they must be the same thing, mustn't they? Well, no, they're not. Although the names are the same in our script, each name actually refers to a different data item. The first one is global, the second is local. The local variable has precedence inside its own function. That means the system will use the local variable whenever it can.

Another question you might ask is "Why bother with global variables?" The answer to *that* is also demonstrated in setLocal(). I've added an alert box which I use to display the value held by one of the global variables. Global variables are used to hold values which need to be accessed by more than one function. Generally such values are not going to change during the runtime of the program and passing them as variables is an unnecessary additional overhead.

Finally, notice that the HTML page is only written out after all of the function calls have been completed. If you try to call a function before you have called `document.close()` you'll get a runtime error in Netscape.

## 5.11   EXERCISES

### Scripting technologies

1. What are the differences between a set of Web pages and a Web application? What technologies are currently available for the creation of such applications?

2. List the technologies that are used to create DHTML pages.

3. Describe the Document Object Model.

4. The DOM is at the heart of the incompatibilities between the main browsers. How might these problems be resolved?

5. How do ECMA Script, JScript and JavaScript relate to each other?

6. JavaScript is an interpreted language. What advantages does interpretation have over compilation when prototyping applications?

7. How does JavaScript compare with other technologies that are available for use on client browsers?

### JavaScript

1. Why do you think JavaScript code closely resembles code in languages such as C?

2. Outline the structure of a JavaScript program.

3. How is JavaScript included in HTML documents?

4. Can JavaScript be executed without using a Web browser?

5. What is the difference between a variable and a value? How should variables be named?

6. What data types does JavaScript use?

7. What are scoping rules – why are they so important in all programming languages?

8. Describe each of the loop constructs that JavaScript provides. Why do languages typically have more than one type of loop?

9. What are functions used for? How are functions defined in JavaScript?

10. How does parameter passing work?

11. Why do some functions return values to the calling statement?

12. How does JavaScript create HTML pages *on the fly*?

## Using JavaScript

1. Write a simple JavaScript that adds some numbers together, concatenates a couple of strings, and then shows the result in an `alert()` dialog and on the page.

2. Create a Web page which uses `prompt()` dialogs to ask a user for their name, age and shoe size. Display the information they enter on the page formatted as a small table.

3. Write a Web page which contain the code from page 123.

4. Try removing the JavaScript code from the HTML page show in Section 6.5. Place the code in a file called `testscript.js`. See if you can link this into the HTML page. Does the page act as you expected?

5. In the discussion of arrays in Section 5.9 I demonstrate some, but not all, of the functions. Write a Web page which prompts the user for six items of input, stores this in an array and displays it using `join()`. Display the data in sorted order. Use `splice()` to add some more elements into the array and display the result.

# 6
# *Objects in JavaScript*

## 6.1 DATA AND OBJECTS IN JAVASCRIPT

The previous section introduced the ideas of variables and control structures in JavaScript. If you worked through it and played around with the exercises then you should by now be comfortable with using functions and returning values. JavaScript has one more concept left that you need to understand before diving into DHTML. JavaScript tries to be an *object-oriented* (OO) language. It's not actually a true OO language like Smalltalk or Eiffel but it tries, the primitive objects that JavaScript does provide are very useful. Because the builtin functions all use these ideas, you'll need to get a grasp of them before going any further, so next up we have JavaScript objects for beginners.

### 6.1.1 Objects – A Brief Introduction

Object orientation is one of the most powerful concepts yet developed by computer scientists. Objects are widely applicable and object-based systems can be developed using many languages. Experienced programmers who are used to developing in traditional languages such as COBOL or FORTRAN, which have historically not supported objects, often find the OO paradigm confusing. Beginning programmers tend to be able to think in object terms right from the beginning.

As you'll see in a while JavaScript objects are easy to understand and use, but the language doesn't support all of the features found in most object systems. Before I discuss JavaScript objects I'll just spin rapidly through the general idea of objects.

### 6.1.1.1 *Objects*

An object is a *thing*. It can be anything that you like from some data through a set of methods[1] to an entire system. The reason that object-orientation is such a powerful idea is that quite simply it lets software designers and developers mimic the real world in their designs. This idea might be so obvious as to be not worth mentioning, after all software is usually meant to solve real-world problems. The benefit of OO is the tight linkage between the description of a problem and the ways in which it can be solved.

Real objects are more than just data or processing: data often describes something but the thing being described also has the ability to act. For instance a student has a name and address and is, usually, enrolled on one or more courses. A piece of software written using any language and any development technique can model the data which describes the student. But students are more than simple data: they each have unique behaviors. Some students attend regularly, others hand all work in early, others change course frequently. Any software which manages data about students needs to track some, or all, of those behaviors. The big win for a software engineer from using OO is that the data and the dynamic aspects of a system can all be included in the finished product.

Objects are described in software and design constructs called classes. A class usually contains some data items and some methods. Each class provides services to other classes in the system. Often programs are composed of a set of class hierarchies in which generic classes are declared which then have their functionality refined and specialized into usable form. This is where more of the power of OO comes from. A single generic class can be specialized in many ways and each of the specialized versions *inherits* some of the properties and behavior of the generic class. That means that common parts of the program can be developed just once and easily reused.

Think about the typical students again. The data describing them and some behavior such as attendance at lectures can be described in a student *base class*. More specialized behavior can be described in *subclasses*. A biochemistry student who attends laboratory sessions would be an example of a different subclass to a literature major who goes to seminars but not labs.

When a program runs, objects are created. An object is a run-time *instance* of a class. The object has all of the behavior that was defined in the class and is able to perform processing. The dynamic aspects of an object are captured through pieces of code written inside methods. When an object needs to do something, the appropriate method is executed. Generally objects don't act independently. Instead their actions are triggered by events throughout the system, in particular the program that they belong to. Usually actions occur because an object somewhere in the system requests a service from another object. In our student example, a record management system might need to know the name of a particular student. It finds this by asking the object which represents that student for its name.

There's one more thing that you ought to know about objects. Very often an object is formed by aggregating together lots of simpler objects. Again this is simply a way of mir-

---

[1]The name for functions in OO.

roring the world around us. We are made from a set of complicated components such as our brains, cardio-vascular system and gastro-intestinal system. If we were modelling an object-oriented human we would start by modelling each of those systems. We would then combine those systems to make more complex pieces, finally we would join all of the pieces together to make a person.

> **Note:**
> A class is a description of something; an object is an instance of a class. It's the object that exists in the computer's memory and which does the work.

In summary:

- an object is described by a class;
- a class can be specialized through inheritance;
- a class usually contains both data items and processing capability.

### 6.1.1.2  *JavaScript Objects*
So does JavaScript implement all of that object stuff? Well it would be true to say that it does and then again it doesn't. The builtin JavaScript objects such as `document` and `window` act, and are used, like standard OO objects. I'll be showing how to use these in Section 6.4.

Where JavaScript diverges from *traditional* OO is in its treatment of user-defined objects. An object is really a data structure that has been associated with some functions. It doesn't have inheritance and the structure of the code can look a little peculiar. The easiest way of understanding how to combine your data and functions into objects is to work through an example. Code first then explanation:

```
<html>
  <head>
  <script language=javascript>
  <!--

  function ObjDemo(){
    popup("Hello");
    myhouse = new house("Dun Hacking", 2, 4);
    alert(myhouse.name + " Has " + myhouse.floors +
        " Floors And " + myhouse.rooms() + " Rooms");
    myhouse.leave("Farewell");
  }

  function house(name, floors, beds) {
    this.name = name;
    this.floors = floors;
    this.bedrooms = beds;
```

```javascript
        this.rooms = frooms;
        this.leave = popup;
    }

    function frooms(){
        var groundfloor = 3;
        var utilities = 2;
        var total = 0;

        if(this.floors <= 0){
            total = 0;
        }
        else {
            if(this.floors == 1) {
                total = this.bedrooms + utilities;
            }
            else{
                total = (this.floors * utilities);
                total += groundfloor;
                total += this.bedrooms;
            }
        }
        return total;
    }

    function popup(msg){
        alert(msg);
    }

    //-->
    </script>
    </head>
    <body onLoad="ObjDemo()">
    </body>
</html>
```

Before reading this explanation try to work out what is happening there yourself. The script is initiated as soon as the onLoad event happens during page loading:

```html
<body onLoad="ObjDemo()">
```

The `ObjDemo()` function performs four tasks. First it calls the popup function which displays an alert box with the string `Hello` displayed. That's simply using functions as I've done before. The next bit of code does something different and new[2].

```
popup("Hello");
myhouse = new house("Dun Hacking", 2, 4);
```

**new**

> The keyword `new` is used to create objects. It allocates memory and storage for them and sets all variables that can be set at this stage. Whenever you define an object you should make sure that all variables are set: strings to `" "` and numbers to 0. `new` calls a function which has the same name as the type of object that is being created. This function is called the *constructor*.
>
> After the call to `new` in this program, the object `myhouse` exists and can be used. If you try rewriting the script so that `myhouse` is used *before* it's created you'll get a JavaScript error.

The object-oriented aspects of the script all revolve around the `myhouse` object which is an *instance* of house. The constructor takes a number of parameters and assigns them to variables.

Objects can have functions as well as variables. These object functions, or *methods*, are *aliased* by giving them a unique name within the object. By doing this aliasing, a function can be accessed either as a top-level part of the script or as part of an object. The local object functions are aliases of, or pointers to if you prefer, the actual functions rather than copies of those functions. This code shows the house constructor:

```
function house(name, floors, beds) {
    this.name = name;
    this.floors = floors;
    this.bedrooms = beds;
    this.rooms = frooms;
    this.leave = popup;
}
```

**this**

> To differentiate between global variables and those which are part of an object but *may* have the same name, JavaScript uses `this`. Whenever you refer to a variable which is part of an object you *must* precede the variable name by `this`. Separate the variable name from `this` with a dot.

**.(dot)**

> When referring to a property of an object, whether a method or a variable, a dot is placed between the object name and the property.

---

[2]No pun intended!

Sometimes it would be useful if you could write information to the screen from within an object and carry on with the processing. Unfortunately JavaScript does not allow you to mix screen output and processing. Instead you need to use your scripts to prepare a complete page and write that before performing more processing. Once you use a statement such as document.write(), the interpreter expects to encounter a document.close() statement before it will handle any JavaScript functions you've written. I mention this because when you use JavaScript objects you often need to write to the screen from those objects. Doing so is *not* easy.

## 6.2  REGULAR EXPRESSIONS

One common task in software development is the parsing of a string looking for a particular pattern. For instance, a script might take name data from a user and have to search through it checking that no digits have been entered. This type of problem can be solved by reading through the string one character at a time looking for the target pattern. Although that might seem like a straightforward thing to do, actually it turns out that it is not. Efficiency and speed matter, and any code which performs these tasks need to be constructed very carefully. The usual approach in scripting languages is to create a pattern called a *regular expression* which describes a set of characters that may be present in a string.

JavaScript versions after 1.1 include a set of routines to manipulate strings and search patterns. These are wrapped up as regular expression objects. JavaScript regular expressions are more than patterns: they include functions which you call from your scripts when you need a pattern finding. You might expect that you would use search patterns by applying a pattern to a string. JavaScript allows this way of working:

```
var pattern = "target";
var string = "Can you find the target?";
string.match(pattern);
```

but you can also work the other way. A string can be passed into a regular expression as a parameter:

```
var pattern = new RegExp("target");
var string = "Can you find the target?";
pattern.exec(string);
```

JavaScript regular expressions are based on those found in Perl. In fact from the programmers point of view, they work in just the same way. Rather than describe them in detail twice, I'm going to point you to the Perl description in Section 8.9. Regular expressions are a fundamental part of Perl, discussion of their complexities sits more naturally in a discussion of *that* language.

### 6.2.1  Creating Regular Expressions

A regular expression is a JavaScript object. As with any other type of object there are multiple ways of creating them. They can be created *statically* when the script is first parsed, or dynamically at run-time. If performance is an issue for your script then you should try to use static expressions whenever possible. If you don't know what you're going to be searching for until run-time, for instance if the search pattern depends on user input, then you'll need to create dynamic patterns. Let's look at an example of each. A static regular expression is created as follows:

```
regex = /fish|fowl/;
```

Dynamic patterns are created using the new keyword to create an instance of the RegExp class:

```
regex = new RegExp("fish|fowl");
```

### 6.2.2  Writing Patterns

Search patterns can be very simple or incredibly complicated. The most difficult thing about them is, probably, working out what you want to search for. Once you've worked that out you need to be able to express the search pattern in a format which can be used by a computer program. Describing a pattern in natural language is relatively easy. Unfortunately few computer programs are able to successfully handle natural language instruction. On the other hand computers are very good at repetitive symbolic manipulation. If your search pattern can be expressed as a set of symbols, a computer can use it, some search rules and a target string very effectively. This is exactly the approach which regular expression systems take.

Patterns are expressed in a cryptic, but powerful, grammar which uses symbols to replace complex statements. As I mentioned earlier, the JavaScript regular expression grammar is identical to that used in Perl. I'm leaving a discussion of the grammar until Section 8.9, but Table 6.1 lists a few highlights. One complication is that some of the characters in the JavaScript grammar are preceded by a backslash character. This is an escape character which is used to tell the browser that the character signifies an operation not a letter. Browsers[3] have a tendency to remove the backslash thus breaking your neatly created expression. The solution is to escape the backslash by preceding it with another one. If you use \\d, for instance in JavaScript, the browser will actually use \d.

### 6.2.3  Remembering the Result

You may be simply looking through a string to see if it matches some particular pattern. At other times, though, you'll be looking for a pattern that you're going to use elsewhere. This

---

[3]Or all those that I've used, at least.

***Table 6.1*** JavaScript Regular Expression Grammar

| Token | Description |
| --- | --- |
| ^ | Match at the start of the input string. |
| $ | Match at the end of the input string. |
| * | Match 0 or more times. |
| + | Match 1 or more times. |
| ? | Match 0 or 1 time. |
| a\|b | Match a or b. |
| {n} | Match the string n times. |
| \d | Match a digit. |
| \D | Match anything except for digits. |
| \w | Match any alphanumeric character or the underscore. |
| \W | Match anything except alphanumeric characters or underscores. |
| \s | Match a whitespace character. |
| \S | Match anything except for whitespace characters. |
| [...] | Creates a set of characters, one of which must match if the operation is to be successful. If you need to specify a range of characters then separate the first and last with a hyphen: [0-9] or [D-G]. |
| [^...] | Creates a set of characters which must not match. If any character in the set matches then the operation has failed. This fails if any lowercase letter from d to q is matched: [^d-q]. |

means that you'll need to remember the result of your search. The RegExp object holds the result of its operations in an array which it returns to the calling script.

Any part of a pattern which you need to remember is placed inside parentheses. You can match, and remember, as many substrings as you want to. These are returned in an array and can be recalled very easily. The order of storage matches the order in which the sets of parentheses appear in the pattern. The first match, therefore, is stored in array[0]. If you wanted to find and use the pattern "fred" in a string and use it later, you'd do something like:

```
<html>
   <head>
      <title>Remembering Patterns</title>
   </head>
   <body>
   <script language=javascript>
   <!--
      var re = new RegExp("[F|f]red");
```

```
        var msg = "Have you met Fred recently?";
        var results = re.exec(msg);
        if(results) {
            alert("I found " + results[0]);
        } else {
            alert("I didn't find it");
        }
    //-->
    </script>
    </body>
</html>
```

The regular expression is designed to search for either 'f' or 'F' followed by the string "red". If the string is found, it is stored as the first element of the results array. If the search fails, nothing is written into results. We can test for the success of the search by testing whether the array has any sort of value. Depending upon the result of that test, an alert message is displayed.

### 6.2.4  Functions

Regular expressions are manipulated using functions which belong to either the RegExp or String classes.

#### Class string Functions

**match(pattern)**
> Searches for a matching pattern. Returns an array holding the results, or null if no match is found.

**replace(pattern1, pattern2)**
> Searches for pattern1. If the search is successful pattern1 is replaced with pattern2.

**search(pattern)**
> Searches for a pattern in the string. If the match is successful, the index, offset, of the start of the match is returned. If the search fails, the function returns –1.

**split(pattern)**
> Splits the string into parts based upon the pattern, or regular expression, which is supplied as a parameter.

#### Class RegExp Functions

**exec(string)**
> Executes a search for a matching pattern in its parameter string. Returns an array holding the result(s) of the operation.

`test(string)`

Searches for a match in its parameter string. Returns `true` if a match is found, otherwise returns `false`.

### 6.2.5 Flags

The default behavior for regular expressions is to work only on single lines of data, to stop as soon as a match is successful and to use the pattern exactly as written. The behavior of `RegExp` objects can be modified using three *flags*.

`i`

Performs searches which ignore the case of the pattern and the input string.

`m`

Allows searching of data which spans several input lines.

`g`

Rather than stopping when the match is successful, this forces global matching across all of the input.

The flags are applied either directly into the regular expression:

```
regex = /fish|fowl/ig;
```

or as an additional parameter to the object constructor:

```
regex = new RegExp("fish|fowl", "ig");
```

### 6.2.6 Examples

The best way of seeing how regular expressions work is to actually use them. The following set of scripts should give you some insight into how this powerful tool can be used.

*Finding a Pattern Match*   The following script prompts you for a string and then a pattern. The pattern is converted into a `RegExp` object which is then used to search the string looking for the pattern. Depending upon the success of the search, a message is written into the browser.

```
<html>
  <head>
    <title>Pattern Matching</title>
  </head>
  <body>
  <script language=javascript>
  <!--
    var msg = prompt("Enter a test string", "");
    var hunt = prompt("Enter a regular expression", "");
```

```
      var re = new RegExp(hunt);

      var results = re.exec(msg);
      document.writeln("<h1>Search Results</h1><p>");
      if(results) {
         document.write("I found " + results[0]);
      } else {
         document.write("I didn't find it");
      }
      document.writeln("</p>");
      document.close();
   //-->
   </script>
   </body>
</html>
```

***Splitting a String***   String splitting is incredibly useful.  If you are getting input data from users then it's likely to come into your script as a string.  The following sample shows how you can take a string and split it into pieces.  The script uses a character which the user enters to perform the split. If you run this script you'll notice that the character which you're splitting on is discarded.

```
<html>
   <head>
      <title>String Splitting</title>
   </head>
   <body>
   <script language=javascript>
   <!--
      var msg = prompt("Enter a test string", "");
      var hunt = prompt("Enter a split character", "");
      var results = msg.split(hunt);
      document.writeln("<h1>Split Results</h1><p>");
      for(var i = 0; i < results.length; i++) {
         document.write("results[" + i + "} " + results[i]);
         document.writeln("<br>");
      }
      document.writeln("</p>");
      document.close();
   //-->
   </script>
```

```
    </body>
</html>
```

*Replacing a Matched String*  This time the user enters the string and any regular expression pattern. If the pattern is matched then it is replaced with a simple string. You could try modifying this script so that it replaces all instances of the search string.

```
<html>
    <head>
        <title>Replacing a Matched String</title>
    </head>
    <body>
    <script language=javascript>
    <!--
        var msg = prompt("Enter a test string", "");
        var hunt = prompt("Enter a  regular expression", "");

        msg = msg.replace(hunt, "REPLACED");

        document.writeln("<h1>Replacement Results</h1><p>");
        document.write(msg);
        document.writeln("</p>");
        document.close();
    //-->
    </script>
    </body>
</html>
```

*Swapping Two Words*  Swapping two words is a very common requirement. It's not too difficult to do either. The regular expression is composed of the words we're looking for and the set of characters which separate them. Each of the target words is placed inside parentheses. If it is matched then the result, the word, is stored in a variable. The `replace` function takes the regular expression as its first parameter and a string made of the two words in reversed order, as its second. In the following example I identify the words in the replacement string using the names of hidden JavaScript variables in which they're stored. Don't worry about the strange syntax there, once you've worked through the Perl sections of this book $1 will look positively normal.

```
<html>
    <head>
        <title>Swapping Words</title>
    </head>
    <body>
```

```
<script language="javascript">
<!--
    initial = "this is a test string";
    re = "(test) *(string)"
    finished = initial.replace(re, "$2 $1");
    document.writeln("<h1>Swapping Words</h1><p>");
    document.write(finished);
    document.writeln("</p>");
    document.close();
//-->
</script>
</body>
</html>
```

## 6.3 EXCEPTION HANDLING

Runtime error handling is vitally important in all programs. Your programs should never simply fall over or stop just because a user enters invalid data or does something unexpected. Many object-oriented programming languages provide a mechanism for dealing with general classes of error. This mechanism is called *exception handling*. JavaScript 1.4 was the first version of the language to include exception handling.

> Note:
> The following discussion and example assumes that you're working with a browser such as Mozilla 0.8 or Netscape 6 which implements at least JavaScript 1.4. If users are likely to be viewing your site on an older browser then don't use exceptions.

An exception is an error which you have designed your program to cope with. Well that pretty much describes all errors doesn't it? If you write robust code then your programs will be able to handle them. After all a user has a finite number of choices at any point in a program so if you know what all the choices are then you can cope with any errors that the user, data or program cause. Can't you? In a small piece of JavaScript the answer is probably *yes*, you ought to be able to cope with any errors. In more complex scripts or large programs that may not always be the case. This is where exceptions come into the picture.

An exception in object-based programming is an object, created dynamically at run-time, which encapsulates[4] an error and some information about it. The great thing about exceptions is that you can define your own exception classes to include exactly what you need to handle the problem successfully. But more than that, if you're using exceptions, you no

---

[4]An OO term which really just means "wraps up".

longer need to think about every single mistake that a user might make. Instead you can wrap whole groups of mistakes up inside a single class. For instance all incorrect input might be described by `UserInputException` objects. This is a real *win-win* situation. Because you have exceptions, your code is more robust *and* it's simpler too. Using exceptions needs two new pieces of the JavaScript language.

**throw**

An exception is an object. It's created using the standard `new` method. Once the exception object exists, you need to do something with it. What you do is `throw` the exception, that is you pass it back up the call stack until there's a piece of code which can handle it. The syntax of the `throw` is:

```
do something
  if an error happens {
    create a new exception object
    throw the exception
  }
```

**try...catch**

Where you have a block of code which *might* cause the creation of an exception, you need to program some code to handle the exception if it should happen. The `try...catch` mechanism is found in many programming languages not just JavaScript. The idea here is that your program is going to try to execute a block of statements. If an exception is thrown by any of those statements, execution of the whole block ceases and the program looks for a `catch` statement to handle the exception. `try...catch` blocks take this form:

```
try {
    statement one
    statement two
    statement three
} catch exception {
    handle the exception
}
```

If `statement one` throws an exception, `statement two` and `statement three` will not be executed. Instead the program will move straight to the `catch`.

## 6.3.1  An Exceptional Example

Exception handling is best demonstrated through an example.

```
<html>
  <head>
    <title>Using Exceptions</title>
  </head>
```

```
<body onLoad="RunTest()">
<script language="javascript">
<!--
     function InputException(msg) {
         this.val = msg;
         this.toString = function () {
             return "Input Exception in " + this.val
         };
     }

     function AreLetters(msg) {
         var input = msg;
         var re = new RegExp("[^a-zA-Z]");
         if(input.match(re)) {
             Oops = new InputException(input);
             throw Oops;
         }
     }

     function RunTest(){
         var input = prompt("Type Something", "");
         try {
             AreLetters(input);
         } catch (e if e == "InputException") {
             alert(e.toString());
         }

         document.writeln("<h1>Using Exceptions</h1>");
         document.writeln("<p>");
         document.writeln("</p>");
         document.close();
     }
 //-->
 </script>
 </body>
</html>
```

Let's look at that example in a little more detail. The first thing to notice is the code to create the exception object:

```
function InputException(msg) {
   this.val = msg;
   this.toString = function () {
```

```
        return "Input Exception in " + this.val
    };
}
```

This has a variable which we're going to use to hold an error message, and a function which will be used to display the message. The `toString()` function is declared *inline*, that is it is declared inside another function. Although you've not seen code created like this before, it is *used* exactly like any other function which is part of an object.

```
if(input.match(re)) {
    Oops = new InputException(input);
    throw Oops;
}
```

The script executes a regular expression match. If the input string matches the regular expression, an object of type `InputException` is created. The script then `throws` the new exception and control transfers back to the calling block.

```
try {
    AreLetters(input);
} catch (e if e == "InputException") {
    alert(e.toString());
}
```

The block of code which handles the exception is a simple `try...catch` statement. This encloses just a single function call to the input function. If an exception is thrown during the execution of `AreLetters` it will be handled by the `catch` which closes the `try` statement. In this example the `catch` only operates if the `InputException` is thrown. I could have written the catch statement to handle all exceptions:

```
catch(e)
```

The `catch` block encloses a set of statements inside braces. In this case an alert box is opened which shows the error message inside the exception object. If no exception is thrown, the program continues execution after the closing brace of the `catch`.

## 6.4 BUILTIN OBJECTS

Most of the objects that you'll use in your scripting will be prebuilt ones that came with the browser. In this section I'll describe a few of these. More detailed descriptions are given in Appendix B and fairly comprehensive use of these objects is made in Chapter 7. This brief introduction is merely a taster for things to come.

### 6.4.1 The Document Object

A document is a Web page that is being either displayed or created. The document has a number of properties that can be accessed by JavaScript programs and used to manipulate the content of the page. Some of these properties can be used to create HTML pages from within JavaScript while others may be used to change the operation of the current page.

**write**

**writeln**

As you've already seen, HTML pages can be created *on the fly* using JavaScript. This is done by using the `write` or `writeln` methods of the document object:

```
document.write("<body>");
document.write("<h1>A test</h1>");
document.write("<form>");
```

**bgcolor**

**fgcolor**

These are the same properties that can be set in the `<BODY>` tag. The difference here is that the values can be set from within a JavaScript. The methods accept either hexadecimal values or common names for colors:

```
document.bgcolor = "#e302334";
document.fgcolor = "coral";
```

Those values can be used in dynamically created documents like this:

```
document.write("<body bgcolor=" + cols[counter] + ">");
document.write("<h1>A Test</h1>");
```

**anchors**

Any named point inside an HTML document is an anchor. Anchors are created using `<a name = ...>`. These will commonly be used for moving around inside a large page as shown in Section 2.4.3. The `anchors` property is an array of these names in the order in which they appear in the HTML document. Anchors can be accessed like this:

```
document.anchors[0];
```

**links**

Another array holding potentially useful information about the page. All links are stored in an array in the same order as they appear on the Web page.

**forms**

Again this is an array in the order of the document. This one contains all of the HTML forms. By combining this array with the individual `form` objects each form item can be accessed.

**layers**

A document can be made from a number of layers of content. This array contains the layer objects. Layers have many methods and properties of their own and will be discussed in detail in Section 4.7.

`close()`

> The document isn't completely written until the `close()` method has been called. If you don't use this method then the browser will keep waiting for more data even if there is none.

## 6.4.2   The Window Object

The browser window is a mutable object that can be addressed by JavaScript code. In Chapter 7 I'll show how new windows can be used to give a controlled Web experience or to break your site out from the mundane. All that I want to do here is to show some of the properties and methods that are available from `Window` objects.

`open("URL", "name")`

> This opens a new window which contains the document specified by URL. The window is given an identifying name so that it can be manipulated individually.

`close()`

> This shuts the current window.

`toolbar=[1|0]`
`location=[1|0]`
`directories=[1|0]`
`status=[1|0]`
`menubar=[1|0]`
`scrollbars=[1|0]`
`resizable=[1|0]`

> Many of the attributes of a browser are undesirable in a pop-up window. They can be switched on and off individually.

`width=pixels`
`height=pixels`

> When positioning content, especially on dynamic pages, it is useful to be able to locate it whatever the resolution of the screen or size of window being used. These values are easily available.
>
> When a new window is being opened then you may choose to open it at a set size, for instance if you are displaying an image there. These properties can be used to set the window size. The following code shows how this might work:

```
newWin = open(address, "newWin", status=0, width="100",
    height="100", resizable=0);
```

`scroll(coordinate, coordinate)`

> The content of the window can be automatically scrolled using this command. As with HTML layers the screen coordinates start from 0, 0, which is the top left corner, and increment as you move across and down. The coordinates are given in pixels.
>
> Later I'll show how to scroll individual layers – which is a more satisfying effect than scrolling the entire screen.

## 6.4.3  The Form Object

Two aspects of the form can be manipulated though JavaScript. First, most commonly and probably most usefully, the data that is entered onto your form can be checked at submission. Second you can actually build forms through JavaScript.

The elements of the form are held in an array (you might have guessed there would be an array in there somewhere!). This rather neatly means that any of the properties of those elements that you can set using HTML code can be accessed though your JavaScript. This example shows a form and a function which reads the properties of the form elements:

```html
<html>
   <head>
   <script language="javascript">
   function validate() {
      var method = document.forms[0].method;
      var action = document.forms[0].action;
      var value = document.forms[0].elements[0].value;
      if(value != "Mary"){
         document.forms[0].reset();
      } else {
         alert("Hi Mary!!");
      }
   }
   </script>
   </head><body>
   <form method="post">
      <input type="text" name="user" size="32">
      <input type="submit" value="Press Me!"
         onClick="validate()">
   </form>
   </body>
</html>
```

I will look at a data validation in more detail in Section 7.1, for now you just need to know which events can be used to trigger validation routines:

**onClick="method"**
This can be applied to all form elements. The event is triggered when the user clicks on that element. It is not triggered if you try to force events through the `click()` method.

**onSubmit="method"**
This event can only be triggered by the form itself and occurs when a form is submitted.

`onReset="method"`

Like the previous one this is a form-only event and is (obviously) triggered when a form is reset by the user.

## 6.4.4 The Browser Object

No two browser models will process your JavaScript in the same way. It's important that you try to find out which browser is being used to view your page. You can then make a choice for your visitors:

- exclude browsers that are unable to use your code;
- redirect them to a non-scripted version of your site;
- present scripts that are tailored to suit each browser. You'll be glad to know that this can be done from within your code and doesn't involve rewriting the entire site.

The browser is a JavaScript object and can be queried from within your code. For historical reasons the browser object is actually called the `navigator` object. The following properties are just some that can be gathered:

`navigator.appCodeName`

The internal name for the browser. For both major products this is *Mozilla*, which was the name of the original Netscape code source.

`navigator.appName`

This is the public name of the browser – navigator or Internet explorer for the big two.

`navigator.appVersion`

The version number, platform on which the browser is running, and (for Internet Explorer) the version of Navigator with which it is compatible.

`navigator.userAgent`

The strings `appCodeName` and `appVersion` concatenated together.

`navigator.plugins`

An array containing details of all installed plug-ins.

`navigator.mimeTypes`

An array of all supported MIME types – useful if you need to make sure that the browser can handle your data.

### 6.4.4.1 *Browser Sniffing* JavaScript implementations are based on the ECMAscript standard and most manufacturers do a pretty good job of implementing the language. You might, therefore, expect that your code will work in the same way in most browsers and on most platforms. As with so many Web technologies the reality is rather different to hype and expectation. The language might be the same, but each browser uses a different Document Object Model, and it is the elements of the DOM which JavaScript manipulates. Code which works in one browser cannot always be guaranteed to work in another simply because the objects that you're trying to manipulate might not exist there.

Some people, probably the majority of JavaScript developers, ignore incompatibilities. Commonly, Web sites include a warning that aspects of the site only work in Internet Explorer 5 or Netscape Navigator 4.7. There are lots of browsers out there, and even choosing between them can be very complicated. However the problem of browser sniffing is compounded because the same version of a browser may operate completely differently on different platforms. For instance, you cannot guarantee that your Explorer 4 compatible code will work on both Microsoft Windows and Apple MacOS.

It's possible to create scripts which work much more generally than that, provided you are willing to invest a little time and effort. You'll see that the scripts in Chapter 7 include many conditional tests for different browsers. I've tried to write those scripts so that they'll work in Explorer 4 or Navigator 4. Inside the scripts I select functions based upon the browser that is being used but how do I find that out? The answer is through the process of *browser sniffing*.

You can easily write your own trivial functions to perform sniffing. If you look around the Web you'll find lots of examples that other people have written and made freely available. Comprehensive examples run to hundreds of lines of code. If you're happy with a limited amount of sniffing then use your own code, if you want total coverage use someone else's. One of the best examples is written by Netscape. It's available from:

`http://www.mozilla.org/docs/web-developer/sniffer/browser-type.html`

and has the great benefit that it is regularly updated.

Browser sniffing functions use the properties of the browser object as the next code sample shows. This is a primitive example which creates a JavaScript object containing data about the browser and then displays that data in a new window:

```
<html>
   <head>
   <script language="javascript">
   <!--

   function Sniff() {
      browser = new Is();
      browser.display();
      }

   function Is() {
      this.app = navigator.appName.toLowerCase();
      this.version = navigator.appVersion;
      this.major = parseInt(navigator.appVersion);
      this.minor = parseFloat(navigator.appVersion);
      this.codename = navigator.appCodeName.toLowerCase();
      this.agent = navigator.userAgent.toLowerCase();
      this.display = showData;
```

```
        }

   function showData() {
       win = open("", "newWin");
       win.document.write("<body>");
       win.document.writeln("<h1>About Your Browser</h1>");
       win.document.writeln("<p><em>Application</em> "
                            + this.app);
       win.document.writeln("<p><em>Agent</em> "
                            + this.agent);
       win.document.writeln("<p><em>Codename</em> "
                            + this.codename);
       win.document.writeln("<p><em>Version</em> "
                            + this.version);
       win.document.writeln("<p><em>Version (major)</em> "
                            + this.major);
       win.document.writeln("<p><em>Version (minor)</em> "
                            + this.minor);
       win.document.writeln("</body>");
       win.document.close();
       }

   //-->
   </script>

   </head>
   <body onLoad="Sniff()">
   </body>
</html>
```

## 6.4.5 The Date Object

Manipulating dates and times is a complicated business. There's plenty of difficulty whether handling leap years or formatting output for different regions. JavaScript includes a well-developed Date class which provides functions to perform many different date manipulations.

In JavaScript, dates and times represent the number of milliseconds since 1st January 1970 UTC. JavaScript, like most programming systems, has two separate notions of time: UTC and local. UTC is universal time, also known as Greenwich Mean Time, which is the standard time throughout the World. Local time is the time on the machine which is executing the script. A JavaScript `Date` object can represents dates from −100,000,000 to +100,000,000 days relative to 01/01/1970. Since this range of dates clearly covers several millennia it is important that you always specify years fully. If you mean 2001, use 2001 not 01.

Table 6.2 lists some of the more useful functions for setting and retrieving values from `Date` objects. I have not included those which manipulate UTC dates since the table would become unwieldy.

**`Date()`**

Construct an empty `date` object.

**`Date(milliseconds)`**

Construct a new `Date` object based upon the number of milliseconds which have elapsed since 00:00:00 hours on 01/01/1970.

**`Date(string)`**

Create a `Date` object based upon the contents of a text string. The string must be in the format which is created by the `Date.parse()` function.

**`Date(year, month, day[, hour, minute, second])`**

Create a new `Date` object based upon numerical values for the year, month and day. Optional time values may also be supplied. January is represented by the integer value 0, December by 11.

**`Parse(String)`**

Returns the number of milliseconds since midnight on 01/01/1970 which the string represents. The string must be in the following format:

```
Mon, 9 April 2001 14:02:35
```

The timezone can be specified at the end of the string. If no timezone is specified then the local timezone of the machine executing the script is assumed. Timezones may be one of the U.S. continental zones or a numerical offset relative to GMT:

- Mon, 9 April 2001 14:02:35 GMT
- Mon, 9 April 2001 14:02:35 EST
- Mon, 9 April 2001 14:02:35 GMT+2

Table 6.2: JavaScript Date Functions

| Function | Description |
| --- | --- |
| getDate | Return the day of the month. |
| getDay | Return an integer representing the day of the week, Sunday is 0 and Saturday is 6. |
| getFullYear | Return the year as a four digit number. |
| getHours | Return the hour field of the `Date` object. |
| getMilliseconds | Return the milliseconds field of the `Date` object as a number from 0 to 999. |

Table 6.2: JavaScript Date Functions

| Function | Description |
|---|---|
| getMinutes | Return the minutes field of the Date object, from 0 to 59. |
| getMonth | Return the month field of the Date object. The month is represented by an integer: 0 for January through 11 for December. |
| getSeconds | Return the seconds field of the Date object. |
| getTime | Returns the number of milliseconds since midnight on 01/01/1970 which the Date object represents. |
| setDate(day) | Set the day value of the object. Accepts values in the range 1 to 31. |
| setFullYear(year [, month, day]) | Sets the year value of the object. Optionally also sets month and day values. All are passed as integers. Year as a four digit date, month in the range 0 to 11, day in the range 1 to 31. |
| setHours(hours [, mins, secs, ms]) | Set the hours value of the object to an integer in the range 0 through 23. Optionally set minutes, seconds and milliseconds values. |
| setMilliseconds(ms) | Set the milliseconds value of the object in the range 0 through 999. |
| setMinutes(min [, secs, ms]) | Set the minutes value using an integer in the range 0 though 59. |
| setMonth(month [, day]) | Set the month value to an integer in the range 0 through 11. |
| setSeconds(secs [, ms]) | Set the seconds value of the object to an integer in the range 0 to 59. |
| setTime(time) | Set the value of the Date object. The parameter is a string representing the number of milliseconds since midnight, 01/01/1970. |
| toGMTString | Returns the Date formatted as a string in GMT format. |
| toLocaleString | Returns the Date formatted in local format. |
| toString | Returns the Date as a string. |

Here's a simple piece of code which demonstrates how easily dates can be manipulated:

```
<html>
  <head>
    <title>Handling Dates</title>
  </head>
```

```
<body onLoad="Dater()">
<script language="javascript">
<!--
   function Dater() {
       var today = new Date();
       var yesterday = new Date();
       var diff = today.getDate() - 1;

       yesterday.setDate(diff);

       document.write("<h3>The date is " + today  + "</h3>");
       document.write("<h3>The date yesterday was ");
       document.writeln(yesterday  + "</h3>");
       document.close();
   }
 //-->
 </script>
 </body>
</html>
```

## 6.5 EVENTS

JavaScript is an *event-driven* system. Nothing happens unless it is initiated by an event outside the script. JavaScript is always reactive rather than proactive, with event triggers coming via the browser. An event is any change that the user makes to the state of the browser. You're used to using a lot of event-driven software, although you may not always recognize it as such. For instance a word processor simply responds to your actions.

Most software you ever use is controlled by you. That's not always true about Web applications. Animations created using Macromedia's Flash software play when the page is loaded provided the browser has the correct plug-in installed. Often users simply have to put up with Flash because they are unable to control it except by disabling the plug-in. JavaScript can work in the same way. Your script can be initiated when the page loads and then run automatically. This is one of the most annoying things about scripted Web pages and is the main reason that many people switch off JavaScript when they configure their browser. Generally you're adding a script to a page to improve its functionality or appearance. Hence the script is an integral part of the page but its operation should always be controlled by the user.

JavaScript event handling can be quite a complex issue. Different manufacturers have implemented their own ways of capturing and handling events. Internet Explorer has a large set of complicated, but useful, event routines which can be used to extend its functionality beyond the Web and onto the Windows desktop. Unfortunately, despite being useful and well-designed, these lack platform independence. I want to show you some ideas that you can actually use and which most visitors to your page can use too. Therefore I'm going to concentrate upon a lowest common denominator set of event handlers.

**Table 6.3**  JavaScript Events

| Event | Handler | Description |
|---|---|---|
| blur | onBlur | The input focus is moved from the object, usually when moving from a field of a form or from the form itself. |
| change | onChange | The value of a field in a form has been changed by the user entering or deleting data. |
| click | onClick | The mouse is clicked over an element of a page. |
| dblclick | onDblClick | A form element or a link is clicked twice in rapid succession. |
| dragdrop | onDragDrop | A system file is dragged with a mouse and dropped onto the browser. |
| focus | onFocus | Input focus is given to an element. The reverse of blur. |
| keydown | onKeyDown | A key is depressed but not released. |
| keypress | onKeyPress | A key is pressed. |
| keyup | onKeyUp | A depressed key is released. |
| load | onLoad | The page is loaded by the browser. |
| mousedown | onMouseDown | A mouse button is pressed. |
| mousemove | onMouseMove | The mouse, and hence cursor, is moved. |
| mouseout | onMouseOut | The mouse pointer moves off an element. |
| mouseover | onMouseOver | The mouse pointer is moved over an element. |
| mouseup | onMouseUp | The mouse button is released. |
| move | onMove | A window is moved, maximized or restored either by the user or by a script. |
| resize | onResize | A Window is resized by the user or by a script. |
| select | onSelect | A field on a form is selected by clicking the mouse or tabbing from the keyboard. |
| submit | onSubmit | A form is submitted (the submit button is clicked). |
| unload | onUnload | The user leaves the Web page. |

The original set of event handlers appeared in Netscape 2 and was broadly replicated in Internet Explorer 3. These still work today, even in version 6 browsers, and are available in all browsers which support JavaScript. Despite the limited number of events which can be handled using these techniques they provide most events that you are likely to need on a Web page. Table 6.3 shows some of the more common JavaScript events. The names of simple event handlers are not case-sensitive; `onload`, `onLoad` and `ONLOAD` all represent exactly the same thing.

Not all objects can create all events. Some HTML objects such as paragraphs and headings can't create any events although this may change in a future version. When an event happens, your script may want to do something with it. Not all events need handling; some can be ignored if they are not relevant. Where you want an action from the user to lead to some action from a script you'll need to implement an *event handler*. Event handlers are JavaScript functions which you associate with an HTML element as part of its definition in the HTML source code:

**`<element attributes event="handler">`**

The handler will be a JavaScript function that you have defined elsewhere and which is available to the element.

Plenty of examples of event handling are given in Chapter 7. For now, the following code demonstrates a few different events being created and handled.

```html
<html>
  <head>
    <title>Handling Events</title>
  </head>
  <body onLoad="ShowLoaded()" onUnload="SayGoodbye()">
    <h1>Handling Events</h1>
    <p>
      <a href="#" onMouseOver="Mouse()">A Hyperlink</a>
    </p>
    <form>
      <input type="button"
        value="Click Me!"
        onClick="Clicked()"
        onMouseOver="Mouse()">
    </form>
  <script language="javascript">
  <!--
      function ShowLoaded(){
          alert("The page has loaded");
      }


      function SayGoodbye() {
          alert("Goodbye, thanks for visiting");
      }
```

```
        function Clicked() {
            alert("You clicked the button");
        }

        function Mouse() {
            alert("The mouse is over the link");
        }

    //-->
    </script>
    </body>
</html>
```

Each of the event handlers performs an identical task. When they are called an `alert` dialog is used to display a message. The messages differ so that we can track which event has just occurred and which object caused it. The relationship between events, event handlers and page elements should be obvious from the code. Notice, though, that the `button` has two event handlers. One is for an `onClick`, the other for `onMouseOver`. If you run the code you'll find that the `button` never creates the `onMouseOver` event. You might think that a button would need to somehow *know* that the mouse was over it before it was clicked. In fact it doesn't. Table 6.4 lists the objects and event handlers which are supported by JavaScript 1.1. These provide a sort of minimal functionality which almost every browser supports. If you work from this list then your scripts will work for almost all visitors[5] to your site.

Table 6.4: JavaScript 1 Objects and Event Handlers

| Object | Event Handlers |
|--------|----------------|
| window | onload |
|        | onunload |
|        | onblur |
|        | onfocus |
| link   | onclick |
|        | onmouseout |
|        | onmouseover |
| area   | onmouseout |
|        | onmouseover |
| image  | onabort |
|        | onerror |

[5]Well, at least, those with JavaScript enabled!

Table 6.4: JavaScript 1 Objects and Event Handlers

| Object | Event Handlers |
| --- | --- |
|  | onload |
| form | onreset |
|  | onsubmit |
| text | onblur |
|  | onchange |
|  | onfocus |
|  | onselect |
| textarea | onblur |
|  | onchange |
|  | onfocus |
|  | onselect |
| password | onblur |
|  | onchange |
|  | onfocus |
|  | onselect |
| button | onclick |
| reset | onclick |
| submit | onclick |
| radio | onclick |
| checkbox | onclick |
| select | onblur |
|  | onchange |
|  | onfocus |
| fileupload | onblur |
|  | onselect |
|  | onfocus |

## 6.6  EXERCISES

### Object-oriented JavaScript

1. Briefly detail the main features of the theory of object-orientation.

2. How does JavaScript fare as an object-oriented language? Would it be correct to say that JavaScript is *object-based* rather than object-oriented?

3. Try the code from Section 6.1.1.2. Does it do what you expected?

4. The new keyword is very special. What does it do?

5. Detail the functioning of the JavaScript keyword `this` and the dot operator.

## Using JavaScript Objects

1. Write a script to create a new browser window and display some text in that window. Put your script inside a suitable HTML page and test it.

2. Modify your window creating script so that it has less *furniture* such as scrollbars.

3. Create an HTML page which includes a simple form. Write a script to extract the data from the form when the `submit` button is clicked. Display the extracted data in a new document.

4. Add the browser sniffer from Section 6.4.4.1 to an HTML page. Modify the script to display more information about the browser being used. Look in Appendix B for possible properties that you could add.

## JavaScript Events

1. JavaScript is *event driven*. What are events? What events can JavaScript handle?

2. Create a Web page containing a form which has a single button and a text input field. When the button is clicked a dialog box should open which displays the contents of the text field.

3. Put an image on a page. Write some JavaScript which displays a message when the mouse is over the image. Try to display the co-ordinates of the mouse if it is clicked on the image.

## Dates

1. Write a script which accepts a date as input from the user, adds 70 years to it and displays the result. The date will come into your script as a string.

2. Display the current date and time in both GMT and locale forms.

## Regular Expressions

1. Write a regular expression which searches strings for non alphabetic characters. Test your script in a Web page.

2. Write and test a regular expression which swaps the first two words of a string.

3. Write an expression which replaces every occurrence of the letter 'a' in a string with the letter 'q'.

# 7
# Dynamic HTML with JavaScript

Much of the JavaScript code that I have shown so far has created new documents and written directly to them. The commonest unit that your JavaScript will have to interact with is the document. Remember that the structure of data and the way that the browser manipulates that data depend upon the document object model (DOM). Almost all of the objects that can be manipulated by a script are part of a document. In the previous chapter you saw how to manipulate some of the elements of the DOM. In this chapter I'll show you how to manipulate the actual browser window. The examples in this chapter demonstrate some of the most popular uses of JavaScript that you'll find on the Internet today.

Dynamic HTML (DHTML) is the combined result of everything that I've discussed so far. It is well structured HTML code which adheres to the standards, it is stylesheets used to present neutral formatting control, and finally it is the use of scripts to make the text, images, and style elements active. In this chapter I'm going to show how to build some of the most common and useful DHTML applications, and how to build applications that are more often associated with Java than DHTML.

I'll show you how to make that popular perennial, the rollover image. You'll have seen these on a lot of Web sites: as your mouse moves over some text or an image, the element changes in some way. Second I'll show a very simple way of moving images around the screen. Third up is the use of layers to reduce downloads. Basically you can put a collection of pages into a single HTML file and use JavaScript to let surfers navigate through them. The great thing about this technique is that your site *looks* like it's a normal download-every-page kind of site but it'll run far more quickly[1]

---

[1] Although it will take longer to load in the first place. The usual caveats that *some you win, some you lose*, apply

Finally I present two big, complex applications which are developed for the bleeding edge of today's Web design. Having all of your navigation support provided by menus is a sensible way of structuring a site. You *can* use Java applications to give drop-down menus, but I'll show a clean and easy way of doing the same with text, stylesheets, and JavaScript. Second, many companies now offer free Web site hosting supported by revenue from advertising. Some of these sites use a neat technique to *brand* all of the pages that they host. This branding is usually an image that floats in the bottom right-hand corner of the screen. The last DHTML application that I'll give you shows how to do the same by floating a layer. In the example I'll use a piece of text rather than an image but, because the technique uses floating layers, you can place any content inside it that you choose to.

## 7.1 DATA VALIDATION

Before doing anything dynamic, I'm going to discuss the validation of data. It would be nice to validate data that is entered into your forms at the client. Existing techniques rely upon the use of server scripting and are very robust. There's a delay between the user entering data, the script performing validation, and an error (or confirmation) being returned to the user. Many potential errors such as entering a space or character other than a digit or a letter into a user name should be spotted at the client and dealt with.

A common technique for restricting access to a site is to check user IDs against a file of valid users. For security reasons it turns out to be a bad idea to do this sort of data validation at the client. Any code or data that you send to the client gets cached there. If you send a long list of items to validate against then that list is available to the user. If they are trying to hack your system then you have given them the key to the door.

Generally the RegExp class discussed in Section 6.2 provides everything that you need to start validating data. Before getting too deeply involved in the *how*, you have to understand *what* validation is and what it is not. Validation is simply the process of ensuring that some data *might* be correct data for a particular application. Broadly speaking data validation is the process of ensuring that users submit only the set of characters which you require. It is *not* the process of ensuring that the data is in any way accurate.

Why can't we test for accuracy? Well under some circumstances we can. If a program accepts data from a remote data logger and that input is always going to be in a particular range, then the program knows that data outside the range is invalid and should not be accepted. What it does with the incorrect data depends upon the way that the application was specified, of course. A Web form is rather different. Most of the data that your scripts get from users will be textual and almost impossible to verify. Consider a form which accepts names. Generally names contain a limited set of characters: the letters a to z in upper and lower case and a few punctuation marks. They don't tend to include digits, exclamation marks or equals signs.

This means that you can write a regular expression which checks that any name entered by users only has allowable characters in it. What you cannot do is check if they've entered a real name. The string `Abcde Fghij-Klmno` has all of the characteristics of a real name, but you're unlikely ever to meet anyone who answers to it.

One common request is for a way of validating email addresses. Many Web sites use email addresses to track users, and their developers would like to be sure that the email addresses they use are correct. Email addresses follow regular patterns and come in a limited number of types so they would appear to be an ideal candidate for automatic validation. The same problem applies to email addresses as to people's names: you can only ever test the validity of the characters and combinations. You cannot tell from an email address if there's a real user on a real system anywhere behind it. So what about testing for valid characters and combinations? Again this is *not* an easy problem to solve. Simple regular expressions can be created which will work on many Internet addresses but a fully featured version is very long and complicated. If you want to see one of these monstrosities, take a look at *Mastering Regular Expressions* by Jeffrey Friedl.

## 7.1.1   Validation: an example

Now that you know what validation is, it's time to see some code. The following Web page has two text fields. One accepts names, the other accepts ages. Both fields are validated using regular expressions and if the data is valid the contents of the form are transmitted in an email message. Look at the code, then I'll show you some of the important pieces in a little more detail.

```html
<html>
   <head>
      <title>Data Validation</title>
   </head>
   <body>
      <form method="post"
        action="mailto:chris@localhost"
        onSubmit="return Validate()">
        <table border="0">
          <tr>
            <th>Your Name</th>
            <td><input type="text" length="24"></td>
          </tr>
          <tr>
            <th>Your Age</th>
            <td>
               <input type="text" size="3" maxlength="3">
            </td>
          </tr>
          <tr>
```

```
            <td><input type="submit" value="Submit"</td>
            <td><input type="reset" value="Reset"</td>
          </tr>
        </table>
      </form>

      <script language=javascript>
      <!--
        function Validate() {
            var valid = false;
            var name = document.forms[0].elements[0].value;
            var age = document.forms[0].elements[1].value;

            name_re = new RegExp("^[A-Z][a-zA-Z '-.]+$", "g");
            age_re = new RegExp("^[\\d]+$", "g");

            if(name.match(name_re)){
                // only validate the age if the name is OK
                if(age.match(age_re)){
                    // name and age are both valid
                    valid = true;
                } else {
                    alert("Age does not match " + age_re);
                }
            } else {
                alert("Name does not match " + name_re);
            }
            return valid;
        }
      //-->
      </script>
    </body>
</html>
```

Very often novice JavaScript programmers find they can write simple validation routines but they cannot find a way of calling the routine before the data is submitted. Or, if they do call the routine, the form is submitted regardless of the validity of the data. The solution is definitely non-intuitive because it relies upon a little documented property of the form tag. forms have an onSubmit event which is generated when the submit button is clicked. Data validation is performed by the event handler which you create for the onSubmit event. So far, so normal. The trick is to make your event handler function return true if the data in the form is valid or false if it is not. The onSubmit event is then assigned the return value from the handler. The form will only be submitted if the event gets set to `true`. This example shows what I mean:

```
<form method="post"
    action="mailto:chris@localhost"
    onSubmit="return Validate()">
```

You can mimic this process from an `onClick` event. Don't use a `submit` button on your form, use a plain `button`, and create an event handler for its `onClick` event:

```
<input type="button" value="Submit" onClick="Validate()">
```

then use the boolean value in the validation function instead of returning it. If the function evaluates to `true`, force the submission of the form:

```
if(valid == true) {
   document.forms[0].submit();
}
```

Back to the example.The value from the `name` field is copied into a local variable and then compared against a regular expression:

```
var name = document.forms[0].elements[0].value;
name_re = new RegExp("^[A-Z][a-zA-Z '-.]+$", "g");
```

The regular expression there checks for a capital letter at the start of the line followed by one or more characters until the end of line is reached. The valid character set I've used includes upper and lower case letters, spaces, hyphens and apostrophes. Your set will differ depending upon your location and requirements. If any invalid character is encountered, the regular expression will return `false`. Notice that I use $ to search all the way to the end of the string. If you leave that out, the regular expression will stop quite happily after the second character and return `true` even if the third character entered is a digit.

Checking the `age` field is a similar process:

```
var age = document.forms[0].elements[1].value;
age_re = new RegExp("^[\\d]+$", "g");
```

This time the regular expression only accepts digits 0 through 9 between the start and end of the string. Again, if you leave out the start and end specifiers, the regular expression engine will be quite happy with the expression, provided, of course, any of the three characters is a digit.

## 7.2 OPENING A NEW WINDOW

Perhaps the majority of the JavaScript coding that you'll do will be based around the use of windows. The typical piece of Microsoft Windows software uses the multiple document interface (MDI) structure. The application has a single *global* frame and when new windows are opened they appear inside that frame. The application frame is said to be the *parent* of all of the internal frames. Web browsers are based around a different model in which each new window is independent of the application from which it was launched. This model is more akin to that typically used in the UNIX world when programming applications for the X Window System.

The Web/X model has some interesting side effects that we can use to our benefit when programming in JavaScript. The main benefit is that because windows are independent of each other, any windows spawned from our code can be made to look and act totally differently from the rest of the application.

Here are the main points from the window object definition given in Section 6.4.2:

```
open("URL", "name")
close()
toolbar=[1|0]
location=[1|0]
directories=[1|0]
status=[1|0]
menubar=[1|0]
scrollbars=[1|0]
resizable=[1|0]
width=pixels
height=pixels
```

A new window can be opened which contains a URL identified resource and the attributes of that window can be tailored to suit the application. Imagine developing a Web site to show off artwork or photographs. You may want to display thumbnail images which when clicked open a larger version of the image for better viewing. However, if for reasons such as copyright protection, you don't want the image to be printed or its location revealed, the options to the window object declaration give you that power. Here's some code that should demonstrate what I mean:

```
<html>
   <head>
      <script language="javascript">
      <!--
      function Load(url){
         var next = url;
         newwin = open("url", "newwin", 'status=0,toolbar=0,
            resizable=0,width=258,height=137');
      }
      //-->
      </script>
   </head>
   <body>
```

```
   <p><a href="" onClick="Load('./pic1.gif')">
   Show the next page</a></p>
 </body>
</html>
```

This code loads an image into a new window. Care has to be taken with this though: I have found that not all browsers open the new window at the specified size. Some open child windows at the same size as the parent window. This may well be due to a problem they have parsing the JavaScript – the only parameters that appear to present random behavior are `height` and `width`. To reduce the chances of seeing random behavior, follow these rules:

---

Rules:

- The parameter list must be inside a single set of single quotes.
- There cannot be line breaks or spaces in the parameter string. In this book I use line breaks so that the code will print properly in book format. Unfortunately much of the code in my JavaScript examples needs reformatting before a browser will handle it successfully.
- Don't have any spaces between the parameters.
- Don't forget the commas between parameters.

---

Those rules assume that the parameter string under discussion contains all optional parts of the `open()` command. The URL and window name are **not** optional, although the URL can be replaced with empty quotes if you need to open a blank window.

## 7.3 MESSAGES AND CONFIRMATIONS

JavaScript provides three built-in window types that can be used from application code. These are useful when you need information from visitors to your site. For instance you may need them to click a confirmation button before submitting information to your database.

`prompt("string", "string")`
> This command displays a simple window that contains a prompt and a textfield in which the user can enter data. The method has two parameters: a text string to be used as the prompt and a string to use as the default value. If you don't want to display a default then simply use an empty string.

`confirm("string")`
> Shows a window containing a message and two buttons: OK and Cancel. Selecting Cancel will abort any pending action, while OK will let the action proceed. This is

useful when submitting form data, or possibly as the user tries to follow a link that leaves your site for another.

**alert("string")**

Displays the text string and an OK button. This may be used as a warning or to provide a farewell message as visitors leave your site.

The next code sample shows how the popup windows can be used. The results of these statements are demonstrated in Figure 7.1.

```
prompt("Enter Your Name", "");
confirm("Are You Sure?");
alert("A Warning");
```

**Figure 7.1**   The Popup Dialog Boxes

## 7.4   THE STATUS BAR

Some Web developers like to use the browsers status bar as part of the site. Text strings can be displayed in the status bar but should be used with care. The status bar usually displays helpful information about the operation of the browser. It can't do that if it is displaying *your* message. Few people ever look at the status bar so if it is showing your message they may well not notice. Finally anything that can be done in the status bar can be done more interestingly using DHTML techniques. If you want to use the idea, the following code, and Figure 7.2, show how:

```
<html>
    <head>
        <script language="javascript">
        <!--
        function Init(){
            self.status = "Chris's Message";
            }
        //-->
        </script>
    </head>
    <body onLoad="Init()">
        <h1>And the Status Bar Says...</h1>
    </body>
</html>
```

**Figure 7.2** Writing to the Status Line

**`self`**

The previous script used the keyword `self` which I haven't introduced you to before. Sometimes the script needs to act upon the browser window in which it is running. Other times objects need to change their own parameters. In both cases `self` is used so that the object can identify itself or its browser.

## 7.5 WRITING TO A DIFFERENT FRAME

In Section 3.2 I introduced the use of frames as a site layout device. Once frames and JavaScript are combined on the same page, a site can begin to develop some interesting interactive aspects. Often developing a site with links in one frame and output in another provides easy movement through complex data. That's pretty straightforward if you are using static HTML pages, but what if you are using a combination of HTML, JavaScript and, for instance, CGI scripting to build pages on the fly? Though certainly more difficult, it's not *that* difficult. One popular use of frames and JavaScript is a color picker.

**Figure 7.3** The Color Picker

The simple color picker that I'm going to build here is shown in Figure 7.3. It has two frames. The upper one contains a form which is used for data gathering. The lower frame shows the result of the color selections but has been created directly by JavaScript code. This application is run totally on the client side. Once you know how to use CGI scripts to handle form data you may want to try adapting it to use both client- and server-side processing.

I'll describe each of the components, although they ought to be fairly self-explanatory if you've read everything up to this point.

### 7.5.1 The Frameset

The whole page is built around a simple frameset. When the page is initially loaded I display the form in the upper window and an empty HTML page in the lower window.

Some browsers will cope if the bottom frame is left empty, others won't. It's better to use a simple empty page in the bottom frame to be totally browser-friendly. The code for the frameset is:

```
<html>
   <head>
      <title>Color Picker</title>
   </head>

   <frameset rows="40%,*">
     <frame name="topone" src="./cols.html">
     <frame name="botone" src="./blank.html">
   </frameset>
</html>
```

Here's the code for the empty frame:

```
<html>
   <head>
      <title></title>
   </head>
   <body>
   </body>
</html>
```

## 7.5.2  The Upper Frame

The top frame (from the file cols.html) is simple enough. The only part that hasn't been introduced already is the use of an external file to hold the JavaScript code. In this case it's in a file called picker.js and is called from the script tag. The JavaScript is loaded by the browser but isn't run until the onClick() action of the button is triggered.

```
<html>
   <head>
      <script language="javascript" src="./picker.js">
      </script>
   </head>
   <body bgcolor="white" text="red">
   <h1 align=center>Chris's HomeBrew Color Picker</h1>

   <form>
      <table align="center" border="0" cellpadding="5">
      <tr>
         <td colspan="4" align="center">
         <h2>Enter Color Values in the Boxes</h2>
```

```
      </td>
   </tr>
   <tr>
      <td>
      <h3>Background Color</h3>
      </td>
      <td>
         <input type="textfield" size="16" name="bgcol"
         value="white">
      </td>
      <td>
      <h3>Text Color</h3>
      </td>
      <td>
         <input type="textfield" size="16" name="fgcol"
         value="black">
      </td>
   </tr>
   <tr>
      <td>
      <h3>Table Headings</h3>
      </td>
      <td>
         <input type="textfield" size="16" name="thcol"
         value="black">
      </td>
      <td>
      <h3>Table Data</h3>
      </td>
      <td>
         <input type="textfield" size="16" name="tdcol"
         value="black">
      </td>
   </tr>
   <tr>
      <td colspan="2" align="center">
         <input type="button" value="Show It!!"
         onClick="ShowIt()">
      </td>
      <td colspan="2" align="center">
         <input type="reset" value="Reset It">
```

```
        </td>
      </tr>
      </table>
    </form>
    </body>
</html>
```

I've placed the JavaScript in a separate file which I'm including in the head section of the document. Each `textfield` is given a unique name when it is created so that it can be easily identified in later code. The `textfields` could have been anonymous, not given names, and accessed through the `forms` and `elements` arrays. This would increase the size of the code and potentially lead to more bugs.

## 7.5.3 The JavaScript Code

The HTML part of the page is simple. The JavaScript is actually not much more complex but because I haven't shown anything quite like it before I'll go into it in some detail. First the code which is stored in a file called `picker.js`:

```
function ShowIt ( ) {
    var topbox = document.forms[0].elements;
    var bottombox = parent.frames['botone'].document;

    // first extract the values from the form
    var bg = topbox.bgcol.value;
    var fg = topbox.fgcol.value;
    var thc = topbox.thcol.value;
    var tdc = topbox.tdcol.value;

    // now build the new page
    bottombox.open();
    bottombox.write("<body bgcolor="
                + bg
                + " text="
                + fg
                + ">\n");
    bottombox.write("<h1 align=center>The Result Is:</h1>");
    bottombox.write("<table align=center border=2"
                + "cellpadding=4 cellspacing=4>\n<tr>"
                + "<th>Plain Heading</th>"
                + "<th bgcolor="
                    + thc
                    + ">Colored Heading</th>"
```

```
                              + "</tr>"
                              + "<th>Plain Data</th>"
                              + "<th bgcolor="
                                  + tdc
                                  + ">Colored Data</th>"
                              + "</tr>"
                              + "</tr>\n</table>");
        bottombox.write("</body>");
        bottombox.close();
        }
```

The page uses just a single JavaScript function called ShowIt which accepts no parameters. The color values that were entered into the form do not need to be passed as parameters. They are available to the script through the frameset itself. When the frames were created they were given the names topone and botone. The script is part of the document that is being displayed in frame topone and is going to create a document to be displayed in frame botone. This structure is shown in Figure 7.4.

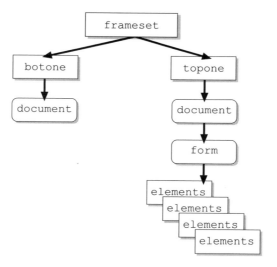

**Figure 7.4** The Structure of Color Picker

Although the structure sounds complex it isn't really. Each frame is a part of the main window and contains a single document. Each frame has a unique name and we can use that name to write to, or read from, those documents.

The first thing that I do is create two local variables:

```
var topbox = document.forms[0].elements;
var bottombox = parent.frames['botone'].document;
```

These variables are used to reduce the amount of typing that is necessary. Let's look at them a little more closely. The first variable, `topbox`, is going to be used to refer to all items in the upper frame. This is the frame with the HTML form and which holds the HTML document containing the JavaScript code. The document only has one form, which is therefore at the start of the forms array on position zero. The values that are entered into the form will be stored in the elements array.

The second variable, `bottombox`, refers to all items in the lower frame. If a method in one frame is going to refer to another frame it must do so via the parent window. The main, or *parent*, window has an array of all frames which can be referred to either by their position in the array or, as in this example, by name. Each window includes a single HTML page. Having referenced the correct frame, the document and elements can be referred to easily.

The alias for the upper frame is able to refer directly to the `document` property because it is referring to the document in which it is contained. The alias for the lower frame first has to reference the frame because that is a separate HTML document in another window.

Once the documents have been correctly aliased the values can be extracted from the form. The aliasing isn't necessary but is desirable. Compare these two:

```
var bg = topbox.bgcol.value;
var bg = documents.forms[0].elements.bgcol.value;
```

Having extracted the parameters, the colored sample page can now be created. First the document has to be opened. If this is not done then the document is unavailable to be written into:

```
bottombox.open();
```

The HTML page can now be created. Notice that you need to make the `<body>` `</body>` pair of tags as well as the visible content. The JavaScript interpreter performs string substitution and concatenation on the fly. The values from the local variables are substituted directly into the strings as they are written:

```
bottombox.write("<body bgcolor="
            + bg
            + " text="
            + fg
            + ">\n");

bottombox.write("</body>");
```

Finally we can close the document. This is the point at which the HTML gets sent to the frame and the page gets displayed.

```
bottombox.close();
```

Most JavaScript tasks are more straightforward than even the color picker. The arrival of browsers which can support complex scripting and which use layers to arrange content has given rise to Dynamic HTML.

## 7.6 ROLLOVER BUTTONS

The most common usage of dynamic HTML, and one that you are bound to have seen, is the image rollover. The technique is used to give visual feedback about the location of the mouse cursor by changing the images on the page as the mouse moves over them. This is a highly effective technique, especially where images are used as the hyperlinks in a menu, or where an image map is being used.

The JavaScript code doesn't directly manipulate the image. If you need to change the actual image then you ought to investigate ActiveX, Flash or Java programming. The JavaScript rollover is far simpler because it uses *two* image files which it swaps between as the mouse is moved. One image is created for the inactive state when the mouse is *not* over it. A second image is created for the active state when the mouse cursor is placed over it. Usually the images are identical apart from some highlighting for the *active* image.

Study the following code[2] then I'll explain what is happening:

```
var showing = -99;
var menu_show = 0;
var browser_is, topon, topoff;

function Init() {
   browser_is = new Is();
   if(browser_is.major >= 4)
      {
      if( (browser_is.browser.indexOf("netscape"))
         || (browser_is.browser.indexOf("explorer")) )
         PreLoad();
      }
   else {
      // don't break strings in "real" code
      alert("This Dynamic HTML Page Only Works in Netscape
      Navigator v4 or Internet Explorer 4 (or Later)");
      }
   } // version 4 browser
```

---

[2]Don't forget that you cannot use line breaks in JavaScript parameter strings. I've done so here to get the code formatted for a book.

```
function Is() {
   // convert characters to lowercase
   // to simplify testing
   var agt = navigator.userAgent.toLowerCase();

   // *** BROWSER VERSION ***
   this.major = parseInt(navigator.appVersion);
   this.minor = parseFloat(navigator.appVersion);
   this.browser = navigator.appName.toLowerCase();
   this.js_ver = "";

   // *** JAVASCRIPT VERSION CHECK ***
   if(this.major > 3)
      js_ver = 1.2;
   else
      js_ver = 1.1;

   } // Is

function PreLoad() {
   // mouseOn
   topon = new Image(60, 37);
   topon.src = "./top_on.jpg";

   // mouseOff
   topoff = new Image(60, 37);
   topoff.src = "./top_off.jpg";

   } // PreLoad

function myMouseOn(n) {
   imageON = eval(n + "on.src");
   document.images[n].src = imageON;
   } // myMouseOn

function myMouseOff(n) {
   imageOFF = eval(n + "off.src");
   document.images[n].src = imageOFF;

   } // myMouseOff
```

This is the HTML page for the rollover:

```html
<html>
    <head>
        <title>Rollover Buttons</title>
        <link rel=stylesheet href="./styles.css">
        <script language="javascript" src="./rollo.js">
        </script>
    </head>

    <body onLoad="Init()">
    <h1>Demonstrating the Mouse-over Effect</h1>
    <a href="#"
            onMouseOut="myMouseOff('top')";
            onMouseOver="myMouseOn('top')";
            return true>
        <img src="./top_off.jpg" alt="Show Next"
            width=60 height=37 name="top">
    </a>

    </body>
</html>
```

### 7.6.1  The Explanation

The obvious place to start the explanation is the HTML page. The JavaScript for the example is stored in a separate file but it doesn't *have* to be. Like any JavaScript the rollover code can be embedded in the HTML page. Including it from a separate file is simpler as it lets you debug the HTML source and the JavaScript independently. The key parts of the HTML revolve around event handling. Three events concern us here:

- The onLoad event happens when the page is first loaded into the browser. As you'll see shortly, handling this event is used to set-up the page and script by acquiring all necessary resources.

- onMouseOver calls a JavaScript function when the cursor passes over the image.

- onMouseOut calls a function when the cursor moves away from the image.

The address tag includes this construct:

```
a href="#"
```

In this, and subsequent, examples I need to use a hyperlink in my code. The rollover is usually applied to links but I don't actually want my code linked to another page. Instead I want the image to change while the content remains the same if the hyperlink is clicked. JavaScript provides a *dummy* target. If you use # as the address of a link, the browser will simply reload the current page. Using this dummy link has many uses when you are developing complex sites or scripts, or if you have incomplete links on your production site. It is certainly better than the alternative. Leaving the address empty will either make the browser load `index.html` if it exists or return a directory listing.

*The JavaScript*   When the `onLoad` event happens, the `Init()` function runs. This starts by creating an object called `browser_is` which holds the results of the browser sniffing routine. If `browser_is` holds values for Netscape Navigator or Microsoft Internet Explorer versions 4 or later, the `PreLoad()` function runs. If the browser is *not* suitable then a warning message is displayed. Because no further JavaScript runs after the warning, early browsers will not try to run the code and hence will not give run-time error messages.

The `browser_is` object contains the browser name which has been converted to lower-case letters, version number, and the version of JavaScript which it supports. When I check the browser type I do so by using the builtin method `indexOf`. This method is part of the JavaScript string object. It searches along the string looking for another string which is supplied as a parameter to the method. If the search is unsuccessful the method returns 0. This 0 can be used as a Boolean value in tests. This is the approach I adopt in this particular browser sniffing routine.

> **Rule:**
> Always use browser sniffing and provide an alternative for those who cannot run your code. The rollover is a nice visual effect which doesn't affect the functionality of the page. The links still work even if the images don't change.

`PreLoad()` makes a new object for each image. These are all instances of the JavaScript `Image` object and you'll need two for each location: one for when the mouse is over the image and one for when it isn't. Each image object holds the size of the image and the location of the actual image file in the `src` parameter. By creating these images early in the loading process, in this case from the `onLoad` event, the objects are available for use even before the image files have been downloaded.

Two functions remain: `myMouseOn` and `myMouseOff`. Both work in the same way so I'll just examine `myMouseOn`. The function is called when the `onMouseOver` event is triggered. The function receives the name of the image as a parameter:

```
onMouseOver="myMouseOn('top')";
```

Notice that it's not the full name. I have deliberately used variable names for the objects created in `PreLoad()` so as to simplify the calling routines. I created two objects called `topon` and `topoff`, each of which contains a link to a different image file. I can choose between the objects by appending the value `on` or `off` to the first part of the name. The following line of code chooses the object and then passes its `src` value (the file name) into a temporary variable:

```
imageON = eval(n + "on.src");
```

If you want to be sure this is really happening, put an alert message at the end of the `PreLoad()` function and see what effect it has:

```
alert("topon " + topon + " src " + topon.src +
"topoff " + topoff + " src " + topoff.src);
```

**eval**

JavaScript can build expressions dynamically as it interprets scripts. This slightly odd feature is available to you through `eval`. When your scripts need to process information which won't be available until runtime you can place that information into an expression as it becomes available. You subsequently execute the expression as if all of the code had been created at the same time.

Remember that the document object holds an array of images. Each object in that array can be identified either by its name or by its position. The image in our link was named `top` (check the code for the HTML page) so to change the image we simply change the file associated with the `src` value of the document image object named `top`:

```
document.images[n].src = imageON;
```

That's quite a complex procedure. To clarify what is happening you should run the code from my example. Use any old images that you might have lying around (your browser cache would be a good place to start looking). Once you have the code working with just one image on the page try adding another image and making them *both* work as rollovers. Here's a hint: the only JavaScript that will need changing will be in the `PreLoad()` function.

Hopefully you'll see that almost all of our rollover code could go into a library and be included in any of your pages. If each page uses different images then simply put the `PreLoad()` routine into the HTML file (between `<script>...</script>` tags) and modify it to suit your needs.

Some HTML authoring packages will create rollover code for you. Some of that code is simple and efficient but much of it is bloated and inflexible. It may take you a while to understand the code I just outlined, but because it can be placed into a library and reused, that effort will be worthwhile. Once you understand the code you can start to modify it. For instance why not move the image slightly as the mouse is clicked to give the impression of a button being pressed in? Or try using three images: one for `onMouseOut`, one for `onMouseOver`, and one for `onClick`?

## 7.7   MOVING IMAGES

Unlike the rollover which takes some understanding, moving images around the screen is pretty simple. I'm not going to show the full code here, just the function that moves the image. In fact this isn't a moving image at all, that's just the effect. What is actually moving is a layer of content. The example flies a logo in from the left of the screen five times before positioning it in the center of the screen. Images (layers) can move around repeatedly but doing so takes up processor cycles. It's more user-friendly if your images only move for a restricted amount of time such as when the page is first loaded or when the user specifically triggers the event.

You might remember from Section 4.7 that content can be created in layers which are stacked vertically by assigning a z-index to them. Each layer can be positioned on the screen by changing the offset of the top left corner of the layer.

This HTML code creates a division of the page named logo and positioned at pixel 5,1000. The layer must be positioned absolutely so that the browser doesn't mess up the look of the page, and must be visible. The sole content of this division is an image:

```
<div id="logo" style="top: 5; z-index: 4; left: 1000;
visibility: visible; position: absolute;">
   <img src="./title.jpg">
</div>
```

Although I've used a division to place the image rather than a Netscape-specific layer, this code will only work in Navigator. If you want to create a browser-neutral version then modify the code using the techniques that I'll show in Section 7.10. Look at the code first, then I'll explain it:

```
var count = 0;
function FlyLogo(){
   if(count < 5) {
      if(document.layers["logo"].left == 200) {
         count++;
         document.layers["logo"].left = 1000;
      }
      document.layers["logo"].left -= 10;
      setTimeout('FlyLogo()', 200);
   }
   else
      document.layers["logo"].left = 200;
}
```

When the function is called it checks the counter to make sure that it should run. If the counter is equal to 5 then the left edge of the logo is placed at pixel 200 and no more processing is performed by this routine.

If the counter is less than 5, the layer containing the logo will be moved. If the left-hand side of the layer is at pixel 200 then the image has finished moving across the screen. The counter is incremented and the layer repositioned to pixel 1000. However, if the left edge of the logo is not at position 200 it is repositioned 10 pixels to the left of its current location.

The `FlyLogo()` routine then calls itself[3] using the builtin `setTimeout()` call. This takes the name of the function and a delay in milliseconds. It will not run the routine until after the delay has elapsed. In this case our image moves 10 pixels left every 200 ms.

If the delay were too short, say 50 ms, then the image would whip across the screen so rapidly that it would not be visible. If the delay were too long, say a second, then the image would crawl across the screen in a really disappointing way.

Some of you will be wondering why I'm bothering to code this rather than use an animated GIF. Writing the JavaScript is easier than creating a GIF, the download is far smaller and this version is very flexible. I might, for instance, decide to move the image vertically instead of horizontally. If I'd used a GIF then I would need to recreate the entire thing. Here I simply alter the code to move from bottom to top instead of right to left.

As an aside, if you want to move an image along a diagonal then move the top left corner horizontally and vertically at the same time. Easy!

## 7.8 MULTIPLE PAGES IN A SINGLE DOWNLOAD

DHTML opens up some interesting possibilities. One that is fairly obvious but rarely used is having several pages in a single download. Instead of using a separate file for each page, why not place each page of content in a separate layer and switch between those layers? This technique will not work if the layers have too much content or too many images, simply because the overhead of downloading the page will be too great. It also won't work well if visitors to your site are unlikely to want to see all of the pages. However, where most of your data is text-based and where users are going to want to see all of that information this is a good trick. It'll also work well as a way of splitting a single large document into several screens of data so that users don't have to scroll up and down.

On the other hand, if you base a site around this technique then you'll find that many people can't use it. This is true of any new idea and as more people use version 4 or later browsers, so more and more people will be able to view your pages.

### 7.8.1 The Stylesheet

This stylesheet is going to be used in this section and the next two. I've included it here for convenience:

```
.SWITCH {
    font-size: 20pt;
    font-family: Arial, helvetica, "sans serif";
    color: ultramarine;
    background: wheat;
```

---

[3]This is called *recursion*. Do it too often in JavaScript and the browser will fall over as it runs out of memory.

```css
}

.OVER {
    font-size: 20pt;
    font-family: Arial, helvetica, "sans serif";
    font-style: italic;
    font-weight: bold;
}

a:link, a:visited, a:active {
    text-decoration:none;
}

p {
    font-family: "Times New Roman", times, serif;
    font-size: 12pt;
    color: purple;
    text-align: justify;
    margin-left: 10%;
}

h1 {
    font-size: 16pt;
    color: teal;
    text-decoration: underline;
    text-align: center;
}
```

## 7.8.2  The HTML Page

The HTML page is rather more interesting than the stylesheet. As usual, take a look at the code before I explain some of what it is doing:

```html
<html>
    <head>
        <link rel=stylesheet href="./styles.css">
        <script language="javascript" src="switch.js">
        </script>
    </head>
    <body onLoad=Init()>

        <div id="menua" style="top: 5; left: 5;
```

```
visibility: visible; position: absolute; z-index: 5;">

    <p class=SWITCH>
    <a href="#" onClick="ChangeLayer(0)">One</a>
    <a href="#" onClick="ChangeLayer(1)">Two</a>
    <a href="#" onClick="ChangeLayer(2)">Three</a></p>
</div>

<div id="content0" style="top: 40; left: 0;
    visibility: visible; position: absolute;">
    <h1>A test header</h1>
     <p>here's some text</p>
     <hr>
</div>

<div id="content1" style="top: 40; left: 0;
    visibility: hidden; position: absolute;">
    <h1>Another test header</h1>
    <p>here's some more text</p>
    <hr>
</div>

<div id="content2" style="top: 40; left: 0;
    visibility: hidden; position: absolute;">
    <h1>Yet another test header</h1>
    <p>here's yet more text</p>
    <hr>
</div>

    </body>
</html>
```

The page contains no JavaScript. Yet again I am loading the script code from a separate file. As with the other examples, the program starts by running the Init() function when the page loads.

The page contains four divisions or layers. The first is a menu layer which holds three hyperlinks. Each hyperlink points to the dummy page # so that the browser doesn't attempt an unwanted page load. We are going to move around totally within this one page so do not need to go back to the server. The links all use the same event handler. When onClick occurs they call the ChangeLayer() routine using the number of the layer that is to be displayed as a parameter.

Division `menua` is formatted using the `SWITCH` style from the stylesheet. It is placed 5 pixels in from the left and top edges of the screen. I've also given the layer a `z-index` of 5 to ensure that it is always at the top of the stack. The layer has to be positioned using `absolute` and `visible`.

The other layers are all content holders. These are all positioned in the same place at 40 pixels from the top of the screen. That value was selected so that the layers appear below the menu on the screen. Only one content layer is visible, the other two are hidden. If more than one of these layers is visible then the content of both will display at the same time, which is obviously not ideal.

### 7.8.3 The JavaScript

```
var active = 0;
var browser;

function Init() {
   browser = new BrowserObj();
   }

function BrowserObj() {
   this.navigator = 0;
   this.explorer = 0;
   this.other = 0;

   if ((navigator.appName.toLowerCase()).indexOf
   ("netscape") >= 0)
      this.navigator = 1;
   else {
      if ((navigator.appName.toLowerCase()).indexOf
      ("explorer") >= 0)
         this.explorer = 1;
      else
         this.other = 1;
      }
   this.major = parseInt(navigator.appVersion)
   this.minor = parseFloat(navigator.appVersion)
   } // BrowserObj


function ChangeLayer(now) {
   if(browser.navigator) {
       document.layers["content" + active].visibility = "hide";
```

```
            document.layers["content" + now].visibility = "show";
            active = now;
            }
        else {
            var current = document.all("content" + active).style;
            var next = document.all("content" + now).style;
            current.visibility = "hidden";
            next.visibility = "visible";
            active = now;
            }
    }
```

The script is quite simple. As ever, it starts by sniffing out the browser being used. Most of the work is done by the `ChangeLayer()` function. The script holds the value of the page that is currently showing in a variable called `active` which is initialized to 0 as we start by showing that layer.

The processing differs depending whether Netscape or Explorer is being used. The two approaches are so different that I'll explain them separately. First Netscape Navigator. The code for this version should be familiar to you as it's similar to the code used in the rollover example:

```
document.layers["content" + active].visibility = "hide";
document.layers["content" + now].visibility = "show";
active = now;
```

In Netscape, layers and divisions have a `visibility` property. When layer visibility is set in the HTML code the browser accepts the values `visible` and `hidden`. When setting layer visibility from JavaScript, Netscape insists on the use of `hide` and `show`. All that is needed to swap the layers is to set the current layer to `hide` and the new layer to `show`.

The layers are named in the form `content0`. Netscape keeps an array of layers which can be referenced by name. Using `"content" + value` concatenates the number in value onto the end of the string. This can then be used to find the desired layer.

Always hide the current layer first. This method lets the user select the current layer for redisplay. Users will sometimes select the current layer by accident. If you display the new layer *then* hide the current one and both have the same value you'll end up with no content showing.

Having displayed the new page the variable needs to be set to the value of the page that is now showing.

So swapping layers in Netscape is easy. What about Explorer? Well, it's no harder but few of the techniques that work for Netscape will work here. Explorer doesn't keep arrays of document contents. Instead it has a single global array from which all page elements must be referenced. Explorer doesn't have a layer visibility property. Instead the visibility of layers is set by manipulating the style object. Many of the configurable properties of the layer are set through the `style` property.

```
var current = document.all("content" + active).style;
var next = document.all("content" + now).style;
current.visibility = "hidden";
next.visibility = "visible";
active = now;
```

I use two temporary variables called `current` and `next` to hold some of the detail. The elements that are being altered are named `content` and a layer number: `content0`, `content1`, and `content2`. The Explorer objects are referenced by passing the element name into a function called `document.all()`. Once the elements are referenced their visibility can be set. Explorer uses the values `visible` and `hidden`.    Once again the variable holding the value of the visible layer is set at the end of the function.

So swapping between layers is yet another simple technique. The most difficult part of this is writing the HTML page. It's probably done most easily if you create each division as a page in its own file, test everything, and then cut and paste the pages into the same file along with all of the division definitions.

## 7.9    A TEXT-ONLY MENU SYSTEM

Clearly the rollover and layer swapping are powerful techniques.  They can make any site look interesting and if used properly they make even relatively mundane sites into bleeding-edge multimedia experiences. They don't seem to satisfy many site builders. In fact many sites use Java programs towards the same ends. Java is not an ideal solution on today's Web. It is slow, difficult, and less popular than an e-mail virus with users.

The most common use of Java is the site menu.  There are many ways of providing navigation but allying a global menu to hyperlinks is one of the most popular.  How do you build a global menu? There are many ways, some of which I've outlined earlier. Java is another option.  What about JavaScript?  Can we use JavaScript to build an interesting menu?  The answer is emphatically yes. By combining the techniques from rollovers and layer swapping we get a simple, fast, and effective menu system.

The menu system that I'll show here is actually incomplete.  What I am trying to do is demonstrate the principles so that you can take and use them in your own pages. This code will demonstrate how to use layers in a rollover, changing the formatting of the page as the mouse moves about. This is yet another example in which the HTML is more complex than the JavaScript. In fact the HTML is *so* complex that you will be rewarded by spending some time studying it in detail.

### 7.9.1    The HTML Page

As usual, look through the code then I'll explain some of the highlights:

```html
<html>
   <head>
      <link rel=stylesheet href="./styles.css">
      <script language="javascript" src="./menu.js">
      </script>
   </head>
   <body>
      <div id="menua" style="top: 5; left: 5;
      visibility: visible; position: absolute; z-index: 5;">

      <p class=SWITCH>
         <a href="#"
            onMouseOver="Highlight(0)"
            onMouseOut="UnHighlight(0)">One</a>
         <a href="#"
            onMouseOver="Highlight(1)"
            onMouseOut="UnHighlight(1)">Two</a>
         <a href="#"
            onMouseOver="Highlight(2)"
            onMouseOut="UnHighlight(2)">Three</a>
      </div>

      <div id="menu0b" style="top: 5; left: 5;
      visibility: hidden; position: absolute; z-index: 5;">

      <p class=SWITCH>
         <span class=OVER>
         <a href="#">One</a>
         </span>
         <a href="#">Two</a>
         <a href="#">Three</a>
      </div>

      <div id="menu1b" style="top: 5; left: 5;
      visibility: hidden; position: absolute; z-index: 5;">

      <p class=SWITCH>
         <a href="#">One</a>
         <span class=OVER>
         <a href="#">Two</a>
         </span>
```

```
        <a href="#">Three</a>
    </div>

    <div id="menu2b" style="top: 5; left: 5;
    visibility: hidden; position: absolute; z-index: 5">

    <p class=SWITCH>
        <a href="#">One</a>
        <a href="#">Two</a>
        <span class=OVER>
        <a href="#">Three</a>
        </span>
    </div>


    </body>
</html>
```

The HTML page has four divisions. The main one is menua which will be displayed when the menu is inactive. This layer is positioned at pixel 5, 5. It contains a single paragraph which is styled by assigning a class from the stylesheet. Inside the paragraph there are three hyperlinks which in this example go nowhere. In an actual site these would point to the linked pages.

Each hyperlink is a piece of text but because they are links the onMouseOver and onMouseOff events still work. These events are tied to the link rather than to an image. The event handling will be shown when I discuss the JavaScript.

The remaining three layers are all hidden. As the mouse moves over the menu these layers will be made visible and hidden. Each sub-menu is basically identical to the main one. Each has one item that is formatted differently. A different class of formatting is applied to the items through the use of .... If you are developing just for Netscape the class can be applied inside the <a> tag. Explorer won't recognize classes inside hyperlinks but as Netscape accepts the Explorer-friendly version we'll use it here.

## 7.9.2  The JavaScript

```
var active = 0;

function Highlight(id) {
    document.layers["menua"].visibility = "hide";
    document.layers["menu" + id + "b"].visibility =
"show";
    }
```

```
function UnHighlight(id) {
   document.layers["menu" + id + "b"].visibility =
"hide";
   document.layers["menua"].visibility = "show";
   }
```

This script should not need any explanation. It's identical to the code from the layerswitch example. I have only included the Netscape version as you ought to be able to code the alternative for yourselves. The `Highlight()` function hides the default menu and makes one of the other layers visible. The `UnHighlight()` function reverses this by hiding the visible layer and making the default menu visible.

## 7.10  FLOATING LOGOS

The final JavaScript example is by far the most complex and took the most time and effort to develop. You may have seen Web sites like Geocities which display a floating logo in the bottom right hand corner of the screen. As you resize the browser or scroll the window the logo remains fast in the corner. Depending upon your point of view this is either an affront to all Web surfers or (in my view) a great way of providing relatively unobtrusive branding.

Sites like Geocities float an image (usually a small GIF), I am going to float some text. I'm actually floating a layer which only holds some text. If you want to float a picture then change the text to the appropriate URL.

If you use this technique be aware that the floating brand will always be on top of the stack. If the brand is too big or garish it will either hide site content or attract attention away from it. That is why Geocities, for instance, uses a mostly transparent image.

### 7.10.1  The HTML Page

The HTML page is nice and simple. It only has two layers. If you are copying these code samples you will have to put more content into the main layer so that you can see what happens during scrolling.

```
<html>
   <head>
      <script language=javascript src="logo.js">
      </script>
   </head>
   <body onLoad=Init()>
      <div id="lay0" style="visibility: visible;
      position: absolute;">
         <!--Your Content Here -->
```

```
    </div>

    <div id="lay10"
       style="visibility: visible;
          position: absolute;
          font-size: 20pt;
          background: aquamarine;
          color: purple;
          text-align: left;">
       <p>LOGO</p>
    </div>

  </body>
</html>
```

## 7.10.2   The JavaScript

The JavaScript is pretty complex. I've shown the browser-sniffing functions a number of times before so I'll ignore them here. There are three other functions and I'll go through them all in detail. As you read this code be aware that it works for both main browsers.

```
var brows;
var orig_width;
var orig_height;
var px;
var py;

function Init(){
   brows = new BrowserObj();
   if( (brows.major < 4) || (brows.other) )
     alert("Only works with version 4 browsers");
   else {
      if(brows.navigator) {
         orig_height = window.innerHeight;
         orig_width = window.innerWidth;
         }
      else {
         orig_height = document.body.clientHeight;
         orig_width = document.body.clientWidth
         }
      SetupEvents();
      PositionLogo();
```

```
      }
   } // Init


function BrowserObj() {
   this.navigator = 0;
   this.explorer = 0;
   this.other = 0;

   if ((navigator.appName.toLowerCase()).
   indexOf("netscape") >= 0)
      this.navigator = 1;
   else {
      if ((navigator.appName.toLowerCase()).
      indexOf("explorer") >= 0)
         this.explorer = 1;
      else
         this.other = 1;
      }
    this.major = parseInt(navigator.appVersion)
    this.minor = parseFloat(navigator.appVersion)
   } // BrowserObj


function PositionLogo() {
   if(brows.navigator){
      var height = window.innerHeight + py;
      var width = window.innerWidth + px;
      }
   else {
      var height = orig_height;
      var width = orig_width;
      }
   var wide = 120; // logo width
   var high = 50; // logo height
   var top = height - high;
   var left = width - wide;

   if(brows.navigator)
      document.layers["lay10"].moveTo(left, top);
   else
```

```
            {
        document.all("lay10").style.left = left;
        document.all("lay10").style.top = top;
            }
    } // PositionLogo


function SetupEvents() {
    if (brows.navigator)
        setInterval("Reposition()", 200);
    else {
        window.onresize = new Function("Reposition()");
        window.onscroll = new Function("Reposition()");
        }
    } // SetupEvents


function Reposition() {
    if(brows.navigator) {
        px = window.pageXOffset;
        py = window.pageYOffset;
        if ( (orig_width != window.innerWidth)
            || (orig_height != window.innerHeight) )
            {
            orig_width = window.innerWidth;
            orig_height = window.innerHeight;
            }
        }
    else {
        px = document.body.clientWidth;
        py = document.body.clientHeight;
        var w2 = document.body.scrollLeft;
        var h2 = document.body.scrollTop;
        orig_width = px + w2;
        orig_height = py + h2;
        }
        PositionLogo();
    } // Reposition
```

*SetupEvents( )*   After sniffing out the browser the script runs the `SetupEvents()` function. This tells the browser what to do when certain events happen. In the ideal situation, supported by Explorer, the processing will happen whenever the window is resized or scrolled. When these events are triggered the `Reposition` function is run. Explorer complicates matters. You can't simply run the function. Instead the function call has to be wrapped inside a call to the builtin `new Function()` call.

```
function SetupEvents() {
   if (brows.navigator)
      setInterval("Reposition()", 200);
   else {
      window.onresize = new Function("Reposition()");
      window.onscroll = new Function("Reposition()");
      }
   } // SetupEvents
```

Netscape doesn't support the `onScroll` event but does support `onResize()`. We need a workaround to cope with the lack of `onScroll` and the workaround will mean that we can also ignore window resizing. We tell the browser that every 200 milliseconds it should run the Reposition function. This delay is short enough to cope with scrolling and resizing but not so short that it takes up too many processor cycles.

*PositionLogo( )*    Once the events are set up, the logo is positioned for the first time. Two variables are set which hold the height and width available for showing pages. The global variables `orig_height` and `orig_width` were set in the `Init()` function. When positioning the logo in Netscape the available height is the height of the window plus the vertical offset of the page (how far it has been scrolled). The available width is the window width plus the horizontal scroll. When the logo is being positioned for the first time the offset values `px` and `py` are both zero.

The top of the logo will appear at 50 pixels above the top of the screen, the left edge will be 120 pixels in from the right side of the screen. These values are based upon the size of the piece of text that I'm displaying and will need altering if, for instance, you are using an image or more text. The exact location at which the layer is placed is stored in two temporary variables: `top` and `left`.

```
function PositionLogo() {
   if(brows.navigator){
      var height = window.innerHeight + py;
      var width = window.innerWidth + px;
      }
   else {
      var height = orig_height;
      var width = orig_width;
      }
   var wide = 120; // logo width
   var high = 50; // logo height
```

```
var top = height - high;
var left = width - wide;

if(brows.navigator)
    document.layers["lay10"].moveTo(left, top);
else
    {
    document.all("lay10").style.left = left;
    document.all("lay10").style.top = top;
    }
} // PositionLogo
```

Once the positions have been calculated the layer can be moved. In Netscape the `moveTo()` function is called for the layer. In Explorer the left and top values of the style for the layer element are set.

*Reposition( )*   So far I have explained how to set the initial position of the logo and how to tell the browser which events it should respond to. All that is left is to move the logo layer when an event is triggered. Examine the code for a moment then I'll go though it:

```
function Reposition() {
    if(brows.navigator) {
        px = window.pageXOffset;
        py = window.pageYOffset;
        if ( (orig_width != window.innerWidth)
            || (orig_height != window.innerHeight) )
            {
            orig_width = window.innerWidth;
            orig_height = window.innerHeight;
            }
    }
    else {
        px = document.body.clientWidth;
        py = document.body.clientHeight;
        var w2 = document.body.scrollLeft;
        var h2 = document.body.scrollTop;
        orig_width = px + w2;
        orig_height = py + h2;
        }
    PositionLogo();
    } // Reposition
```

You'll have guessed that the `Reposition()` function needs to be coded differently so that it works in each browser. I'll examine the Netscape alternative first.

The function starts by setting the vertical and horizontal offsets. If the page has not been scrolled these will remain at 0. Next the stored window size is compared with the actual window size:

```
if( (orig_width != window.innerWidth)
  || (orig_height != window.innerHeight) )
```

If the window has been resized the new values are stored. Finally the `PositionLogo()` function is called.

Explorer works rather differently. First the window size is ascertained by checking the size of the client:

```
px = document.body.clientWidth;
```

Because Explorer supports the `onScroll` event it also has properties which hold the amount that the window has been scrolled:

```
w2 = document.body.scrollLeft;
```

In Explorer the location of the bottom right corner of the screen comes from adding the window size to the distance scrolled. Once that value has been found the `PositionLogo()` function is called.

If you search the Internet you'll find many different ways of creating this effect. My method has a couple of advantages: it's simple and flexible; and it definitely works in version 4 of both major browsers. I've seen a number of versions which despite the claims of their authors were specific to one browser or only worked in one application. I even saw one which was so badly coded that it didn't support resizing or scrolling: the author had cheated by fixing the size of his page.

## 7.11 EXERCISES

### Basic dynamic HTML

1. Find a large image and modify the script in Section 7.2 to display it in a window of its own.

2. Write a page which demonstrates the use of the different types of popup window that are available in JavaScript.

3. What are the benefits of using the browser status bar to pass messages to the user?

4. Implement the Color Picker from Section 7.5. Modify it to color more page elements.

5. List the difficulties that you might experience if you use JavaScript to perform data validation.

6. Create a simple form and write a script that performs primitive checking of data.

## Advanced DHTML applications

1. Why is it better to use the `div` tag rather than the `layer` tag to create movable layers of content?

2. Why are rollover images *so* popular among Web developers?

3. Implement a site menu system based around rollover images. Try to write the main code so that it can be placed in a library of useful JavaScript routines.

4. What are the main benefits of creating a library of code rather than rewriting everything each time that you create a site?

5. Will your rollover images still work as hyperlinks if someone fails to download the images?

6. Is it generally better to write your own code for something like a rollover image or to use the code that some authoring tools can generate for you?

7. Create a library of routines to move images around the screen in the following ways:
   - vertically up
   - vertically down
   - horizontally right to left
   - horizontally left to right
   - diagonally from top left to bottom right corners
   - diagonally from top right to bottom left corners
   - diagonally from bottom right to top left corners
   - diagonally from bottom left to top right corners

8. Try moving a number of images around the screen at the same time.

9. Look at your site and see where you might be able to download a number of pages at the same time. Try implementing the site to work in this way. Is this an improvement over the original version?

10. Can you make the site work in both Netscape Navigator and Internet Explorer?

11. What are the advantages of using JavaScript rather than Java for a site menu?

12. Put the flying logo code from Section 7.7 into a page and see if you can get it to work. Try using as many browser as possible to see how platform independent JavaScript is.

13. JavaScript has some disadvantages when used for menus. List three of them.

14. Expand the code in section 7.9 to work as a full-text menu system.

15. Implement a floating logo on your site. Try floating the logo in each corner of the browser in turn. Again, try to make this work in both major browsers.

16. Why do many people object to having floating logos placed on their pages by companies such as Geocities?

# 8
# Programming in Perl 5

So far I have shown you the basics of creating Web pages using HTML, JavaScript, and Cascading Stylesheets. These are enough to create most of the pages that you find on the Internet. In fact, if you combine the ideas we've seen already alongside a few well-chosen plug-ins, sound effects and moving images, *and* a sense of good design, you could soon be writing award winning Web pages. Add in some Dynamic HTML, possibly using JavaScript and you've got a really exciting Web experience.

Design, layout, and the look and feel of a Web site are only part of the story once a business decides to use the Internet. Businesses need enhanced revenue, or new revenue streams, from their sites. This means that not only does the Web site provide a leading edge advertising tool, which is particularly useful if the company wants to be seen as go-ahead, youthful or thrusting, it must generate sales. Sales do not *have* to come through the familiar e-commerce route where product selection, purchase and payment all happen on-line. Web sites may be used simply to raise brand awareness or to increase customer loyalty. Many organisations already have well established sales routes through catalogs. A Web site can be used to enhance this type of business, for instance by giving customers more information on products which they can order through conventional paths.

For the developers of commercial sites anything which is robust and powerful enough to be used for revenue generation has to go beyond simple HTML. When data has to be gathered about customers and their needs the Website has to become part of a comprehensive business application. The incorporation of forms which are used to enter data into the system, business rules to govern how that data is processed and database systems to store it, mean that significant amounts of processing must be performed on the server.

Getting a Web server to perform application processing is not difficult: most support the Common Gateway Interface, CGI, protocol which allows a degree of interaction between the client browser and the server. Assuming that your Web server is set up to allow CGI then all that you have to do is write some programs which can process data from the client and place them on your server. The difficult part of the whole process is writing the server-side applications. These have a few common characteristics:

- processing of textual data,

- output of text, images, sound etc.,

- errors must be returned to the client browser

- fatal exceptions[1] should be logged for the system administrator,

- short residency – generally a CGI program executes then quits and is restarted each time it is needed,

- each Web site requires a unique solution – off-the-shelf CGI programs are always inadequate,

- the ability to port programs to new servers and operating systems is desirable: you don't want to have to rewrite your whole Web site if you change ISP,

- short development times and rapid prototyping are used to encourage flexible, readily updated Web sites,

- no concept of state. Each time a user accesses a new page or uses a new service the server considers it to be a new interaction. Some applications such as shopping carts require that a set of interactions be created for each user. We shall examine ways of maintaining state between transactions.

CGI applications can be written in any language – the set of requirements given above does not dictate any particular solution. However, we can make some general observations about the suitability of certain languages. The standard languages today for most solutions are C and C++. These are powerful and general purpose, but compiled code is not platform-independent. They provide poor text handling facilities and may be overkill for programs with such short residency. Java is platform independent and has some very good text-handling classes, an excellent exception handling mechanism, and inherently supports the common Web data types such as GIFs and WAVs. However, Java is also too powerful for simple CGI unless you choose to write a multi-threaded Java program to handle all of your needs. This would be an excellent solution but the development time would be comparable to building any other large application. Section 13.2 demonstrates the use of Java *servlets* to process data in similar fashion to the way that CGI scripts operate.

The favored solution is to use a scripting language. Scripting languages have been around in the UNIX world for many years and are used to develop many complex, site-specific system administration tools. Programming support applications such as make-files, source-code control systems, and configuration utilities are extensions of sophisticated scripts. The UNIX world also provides many powerful text and file management

---

[1]Run-time errors which mean the program cannot safely continue.

tools such as sed, grep, awk, and find. These tools have few direct equivalents in the world of the PC desktop where graphical tools are more commonly used.

Increasingly, scripting languages are being made available under Windows. The commonest language for that platform is Visual Basic which comes in a number of variations, including a command-line version called VBScript. In the ideal world a common scripting language would be available across all platforms. A number of such languages exist, including established favourites such as Tcl/Tk, Scheme, Python, and Perl. Of these I would argue that Perl is the best established, especially in the CGI scripting arena.

Although this book concentrates on using CGI scripts on the server, Microsoft provides a powerful technology called Active Server Pages which is designed to achieve much the same ends. ASP scripts are usually written in VBScript and less often in JScript. This is simply because those are the languages which Microsoft pushes as being best suited to ASP scripting. In fact, as I'll demonstrate in Section 13.1, Perl can be used here as well. ASP is an example of a *templating* system which embeds scripting commands inside Web pages for processing by the Server before the pages are sent to the user. Templating is a widely used alternative to CGI scripting and in Chapter 12 I'll examine an open-source language called PHP4 which is starting to rival Perl in popularity.

## 8.1 WHY PERL?

Having been told that you're going to have to learn yet another programming language it would be understandable if you simply asked, *Why?* A number of answers leap to mind. First, I've shown that the languages that you may already know are not suitable for the task. Second, each programming language carries a certain intellectual stance around with it. C++, for instance, in its design encourages the building of complex systems and monolithic applications, Java makes it easy to network and distribute an application, Visual Basic naturally leads to solutions that concentrate on the user interface. Perl has its own approach and culture which is best summed up in the peculiar acronym TMTOWTDI, There's More Than One Way To Do It.

Perl gives programmers freedom: freedom to develop their own solutions in their own way. It can be an interpreted scripting language, it can produce compiled code, you can write monolithic scripts or use structured procedures, if you want to use objects then that's fine, Perl can do that too. Variables can be declared and initialized before use or can pop up inline, non-fatal errors can be caught or ignored. Perl solutions can be quick and dirty or highly sophisticated; rapid prototypes or fully-fledged applications. One of the more interesting aspects of Perl is that you don't need to know much of the language to develop real applications. Given just a few simple commands you can be writing CGI scripts that are sufficiently powerful for most needs. As you learn more of the language your solutions become more complex, as do the types of problem that you can tackle. Learning Perl is supposed to be like learning a natural language: a gradual and evolutionary approach.

### 8.1.1   A Brief History Lesson

Perl is a growing and evolving language which continues to change, and for which major new versions are released every few years. Its originator, and the man who remains its creative and driving force is Larry Wall. Larry Wall currently works for the leading publisher of UNIX books O'Reilly and Associates where he is one of the associates. At some point in the mid-80s Larry needed a text manipulation tool and quickly realized that sed, awk, and related tools wouldn't get the job done so he wrote his own. That tool evolved over time and was released as version one of Perl in early 1988.

That first version of Perl, plus all subsequent ones and thousands of extensions supplied by users and developers, was given away, released onto the Internet so that people could freely use and adapt it. Prior to releasing Perl, Larry had already written, and given away, `metaconfig`, `rn`, and `patch`, all of which turned out to be useful and successful UNIX utilities. Like many people who have been around the Internet community for a long time, Larry Wall has always been committed to the idea of free software and free support. Free software does not mean software which is given away by its developers without charge. Instead it is a term which encapsulates a whole slew of philosophical ideas about the best way to produce software.

The free software idea lets developers release not only compiled and executable programs, but also the source for their programs under a legally binding licence. Wherever the code goes, the licence goes too. Anyone can modify the source of such programs provided that they make their changes freely available and use the original licence for their modified code. This doesn't mean that you can't charge for free software but it does give the end-user the right to further modify and distribute what they've bought provided the original licence accompanies it. You may have heard of open-source software. This is a variation of the free software concept which is said to be more *business friendly*. Open source software has the source code freely available but, generally, if you modify the code you cannot distribute your changes.

The dominant free software licence is the GNU Public Licence, GPL, developed by Richard Stallman and the Free Software Foundation. It is exceptionally restrictive in the way that it enforces the free software concept. If you modify code which is licensed with the GPL then your work is licensed with GPL too. You have no choice. Because the GPL is so restrictive, many alternative licences are available. Perl is developed and distributed using two licences: GPL and the Artistic Licence. The latter gives users more freedom about how they manage source code.

## 8.2   ON-LINE DOCUMENTATION

The Perl distribution is exceptionally well documented  but many beginners seem to have difficulties finding or using the documentation. Three types of help system are available: all provide the same content but deliver it in different ways. The major Perl files contain inline comments which describe how they should be used, structured in a special way which can be interpreted by Perl scripts and translated into a variety of formats. This documentation is called *POD*, which is short for plain old documentation. POD can be viewed using a utility called perldoc which comes with all of the Perl distributions. If you don't like the way that the documentation viewer works, POD can be converted into standard UNIX manual pages or HTML Web pages. The manual pages can be viewed using the man utility, the HTML pages with any Web browser.

To access POD directly from a UNIX command-line you use a utility called `perldoc`. The name of the documentation file which you want to read is given as a parameter:

```
perldoc <file>
```

This launches the POD viewer. To page down press the spacebar, to move down by one line press the down arrow, to move up by one line use the up arrow. You can also move in page sized steps by using the Page Up and Page Dn keys. To leave the viewer press q.

Table 8.1 lists some of the key commands which you should investigate. Perl comes with a *very* comprehensive on-line manual. In fact over 100,000 lines of documentation are said to be provided as part of the standard distribution. The manual is broken into a number of sections, an index for these is available by typing:

```
perldoc perl
```

One of the best pieces of advice I can give to someone learning Perl is to consult this documentation whenever they get stuck. Using it can be difficult as material is often not where you expect it to be, but the sheer scale and depth of knowledge you're being given here is breathtaking. Personally I prefer the HTML version of the material. If you struggle to use `perldoc` or find it too unfriendly, see if the HTML files are available for your particular installation.

If you are using Perl on a Windows machine and have installed a recent version from ActiveState[2] then you already have all of the documentation that you'll need to get going. This distribution has documentation as both HTML and POD. Briefly this is how to use them.

- **HTML** Viewing the HTML documentation could not be easier. When you install Perl a new tree of directories is created:
  - bin which includes executable programs such as the Perl interpreter,
  - lib includes all of the standard libraries that come with the distribution,
  - site holds any additional modules which you choose to install to modify the distribution to meet your personal needs,
  - html has all of the documentation in HTML format.

---

[2]http://www.activestate.com

***Table 8.1*** `perldoc` Commands

| `perldoc command` | Description |
|---|---|
| `perldoc` | Displays a brief version and help message. |
| `perldoc -h` | Verbose help, including listing all command-line parameters. |
| `perldoc -q` *expression* | Searches questions (not answers) in parts 1 to 9 of the Perl FAQ for the string contained in *expression*. For instance `perldoc -q CGI` lists all items which directly discuss CGI scripting. |
| `perldoc perldoc` | Displays the POD for the perldoc program. |
| `perldoc perl` | Displays the top-level of the Perl manual which includes a comprehensive index of the included documentation. |
| `perldoc` *manual section* | Displays the POD for a particular section of the manual. |
| `perldoc` *module name* | Displays the POD for the named module. For instance `perldoc CGI` displays the POD from the CGI.pm module and `perldoc perlwin32` shows information relating to building and using Perl on Microsoft systems. |

To access the HTML documentation open the file `index.html` in the `html` directory in a Web browser. In the frame on the left of the screen you'll see all of the help files listed. Choose one and the file is displayed in the right-hand frame. As you scroll down the list of contents you'll see that the distribution includes many modules which are especially created for programming Microsoft systems (listed under Win32). These are obviously not available on the UNIX distributions of Perl.

- **POD** Viewing the POD directly under Windows works just like it does under UNIX. You need to open up a DOS command box. At the prompt, type `perldoc` which will give you a brief help message. Again, Table 8.1 lists some of the more useful things that you can try with perldoc and POD.

## 8.3 THE BASIC PERL PROGRAM

The simplest Perl script is a one-line print statement run from the command-line. If you are using UNIX it's a relatively easy thing to do; if you're using Windows then the process is slightly more complex. If you have a Macintosh you'll need to consult the documentation for your version of Perl to find out how to compensate for the lack of a command shell[3].

---

[3]In MacOS X use the UNIX versions in the builtin shell.

First the easier situation from UNIX. From a command prompt enter this:

```
perl -e 'print "Hello World\n"'
```

Make sure that you get all of those quotes correct – the script uses three different types. Press Enter to execute the script.

Under Windows you must first start a DOS shell. The quotes need to be *escaped* so that DOS doesn't try to interpret them as commands meant for it, but instead passes them to the Perl interpreter. This can be done in one of two ways. Try each of these in turn:

```
perl -e "print \"Hello World\n\""
perl -e "print qq(Hello World\n)"
```

In the second example you'll see a command called qq being used. Often in scripts you'll need to put quotes around strings or words but doing so may be impossible due to the structure of the code. In JavaScript it was important to use single quotes inside double quotes. Well, it is just the same with Perl. The commands qq and qw provide a safe way of quoting. The former puts a single pair of quotes around its entire parameter. The latter takes a list of words as its parameter and places quotes around each one:

qq(Hello World) produces "Hello World" while qw(Hello World) gives "Hello" "World".

Before moving on to writing complex programs it is useful to test your Perl installation. Find out exactly what version you have available by typing perl -v at a command prompt. This should display version information. If it doesn't you'll need to check your installation and environment variables.

Create a file using your favorite editor and enter:

```
print "Hello World!\n";
```

Save the file as hello.pl. Notice that the line is terminated by a semicolon: all statements in Perl have to be terminated in this way. Missing the semicolon is one of the easiest mistakes for a beginner. To run your Perl scripts you'll need to change to the directory in which you are editing the file[4] in a command shell and type:

```
perl -w hello.pl
```

Hopefully that ran the "Hello World" program which you saved a moment ago. If there are any problems with your code, the -wflag makes the interpreter print lots of useful information to the command shell. Using this is so useful that it is usually considered to be an essential part of good Perl programming style.

Let's try a slightly more complicated example. Modify hello.pl so that it contains *just* the following code:

```
#!/usr/bin/perl -w
print "Hello World!\n";
exit(0);
```

---

[4]I'll assume that you know how to do this for the particular operating system that you are using.

The first line of that short script is the magic *shebang* line. This is made from the characters # ! and the full path to an application. In that simple script the path points to the Perl interpreter and includes a *flag* which I am passing to the interpreter to change its behavior. The shebang line *must* be the first line of the file since the # ! character pair are an instruction to the shell telling it to pass the rest of the file to another application. In your particular situation the Perl interpreter may be stored in a different directory to mine. You'll need to find out where it is and change the line to suit your local conditions. The following lines show possible alternatives:

```
#!/usr/local/bin/perl
#!/bin/perl
```

Microsoft Windows does not use the same mechanism. It generally associates a type of file with a particular application which it uses to process the file. If you've installed ActiveState Perl this association will have been automatically set-up for you so that all files which end .pl are passed to the Perl interpreter. If you need to set flags when the script is run you have a problem with this mechanism. This particular distribution lets you use the shebang mechanism to execute the script and control its behavior. This means that you can run these from the prompt in exactly the same way that you would under UNIX by just typing the file name. Use the following line:

```
#! perl -w
```

Now it's time to execute the script we created and saved earlier. Open a command shell and change to the directory in which you saved the file. At the prompt type:

```
hello.pl
```

On a Windows machine, that should run the script which displays a simple message. On a UNIX machine you should get a message telling you something like:

```
bash: ./hello.pl: Permission denied
```

UNIX uses a system of permissions to control access to files. Each Perl script that you write, whether saved as .pl or as .cgi, needs to be made executable with the chmod utility. This is done by entering the following at a command prompt:

```
chmod 755 <scriptname>.pl}
```

This gives the owner of the file, usually its creator, permission to read, write, and execute the file as a program. Other users on the system can read the file or execute it but cannot edit its source. To run a Perl script you simply type the file name at the command prompt, there is no need to place the perl command before it. The operating system uses the shebang line to find out how to run the program, in this case it will pass it to the Perl binary.

Perl doesn't use normal data types such as integers, floats or chars. Instead data items are simply things which are accessed through a variety of structures. Control over the operations which you perform on a data item is pretty much left up to you. If you want to try adding a string of characters to a floating point number then the Perl interpreter isn't going to stop you.

In this book I'll use the primitive data types: scalar, array and associative array. Because they are rather different to data types in other languages there should be plenty to keep us all busy. Perl can be used for object-based programming, just as JavaScript can, but generally it is used to develop simpler, procedural programs.

## 8.4  SCALARS

The basic data type is called the *scalar*. Scalar items are identified by having a $ at the front of their name.

> **Note:**
> In Perl, the data type of a variable is identified by a character symbol which precedes its name.

So what is a singular piece of data? Well, single data items might be numbers or characters, strings or individual data items inside a structure such as an array. Table 8.2 shows some examples of this.

*Table 8.2*  Scalar Data Assignments

| Assignment | Explanation |
| --- | --- |
| `$item = 0;` | Scalars can be simple integers. |
| `$item = 0.32536;` | A scalar can also hold a float. |
| `$item = " ";` | This scalar is initialized as an empty string. |
| `$item = "fred";` | Here we assign a string to the scalar. |
| `$item = 23.03e4;` | Scalars can use scientific format. |
| `$item = 34 * 56.78;` | The result of any operation can be assigned to a scalar. It will be typed correctly for the context. |
| `$item = "A whole sentence";` | Scalars can hold strings with spaces – which will turn out to be very useful. |
| `$new = $item;` | Scalars can be assigned the value of other scalars. |
| `$item = $array[3];` | A scalar can be assigned a value from an array. |

Because the type of a scalar is not predetermined they can be used rather creatively. Try saving the following script in a file called `scalar.pl`.

```
#!/usr/bin/perl -w

$item = 0;
$item = 34 * 54.364762;
$item .= " fred";
print $item."\n";
print "$item\n";

exit(0);
```

Make the script executable if you're using UNIX with the chmod command:

```
chmod 755 scalar.pl
```

Run the script by entering the following command at a prompt, then pressing Enter:

```
scalar.pl
```

In the script, $item undergoes the following set of operations:

- It is initialized as a number with the value 0.
- It then takes the result of the multiplication operation.
- A string is then joined onto the end of the numerical value. Notice the .= construct which is used for certain string concatenation operations. See Section 8.8 for more details on this and similar operators. What's important for now is that the scalar was able to act as a number and then become a string when it needed to.
- The scalar is then displayed, using the print function, with a newline character joined to its end.
- Finally the scalar is displayed from within a string.

Perl has a rich set of printing operations which are borrowed directly from C. Most of the examples in this chapter use the most primitive print operation. Detailed descriptions of the printing and display operations can be found in Section 8.8.5.

Within the script, whenever it was necessary, $item was automatically converted into a string so that fred could be concatenated onto it. But what happens if we insert the following code:

```
$item = $item * 3;
```

just before the print statements?

```
#!/usr/bin/perl -w

$item = 0;
$item = 34 * 54.364762;
```

```
$item .= "fred";
print $item."\n";
print "$item\n";

# new things below here...
$item = $item * 3;
print $item."\n";
print "$item\n";

exit(0);
```

The interpreter throws out an error message saying that $item, or rather the argument to the operation on line 10 (1848.401908fred), isn't numeric. Once you have non-numerals in a string you can't convert it into a number. But...notice what the final two print statements output:

```
5545.205724
```

That's the result of the multiplication the script performed before fred was concatenated onto $item. Strings which could represent valid numbers such as "54.123" or "54.3e02" can be used in either string or numerical operations as the following example shows:

```
#!/usr/bin/perl -w

$item = "3245.02e4";
$item2 = $item;

$item .= "12";
$item2 = $item2 + "12";

print $item."\n";
print $item2."\n";
exit(0);
```

Initially both variables are set to string values. The first, $item, then has a string concatenated on. When displayed this scalar holds the value

```
3245.02e412
```

The second scalar is used in an arithmetical operation although both of the operands[5] are strings. Since both operands contain only digits the operation can be performed legally and the result displayed:

---

[5]The values used in the operation.

```
32450212
```

If the line were changed to:

```
$item2 = $item2 + "q";
```

the addition operation would no longer be legal. The interpreter would display this message instead:

```
Argument "q" isn't numeric in add at ./test.pl line 7.
```

> Note:
> I can't stress the importance of thorough testing and debugging, when developing in Perl, strongly enough. Even a very simple script can contain hidden errors and potential side-effects.

### 8.4.1   Functions Which Operate On Scalars

A number of Perl functions operate on scalar data. I've defined some of the more useful ones in this section.

**chomp[(variable)]**

Usually used to remove the newline character from the end of the scalar. If no scalar variable is specified chomp will operate on data coming from the standard input. Standard input is usually the keyboard.

**chop[(variable)]**

Works exactly like chomp but returns the character which was removed.

**lc[(parameter)]**

Returns its parameter with all characters converted to lower case. If the parameter is omitted lc will operate on standard input.

**length[(parameter)]**

Returns the length in characters of its parameter. Operates on standard input if no parameter is specified.

**q/string/**

Places single quotes around the string.

**qq/string/**

Places double quotes around the string.

**substr(string, offset[, length])**

Extracts and returns a substring from the string, starting at the supplied offset. The first character of the expression is at position 0. An optional length may be supplied to indicate how many characters are returned. If this is omitted the substring continues to the end of the string.

**uc [(parameter)]**

   Returns its parameter with all characters converted to upper case. If the parameter is omitted uc will operate on standard input.

## 8.5  ARRAYS

The first of the plural data types is the array. These have an @ before their name and are, broadly, like those which you may have met in JavaScript. Although you've already used arrays, it is probably worth giving a quick refresher on arrays in general before I write about how they're used in Perl. If you know your array from your linked list, your stack from your queue, feel free to skip the next bit and leap to the discussion of arrays in Perl. A couple of warnings: in Perl an array can be used as a stack so you need to keep your wits about you; and Perl arrays are not type sensitive – we can mix and match numbers, strings, arrays, and hashes as items in an array.

   The array is a common, popular, and useful data structure which is found in most programming languages. An array is an ordered list of scalar variables. To access an item in an array you use its position in the list. This is called its index. If we take some simple items: "dog", "cat", 234, "Uncle Bill", we can put them into an array. The following code creates an array and displays its contents:

```
#!/usr/bin/perl -w

@firstarr = ("dog", "cat", 234, "Uncle Bill");
print "@firstarr\n";

exit(0);
```

   Having put our strange list into an array, it is now ordered and we can access items based upon that order. The first item in the array is at index 0 (zero), not index 1, many programming languages count from 0 and Perl is no exception. This is not simply a convention designed to trap the unwary novice, but is very useful in counting through loops. In Perl, as in JavaScript, you need to get used to counting the first instance of anything as instance zero. The index of the last item in our array isn't the same as the number of items in the array. In the example I have 6 things in the array, yet if the first is at index 0 the last must be at index 5. That is, the last item is at index "number of items in the array" – 1.

   Let's now consider the matter of ordering. I said that the items in an array are ordered. That ordering is due to their being in the array and is not an artifact of any property of the array items themselves. If I swap "cat" and "my uncle Bill" the array remains ordered. This is one way in which an array differs from a list. Another is that deleting an item from an array does not affect the other items in the array. If I delete cat, which was at index 1, the array still has 6 items, the only difference is that the item at index 1 is empty. If this data structure worked like a list then deleting cat would reduce it to 5 items. I could easily write a function which would delete an item from an array and shuffle the other items along one place so that there is no gap. Similarly I could write a function to insert items into an array but these are add-ons to the array rather than inherent within the data structure.

Arrays in Perl are nice and straightforward with a couple of useful enhancements over the traditional array. You create an array by assigning it a list of values:

```
@myarray = ("dog", "cat", "mouse", 234, "my uncle Bill");
```

You can also set the value of an individual array item:

```
$myarray[5] = "horse";
```

Perl supplies two operations which allow you to manipulate the last item in the array. These are called push and pop. The following code shows these functions in action:

```
#!/usr/bin/perl -w

@myarray = ("dog", "cat", "mouse", 234, "my uncle Bill");
$string = "foobar was my uncle";
print "@myarray\n";

push(@myarray, $string);
print "@myarray\n";

$item = pop(@myarray);
print "$item\n";

exit(0);
```

Using push then pop can leave the array in its initial state:

```
#!/usr/bin/perl -w

@myarray = ("dog", "cat", "mouse", 234, "my uncle Bill");
$string = "foobar was my uncle";
print "@myarray\n";

push(@myarray, $string);
print "@myarray\n";

pop(@myarray);
print "@myarray\n";

exit(0);
```

You won't find these operations in a traditional array implementation, rather they are usually reserved for use with stacks. However, they are very useful if you want to swap things. If you push items into one array and pop them off into another you've quickly reversed their order.

The following script shows most of the array syntax in operation. Try it out:

```perl
#!/usr/bin/perl -w

$array = "";
$discard = "";
for($i = 0; $i < 12; $i++) {
  $array[$i] = $i*1000;
}

$i = 0;
foreach $t (@array) {
  print("$i    $t\n");
  $i++;
}

$discard = pop(@array);
push(@array, "uncle Jack");
$i = 0;
foreach $t (@array) {
  print("$i    $t\n");
  $i++;
}

($fred, $jack, $mary) = @array;
printf("$fred, $jack, $mary");
exit(0);
```

Let's look at the interesting behavior that we see there. I'll go through each loop in turn. First we initialize two scalars then iterate through the first simple loop writing a value into an array on each loop. You should notice that the array is declared and referenced as a scalar. This works because Perl is fairly flexible about data management, once the Perl interpreter sees something like $var[$count] it knows that it is dealing with an array. In writing to an individual array cell we are addressing part of the array not all of it, therefore we can't use @array as this means the whole array. The loop writes a number to each cell of the array but, of course, later we may treat this number as a string if we have to.

> Rule:
> If we want to perform an operation on the whole array we use @arrayname;
> if we want to perform an operation on an individual item in the array we use
> $arrayname[$index].

The second loop iterates through the array, copies the value at each index, and displays it on the screen. This time a `foreach` loop is used as the size of the array is fixed. Once the end of the array is reached the loop will terminate. The notation:

```
foreach $t (@array)
```

is used to set the value of $t on each loop. After displaying the array we remove the last item using pop, the array now has only 11 items. We then replace the popped item with a string and once more print the array.

Finally three new scalars are declared and assigned values. This type of assignment starts from the beginning of the array (index 0) and assigns to as many variables as are declared. If you try to assign to more variables than you have items in your array you will get a run-time error. The assignment statement will work perfectly but once you try to use the variables which did not get a value from the array you will be warned that you are trying to use an uninitialized value. This can lead to undefined behavior so care needs to be taken when using arrays.

> **Rule of Thumb:**
> Although Perl is more flexible than C about arrays, using variables with an indeterminate value will still give problems. The safest approach is usually to track the length of the array manually so that you can never fall off the end.

Here's a final useless but amusing thing that you can do with arrays and pop. You can pop items off the end of your array whilst manipulating it in a loop:

```perl
#! /usr/bin/perl -w

$array = "";
$discard = "";
for($i = 0; $i < 12; $i++) {
  $array[$i] = $i*1000;
}

$i = 0;
foreach $t (@array) {
  $discard = pop(@array);
  print("$i    $t\n");
  $i++;
}
```

I honestly cannot think why anyone would want to do this, and it could be really dangerous. It does, though, demonstrate just how flexible Perl is.

## 8.5.1 Functions Which Operate on Arrays

A number of Perl functions operate on arrays of data. I've defined some of the more useful ones in this section.

**join(separator, item[, item[, item]])**

joins the items specified in the comma separated list into a single string. The items in the new string are separated by the character passed in as the first parameter:

```perl
#! /usr/bin/perl -w
print join("!", "Jack", "Mary", "Fred", 32),"\n";
exit(0);
```

which displays

```
Jack!Mary!Fred!32
```

**push(array, scalar)**

adds a scalar item to the *end* of the array.

**pop(array)**

removes one item from the end of an array, returning it so that it can be used.

**qw/string/**

Places quotes around the scalar values in the array.

**reverse(item[, item[, item]])**

Returns the list of items in reversed order:

```perl
#! /usr/bin/perl -w
print reverse("Jack", "Mary", "Fred", 32,),"\n";
exit(0);
```

which displays

```
32FredMaryJack
```

**shift**

takes the first item off the array and returns. After this operation the array is shortened by one item.

**sort**

sorts the elements of the array and returns them in sorted order.

**splice(array, offset, length, item[, item[, item]])**

works in the same way as the JavaScript `splice` function which was described in Section 5.9.2. Items from `offset` to `length` are removed from the array and replaced by the items in the comma separated list. The following example shows how this works:

```perl
#! /usr/bin/perl -w
```

```
@orig = ("first", "second", "third", "fourth", "fifth", "six");
print "@orig\n";

splice(@orig, 2, 3, "new 1", "new 2");
print "@orig\n";

exit(0);
```

which displays

```
first second third fourth fifth six
first second new 1 new 2 six
```

## 8.6  HASHES

The second, and last, of the plural data types is the hash. Identifiable by the % before their unique name, hashes consist of a series of pairs of items with each pair comprising a **key** and an associated **value**. Hashes are formally called *associative arrays* but that is rather long-winded so I prefer to stick to the simpler name. The clearest way of getting a grasp on the hash concept is to see some examples. Hashes can be declared in one of two ways:

```
%myhash = ("key", "value",
    "Mon", "Monday",
    "Tue", "Tuesday",
    "Dog", "Rover",
    "Cat", "Fluffy");
```

or:

```
%myhash = ("key" => "value",
    "Mon" => "Monday",
    "Tue" => "Tuesday",
    "Dog" => "Rover",
    "Cat" => "Fluffy");
```

In my opinion, the second version makes the relationship between the key and its value obvious while the first could be a mislabelled array. In the first example I'm going to write some values into a hash and then read them back and display them. Code first, then some explanation:

```
#! /usr/bin/perl -w

%myhash = ("key" => "value",
    "Mon" => "Monday",
    "Tue" => "Tuesday",
```

```
        "Dog" => "Rover",
        "Cat" => "Fluffy");

foreach $key (keys %myhash) {
    $value = $myhash{$key};
    printf("Key: %s\tValue: %s\n", $key, $value);
}

exit(0);
```

Save that code in a file called `hash.pl` then run it. The output should look like this:

```
Key: Cat        Value: Fluffy
Key: key        Value: value
Key: Dog        Value: Rover
Key: Mon        Value: Monday
Key: Tue        Value: Tuesday
```

When you run this script you will find that the key/value pairs are printed in a different order to the one in which you entered them. You haven't made a mistake and this is not a bug but a powerful feature. Clearly something more than simple storage is going on.

---

**Rule:**
What happens when you add something to an array is that Perl applies a *hashing* algorithm to the key. This is then assigned to one of eight buckets depending upon the result of the hash. A hash array is called that because it uses a hashing algorithm to optimize storage.

---

That seems a lot of effort. Why bother? Imagine that you have a large database to manipulate and that you are using Perl, which is free, rather than Oracle which is immensely expensive. You wouldn't want all of your data items placed into the same data structure: searching for a specific item would take an eternity. By creating eight data structures Perl is able to radically reduce search times. The reduction is by at least 7/8th as Perl applies the hashing algorithm to your search request and will only ever search one bucket. If you want to know how many buckets have been used to store your data, try this which will tell you:

```
print %myhash."\n";
```

It is important that you realize that every key must be unique. If you add something to your hash and later reuse the same key, the second value will overwrite the first which will be irretrievably lost.

Let's look at the script to see how it works. The first thing to notice is the line which reads the *keys* out of the hash.

```
foreach $key (keys %myhash) {
```

Before we can operate on the data values we need to get them out of the hash. We can't access them directly[6], instead we'll get at the values through the indexed keys. To get all of the keys from the hash we use the `keys` function.

The keys come out of the hash in an array. I want to iterate across this list of keys and extract and display each associated value. The easiest way of moving across a structure like an array is to use a `foreach` loop. Once we have a key we can apply this to the hash to access its associated value. In this program I'm going to copy the value into a scalar so that I can display it. As with the array if we only want to work on a single item we treat the hash like a scalar by calling it using the $ notation. Notice that the key is surrounded by curly brackets not parentheses:

```
$value = $myhash{$key};
```

> **Note:**
> This is an opportunity for errors which are difficult to spot when debugging your code: if you're reading from a hash by applying a key, use curly brackets.

Sometimes you will not be interested in the keys but will want to look at all of the values. As well as the `keys` function, Perl has a function to return a list of values from a hash. Not surprisingly it is called `values`.

```
foreach $value (values %myhash) {
  printf("Value: %s\n", $value);
}
```

You cannot reverse engineer the hash to get the keys from their associated values but there should never be any reason to do that unless you got the key/value pair the wrong way round.

> **Rule of Thumb:**
> Try to think in hashes. Although you'll use arrays and scalars more often, much of the real power and flexibility of Perl lie in the murky recesses of the hash.

You put ordered data into your hash, you get unordered data out. Doesn't seem to be a very useful solution does it? Fortunately you can sort your data as it comes back using the, rather appropriately named, `sort` function.

Try this in the earlier hash example:

```
foreach $key (sort keys %myhash) {
  $value = $myhash{$key};
  printf("Key: %s\tValue: %s\n", $key, $value);
}
```

---

[6]Yet, I'll show you how to do that in a moment.

There's a lot more that you can do with sort but I haven't shown you enough Perl yet to use it. One thing to note is that sort puts the data into ascending alpha-numerical order. It has no understanding of context so although Monday comes before Wednesday in sorted data that is simply a result of "M" being before "W" in the ASCII table. If you want context sensitive sorts then you have to craft them for yourself.

Here's a complicated way of displaying data in reverse sorted order. It's a slow and dirty approach which involves reading and sorting from the hash, putting the keys and values into a pair of arrays and then popping the arrays. To use this program, enter pairs of keys and values separated by colons at the command line until you're finished or fed up. Then type quit and the sorting will start:

```perl
#! /usr/bin/perl -w

$in = "";
print "Enter a key/value pair separated by a colon
(quit to finish)\t";
$in = <STDIN>;
chomp $in;

while($in ne "quit") {
   ($key, $val) = split(/:/, $in);
   $myhash{$key} = $val;
   print "Enter a key/value pair separated by a colon
   (quit to finish)\t";
   $in = <STDIN>;
   chomp $in;
}

$cnt = 0;
foreach $temp (sort keys %myhash) {
   $keyarray[$cnt] = $temp;
   $valarray[$cnt++] = $myhash{$temp};
}

while($cnt > 0) {
   $t = pop(@keyarray);
   $tt = pop(@valarray);
   print("Key: $t    Value: $tt\n");
   $cnt--;
}

exit(0);
```

The only unfamiliar thing left in that script should be:

```
($key, $val) = split(/:/, $in);
```

Which will split the input into pieces each time it finds a colon. The pieces are then stored into two scalar variables. String manipulations like this will be explained in Section 8.8. For those of you who like quick solutions to your problems, here's how to print out an array in reverse order using the `reverse` function:

```perl
#! /usr/bin/perl -w

$in = "";
print "Enter a key/value pair separated by a colon
(quit to finish)\t";
$in = <STDIN>;
chomp $in;

while($in ne "quit") {
   ($key, $val) = split(/:/, $in);
   $myhash{$key} = $val;
   print "Enter a key/value pair separated by a colon
   (quit to finish)\t";
   $in = <STDIN>;
   chomp $in;
}

@revkeys = sort keys %myhash;
print "@revkeys\n";

foreach $key (reverse @revkeys) {
   $value = $myhash{$key};
   print("Key: $key  Value: $value\n");
}

exit(0);
```

Notice how that looks just like the earlier sorted array but uses a different function? This is a good example of reusing your knowledge to good effect.

## 8.6.1 Functions Which Operate on Hashes

A number of Perl functions operate on associative arrays, hashes, of data. I've defined some of the more useful ones in this section.

**delete $hash{$key}**
>   Deletes the specified key and its associated value from the hash.

**each %hash**
>   Returns a list of pairs of keys and values. This function is used to iterate over the contents of the hash:

```
#! /usr/bin/perl -w

%myhash = ("key", "value",
    "Mon", "Monday",
    "Tue", "Tuesday",
    "Dog", "Rover",
    "Cat", "Fluffy");

while(@pair = each %myhash) {
    print "@pair\n";
}

exit(0);
```

**exists %hashvalue**
>   returns TRUE if the value exists as a *key* in the hash. Try adding this to the previous example:

```
if(exists $myhash{"Dog"}){
    print "It's there\n";
}
```

**keys %hash**
>   returns all of the keys from the hash as an array.

**values %hash**
>   returns all of the values from the hash as an array.

## 8.7 CONTROL STRUCTURES

Perl is a block structured language like JavaScript. This means simply that operations can be grouped into blocks so that they can be performed repeatedly, or not at all. Blocks have to be delimited by curly brackets, {...}.

> Note:
> In JavaScript you can leave the brackets out if the block consists of only one line.
> Not so in Perl: you must use the brackets.

Perl coders also tend to be fussy about the way that brackets are used and how the program is laid out. Partly this is because Larry Wall has made his own somewhat idiosyncratic views known, and partly because so many Perl loops do have just a single line. If you are not careful you can end up with lots of white space in your scripts, which can be as unreadable as not having enough space.

The *approved* approach looks like this:

```
condition() {
    rest of block;
}
```

A common alternative which uses an extra line is:

```
condition()
  {
    rest of block;
  }
```

I tend to use the approved style for Perl, although I use the alternative for languages such as C, C++, and Java. For some reason I can't read my programs if I get the indentation wrong. More important than whether you can read your own code, other people may need to read it. If you are writing code for yourself, that code may never be read again, most developers work in teams and share code. Many organizations use the same code for years. Over time this code will need regular maintenance and updates. The person who originally wrote the code is unlikely to be the one who modifies it five or ten years later. All code needs to be neatly structured with liberal use of comments throughout. Perl is an especially messy language because it uses *lots* of characters which have special meanings. One of the easiest ways of making Perl code more legible is to use consistent blocks. As you read some of the larger pieces of code in this book, you'll see that consistent layout really *does* make the code more readable.

There are three basic types of block in Perl: subroutines which I'll consider later, repetition, and conditional loops. Conditional loops form if...elsif...else structures; repetition is achieved by while, for, and foreach loops. Looping is terminated when a controlling condition is true. In Perl almost everything is true, in fact generally speaking only two conditions are considered false:

- the integer 0
- the strings " " and "0"

### 8.7.1 Loops

**for**

for loops in Perl work exactly as they do in languages like C and JavaScript. They repeat the same operation, or set of operations, until the looping condition becomes false. The counter is a scalar value.

```
for($i = 0; $i < 10; $i++) {
    print "The Counter is $i\n";
}
```

This simple loop will repeatedly print its message to the screen and terminate once the value of $i is no longer less than 10. The $ declaration of variables will be explained later, as will the syntax of the `print` statement.

### foreach

Sometimes you want to perform the same operation on each item of an array. It is perfectly possible to use the `for` statement but `foreach` makes for neater code. In the following example I use a `for` loop to set the value of each element of an array and then use a `foreach` loop to print those values to the screen. Notice the strange @ symbol which is used to indicate an array, and the different ways that an array can be referenced. Section 8.8 will cover this in detail.

```
for($i = 0; $i < 10; $i++) {
    $array[$i] = $i;
}
$j = 0;
foreach(@array) {
    print "value: ".$array[$j++]."\n";
}
exit(0);
```

### while

`while` loops are best used if you don't know in advance when the loop will terminate. In this example I print a message to the screen prompting for some input, receive the input, and display it back to the user. When the string `quit` is entered, without the inverted commas, the program terminates:

```
#!/usr/bin/perl -w

$in = "";
while($in ne "quit") {
    print "Enter a String (\"quit\" to terminate): ";
    $in = <STDIN>;
    chomp $in;
    print "You Entered $in\n";
}
exit(0);
```

The next example is the same program but manipulating numbers. Try running them both, and in the second example enter a mix of integers and floats. What happens if you enter a string?

```
#!/usr/bin/perl -w

$in = 0;
while($in != -99) {
    print "Enter a Number (\"-99\" to terminate): ";
    $in = <STDIN>;
    chomp $in;
    print "You Entered $in\n";
}
exit(0);
```

Finally a simple program that reads parameter values from the command-line and displays them back.

```
#!/usr/bin/perl -w
$i = 0;
while($array[$i] = shift @ARGV) {
    print "Item $i: $array[$i]\n";
    $i++;
}
exit(0);
```

Save that code in a file called `param.pl`. Run it like this:

```
param.pl Mary, Jane, Susan
```

There's quite a lot to consider in these simple programs. I'll give a full treatment of data types later, for now some basic information will suffice.

Just like JavaScript, Perl is not a strongly typed language; which means that you don't have to declare the type of a variable when you create it. The context in which the variable is used will give the interpreter sufficient information to process it correctly. Data values occupy a different namespace to Perl keywords; in Perl it is not possible to declare a variable which has the same name as a keyword. This is achieved by preceding the name of the variable with a special symbol: $ for scalars, @ for arrays and % for hashes. Notice that in the final example I refer to two arrays: `array` and `ARGV` but that I use `$array` and `@ARGV`.

In the first `while` example I read values from the keyboard and assign them to a scalar using:

```
$i = <STDIN>
```

Like most languages Perl uses three standard streams, `STDIN` for input, `STDOUT` for output, and `STDERR` for error messages. You can use these streams as if they were files. We shall look at input and output in more detail in section 8.8. I then removed the return character from the end of the input using `chomp $i;` There are two ways of chopping the last character from a scalar: `chop` removes the last character, `chomp` is more friendly and removes the last character only if it is a newline. The sample programs demonstrate a number of Boolean checks. The use of the Boolean operators `eq`, `ne`, `==`, `!=`, etc. is considered in Section 8.7.2. Postfix incrementing of scalars works just as in JavaScript (`$i++`).

## exit()

Ultimately even simple programs have to work with the operating system. It is always a good idea to use:

```
exit(0);
```

to terminate your programs as this ensures that all processes finish safely.

## last <label>

Although teachers of structured programming sometimes tell students that loops should have a single entry point and a single exit point, they shouldn't. Any loop must have a single entry point otherwise your code can have all sorts of side-effects and will be impossible to maintain. Having a single exit from a loop leads to contrived and often inefficient code.

Consider the problem of reading through a text file looking for a specific line. Ideally when (or if) you find the line you want, the reading of the file should end so that you can get on with processing the text. The following pseudocode examples show differing approaches to this problem. Example one reads the whole of the file regardless of how quickly the line is found, example two uses a Boolean test to control the reading of the file.

### Example one

```
while(not end_of_file) {
  read next line;
  if(next line equal test){
    process line;
  }
}
```

### Example Two

```
done = false;
while(done equals false) {
  read next line;
  if(next line equals test){
    process line;
    done = true;
  }
}
```

Both of these examples are common approaches to this type of problem. It makes much more sense to break out of the loop either when the end of file is reached or when the required line is found. In C this might be done by adding a break statement into the first example:

```
while(not end_of_file) {
  read next line;
  if(next line equals test){
    process line;
    break;
  }
}
```

Perl has a similar mechanism. The start of the loop is given a label and the `last` operation is provided. This is used to jump out of the loop:

```
TEST: while($in = <INPUT_FILE>) {
  chomp $in;
  if($in eq "quit"){
    last TEST;
  }
}
```

This example reads from INPUT_FILE until the line entered, and chomped, equals the test. The program then jumps out of the loop.

Here is the script which reads numbers from the command-line rewritten to use LAST:

```
#! /usr/bin/perl -w

$in = 1;
$total = 0;

CHANCE: while( ) {
    print qq(Enter a Number ("0" to terminate): );
    $in = <STDIN>;
    chomp $in;
    $total = $total + $in;

    print "You Entered $in\n";
    print "The running total is now $total\n\n";

    if ($in == 0) {
        last CHANCE;
    }
}
exit(0);
```

> Note:
> Iteration is one of the most common things that you'll be doing in your Perl programs. Many simple CGI scripts contain no iteration but simply return a series of strings; I will be looking at how we develop more complex CGI applications. The scripts that we look at later in this book perform real processing; they use the excellent string handling capabilities of Perl and are required to iterate through files, strings, and values returned by the user. If you want to do any serious work with Perl you must be comfortable with its loop constructs and the way that it checks for truth.

### 8.7.2  Boolean Conditions

The status of operations, return values from subroutines, and the existence, or not, of data values can be checked in Perl, just as in other languages using Boolean conditions. A Boolean condition is a logical operation which evaluates to either true or false. Perl has two Boolean operators that are specifically used for operations on strings and four which are used for operations on numbers.

The string operators are eq and ne. The first test will return true if the two strings are equal; the second will return true if they are not equal. When comparing strings it is important that you consider exactly what the values are that you want to compare. In the following example I want to read input from the keyboard and compare it to the string quit. If the user types in quit the program will terminate. Consider what the user actually enters: they type quit followed by the <ENTER> key which appends a newline character onto the string. If I simply compare the input with quit, the program will never terminate:

```
if($input eq "quit")
```

The test will always be false because I am not testing for the newline at the end of the input. Therefore I must remove that newline character before I perform the test. To do this I use the builtin chomp function. Here's the code:

```
#!/usr/bin/perl -w

DONE: while( ){
   print qq(Enter a string ("quit" to finish)\t);
   $in = <STDIN>;
   chomp $in;
   if($in eq "quit"){
     last DONE;
   }
}

exit(0);
```

That code can be rewritten to use a Boolean condition to control looping:

```
#!/usr/bin/perl -w

$done = 0;
while($done != 1 ){
    print qq(Enter a string ("quit" to finish)\t);
    $in = <STDIN>;
    chomp $in;
    if($in eq "quit"){
      $done = 1;
    }
}


exit(0);
```

When evaluating numerical conditions we have four Boolean operations available. These should be familiar from JavaScript:

- `==` is used to test if the two values are equal,
- `!=` evaluates to true if the two numbers are not equal,
- `<=` is true if the value on the left is less than or equal to the value on the right,
- `>=` is true if the value on the left is greater than or equal to the value on the right.

These operations work exactly as they would in JavaScript or the vast majority of conventional programming languages. In the following example the program repeatedly executes a loop, and at the end of each iteration a variable is incremented. When the value of the variable equals 13 the program terminates. Notice that rather than testing for $i == 13 I test for $i <= 12. This gives me no performance benefits and, in fact, makes the code slightly less readable, but does demonstrate the use of a different operator. Without running the program, work out how many messages are displayed on the screen.

```
#!/usr/bin/perl -w

$i = 0;
$done = 0;
while($done == 0) {
    if($i <= 12){
      print "$i\tIt's a boy!\n";
  }
  else {
    print "$i\tIt's a girl!\n";
    $done = 1;
  }
```

```
   $i++;
}

exit(0);
```

## if ...elsif ...else

Not all conditions have only two correct answers. Often you will want to test a condition against a range of values and perform different operations for each possible value returned. In JavaScript we might use a `switch` statement:

```
switch(fred) {
   case(0):
       do something;
       break;
   case(1):
       do something else;
       break;
   default:
       do another thing;
   }
```

Perl doesn't have a switch but does provide a simple construct to perform almost the same operation. Subtle differences exist because of the need for a break statement in JavaScript, and the fact that you can only switch on an integer value. In Perl that statement would be written as:

```
if($fred == 0) {
  do something;
}
elsif($fred == 1) {
  do something else;
}
else {
  do another thing;
}
```

The Perl version is more difficult to write and maintain and less efficient at run-time. If you have 20 options instead of three, the JavaScript `switch` statement needs to make only a single check on the conditional value to switch to the correct next operation. In Perl if you wanted the last of the 20 options you would be making 19 conditional checks.

> Rule of Thumb:
> Structure your Boolean operations carefully to minimize the run-time overhead. When writing `if...elsif...else` take care that you type `elsif` rather than `elseif`: it's an awkward one to spot when debugging!

## 8.8  PROCESSING TEXT

Perl is a text processing language. Its facilities and optimizations are there to make the manipulation of text strings and plain text files fast, and relatively easy. UNIX systems generally have far richer text manipulation tools than Apple or Microsoft systems. These tools tend to be command-line based and work very well in automated applications such as batch processing. If you wanted to search for an individual sentence among all of the files in a directory on a PC you might open each file into a text editor and perform an individual search. Alternatively you could use the graphical `Find` utility which Windows provides. To perform the same operation on a UNIX box you would write a one-line `grep` script and run it. The advantage of the graphical approach is that novice users can perform relatively complex operations without needing to acquire too much knowledge. The command-line approach provides more flexible tools which can be embedded within scripts and called programmatically, that's clearly better if you need to repeat an operation in the future.

Here we see just one of the benefits of Perl: it brings programmatic access to a range of utilities to all platforms. Perl is available on many different systems and it always works in the same way on each of them. Perl can therefore be used to bring the power of UNIX text manipulation to every desktop.

Perl is much more than an extended grep, sed, and awk clone. Because it is a proper programming language you can use it to perform all manner of complex text transformations. Many computer-based operations need databases of information which are usually too small to need the services of fully fledged database management software. For example, system administrators need to know things such as which system log-on codes have been assigned, which workgroup a user belongs to, which printers they have permission to use, and how often systems are accessed. Webmasters may want to know where most accesses to their Web site are from, which pages are accessed most often, how accesses map throughout the day, and where the peaks are. All of this information is available to them but hidden in system log files. They could read through the logs and extract the information for themselves but many sys-admins now choose to write Perl scripts which extract and process their data. They can then present themselves with pre-digested summary information which they can usefully use.

Perl provides at least the following facilities:

- searching files for strings,
- searching strings for substrings,

- extraction of substrings into summary files,
- copying of data from one file to another,
- replacement of one substring with another,
- manipulation of individual characters,
- displaying strings,
- formatted report generation.[7]

## 8.8.1  Splitting Strings

The two operations that you'll encounter frequently, especially once we start to look at CGI programming, are splitting strings into lists and building strings from lists. To take a string apart we use the `split` function which is defined as:

**split /pattern/, [expression], [limit]**
>     The function takes a string and searches it for a specified pattern of characters; each time it finds that pattern it returns a substring. This operation is repeated either until the end of the string is reached or the number of substrings is equal to the optional limit. Where multiple strings are being returned they are usually made available in an array.
>     The string itself may optionally be specified in the expression field. If no string is specified the default input, called $_ is used. The default input is usually the standard input but may also be any arguments to the function. The substrings run from the start of the string previously found delimiter to the most recently found delimiter, but do not include the delimiters, which are discarded.

That definition might be quite confusing so here's a simple example that shows most of what you can do. Try running the code before you read the explanation:

```
#! /usr/bin/perl -w

# create a text string
$test_string = "cake::cookies::candies::chocolate";

# split the strings into the elements of an array
@nice = split(/::/, $test_string);
foreach $t (@nice) {
   print("Item: $t\n");
}

# split the items into a list of scalars
```

---

[7]I'm not going to look at this as the facilities are rather limited and the output looks a little old-fashioned.

```
($first, $second, $rest) = split(/::/, $test_string);
print("Items: $first, $second, $rest\n");

($first, $second, $rest) = split(/::/, $test_string, 3);
print("Items: $first, $second, $rest\n");

exit(0);
```

I start by creating a string in which the data items are separated by pairs of colons. If you are using strings to store data it is important that your separators are characters, or combinations, which are not going to appear in the data items. If they do appear in the data you'll get unforeseen side-effects – incorrect substrings. This might seem obvious, but when you write the script you may have little idea about the content of the data your users will enter. This can make the selection of a delimiter fraught. Popular choices for delimiters include pairs of colons (: :) and the pipe character ( | ) which almost never appear in English text.

In the first split I put all of the items into an array called @nice. I always put the operands of split inside parentheses as this makes them more readable, but this is optional. The pattern that we're going to split on can be written in one of two ways: /pattern/ or "pattern". The former is usually preferred as it matches the notation used in regular expressions, see Section 8.9, but the latter may be more legible: especially for beginners.

If you return the result of split to an array it will push each item onto the end of the array as it is split off. If you give it a list of scalars, each will, in turn, be assigned a substring as these are split off. The second split assigns the substrings into three scalars, the fourth substring is discarded as there is nowhere to put it. This is somewhat corrected in the third split. This time I give split a limit of three substrings. The first two scalars get the values you would expect of cake and cookies respectively. The third scalar is set to candies::chocolates. Everything remaining goes into the final substring once limit is reached. Specifying the number of output values ensures that split does not lose any data. The final type of split can be very useful in searching text databases on key fields:

```
#! /usr/bin/perl -w

$test_string = "cookies::multipack::chocolate::brownies";

($first, $rest) = split(/::/, $test_string, 2);
if($first eq "cookies") {
  ($pack, $flavour, $type) = split(/::/, $rest);
  if($type eq "graham") {
    print "found it\n";
  }
  else {
```

```perl
        print "not this one\n";
    }
}


exit(0);
```

If `$test_string` were being read from a file of product descriptions I could easily search for all relevant items and then further refine my search on that subset of the original database. If I only wanted to find information on graham crackers I would split all strings into two parts and a few strings into three parts instead of having to split all the strings into four pieces:

```perl
#! /usr/bin/perl -w

$test_string = "cookies::multipack::chocolate::brownies";

($prod, $pack, $flav, $type) = split(/::/, $test_string);
if($type eq "graham") {
  print "found it\n";
}
else {
  print "not this one\n";
}


exit(0);
```

If you know that the key values in your database are unique you can write the result of the first split into a hash which will speed up data retrieval. However, in this example there is likely to be more than one type of cookie and so hashing wouldn't work.

```perl
#! /usr/bin/perl -w

$test_string = "cookies::multipack::chocolate::brownies";
($product, $rest) = split(/::/, $test_string, 2);
$foodhash{$product} = $rest;

foreach $t (keys %foodhash) {
  if($t eq "cookies") {
    print "found it\n";
  }
  else {
    print "not this one\n";
  }
```

```
}
exit(0);
```

I will be examining pattern matching in more detail in Section 8.9 but a few comments are worth making here.

- If you want to split on white space, use either `split(/ /)` or `split(" ")`.
- To split every character out of the string use `split(//)`. Notice that no space is left between the slashes.
- Some characters must be *escaped* before being used in pattern matching. If Perl is going to interpret the character as a control string you need to make clear that it should not be expanded. Such characters have a backslash placed in front of them in the pattern:

  `\", \n, \t,\$`

- The pattern can become quite complex. Items can be grouped together using `[ ]`, options can be separated using pipe `|`:
    - `split(/[0-9]/, string)` splits on any digit,
    - `split($/::|\|/$, string)`
      splits on either paired colons or pipe. Notice that the pipe character has to be escaped.

## 8.8.2 Building Strings

Building strings is easier than splitting them apart. You've already seen a lot of string concatenation in my sample code although you may not have recognized it as such. Many of the print statements that I've used have a newline character appended onto the string. To concatenate[8] substrings into a string use the dot operator:

```
$next = "world";
$fred = "hello ".$next."\n";
```

It is also possible to put scalar values directly into the middle of strings:

```
$fred = "hello $next\n";
```

If you want to append something onto the end of a string, use the `.=` operator:

```
$fred = "hello ";
$fred .= "world\n";
```

Finally to concatenate lots of items use the `join` function rather than the dot operator.

**`join(separator, item[, item[, item]])`**
    Joins the items specified in the comma separated list into a single string. The items in the new string are separated by the character passed in as the first parameter.

---

[8]Join.

### 8.8.3 Formatting Date and Time

This sample program uses two built-in Perl functions to get the current system time and date, formats that information and prints it to the screen. Look for the various ways that strings are concatenated:

```perl
#!/usr/bin/perl -w

print &GetTime();
exit(0);

sub GetTime {
  ($sec, $min, $hour, $mday, $month, $year, $wday,
   $yday, $isdst) = localtime(time);

  $day = (Sunday, Monday, Tuesday, Wednesday, Thursday,
  Friday, Saturday)[$wday];

  $month = (January, February, March, April, May, June,
  July, August, September, October, November, December)
  [$month];

  # future proof the year field
  # time returns years from 1900 so 2000 is 100 in Perl
  $year = 1900 + $year;

  # add the correct *ending* onto the day e.g. to make
  # 21->21st or 13->13th
  if( ($mday == 1) || ($mday == 21) || ($mday == 31) ) {
     $mday = $mday."st";
  } elsif ( ($mday == 2) || ($mday == 22) ){
     $mday = $mday."nd";
  } elsif ( ($mday == 3) || ($mday == 23) ) {
     $mday = $mday."rd";
  } else {
     $mday = $mday."th";
  }

  $today = join ' ', $day, $mday, $month, $year;

  # put in the leading 0 if it's less than 10 minutes
  # past the hour
  if($min < 10) {
```

```
        $min = "0".$min;
    }

    $time = join ':', $hour, $min;

    return "The time is $time on $today\n";

}
```

This script is based around the output from the `localtime` function. This function takes the time as returned by the `time` function and converts it into an array of 9 elements. The elements are formatted for the locale of the particular Perl implementation.

Notice how I apply an index to the `$day` and `$month` lists to convert a numerical representation of the date into a textual one. Neat, though I say so myself.

### 8.8.4   Character Manipulation

Sometimes it can be useful to have all characters in a string in the same form. For instance if you want to perform a comparison it might be useful if all the letters were in the same case. To convert an expression to lower-case through brute force you could use the `tr` function which works like the one in `sed`. `tr` takes two arguments separated by forward slashes; the first is the set of characters to be altered, the second is the set of characters they'll be altered to:

```
#!/usr/bin/perl -w

$fred = "SOme sTrinG";
$fred =~ tr/[A-Z]/[a-z]/;
print $fred."\n";
exit(0);
```

The `=~` operator takes the string on the left, applies the function on the right, and returns the result as the scalar on the left. You can have some, not especially useful, fun with this. The following script uses the `tr` and `uc` functions:

```
#!/usr/bin/perl -w

$fred = "SOme sTrinG";

$fred =~ tr/[A-Z]/[a-z]/;
print $fred."\n";

$fred =~ tr/[a-i]/[0-9]/;
print $fred."\n";
```

```
$fred = uc $fred;
print $fred."\n";

exit(0);
```

## 8.8.5 Printing Strings

There are two functions which can be used to `print` strings. The `print` function performs no additional formatting on the string before printing it; `printf` is used to format a string before it is displayed. You can also print large blocks of pre-formatted text using what is called the "here" syntax of the shell.

### `print [filehandle] list`

This is the simpler print routine. It takes a string, or a comma-separated list of strings and prints them. If a filehandle (see Section 8.10) is given, the string will be written to the file that it references. If no filehandle is given, the strings will usually be written to the screen. When using `print` in CGI scripts on a Web server the data will automatically be returned back to the client browser because the default filehandle for `print` is actually `STDOUT`. If your printing requirements are simple you should use `print` rather than `printf`: it is quicker because it does less processing, and you are likely to make fewer errors with it.[9]

*Table 8.3*  `printf` Formatting Controls

| Code | Meaning | Code | Meaning |
|------|---------|------|---------|
| c | Character. | lo | Long octal integer (base 8). |
| d | Decimal integer. | lu | Long unsigned decimal integer. |
| e | Floating point number in exponential format. | lx | Long hexadecimal integer (base 16). |
| f | Floating point number in fixed point format. | o | Octal integer (base 8). |
| g | Floating point number in compact format. | u | Unsigned decimal integer. |
| s | String. | x | Hexadecimal number with lower-case letters (base 16). |
| ld | Long decimal integer. | X | Hexadecimal number with upper-case letters (base 16). |

[9]C coders may prefer to regard this advice with the sniffy disdain it probably deserves!

**`printf [filehandle] format, list`**

This is the more complex, and more flexible printing routine. Again, a string, or comma-separated list of strings, is printed to either STDOUT or a named filehandle. The big difference here is that the output must be formatted before it is printed. The formatting operators are listed in Table 8.3. First look at an example, then I'll describe the formatting:

```perl
#! /usr/bin/perl -w

$string = "Some Examples:";
$number = 76523;
$decimal = 34.5612;
$float = 23.08e35;
$hex = 0x23a7;

print("$string, $number, $decimal, $float, $hex \n");

printf("%s\t%d\n\t\t%f\n\t\t%e\n\t\t%x \n", $string,
$number, $decimal, $float, $hex);

printf("%s\t%d\n\t\t%3.3f\n\t\t%1.3e\n\t\t0x%X \n",
$string, $number, $decimal, $float, ($hex + 0xa));

exit(0);
```

Which produces the following on my system:

```
Some Examples:, 76523, 34.5612, 2.308e+36, 9127
Some Examples:  76523
                34.561200
                2.308000e+36
                23a7
Some Examples:  76523
                34.561
                2.308e+36
                0x23B1
```

Formatting information is embedded in the format string, but you can also put *raw text* in there. The formatting commands take the form:

`%m.nx`

where % is used to tell the interpreter that there are formatting commands next. m and n are optional integer values which indicate how many characters should be displayed.

In the example script I display some numbers without formatting before redisplaying them using formatting to restrict the sizes of fields. Notice also that in the second example I perform hexadecimal arithmetic from within the `printf` statement.

### special characters

When printing you will want to use tab characters to easily format messages and, of course, you will need to use newlines in your print statements. The correct way of specifying a tab is by using backslash-t and to specify a newline use backslash-n. If you want to display any character which Perl interprets as a command you will need to first escape that character with a backslash:

```perl
#!/usr/bin/perl -w

printf("Printing Special Characters:
\tbackslash \\
\tinverted commas \"
\ttab.\t.
\tdollar \$
\tnewline \n
\texclamation mark \!\n");


exit(0);
```

which looks messy but shows what is going on. If your `printf` statements are not working as you expect check for the presence of special characters.

### sprintf format, list

This works exactly like `printf` but instead of displaying a string it returns it to be used by the program:

```perl
#!/usr/bin/perl -w

$msg = sprintf("Printing Special Characters:
\tbackslash \\
\tinverted commas \"
\ttab.\t.
\tdollar \$
\tnewline \n
\texclamation mark \!");

print $msg."\n";


exit(0);
```

### print «identifier;

This function is used to print here documents. Perl provides a line-oriented form of printing. The delimiters used in formatting strings for printing are end-of-line markers rather than display characters. The syntax for using this printing style is:

```
print <<END_OF_TEXT;
    Print this line
    and this one!
Here's another with a scalar $value.
END_OF_TEXT
```

Printing starts on the line following the function call. The call must be written as shown, although the identifier can obviously be changed. The string is printed until the terminating identifier is reached. This identifier must be on a line of its own with no characters before it and only a newline character after it. It is also useful to put a blank line after the terminating identifier. This is not strictly necessary although some ports of Perl will throw out error messages without it. The blank line won't do any harm so use it to be safe. The text will print exactly as you have formatted it in the script code. This will turn out to be very useful when we come to display HTML pages from our CGI scripts in Section 9.4.

## 8.9 REGULAR EXPRESSIONS

Now you've tried a bit of Perl, hopefully you like it. It probably meets some of your needs, it isn't as rigorous as C, or as mind-numbingly vast as C++ and is sufficiently different to give you an edge in the jobs marketplace. How do you go from hacking a few Web pages to developing serious applications? Just what does it take to move from acolyte to guru, from sweaty-palmed novice to sneering, disdainful expert? Regular expressions, that's what. Learn a little of using regexes and you'll be able to perform complex text manipulations easily and rapidly; learn a lot and you'll be able to solve apparently insoluble problems automatically. Regular expressions cannot meet all of your text manipulation needs but they can meet many of them.

Of course other languages have regular expression facilities. They are now an integral part of JavaScript, for instance. The reason that regular expression facilities are so widespread is quite simple: they are extremely useful when you are processing text. So why do they matter so much in Perl? Basically Perl is designed and optimised for text manipulation. It's generally used for that purpose and, realistically, the sort of processing that you do on the Web is just handling large quantities of text. Therefore anything which simplifies that whole process is important to Perl programmers.

A regular expression is a meta-description of a piece of text, it's a grammar for a mini language. A regular expression is a method of describing patterns so that software can match text against them. Perl uses pattern matching in these places:

- we have already seen and used `split` which takes a pattern as its first argument, and a string as its second, and returns a list of substrings which match the pattern,

- we've used `tr///` to change individual characters within a string,
- the match operator `m//` in Perl is used to find matching substrings,
- the `s///` operator is used to replace substrings matching the pattern with a replacement string,
- checking if a particular combination of characters exists inside a string. This use is the one that is most commonly associated with the idea of regular expressions.

When the pattern matching routine runs, a number of things can happen. You might simply want to know that your pattern, or part of it, matches something in the search string, for instance to test a Boolean condition. You might want to know where in the string the match is. You might choose to delete matching substrings or to replace them with another string.

## 8.9.1   Using Regular Expressions

Before looking at what makes a regular expression, I'll show you how to use them. They are generally used in just two ways. The expression is applied to a string and the result of the expression is used to replace the value of the string:

```
$string =~ s/foobar/fred/
```

Alternatively a string is tested against the expression and a Boolean value returned. This is useful when, for instance, you want to see if a string contains a particular substring before performing any more processing upon it:

```
$value = ($string =~ m/foobar/)
```

Before trying to use regular expressions I'll list all of the components which combine to make them. It is important to know how they are constructed before seeing too many examples as they can become very complicated very quickly.

## 8.9.2   Pattern Matching Operators

Each of the operators which use regexes can be modified to work slightly differently. Before I describe the regex grammar that Perl uses I'll get the operator modifiers out of the way.

**m/pattern/gimosx**

>   Pattern matching returns either 1, if the pattern matches, or 0, if it doesn't. You must either specify a string through `=~` or allow `m//` to search `$_` which is the default input. The six available modifiers are shown in Table 8.4.

**s/pattern/replacement/egimosx**

>   Replaces `pattern` with `replacement`. If the pattern is found the function returns the number of matches made (will only be > 1 if you specify /g) or 0 if the pattern doesn't match. The flags which modify the behavior of `s//` are listed in Table 8.5.

***Table 8.4*** Modifiers for Pattern Matching

| | Meaning | | Meaning |
|---|---|---|---|
| g | Find all occurrences of the pattern. | o | Only compile pattern once. |
| i | Case insensitive matching. | s | Treat string as single line. |
| m | Strings are treated as multiple lines. | x | Use extended regular expressions. |

***Table 8.5*** Modifiers for Pattern Replacement

| | Meaning | | Meaning |
|---|---|---|---|
| g | Find all occurrences of the pattern. | o | Only compile pattern once. |
| i | Case insensitive matching. | s | Treat string as single line. |
| m | Strings are treated as multiple lines. | x | Use extended regular expressions. |
| e | The replacement is treated as an expression and evaluated. | | |

`tr/searchlist/replacements/cds`

replaces occurrences of the searchlist with the corresponding value from the replacement list. The modifiers which can be applied to `tr` are shown in Table 8.6.

***Table 8.6*** Modifiers for List Replacement

| | Meaning |
|---|---|
| c | The search list is complemented (logically NOTted). |
| s | Duplicate replaceable characters are given a single character. |
| d | Any characters which are not replaced will be deleted. |

## 8.9.3 Components of Regular Expressions

A regex is made up of a number of different types of component. If you want to read and understand them you need to know what the components are.

### 8.9.3.1 *Alphanumeric Characters* A regex can contain literal strings and ordinary ASCII characters. These can be composed of any character which is not a metacharacter (see next). Characters can become special characters by putting a backslash in front of them. In regular expressions this is called quoting[10].

---

[10]To be awkward, in `printf` it was called escaping.

The following script matches all instances of the patterns "grommit", "Grommit", and "grOmmiT" including the inverted commas. It also includes a match which will find those strings *without* the inverted commas:

```perl
#!/usr/bin/perl -w

push(@strings, "Wallace and Grommit");
push(@strings, qw(Wallace and "Grommit"));
push(@strings, "Wallace and grOmmit");

foreach $item (@strings) {
    if($item =~ m/\"Grommit\"/ig) {
        print "$item matches\n";
    }
    if($item =~ m/[G|g]rommit/ig) {
        print "$item matches\n";
    }
}

exit(0);
```

### 8.9.3.2 Metacharacters

Metacharacters are control sequences. They are not themselves matched but they alter the way that the system matches alphanumeric characters. If you want to match against a metacharacter you have to quote it with a backslash. I'll explain how metacharacters work in Section 8.9.4. The list of metacharacters is:

```
\ | ( ) [ { ^ $ * + ?
```

To match for the pattern "Grommit$$$" try the following match:

```perl
#!/usr/bin/perl -w

push(@strings, qw(Wallace and Grommit));
push(@strings, qw(Wallace and Grommit$));
push(@strings, qw(Wallace and Grommit$$));
push(@strings, qw(Wallace and Grommit$$$));

foreach $item (@strings) {
    if($item =~ m/\"Grommit\${3}/ig) {
        print "$item matches\n";
    }
}

exit(0);
```

### 8.9.3.3 *Special Characters and Operators*  Some ordinary characters can be
used as operators. The set of characters is listed in Table 8.7, you met this table earlier when
I was discussing regular expressions and JavaScript. I'm reproducing it here to emphasise
the similarities between the two languages in this respect.

**Table 8.7**  Special Characters

| Token | Description |
|---|---|
| ^ | Match at the start of the input string. |
| $ | Match at the end of the input string. |
| * | Match 0 or more times. |
| + | Match 1 or more times. |
| ? | Match 0 or 1 time. |
| a\|b | Match a or b. |
| {n} | Match the string n times. |
| \d | Match a digit. |
| \D | Match anything except for digits. |
| \w | Match any alphanumeric character or the underscore. |
| \W | Match anything except alphanumeric characters or underscores. |
| \s | Match a whitespace character. |
| \S | Match anything except for whitespace characters. |
| [...] | Creates a set of characters, one of which must match if the operation is to be successful. If you need to specify a range of characters then separate the first and last with a hyphen: [0-9] or [D-G]. |
| [^...] | Creates a set of characters which must not match. If any character in the set matches then the operation has failed. This fails if any lowercase letter from d to q is matched: [^d-q]. |

### 8.9.3.4 *Alternatives*  If you need to match one, or more, from a set of patterns
they are separated by |. The following example matches letters w through z or the string
Wallace.

```
#!/usr/bin/perl -w

push(@strings, qw(Wallace and Grommit));
push(@strings, qw(wallace and Grommit));
push(@strings, qw(allace and Grommit));
push(@strings, qw(Walace and Grommit));

foreach $item (@strings) {
    if($item =~ m/[w-z]|Wallace/) {
```

```
        print "$item matches\n";
    }
}

exit(0);
```

#### 8.9.3.5 Quantifiers

Sometimes you want to look for repeated patterns. The pattern matching operators attach only to the previous character, or set of characters if that set is placed inside parentheses. The quantifiers are shown in Table 8.8.

The next script shows how to specify the number of times a character must be matched. The first match looks for the string `allace` which must contain the repeated letter `l`. The second match will only succeed if the string has a single `l`:

```
#!/usr/bin/perl -w

push(@strings, qw(Wallace and Grommit));
push(@strings, qw(wallace and Grommit));
push(@strings, qw(Walace and Grommit));
push(@strings, qw(allace and Grommit));

foreach $item (@strings) {
    if($item =~ m/al{2}ace/) {
        print "1. $item matches\n";
    }
}
foreach $item (@strings) {
    if($item =~ m/al?ace/) {
        print "2. $item matches\n";
    }
}

exit(0);
```

**Table 8.8**  Pattern Matching Multipliers

|          | Meaning                      |         | Meaning                  |
| -------- | ---------------------------- | ------- | ------------------------ |
| {n, m}   | match between n and m times  | {n, }   | match at least n times   |
| {n}      | match exactly n times        | *       | match 0 or more times    |
| +        | match 1 or more times        | ?       | match 0 or 1 time        |

### 8.9.3.6 *Character Classes*   It is possible to group together sets of characters when you want to perform the same operation using the whole set. Character classes are placed inside square brackets thus [class]. For instance if you want a class containing all of the ASCII lower-case characters you would use [a-z]. Notice the minus sign which indicates that you want to use a range. The character class works exactly like the same set of individual characters separated by |. These are equivalent:

```
m/[a-e]/
m/a|b|c|d|e/
```

Any of the special characters can be used in a class, and metacharacters are not interpreted as such inside square brackets. The exception to that is ^ which will be treated as a metacharacter if it is the first thing inside the brackets: it will invert the search so that it matches things not in the class. To match all of the metacharacters you could use:

```
m/[\|()[{^$*+?.]/
```

## 8.9.4  Rules for Matching

First it's probably important to realize that the matching algorithm is not intelligent – it simply applies patterns in the order that you specify along the string until it either runs out of string or matches successfully. The matching engine will keep trying things until the end of the string then back up to its last success, or the start of its last failure, and continue from there. Larry Wall codifies this behavior as *think locally, act globally*.[11]

**rule one**
> The engine matches as far left in the string as it can. Having found a match it will stop, unless you specify otherwise, it will not continue to search in the hope of finding a better match.

**rule two**
> The regular expression is a set of alternatives. If any one of the alternatives matches then the whole set is deemed to have matched. The alternatives are tried left to right in the order in which you specified them. Put the most likely alternative first and you'll get more efficient code.

**rule three**
> An alternative will match if every item within the alternative matches in the left to right order.

**rule four**
> Each unit of the regex matches according to its type: brackets group items and store them for back-referencing. The dot . matches any character; a character class matches any character in the list

[11]These rules are abridged, simplified and further explained from the versions in *Programming Perl*.

## 8.9.5   A Few Other Things That You Should Know

**backreferences**

Are assigned according to sets of parentheses. A match from the first set will be assigned to $1, a match from the second set to $2 and so on. These backreferences are then available for further manipulation. Outside the pattern matching they are available as the scalars $1, $2 etc. The backreference holds the actual match, not the rules for that match taken from the regex.

Here is some code to swap the first two words in a string:

```perl
#! /usr/bin/perl -w

$string = "here is a string string to test";
$string =~ s/^([^ ]+) +([^ ]+)/$2 $1/x;
print "$string\n";
exit(0);
```

How does that work? Here's the regex set out neatly with comments. Notice that the x flag lets me place comments inside the regex and set it out over a number of lines. I've included the flag in the one line version simply to be consistent:

```
s/              # perform substitution
    ^           # at the start of the string
  ([^ ]+)       # find repeated non-space characters
                # store that as \1
  +             # move along the string
  ([^ ]+)       # find repeated non-space characters
                # store that as \2
  /$2 $1/       # substitute $2 for the value in
                # position 1 and $1 for the value
                # in position two
  x;            # added to allow pretty printing
```

### 8.9.5.1   Backreferences – An Example

```perl
#! /usr/bin/perl -w

my $string = "here is a string string to test";
my $found = 0;
$found = ($string =~ m/\b(\w+)(\s+\1)+\b/ix);
print "$found $1 $2\n";
exit(0);
```

That's quite a complex regex. Before reading this explanation try to work it out for yourself.

```
m/          # it's a pattern match
  \b        # find a word boundary
  (\w+)       # followed by repeated word characters
            # save this as \1
  (\s+\1)     # find repeated space followed by the
            # result of the first match
  +         # do this repeatedly
  \b        # finish at a word boundary
/ix         # be case insensitive and allow pretty
            # layouts
```

Does that make sense? Well the regular expression in there simply finds the first instance of a repeated word in the test string and displays it to the screen. Try reading the code again now that you know what it does.

## 8.10   USING FILES

Perl makes using files very simple, certainly compared to the myriad subtle complexities of C or C++. The file is used through the mechanism of the filehandle. Filehandles are one of Perl's basic data types and are simply names which the programmer allocates to files, devices, sockets, or pipes. A large part of the complexity of using files is actually hidden behind the filehandle which presents a very clean interface.

**open(FILEHANDLE,   "[>|»]filename")**
**open(FILEHANDLE)**

To use a file you have to open it either for reading or writing. If you want to read from a file you supply a filehandle and the name of the file, which must be in quotes. To write to a file precede the filename by >, to append to the end of an existing file use >>. When you use the filehandle you can omit the $ sign, as you'll see in the following examples. If the file doesn't exist then writing to the filehandle will create it. You'll need to include error checking so that your script operates properly if you try to open a non-existent file:

```
$INPUT_FILE = "./datafile.dat";
open($INPUT_FILE) or
    die("Unable to open $INPUT_FILE\n Program Aborting\n");

$OUTPUT_FILE = ">./storage.dat";
open($OUTPUT_FILE) or
    die("Unable to open $OUTPUT_FILE\n Program Aborting\n");
```

You need an error message when trying to open a file for writing in case the operating system prevents you opening the file. Once you get this sort of major run-time error the only answer is to abort the program.

**close(FILEHANDLE)**

You can read from a file repeatedly until it is closed, although you wouldn't want to read past the last line. If you try to open a file which is already open it will be closed then re-opened for you.

**<FILEHANDLE>**

To read from a file you use the line reading operator: <>. This reads and returns all characters up to and, including the newline. If you don't want the newline character, use chomp to remove it.

Create a simple data file containing:

```
cookies::chocolate::grahams
cookies::fruit jelly::raspberry chewies
cake::chocolate::black forest gateau
cookies::plain::grahams
```

save it as cakes.dat and try the following script. This reads each line from the file, splits out the component substrings and prints them to STDOUT.

```perl
#!/usr/bin/perl -w

$CAKES = "./cakes.dat";
open(CAKES) or
    die("Unable to open file $CAKES\n Program Aborting\n");

print "Cake-a-base\n";
while($line = <CAKES>) {
  chomp $line;
  ($type, $filling, $style) = split(/::/, $line);
  printf("%s\t%s\t%s\n", uc($type), $style, $filling);
}

close CAKES;

exit(0);
```

Hopefully that now makes sense. The line

```perl
while($line = <CAKES>) {
```

reads from the file until it reaches the end of the file. At this point the loop will terminate. When reading from file in this way the data comes out one line at a time. This is extremely useful because it means that processing file data does not require any extra effort on the programmer's part. Altering that program so that it writes its data into a file is very easy:

```perl
#!/usr/bin/perl -w
```

```perl
$CAKES = "./cakes.dat";
open(CAKES) or die("Unable to open source file $CAKES\n
Program Aborting\n");

$NEWCAKES = ">./new.dat";
open(NEWCAKES) or
   die("Unable to open target $NEWCAKES\n Program Aborting\n");

print NEWCAKES "Cake-a-base\n";
while($line = <CAKES>) {
  chomp $line;
  ($type, $filling, $style) = split(/::/, $line);
  printf NEWCAKES ("%s\t%s\t%s\n", uc($type),
      $style, $filling);
}

close CAKES;

exit(0);
```

Writing to a file uses lines of text. In this script I use `printf` to write a formatted string to the file:

```perl
printf NEWCAKES ("%s\t%s\t%s\n", uc($type),
    $style, $filling);
```

When the end of the file is reached the line reader returns an undefined value, equivalent to false, and reading ceases. I use the `close` function in these programs to shut the files after I've finished with them. In Perl, unlike some other languages, you don't always have to *explicitly* close files but it is good practice to do so.

## 8.11 SUBROUTINES

Basic software engineering practice dictates that we don't write monolithic slabs of code. To make code readable, and hence maintainable, frequently used sections are placed in subroutines. If you're working through the book, you'll already have used this idea successfully in JavaScript. In fact, if you've done much programming at all, you'll have used subroutines, although they might have been called methods, operations, procedures, or functions in the language you were using. Subroutines are user-defined pieces of code which get used as if they were functions supplied with Perl, or downloaded as modules or libraries.

`do subroutine([list])`

`use module_name`

`require expression`

These are all ways in which code from another file can be included in the current script. In the chapters on CGI scripting, I'll be demonstrating how to include other code in your scripts. Usually, though, you'll be using subroutines that you've defined and which live in the same file as the calling procedure.

`sub function_name`

Subroutines are declared like this. Simply put `sub` before the function name and enclose its code in brackets.

`&subroutine([list])`

Yet another funny symbol there. This is the way that you call subroutines. The ampersand is used to stop the namespace getting cluttered[12]. Strictly speaking the ampersand is not needed in Perl 5; however, I find that using it makes function calls nice and clear. You optionally pass a list of parameters into the subroutine. The list can, of course, contain just a single item:

```
#! /usr/bin/perl -w

$a_number = 34.5;
$square = &mysquare($a_number);
print "$square\n";

exit(0);

sub mysquare {
    $in = @_[0];
    return $in * $in;
}
```

Perl doesn't require function[13]prototypes so there is no way of knowing in advance (i.e. when interpreting the code) how many parameters a function will get. Each function receives its parameters as an arbitrary list, which is in fact passed as an array. This array of parameters is called `@_` and can be manipulated just like any other array. Therefore parameters are accessible through `@_[0]` etc. (strictly that's `$_[0]` of course), and can be copied into scalars or into other arrays.

`return expression`

This is used to get values back from a subroutine. If you send just a single scalar as a parameter then you can only return a scalar; if you called the subroutine with a list of values then you will be able to get a list back.

---

[12]You'll find that this namespace stuff really stands out. Once you know what's going on it makes the code far more readable.

[13]Or subroutine, or whatever you want to call them.

**local (expression)**

Sometimes you want to temporarily manipulate a global variable before resetting it to its previous value. This is especially useful with arrays and hashes, and Perl provides a scoping mechanism to allow this. Within a subroutine, or any other block structure, you can declare a local version of the variable using the `local` keyword. This local variable can be manipulated in any way that you like but when you leave the block the global will still be there unaltered. Subroutines called from the block will see and be able to use the local version of the variable rather than the global one.

**my (expression)**

If you don't need the danger and power of local variables, or you want to declare a variable which can't be seen by subroutines you modify it using `my`. These private variables are not visible until after they have been declared so you have to take care to declare and initialize them before you use them.

### 8.11.1  Parameters into an Array

Subroutines are fairly straightforward to use once you understand the `@_` array and how you can manipulate it. We have already looked at arrays in some detail, so this next example should be pretty straightforward. What you will notice is that the parameters are passed into an array inside the subroutine. Each parameter becomes a new array item. This is often more useful than passing the parameter values into a set of scalars as the array can be easier to manipulate. The mechanism also lets you pass a *lot* of parameters – try passing twenty parameters and then copying each one into a separate scalar!

The script takes a number of strings as arguments and returns the longest string and its length:

```
#! /usr/bin/perl -w

# find the longest of a set of strings
$fred = "Hello, I'm Fred";
$jack = "Hi!, Jack's the name";
$jill = "I'm Jill, but then you knew that anyway!";
$mary = "Wibble";

@answer = &Longest($fred, $jack, $jill, $mary);
$size = pop(@answer);
$long = pop(@answer);
printf("%s : %s\n", $long, $size);

exit(0);

sub Longest {
```

```perl
  my @param = @_;
  $long = shift(@param);
  $next = "";

  $size = length($long);
  foreach $next (@param) {
    if($size < length($next)) {
      $long = $next;
      $size = length($long);
    }
  }

  push(@it, $long, $size);
  return @it;
}
```

Notice that I call the subroutine with a list and am able to return an array. I use this to get two values back, rather as you might use a structure in C or a small class in C++ to get a set of values back from a function. The Perl implementation looks neat and is easy to use[14].

Once the parameters have arrived at the function, they need to be made available to it. Even if you are only passing a single value it will be passed as an array. Of course that array will only have one item, nonetheless you need to be aware that you're going to be handling arrays of parameters. The parameter array always has the strange name of @_. In the example I copy the values into a local array within the function using:

```perl
my @param = @_;
```

If I had only wanted to use a single parameter value inside the function I might have written something like:

```perl
my $param = $_[0];
```

Which would extract the first item from the parameter array. Remember if you want to use an array as if it were a single entity you need to refer to it with a $ rather than @.

## 8.11.2 Parameters into a Hash

The parameter set can be passed into a hash as well as a scalar and an array. If the data structure which is going to receive the parameters is a hash then Perl takes the parameters in pairs. The first parameter in each pair becomes the key, the second becomes the value.

---

[14] As you use Perl more and more, you'll find lots of these excellent design features. This probably results from its being an evolving language.

It is therefore important if you are going to use this technique that you supply pairs of parameters in the correct order.

```perl
#! /usr/bin/perl -w

$fred = "Hello, I'm Fred";
$jack = "Hi!, Jack's the name";
$jill = "I'm Jill, but then you knew that anyway!";
$mary = "Wibble";

@answer = &HashParam("fred" => $fred,
    "jack" => $jack,
    "jill" => $jill,
    "mary" => $mary);

exit(0);

sub HashParam {
  my %param = @_;
  foreach $key(keys %param){
    printf("%s : %s\n", $key, $param{$key});
  }
}
```

## 8.12  BITS AND PIECES

### 8.12.1  Operators

I've already used and described a few of the operators which Perl provides. Table 8.9 lists the others.

When discussing scalar variables I used this simple script:

```perl
#!/usr/bin/perl -w

$item = "3245.02e4";
$item2 = $item;

$item .= "12";
$item2 = $item2 + "12";

print $item."\n";
print $item2."\n";
exit(0);
```

**Table 8.9**  Logical Operators (text and numerical)

| Op | Meaning | Op | Meaning |
|---|---|---|---|
| > | Numeric greater than | gt | String greater than |
| < | Numeric less than | lt | String less than |
| <= | Less than or equal | le | String less than or equal |
| == | Numeric equals | eq | String equals |
| != | Numeric not equals | ne | String not equals |
| <=> | Numeric comparison | cmp | String comparison |
| && | Logical AND | \|\| | Logical OR |
| = | Assignment | += | Add two values then assign the result to the operand on the left |
| -= | Subtract then assign the result to the operand on the left | *= | Multiply then assign the result to the operand on the left |
| /= | Divide then assign the result to the operand on the left | .= | Concatenate two strings then assign the result to the operand on the left |
| %= | Modulus division then assign the result to the operand on the left | ++ | Autoincrement |
| -- | Autodecrement | ! | Logical not |
| =~ | Apply a pattern matching operation to a string | | |

The numerical operation could have been written more concisely as

```
$item2 += "12";
```

Unless you've used languages such as C, C++ or Java, that's pretty cryptic stuff. It's not as awkward as it appears to be. In fact it's a more efficient way of incrementing and decrementing values. If you haven't seen this sort of thing before, read this explanation carefully; this is an important piece of notation as the same idea is used with many string and regular expression operations.

First the easy case. It is common in programs to want to alter the value of a numeric variable by 1, for instance when iterating through a loop or moving along an array. You could write that change as:

```
$variable = $variable + 1;
$variable = $variable - 1;
```

but that can be time consuming, especially if you use meaningful variable names, which can get quite long. Therefore C and its descendants allow you to use what are called prefix and postfix incrementation and decrementation. To change a variable by 1 write this:

```
$variable++;
$variable--;
```

You'll see these conventions used in a lot of loops. In the `for` loop we write:

```
for($variable = 0; $variable < $enough; $variable++) {
...
}
```

The value of variable is increased by 1 at the end of the loop, just before the closing bracket and is checked against the terminating condition just as the loop restarts. To move along an array we might use[15]:

```
$count = 0;
while($count <= $arraysize) {
    print $array[$count];
    $count++;
}
```

So that's the simpler example. What of `$item += "12"`? Well instead of increasing the value on the left by 1, here we are increasing it by more than 1. In this case `$item` becomes equal to it's current value plus 12. Again, it is quick to type and, once you are used to it this sort of notation is much easier to read when looking at a piece of code. So we use:

```
$variable += $amount;
$variable -= $amount;
```

rather than:

```
$variable = $variable + $amount;
$variable = $variable - $amount;
```

Other operations such as modulus division, multiplication and even string concatenation can work in similar ways. Strings are concatenated using the dot operator:

```
#!/usr/bin/perl -w

$item = "Chris";
$item .= " Bates";
print "$item\n";

exit(0);
```

When using regular expressions, or performing more straightforward pattern matching, the operation has to be applied to a string. The following example shows how the notation is used:

---

[15]Yes, I could combine the increment and the print into one statement. I didn't do that because I wanted the code to be clear.

```
#!/usr/bin/perl -w

$string = "foobar was my Uncle";
print "$string\n";

$string =~ s/foobar/Fred/

print "$string\n";
exit(0);
```

The =~ operator applies the pattern matching operation on its right side to the string value on its left. In the example a string substitution is performed and the value held in the scalar is altered.

### 8.12.2 Comments

Any program that you write, apart from the sort of trivial examples I have used here, needs comments. Comments are useful when you are developing the code and even more so when you come back to maintain it. Start your scripts with some comments which describe what the program should do, who wrote it and when. Also if you're updating the script you need to include a version number so that users know they have the most recent. Each subroutine and any complex loops need comments explaining what you are trying to achieve. Perl can be fairly self-documenting but when you're using regular expressions it can also be pretty cryptic.

In Perl, comments start with the hash symbol # and run to the end of the line. They're easy, so use them!

### 8.12.3 Special Characters

Perl has many special variables which mean something to the interpreter. These are accessible to the programmer but you will probably never need most of them – they provide a shorthand for the gurus. These are the ones that you ought to recognize and be able to use.

$_

the default input, the default pattern-matching space. Perl often assumes that you want to use $_ unless you tell it otherwise. It will be used by:

- functions such as print,
- pattern matching operations such as s///, tr///, or m// if they're called without =~,
- the foreach loop as default iterator.

$0

The name of the script currently being executed

**$ARGV**

> The name of the current file when reading from <ARGV>

**%ENV**

> The hash containing the current environment. We'll be using this when we start writing CGI scripts.

### 8.12.4   Garbage Collection

Some of the commonest mistakes that all programmers make involve memory allocation and deallocation. Languages such as Perl automatically manage memory for the programmer in a process called garbage collection. The mechanism used by Perl involves tracking references to variables: once they are no longer referenced they can safely be removed from memory.

You can create data structures which can never be deleted in this way: some tree structures for instance involve circular links. If you don't understand what I am writing then you probably couldn't create such a structure anyway. If you do know what I mean, take care with your complex data structures.

### 8.12.5   Command-Line Parameters

Perl has various command-line switches. I've already shown you -w: here are some more that you might want to use:

`--`

> Ends switch processing. Any switches which follow this will be ignored.

`-c`

> Checks the syntax of the script and exits without executing it.

`-d`

> Runs the debugger.

`-e`

> Allows you to run scripts from the command line. If you use this switch then Perl won't bother looking for a filename on the command line.

`-I`

> Followed by directories which are to be added to the search path for modules.

`-S`

> Forces Perl to search your PATH environment variable. Can be useful if your operating system doesn't support #!.

`-T`

> Switches on taint checking. This is useful when developing/running CGI scripts. See Chapter 9 for more on this.

-v

Prints the version of the Perl executable you're running.

-w

Prints useful warnings about the syntax of the script.

### 8.12.6  Things I've Left Out

There is much to Perl that I've not covered. I have shown you enough of the language to start writing CGI scripts. These are relatively simple applications; if you want to know more, or all, about Perl buy one of the books listed in the reading list. I have not said anything about:

- references, hard and otherwise,
- nested data structures, hashes of arrays or hashes of hashes or arrays of arrays or arrays of hashes,
- objects, Perl is now an OO language too,[16]
- cooperating with other languages such as C,
- cooperating with shells,
- the standard Perl libraries,
- error messages.

## 8.13  EXERCISES

## Perl

1. List five benefits that Perl can bring if used for solving text-based problems.
2. How does the flexibility of Perl affect the way that programmers attack problems?
3. Briefly outline the advantages and disadvantages of the open-source or free software model of development.
4. If you don't have access to Perl either install it on your own system or ask your site system administrator for help. Look through the documentation that accompanies your distribution. It is especially important that you find out how to use the perldoc utility to read POD documents.
5. Open a command shell and type `perl -v`. What happened?
6. Create a directory for your Perl scripts. Enter and execute a simple version of the classic "Hello World" program.
7. Try using a number of editors and find one that suits the way that you will work with Perl.

---

[16]It's sort-of OO-ish, but not in the way that Smalltalk or Python (for instance) are.

## Basic Perl Exercises

1. Write a script which contains the various types of loop. Print out the loop counter each time that the script iterates.

2. Enter and execute the script from Section 8.7.1 which prompts for user input then displays the input back to the user. Try running the script using the -w flag.

3. Write a loop in which your code leaps out of the loop if a boolean condition is met.

4. Write an if...elsif...else structure which chooses between four alternatives.

## Perl and Data

1. What are the basic data types in Perl?

2. Write a script which accepts different data types at the command line and performs some simple processing on them. Try some basic arithmetic functions and string concatenation to start with.

3. How can a Perl variable act as a string and a number?

4. What is an array?

5. Write a script which accepts inputs from the user, stores all of the strings in an array, and then displays them in reverse order.

6. Create a hash array of the days of the week. Print out the key:value pairs from the start of the array. Try printing individual values by accessing them through their key.

7. Make a list of six uses for each Perl data type.

8. Modify your script from exercise 6, to read out the values from the hash and sort them into ascending alphabetical order.

9. Run the script from Section 8.6. Can you modify your days of the week script to split the syllable day from each value as it is read out?

10. Try this larger problem:

    Create two text files. Each needs to contain a number of lines of data. The first should be a list of unique identifiers (keys), names, and addresses. In the second file put the unique identifiers and information such as favourite food, hair color, shoe size. Separate the fields of each database table with pairs of colons : :.

    Write a pair of loops which read the data from the files into arrays and which display the contents of those arrays. You may choose to place whole lines into each array cell or to use arrays of arrays.

    Read all of the keys and one associated field from each file. You will have to use a pair of hashes for this. Now search the arrays and print out the keys and pairs of values. Do this only where a key occurs in both hashes. For instance:

    from file one the script reads:

    ```
    1 jack
    ```

```
2 mary
3 harry
34 mary2
56 fred
```

from file two the script reads:

```
1 beer
2 icecream
34 butterscotch
```

the script displays:

```
1 jack beer
2 mary icecream
34 mary2 butterscotch
```

## Text Processing

1. List the text handling facilities which Perl provides.

2. Write a script which splits strings apart on predefined characters. This is the type of script that you might use to handle simple flat-file databases.

3. Modify your string splitting script so that it will accept a sentence as input from the user and split it apart into individual words.

4. Now alter your script so that it builds a new string which is made by reversing the order of all of the words in the input string. Use only string splitting and concatenating functions if possible.

5. Enter and run the date creation script from Section 8.8.3. Make sure that you understand how this works.

6. Modify your string manipulating script so that alternate words appear as either all upper-case or all lower-case letters.

7. Using the script in Section 8.8.5 as a starting point write a script which manipulates the printing of numbers and strings through the `printf` function.

8. Try printing a large block of text by using the « operator.

## Pattern Matching

1. The next several exercises all involve manipulating a string through pattern matching. Start off with this first example and once you understand it add in the code for succeeding examples. Don't move on until you understand what the code does *and* how it works.

```
#! /usr/bin/perl -w
$replace = $ARGV[0];
$line = "this is a test test string string";
```

```
      if($line =~ /$replace/) {
         print("$replace was found\n");
      }
      exit(0);
```

2.
```
   if($line =~ m/$replace/) {
      print("$line\n");
   }
```

3.
```
   if($line =~ s/($replace#) \1/$1/g){
      print("$line\n");
   }
```

4.
```
   if($line =~ /\b(\w+?)\s+ \1/mxgi) {
      print "Duplicate word: $1\n";
   }
```

5.
```
   $line =~ s/^([^ ]*) *([^ ]*)/$2 $1/;
   print "$line\n";
   $line = "this is a test";
```

6.
```
   $line =~ s/^([^ ]*) *([^ ] *)/$2 $1/;
   print "$line\n";
   $line = "this is a test";
```

7.
```
   $line =~ s/^([^ ]*) *([^ ])*/$2 $1/;
   print "$line\n";
   $line = "this is a test";
```

8.
```
   print uc($line)."\n";
   $line =~ tr/[a-z]/[A-Z]/;
   print "$line\n";
```

9.
```
   $line = "this is a test";
   $line =~ s/(\w+)/\U$1/g;
   print "$line\n";
```

10.
```
   $line = "this is a test";
   $line =~ s/(\w+)/\u$1/g;
   print "$line\n";
```

11. Try to write a function which finds the first two pairs of matching words in a string.

## File Handling

1. List the differences between a program file and a data file.

2. What is meant by the terms *reading* and *writing* when thinking about file handling?

3. What does *appending* mean?

4. To master file handling, code and run the "cake-a-base" example from this chapter.

5. What is a subroutine?

6. Can you list five reasons for using subroutines in your programs?

7. Can you think why code based around subroutines might be less efficient when the program is running?

8. Run the following simple example, then modify the code to perform some useful function!

```perl
#!/usr/bin/perl -w

print "In the main program\n";
&mySub();
&mySub();
print "In the main program\n";

exit(0);

sub mySub {
    print "\tNow in the subroutine\n";
}
```

9. Next try running the following, more complex, example. Once it works modify the script so that the user can interactively choose which function is run. Can you also modify the script so that the selection of function takes place from the command line?

```perl
#!/usr/bin/perl -w

$value = 32;
print "Value starts as $value\n";
&mySquare($value);
print "Value now $value\n";
$value = &myCube($value);
print "Value finishes as $value\n";
exit(0);

sub mySquare {
    $input = shift(@_);
    $square = $input * $input;
    print "Value of input to subroutine is $input\n";
    print "Value of square is $square\n";
}
```

```
sub myCube {
    $input = shift(@_);
    $cube = ($input * $input) * $input;
    return $cube;
}
```

10. What does the shift function do?

# 9
## CGI Scripting

The Internet has become a network of interactive, distributed applications. Client software based anywhere in the world can access remote data stored on Web servers and can even modify that data. Clearly the majority of Web-based data is not modifiable but when we design and build commercial Web sites we have to allow users to update our databases. That sounds rather worrying: it could be a security nightmare but I am not talking about allowing access to an organization's key data, rather I am simply suggesting that Web surfers must be able to give you information which you may choose to store and later use.

The basic mechanism for getting feedback from users is the HTML form which we looked at in Section 3.3. Having supplied a form through which the user can supply information we must create applications which extract that data and process it. These might simply send an e-mail thanking the browser for their visit or might process credit card details, product orders, and address information, update stock databases, request delivery dates, and return an appropriate confirmation to the browser. Between these two extremes lie a plethora of approaches to making commercial Web sites interactive. In this chapter I will be examining some of the techniques that are used to process information and explaining some of the reasoning that lies behind them. In the accompanying exercises I'll be demonstrating how to apply these ideas. By the end you will be capable of building a primitive site with some form of shopping cart application.

## 9.1 WHAT IS CGI?

CGI is an acronym for the Common Gateway Interface which is a standard protocol for running programs within a Web server. The CGI protocol allows external programs, those you develop, to interface with programs such as database management software and to access the networking facilities provide by the HTTP server software. HTML documents are generally static once created;[1] they don't change while displayed on the browser. CGI programs are dynamic; the state of their variables alters as they execute.

## 9.2 DEVELOPING CGI APPLICATIONS

A CGI script can be developed in any language. The only limitation is provided by the software that your Web server can run. You can write CGI applications in either interpreted or compiled languages so Perl, Basic, Python, Java, C, and C++ would all be good choices. There are security issues related to running compiled programs, and because CGI applications tend to be fairly trivial, large languages such as C++ and Java are often overkill. The general consensus is that interpreted languages provide the best solutions, with Perl and Visual Basic clearly leading the field.

The vast majority of Web servers run on UNIX boxes. Most CGI scripting involves manipulation of text data and many Web masters prefer to use software which is both free[2] and which has wide ranging technical support available on the Internet. Perl is the *de facto* standard CGI scripting language for all of these reasons, and as we saw previously it is also immensely powerful. Perl is continually being developed and enhanced, there are very many freely available modules created by other Perl users which support and ease the development of Web scripts. We shall be looking at a few of these modules later in this section.

Visual Basic is being heavily pushed by Microsoft along with the Active Server Pages (ASP) technology. Both are proprietary products, VB will not run on most servers, and the majority of HTTP server software does not support ASP at the moment. VB is an interface-driven development system, whereas CGI scripts are command-line based, leading to a fundamental conflict between what the product is designed to do and what CGI script developers require.

Having selected a development language you need to choose a method for developing your scripts. The obvious choice is to hack some code, upload it to the Web server, and try to run it. Obvious, but not a good choice: imagine a script with a non-terminating loop. How would you spot that bug when running it remotely? How would you examine any error messages that you might be directing to STDERR? What sort of load would an

---

[1]We've seen how to add dynamics on the client-side through JavaScript applications.
[2]Free in the free-source sense rather than the monetary sense. Take a look at the Free Software Foundation Web site (http://www.fsf.org) for more details.

unfinished script put upon the server? The sensible approach is to develop your scripts on your local PC or workstation, test that they run from the command-line, or a Web server installed on your PC, and only upload them to the server once the logic of the scripts has been debugged. The only areas left for bugs are then interaction with the server: parsing incoming data and returning data. If you've developed sensibly, even these will not be major problems.

In the rest of this chapter I'll introduce a number of routines which can be used to handle many simple CGI tasks. These emphatically don't make a robust library that could be used on production code. For that you ought to look to the `CGI.pm` module. The routines in this chapter can be used to extract simple data returned from the form using GET and create a response. The weakest of the routines is the input parser. The rest provide code which can be used in production systems with just a few tweaks. As you'll see when we look at Perl and Active Server Page applications in Section 13.1, `CGI.pm` can't be used there. It makes sense to have a library of simple page creation routines which you can use in either CGI or ASP, as I do.

## 9.3 PROCESSING CGI

### 9.3.1 Rationale

There are a number of libraries available from the Comprehensive Perl Archive Network, CPAN, sites which help with the problem of parsing input from the user. Whenever possible these should be used. They handle difficult MIME types very effectively. I'll be discussing the most popular of these, `CGI.pm`, in Section 9.5. First, I'll spend some time discussing, and demonstrating, how to parse the response from a browser. Why don't I simply tell you how to use the module? Frankly, if you look around for help, most authorities will tell you to use it. I tend to agree that for *production* code `CGI.pm` is the right way to go. When you're learning though, you can afford to find out *how* things work. Therefore I'm going to start by showing you some code that you can use to build your own, simple, CGI library. Here are a few more reasons:

- there's some good Perl code hiding in here which you will find generally useful,

- if you are going to use a library it is always a good idea to have some understanding of how it does what it does,

- the examples will give you a good feeling for the structure of the data which client software should be returning.

Before looking at some code let's consider what CGI data is, where it comes from and how our scripts are expected to deal with it. When a user submits a Web form, the contents of that form are extracted by the browser and packaged as a message which is returned to a Web server. We saw in Section 3.3 that a form contains the URL of a server and the name of an application on that server. The browser transmits the data to the server. The server must then pass the data to the appropriate application for further processing. So what's a server? Well, in the example of a Web server, it's simply a piece of software executing on a machine which can process requests from Web browsers.

> Note:
> If you want to learn to develop CGI scripts, or ASPs or Java Servlets you'll need access to the appropriate Web server. If you're learning this stuff at work or in education you may already have access to a Web server: ask the system administrator how to use it. If you're learning on your own machine you can download and install a Web server of your own. I'm not going to tell you how to configure or administer your own set-up since the variations between systems are extremely complex. Most come with lots of documentation, and you can buy good quality texts about popular servers such as Apache.

Creating an application from the ground up which can handle data sent from a Web form is a non-trivial piece of programming. It's not difficult once you've seen it done, on the other hand it does require quite a lot of code. I'm going to describe the necessary code over the next few pages before I show you how to use it. The code is split into two logical components:

- something to extract the data which is returned from a Web form,
- and something to create a new page which is sent back to the browser.

You can't simply write a script which handles the first part but doesn't do the second. The CGI protocol expects that you're going to be sending some data back to the browser. If your script doesn't do this then the Web server will do it for you. The Apache server sends back an HTML page which says there has been an *Internal Server Error* due to a misconfiguration of the Web server. It also writes a message into the error log it maintains which on my systems says:

```
[Sat Apr 28 21:12:03 2001] [error] [client 127.0.0.1]
   Premature end of script headers:
   /home/httpd/cgi-bin/sample.cgi
```

That simply means that your script didn't obey the protocol by returning a correctly formatted HTTP message in response to data from a Web form.

So, before I can show you a working script, I'll have to show you the individual components, starting with the function which parses data.

## 9.3.2  Parsing The Data

Data can be sent from a form using either the GET or POST methods. The two methods have to be handled in different ways, but once you've extracted the data from the message you need to store it in a hash for later use. The keys for the hash are going to be the name attributes from the HTML form, the values are going to be the data items which the user entered into the fields of the form. The following function extracts the data and stores it in a hash called %VALS which must be declared elsewhere in a script. You'll see it being used in a while:

```
sub ParseInput {
    $meth = $ENV{REQUEST_METHOD};
    $meth = uc($meth);

    if($meth eq "GET"){
        $in = $ENV{QUERY_STRING};
    } else {
        $length = $ENV{CONTENT_LENGTH};
        read(STDIN, $in, $length);
    }

    @pairs = split(/[&;]/, $in);
    foreach $pair(@pairs) {
        ($key, $val) = split(/=/, $pair);
        $val =~ tr/+/ /;
        $val =~ s/%([a-fA-F0-9][A-Fa-f0-9])/pack("C", hex($1))/eg;
        $VALS{$key} = $val;
    }
}
```

Operating systems keep a table of information about the user and running applications, this table holds a record of the current system *environment*. In Perl this can be accessed through a builtin variable %ENV. When the Web server receives data it stores both the data and information about it in a set of environment variables. Parsing CGI data basically means extracting the data from the environment and formatting it so that it can be used by an application. My parser routine starts by finding out which method was used to send the data:

```
$meth = $ENV{REQUEST_METHOD};
```

and then converting it to uppercase for use in a comparison operation. When data is sent in a GET message, it forms part of the URL. Figure 9.1 shows how this looks. The same HTML form but rewritten to use the POST method is shown in Figure 9.2.

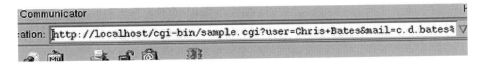

**Figure 9.1** Using GET To Transmit Data

**Figure 9.2**   Using POST To Transmit Data

> Rule:
>
> **Never,** ever use GET for sensitive data. It's OK for page and file addresses but not for customer information. I have heard of major international companies sending customer account information using GET. Anyone with malicious intent can *hack* such systems simply by manually creating URLs which contain other people's data.

Data is extracted from a GET like this:

```
$in = $ENV{QUERY_STRING};
```

which copies the data into a local variable. When a POST has been used, the process is slightly more complicated:

```
$length = $ENV{CONTENT_LENGTH};
read(STDIN, $in, $length);
```

First we need to know how many bytes of data were sent, then we use the read function to extract that data from the standard input, STDIN. Whilst STDIN is usually the keyboard on interactive systems such as desktop PC, on a Web server it is actually the Web server process. The data is sent to our application as a stream of bytes which we simply read in.

`read(FILEHANDLE, SCALAR, LENGTH, [OFFSET])`

attempts to read LENGTH bytes from the file pointed to by FILEHANDLE and place them in SCALAR. If an OFFSET is supplied it will indicate the character position in SCALAR in which the function should start to place characters. This allows you to read into the middle of an existing string. If the value of LENGTH is greater than the size of the file, read will return all characters up to the end of file marker. On error it returns false, the undefined value.

The parsing of input has involved three aspects:

- first decide what type of response you're getting;
- if response is a GET simply parse the input into a suitable hash;
- if the response is a POST check if data is sent in multiple parts. If it is then assemble the parts into a whole;[3] if not, simply process as if a GET.

---

[3]I'm not looking at multi-part and MIME data here. On a production site you should use the libraries that are examined later rather than building your own (probably less successful) versions.

Response data from GET is usually delimited by & which separates key:value pairs, although ; may occasionally be used. I split the input into the @pairs array, each array item contains a key:value pair, with the key and the value separated by =. We now have to extract the actual keys and values from this array.

The pieces are extracted from @pairs using a foreach loop and split into key and value on =. Now we have to manipulate the data that we got from the form. If the user entered a series of items with a space between each word the browser will have converted the spaces into +. Any non-alphanumeric characters entered will have been converted into % followed by their hexadecimal value from the ASCII chart. The + needs converting back into whitespace and the %hex back into the actual character. This is easily done using two pattern matches:

```
$val =~ tr/+/ /;
$val =~ s/%([a-fA-F0-9][A-Fa-f0-9])/pack("C", hex($1))/eg;
```

The first call removes the + signs and writes the result back to $val. The second call may take a little study. Try to work out what it is doing before you read the rest of this explanation.

Obviously it's a split function which will take $val, manipulate it and store the result back in $val. The options mean that the right-hand side is to be evaluated as an expression and that the function is to be applied to every possible instance in the string. The left-hand side selects a character pattern of % followed by exactly two alphanumeric characters. The result of this is taken by the right hand side as $1, converted into its hexadecimal representation, and then packed into an unsigned character. This would, for instance take %40 and output @.

Finally, having put all of the characters correctly into the string, the key:value pairs are written into the global $VALS hash for later use.

## 9.4 RETURNING A BASIC HTML PAGE

Every CGI interaction that you develop will need to send an HTML page back to the user. Even if they have only updated a file, or registered for more information, you have to let them know that the operation was successful, otherwise they may well retry a few times. And, if the operation failed you need to be sure that they'll come back and try again later.

An HTML page has three sections: the header, the body, and a footer which rounds the whole thing off. In addition you have to send an HTTP header which tells the browser how to process the incoming data. I'm going to outline some simple Perl functions which you can use to create Web pages. These functions all create strings which they return to the main script. As you'll see later, the script will print them and the Web server will then redirect that output back to the browser. I could write this code into every script that I create but I prefer to save it in a file called cgiroutines.pl and include it in my code with:

```
require "cgiroutines.pl";
```

## 9.4.1 The HTTP Header

All responses from servers to HTTP requests have to include a line at the top which tells the client what type of data is coming. This takes the form of the `Content-type` variable. The HTTP protocol then requires a completely blank line before any more data. This is achieved by putting the string `\r\n\r\n` at the end of the `Content-type`. Although you *ought* to use two pairs, each made of a carriage return and a newline, all browsers are happy to accept just the newline characters in the form `\n\n`.

It is usually a good idea to follow the `Content-type` with a Document Type Declaration[4] which can be handled by any SGML tool that is accessing your document. The full code for the `Header` function is:

```
sub Header {
    $head = "Content-type: text/html\n\n";
    $head .=
        qq(<! doctype html public "-//w3c//dtd html 3.2//en">);
    return $head;

} # Header
```

## 9.4.2 The HTML Header

The HTML page header should be as complete as possible. There is often a temptation when hard-coding HTML to leave this stuff out, after all it can seem rather superfluous. If we use Perl scripts to create our pages on the fly there can be little justification for the omission. The code only has to be written once and is then re-used often.

The `TopOfPage` function has a single parameter which is used in the `title` element and as an `<h1>` level title on the page. I've included a link to a stylesheet. If you do not want to use one or you already have a stylesheet that you intend to use, change this line to meet your local conditions. Notice that I use the here documentation («) style of printing to return a string.

```
# TopOfPage prints all the stuff that we need at
# the start of an HTML page. Accepts the page title
# as a parameter.
sub TopOfPage {
    local($title) = @_;
    return <<_END;
<html>
```

---

[4]See Section 3.4.1

```
<head>
    <!-- base href="http://localhost/"-->
    <meta name="author"
          content="Chris Bates">

    <meta name="description"
          content="$title - automagically created via CGI">

    <link rel="StyleSheet"
          href="./mainstyle.css"
          type="text/css"
          media="screen">

    <title>$title</title>
</head>
<body>
<h1>$title</h1>\n
_END
```

`} # TopOfPage`

A possible refinement of this script would allow for automatic creation of an expiry date for each page. You would need to include another meta-header of the form:

```
<meta http-equiv="Expires"
      content="Tue, 20 Aug 1996 14:25:27 GMT">
```

Rather than hard-coding the expiry date and time, why not use the `GetTime()` function that I demonstrated in Section 8.8.3 and add, for instance, 30 days onto the date value to get a reasonable expiry time. Here's a clue on how to do that: split the result of the date/time creation function into an array and then play around with the split version in a further function. That way you don't have to alter the code in the original function.

## 9.4.3   The HTML Footer

The HTML document that you're creating needs finishing off nicely. Useful things to include at the bottom of each page might include:

- the date that you served the page so that readers can tell if they're looking at a cached version which may need updating,

- copyright information,

- the name and e-mail address of the Webmaster. If you use a `<mailto>` tag also include your full e-mail address in the text of the page. That way people who make a hard copy of the page will still know how to contact you.

This simple subroutine closes the HTML body and page and uses a call to `GetTime()`. This is useful to timestamp pages so that users know they are accessing a recent page rather than one which expired some time ago and may have been cached somewhere.

```
# Footer prints the stuff that closes the HTML page
sub Footer {
    my $msg = &GetTime();
    return("$msg</body>\n</html>\n");

} # Footer
```

Again you should modify this to suit your personal needs and conditions.

## 9.4.4   The Whole Program

The routines that I have just shown are demonstrated in the following program. First the HTML page:

```
<html>
    <head>
        <title>A CGI Handler</title>
    </head>
    <body>
        <h1>A CGI Handler</h1>

    <form action="http://localhost/cgi-bin/sample.cgi"
            method="POST">

        <table border="0">
          <tr>
            <td>Your Name:</td>
            <td><input type="text"
                        maxlength="32"
                        size="20"
                        name="user"></td>
          </tr>
          <tr>
            <td>Your Email Address:</td>
            <td><input type="text"
                        maxlength="32"
                        size="20"
                        name="mail"></td>
          </tr>
          <tr>
```

```
            <td><input type="submit"
                       value="Submit Details"></td>
            <td><input type="reset"
                       value="Reset The Form"></td>
        </tr>
      </table>

    </form>
  </body>
</html>
```

Now for the CGI script:

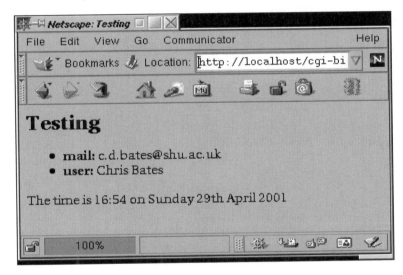

**Figure 9.3**  A Dynamically Created Page

```perl
#!/usr/bin/perl -w

$VALS = "";

&ParseInput();
print &Header;
print &TopOfPage("Testing");

print "<ul>";
foreach $key (keys %VALS) {
    $val = $VALS{$key};
    print("<li><b>$key:</b> $val</li>");
```

```
}
print "</ul>";

print &Footer();

exit(0);

# Place the code for the following routines here:
#     ParseInput
#     Header
#     TopOfPage
#     Footer
#     GetTime
#
# I've omitted the code from the CGI functions
# to save space and reduce repetition.
```

The CGI script has a single global hash variable $VALS which is going to hold the key:value pairs when they are extracted by the ParseInput function. After calling ParseInput, the script prints the strings which my page creating routines return. The body of the page is made by printing the HTML elements and extracting keys and values from the hash and printing those inside the elements. The result is shown in Figure 9.3.

## 9.5 INTRODUCTION TO CGI.PM

CGI.pm is a library of routines that simplify the creation and processing of HTML Web forms. It has two aspects: the processing of data returned from client browsers and the dynamic creation of HTML pages containing Web forms. The ability to easily extract values from returned data and create dynamic forms gives the developer a relatively simple way of maintaining state across the Web. Later in this chapter I'll give examples of how to do just that, one using cookies, others without.

Some of the basic functionality of CGI.pm mirrors the functions that I have just described, although it handles the same processes in an object-oriented rather than a functional manner. My code was included so that you can understand *how* forms are processed; it is not meant to be safe code. Whenever you write a Web application you should use CGI.pm, at least for extracting data from forms. It does this safely and can handle POST, GET, and multi-part MIME data. Mostly you should use CGI.pm because it is safely and securely used by untold thousands of commercial sites around the Web and any problems with it have long since been ironed out.

Copious documentation is supplied with the `CGI.pm` module. If you want to do anything even remotely challenging with the module you must read it. You can get at the documentation by giving the following command at a system prompt:

```
perldoc CGI
```

Method calls in `CGI.pm` are written using the normal referencing notation – the arrow (`->`). Most of the methods can accept a list of parameters, some or all of which may be optional. The parameter passing style is unique. Each parameter name is preceded by a - sign. Parameter values are passed as quoted strings and are separated from the parameter by the `=>` notation that can be used when creating hashes. Here's an example, taken from the `CGI.pm` documentation, of how that might look in practice:

```
#!/usr/bin/perl
use CGI qw/:standard/;

$q = new CGI;
print $q->header,
      $q->start_html('hello world'),
      $q->h1('hello world'),
      $q->end_html;
```

## 9.6 CGI.PM METHODS

`CGI.pm` has a lot of methods. If you want to know how they all work you'll have to read `perldoc CGI`. That is a long document and I don't feel that I need to cover the same ground here. Instead I'll just cover the main points of extracting form data and creating simple pages. In the example that follows I'll show how to use form data to maintain state between interactions without recourse to the dreaded cookie file. And at the end of the chapter I'll show you how to use cookies too.

The main way that `CGI.pm` is used is to safely extract data and keywords returned from a Web form. These values may then be manipulated by any Perl script and can even form the basis of new HTML pages.

### 9.6.1 Creating CGI objects

The basic CGI object is created at the start of a script and contains all of the data and keywords that the form has returned. The following line of code parses the input and stores it in an object:

```
$query = new CGI;
```

Notice that you don't have to tell the program to extract the data. That is done automatically as part of the object creation routine. Sometimes you will want to create an empty

CGI object. This is useful if you are dynamically creating an HTML page whose content is based upon the current state of your script. You might, for instance, want to do this so that you can send customized error pages back to users. To create an empty CGI object:

```
$page = new CGI("");
```

### 9.6.2  Extracting Parameter Names

If your object contains returned data, you need to be able to extract that data so that you can manipulate it. Again CGI.pm makes this *very* simple. The first thing that you must do is extract a list of the parameters from the GET or POST data. The following method call puts all of the parameter names into an array:

```
@parameter_array = $query->param;
```

The parameters are ordered as they were submitted by the user, which may not be the order that you expect. Therefore writing something like

```
$value = $parameter_array[0];
```

may not give you the outcome that you expected.

### 9.6.3  Fetching Parameter Values

Once you have an array of parameter names you can start to extract the values that are associated with those parameters. Again this is easy with CGI.pm. Simply use the parameter name in a method invocation:

```
$name = $parameter_array[0];
$value = $query->param($name);
$value2 = $query->param('date');
```

To set the value of $value the parameters array is accessed and the returned parameter name used for the lookup. This is safer than the previous example simply because having acquired the parameter name it can be checked against expected names and processed properly. The second scalar $value2 is set using a call with an explicit parameter name. Often this is the way that you'll extract values. Most of your CGI scripts will be responding to data from Web pages that you have also designed. Therefore you'll know the names of the parameters that you are getting back and won't need to use the parameter array.

## 9.7  CREATING HTML PAGES DYNAMICALLY

Many of the methods that CGI.pm provides are designed to simplify the creation of forms based upon data values that have been returned by the client. I'll use some in Chapter

10 but I'm not going to discuss them here. You can look them up in the documentation. Instead I'll concentrate on showing how to return a basic HTML page.

The methods described here largely cover the same ground as the code I've already shown. You will have to decide for yourselves whether you'd rather use your own potentially buggy implementations of my routines or use the established `CGI.pm` code.

## 9.7.1 The HTTP Header

Remember that every page needs to send some MIME information to the browser so that it knows how to handle the data. Getting this bit wrong, or missing it altogether, causes the frustrating `incomplete headers` error messages that all CGI developers see so regularly.

To send the standard HTTP header using CGI.pm simply:

```
print $page->header;
```

That prints `Content-type: text/html`. If you want to send a different MIME type, for instance `image/gif` then you should supply it as a parameter:

```
print $query->header('image/gif');
```

## 9.7.2 Starting and Finishing a Page

Anything that you want to place in either the `<head>` section or the `<body>` tag must be passed as a parameter to the `start_html` method. Useful information that you can give here includes the page title, author name, meta information, address of the stylesheet (if any), and basic page formatting information. The basic form of the method call is:

```
print $page->start_html(-parameter1=>'value',
                        -parameter2=>'value');
```

The following parameters are commonly used:

**`title`**
> This sets the title of the document through the `<title>...</title>` attribute.

**`author`**
> This sets the author through the `author` attribute of the document `<head>` section.

**`meta`**
> Used to create meta information. Multiple data items can be passed in the one parameter. Note the use of curly brackets to surround the list of values:
>
> ```
> -meta=>{'keywords'=>'some important words',
>         'expires'=>'expiry date'}
> ```

```
style
```

This identifies an external stylesheet that you want linked into the document.

```
-style=>{-src=>'somepath/somestyle.css'}
```

**other parameters**

If you pass in parameters which `CGI.pm` does not support it will include them in the `<body>` tag. Instances of this might include the use of `bgcolor`or `text` formatting attributes.

Here's some code showing how `start_html` can be used:

```
print $page->start_html{
   -title=>'A Web Page',
   -style=>{-src=>'./main.css'},
   -bgcolor=>'#e3e3e3',
   -text=>'red'};
```

To finish off the page with the `</body></html>` tags use

```
print $page->end_html;
```

## 9.7.3 The Body of the Page

If you want to create non-form pages, then `CGI.pm` isn't going to give much help with the body of your page. Although it has some *HTML shortcuts*, in my view these are actually more complex than writing your own print statements. Look at these two code fragments and decide which you prefer:

```
print a({-href=>'nextpage.html'}, "Next");
```

or

```
print "<a href="nextpage.html">Next</a>\n";
```

I'll briefly describe how to use the shortcuts. For more detail, as ever, read the `perldoc` supplied with the module. To get access to these shortcuts you need to use a special declaration when including the module:

```
use CGI /qw:standard/;
```

Some HTML tags have attributes; most have values. These are provided as parameters to the shortcut. To give a value use:

```
   h1("A Title")
```

and to supply values for attributes:

```
a({-href=>'index.html',
   -target=>'_TOP'
});
```

Notice that the attributes have their standard HTML names and are preceded by a dash. The values are passed in using the syntax that we saw when looking at hashes. Guess how the attribute-value pairs are stored?

Finally, you can pass an array of values to some shortcuts and magical things happen. Imagine that you wanted to create a list of items. Coding something like:

```
li(-type=>'square',
   "first"
);
li(-type=>'square',
   "second"
);
li(-type=>'square',
   "third"
);
```

would be rather tedious. CGI.pm has the capability to distribute values for you:

```
li({-type=>'square', ["first","second","third"]});
```

would give the same set of list items. You'll see some of this in action during the examples later in this chapter. The CGI.pm documentation includes the following example to show how this distribution of values can be used to dynamically create tables:

```
print table({-border=>undef},
caption('When Should You Eat Your Vegetables?'),
   Tr({-align=>CENTER,-valign=>TOP},
      [
      th(['Vegetable', 'Breakfast','Lunch','Dinner']),
      td(['Tomatoes' , 'no', 'yes', 'yes']),
      td(['Broccoli' , 'no', 'no', 'yes']),
      td(['Onions'   , 'yes','yes', 'yes'])
      ]));
```

Well you can also create those arrays of parameters dynamically and pass references to them:

```
#!/usr/bin/perl -Tw

use CGI qw/:standard/;
use CGI::Carp;
use strict;

my $page = new CGI;
my $refval = ['Broccoli' , 'no', 'no', 'yes'];
```

```
print(
    $page->header(),
    $page->start_html("Menu"),
    $page->h1("Menu"),
    print table({-border=>undef},
            caption('Should You Eat Your Vegetables?'),
            Tr({-align=>"CENTER",-valign=>"TOP"},
              [
              th(['Vegetable', 'Breakfast','Lunch','Dinner']),
              td(['Tomatoes' , 'no', 'yes', 'yes']),
              td($refval),
              td(['Onions'    , 'yes','yes', 'yes'])
              ])),
    $page->end_html
);


exit(0);
```

## 9.8   USING CGI.PM – AN EXAMPLE

Some of the greatest benefits that CGI.pm brings include, of course, robustness and also a reduction in the amount of code which developers have to craft for themselves. To show the module in action I'm going to rewrite the CGI script that I showed you in Section 9.4.4. The HTML page remains the same, I'm not going to reproduce it here. Here's the new CGI script:

```
#!/usr/bin/perl -Tw

use CGI qw/:standard/;
use CGI::Carp(fatalsToBrowser);
use strict;

my $data = new CGI;
my @params = $data->param;
my $k = "";

print($data->header,
      $data->start_html("Using CGI.pm"));

# the body of the page starts here
print "<h1>Using CGI.pm</h1>";
```

```
print "<ul>\n";

foreach $k (@params) {
    print "<li>";
    print "<b>$k</b>: ";
    print $data->param($k);
    print "</li>\n";
}

print "</ul>";
# that's the body of the page finished

print ($data->end_html);
exit(0);
```

That script is somewhat shorter than the full text of the earlier example. Mostly, of course, because I didn't have to write lots of library code. It uses all of the techniques that you've seen in this chapter. It isn't, though, the fastest code you'll ever see. Rather than perform nine calls to the `print` function, those *could* be optimised so that the page is dumped out as one or two much larger prints. That'll certainly give a performance increase since input and output are some of the commonest bottlenecks in all types of program.

## 9.9  ADDING ROBUSTNESS

In Chapter 8.3 I said that you should develop your Perl scripts using the -w flag. That prints out some moderately useful warnings from the compiler which will help you to narrow down problems in your code. Using -w is only the first step that you can take in the process of creating good Perl scripts. In this book I'm not going to describe how to use the Perl debugger – if you want information on that try looking in the documentation that came with your Perl installation.[5] I am, however, going to give you some guidance through a few topics that will help. Most errors that you'll make writing CGI scripts can be trapped, analyzed, and repaired fairly easily and you'll probably only invoke the debugger on a few occasions.

Writing safe scripts has two aspects: first ensuring that your code is correct, and does what you expect; second ensuring that the data you are handling is not likely to corrupt or damage your system. I'll deal with the data first.

---

[5]`perldoc perldebug` on UNIX, somewhere in the HTML documents if you're using the ActiveState port to Microsoft Windows.

### 9.9.1   Taint Checking

Any CGI script that processes information from users is a security risk. The biggest risk with such scripts is that unchecked variables supplied by the user can be passed directly to the operating system shell. Perl has a mechanism called taint checking which forbids such dangerous practices. Variables which are set using data from outside the script are tainted and cannot be used to set values outside your script.

If such care is not taken the taint can spread. Your tainted variable might be sent to the shell which opens a pipe to a shell command and passes your variable through. Now three different programs have been affected by an insecure value. When you use taint checking in Perl the script will fail, the Perl interpreter exiting, if you try to pass variables along like this. To use taint checking you change the shebang line on UNIX systems to:

```
#! /usr/bin/perl -Tw
```

On NT systems, run all of your CGI scripts with the -T flag as well as -w. Having set taint checking you may find that your scripts die when they try to use external programs even if values are not being passed into them. If you get an error message like:

```
Insecure $ENV{$PATH} at line xx
```

you need to actually set a path at the top of the script. Using something like the following code at the top of your script avoids this problem:

```
$ENV{'PATH'} = '/bin:/usr/local/bin:/usr/bin';
```

but don't include the current directory . in this path. Once you've tainted a variable you cannot use it in system(), exec(), open(), or eval() or any function that affects external data through other programs. If you absolutely must use such a variable then you should first perform a pattern match on it to extract the substrings and rebuild the string. The importance of this is that during the extraction process you will be checking that you have received valid data.

The following subroutine is used to examine each data item and check that it contains only word characters, digits, dots, forward slashes, and ampersands.

```
sub Untaint {
    # untaint the input
    # if it cannot be untainted the program will abort
    $val = lc($_[0]); # function returns lower-case only

    if($val =~ /(([&0-9a-z.@\/]+)/) {
        $val = $1;
    }
    else {
        &Death("$_[1]", "Program aborting: Tainted Data");
```

```
    }
    return $val;
} # Untaint
```

The Death subroutine returns an error message to the client and writes it into the system error log using die. Notice that Death uses functionality from CGI.pm and, for improved readability in the error log, should also be used with CGI::Carp.

```
sub Death {
    # prints an error back to the user if the script dies
    # e.g when opening a file
    $script = $_[0];
    $msg = $_[1];

    $return = new CGI("");
    print $return->header();
    print $return->start_html(-title=>"Fatal Runtime Error");
    print <<_DONE;
        The script <em>$script</em> returned the following
        error message:
        <p><strong>$msg</strong>.
        <p>Please report this error to <a href="mailto:
        yourid@yourserver">yourid@yourserver</a></p>
        <hr>
_DONE

    print $return->footer();
    die("Fatal Error: $msg");

} # Death
```

## 9.9.2  Strict

Like most programming languages Perl supports the use of compiler directives. These are additional commands placed in the code which are used by the compiler rather than processed by it. The most useful of these for the CGI script developer is:

```
    use strict;
```

This makes the compiler print an error every time that it encounters a potentially unsafe construct in your code. The benefit of this for the CGI author is that to avoid these errors you must properly scope all of your subroutines and variables. Typically this is done by making them all local to a package through the use of the my keyword. Some variables and references cannot be made safe so simply. Filehandles present a particular difficulty and

must be *quoted* if you want your scripts to execute. The following code shows how to use
strict in a simple script that reads data from a file and returns it inside an HTML page:

```perl
#!/usr/bin/perl -Tw

# packages to be imported
use CGI qw/:standard/;
use strict;
use CGI::Carp;

# first quote the filehandle
# to reduce the warnings from strict
use vars qw($GBOOK);

# next declare the local variables
my ($name, $mail, $words, $line, $msg);
my $msg = new CGI("");

# finally the code starts here
# ---------------------------

$GBOOK = "./guestbook.dat";
open(GBOOK) or die("Unable to open guestbook.dat");

print $msg->header;
print $msg->start_of_html(-title=>''Guestbook'');

print <<EOT;
<p>The guestbook for this site is shown below
<hr>
<dl>
EOT

while($line = <GBOOK>){
    chomp $line;
    ($name, $mail, $words) = split(/::/, $line);
    print<<DONE;
    <dt>$name [$mail]</dt>
    <dd>$words</dd>
    <br><br><br>
DONE
}
```

```
print "</dl>";
print $msg->end_html;
exit(0);
```

Using `strict` and `-Tw` might seem like a lot of effort. Actually it *is* a lot of effort in many ways, yet it's worth doing if it reduces the number of errors that your scripts write to the server logs and increases the safety of your applications and data. For an explanation of `qw/:standard/` see Section 9.7.3.

## 9.10 EXERCISES

1. If possible start by installing a Web server on your local PC. This can be accessed from address 127.0.0.1. Configure the server to correctly run CGI scripts written in Perl.

2. Write a script which returns an empty HTML page. Test this first from the command-line, then by accessing it with a browser via its URL, ensure that it runs from a Web server.

3. Modify `ParseInput()` so that it handles both GET and POST methods.

4. Modify the `ParseInput()` routine to meet your needs. Test its ability to handle data by writing a simple guestbook application.

5. Test your guestbook by having the script write parsed data to a file. Write a second application which reads the guestbook data back from file and displays it formatted in an HTML page.

### The CGI module

1. List six benefits of using a library such as `CGI.pm` rather than writing your own code.

2. Use `CGI.pm` to write a script which returns an empty HTML page.

3. Modify your guestbook applications so that they use `CGI.pm`.

### CGI Scripting

1. Create a simple Web database application using `CGI.pm`. Use the database to hold details of your CD and MP3 collections.

2. Test your applications from the command line. Is this a useful way of testing and debugging scripts?

# 10
## *Some CGI Examples*

The theory behind CGI scripting in Perl is all very well. That information is useful if you know *what* you want to do. So often, though, designers have a goal in sight but little idea of how to achieve it. Program design and development is a process by which we reach those remote goals, hopefully using ideas and techniques which we know will work. In this chapter I'm going to show you examples of a few different types of processing that you might want to perform on your Web site. These aren't comprehensive solutions, instead they're intended to give you a feel for what you can achieve with Perl.

## 10.1 UPLOADING FILES

I'll start with a process which you might find on people's individual homepages or on corporate Intranets: the file upload. Most Web sites are *read only* for visitors. Authors take the view that the site is their work and they don't want it altered by random passing surfers. There are sites which take a different view and which are meant to be altered by readers. The most famous of these is probably `WikiWikiWeb` which can be found at `http://www.c2.com`. Many applications require a third type of site which, whilst it cannot be altered by readers, does allow them to add their own material.

Consider, for instance, an on-line photo album. You'll see these all over the Web. People place scanned copies of their photos, or more commonly today digital photos onto their homesite so that friends and family can view them. This is really a very good idea but pretty time-consuming. It's also a one-way street: imagine that Auntie Mabel has some snaps of her holiday in the Caribbean to share and she wants to use your Web site to do it. How will she get the photos to you? Well she could send you a CD-ROM with the photos stored on it and a letter which lists all the captions she wants. She could email that same information to you, although the email would be prohibitively large, or she could place all the pictures on an FTP server so that you can download them. Whichever approach she takes is going to involve you in a lot of work. You'll have to write the Web pages, copy all the files to their end location and deal with the inevitable changes which Auntie Mabel will require.

If the family photo album is a lot of hassle, what about the corporate Intranet? Here you've got the same problem magnified ten-fold. Your users are creating reports and memos all day which others on the system *may* need to read. You want to archive all of this material so that it can be used in, for instance, later audit trails. If users simply email their memos to everyone, that quickly becomes irritating and after a while people stop reading the messages. Why not place all of the memos, reports etc. on an Intranet site so that co-workers can access them when they *need* to? Great idea, but potential implementation nightmare. How do the documents get onto the site? Your organisation could employ someone to perform the uploads and maintain the site, you could buy a proprietary Intranet system such as FirstClass or Lotus Notes, or you could create upload pages on an internal Web site.

Building a full application based around a file upload page can be a very complicated process. For either of the applications I've just described, you'll need to enforce access controls, restrict who is allowed to upload files, create a usable directory structure then index that, and finally use some sort of templating system to create the pages. You need:

- a form in which details of files are entered,
- a script to perform the upload and save the file,
- a database to hold the files and index them,
- page templates created using the `HTML::Mason` module.

## 10.1.1 The HTML Page

OK, that's enough advertising, let's look at some code. I'm going to show you how to write an HTML page which includes all of the fields you'll need to upload files, and then a simple script which processes the data it gets from the browser. First the HTML page and the form:

```
<html>
<head>
   <title>File Uploader</title>
</head>
<body>
   <h1>File Uploader</h1>

<form method="post"
      enctype="multipart/form-data"
      action="../cgi-bin/upload.cgi">

   <table border="0" align="center">
      <tr>
        <th>Enter A File Name: </th>
        <td>
           <input type="file"
                  name="original"
                  value="starting"
                  size="40"
                  maxlength="120">
        </td>
      <tr>
        <th>What Shall I Call The Saved Version?</th>
        <td>
           <input type="text"
                  name="newname"
                  length="40"
                  maxlength="120">
        </td>
      </tr>
      <tr>
          <td><input type="submit" value="Submit File"></td>
          <td><input type="reset" value="Reset Form"></td>
      </tr>
   </table>
   </form>
```

```
</body>
</html>
```

The HTML page has two new additions which you've not seen before. Firstly I'm using a new attribute in the `form` tag:

```
<form method="post"
      enctype="multipart/form-data"
      action="../cgi-bin/upload.cgi">
```

We've got no way of knowing how large the files are which users will try to upload. A maximum file size could be enforced with a client side scripting language such as JavaScript or Visual Basic, although those types of solution tend only to work on Windows based machines since they require access to operating system facilities. Instead we'll let users send us as much data as they want to, the problem of sorting out how much to save is then left to the CGI script. Since files tend to be at least 1K bytes, the browser must use the `post` method to send data. The new attribute here is `enctype` which identifies the way in which the form will submit its data. In this case I'm gong to send form data in multiple pieces.

Now we need a way for the user to tell us what file they're going to send. This is done using a Netscape 2 file input field. This is a combined field which has a text box in which a file name can be typed, and a button which can be used to open file dialog to search for the file. This type of input is not standard HTML and may not be available in all browsers, although it works in all of those which I have used. Here's the code:

```
<input type="file"
       name="original"
       value="starting"
       size="40"
       maxlength="120">
```

When the file gets to the server it'll need a new name. The name which accompanies it from the file box will be the complete operating system-dependent name. This will have no meaning on your server so you'll need to save the data in a file with a different name. In the example, I get this information from another `text` box:

```
<input type="text"
       name="newname"
       length="40"
       maxlength="120">
```

## 10.1.2 The CGI Script

When I came to write a script to process uploaded data files, I realized that there are many possible ways of handling this. You might want to save the data in a file, add it to a database or alter it before returning it to the browser. Data files may be plain text or one of hundreds of binary formats. They may be data or applications or images or… You get the picture. This is a complex area, much of the processing is application dependent. I've chosen to simplify the entire thing so that you can see the basic principles in action.

This CGI script reads in the data, saves it into a file on the server and copies the whole thing back to the browser inside an HTML page. If you read `perldoc perlfunc` and `perldoc perlopentut`, you'll find more information about opening files than you can probably imagine ever needing. They'll tell you how to safely handle binary data of all types.

As ever, read the script first, then I'll explain it:

```perl
#!/usr/bin/perl -w

use CGI qw/:standard/;
use CGI::Carp(fatalsToBrowser);

$in = new CGI();
$INPUT = $in->param('original');
$outtie = $in->param('newname');
$OUTPUT = ">./$outtie";

open (OUTPUT) || die "Unable to open file for writing";

print $in->header();
print $in->start_html("Thank You");
print "<h2>Thank You For Sending $INPUT</h2>";

while($line = <$INPUT>) {
    print $line; # display contents back in browser
    print OUTPUT $line; # save in a file
}

close OUTPUT;
print $in->end_html();
exit(0);
```

On the whole that's a pretty standard CGI script which uses the CGI.pm module. I start by creating a CGI object and extracting the parameter values from it. The value sent from the file input field is the *name* of the source file rather than the file itself. I then prepare the output file to be opened for writing:

```perl
$in = new CGI();
$INPUT = $in->param('original');
$outtie = $in->param('newname');
$OUTPUT = ">./$outtie";
```

If I can't open the file, the script dies:

```
open (OUTPUT) || die "Unable to open file for writing";
```

at which point an error will be logged and sent to the browser. If you're running this script on a UNIX server, you'll need to set the permissions correctly so that it can write data to files.

Once the file is open I start to send an HTML page back, using some of the function provided by CGI.pm. The script loops through the incoming data, saving it into a new file and echoing it back:

```
while($line = <$INPUT>) {
    print $line; # display contents back in browser
    print OUTPUT $line; # save in a file
}
```

That's all there is to performing file uploads. You can add plenty of refinement to the script to make it more robust, but the actual upload procedure never gets any more complex than this.

## 10.2 TRACKING USERS WITH COOKIES

The ActiveState version of Perl provides two different modules for cookie creation. If you are developing on a non-Microsoft operating system you can install both of these from CPAN. You can also get updated Windows versions from ActiveState using PPM. The modules are CGI.pm and Cookie.pm, and both are written by Lincoln Stein. Because I've been using CGI.pm throughout this book, and because I am trying to introduce you to some of its key facilities, I'll use it here. The Cookie.pm module comes with full documentation and works in the same way. That's good because it means that you're getting some transferable skills here.

You will be familiar with the format of the CGI.pm methods if you've read Chapter 9. It works just like the commands for creating standard HTML elements but this time the data goes into the HTTP header rather than into the actual HTML document.

### 10.2.1 Creating a Cookie

Creating a cookie is easy. The simplest way is to make a cookie object and then to pass this into the routine which creates the HTML page header. Here's an example which I'll explain in a moment:

```
#!/usr/bin/perl -Tw

use strict;
use CGI qw/:standard/;
```

```
use CGI::Carp(fatalsToBrowser);

my %txtValues = ('Visit'=>'1');
my $this_cookie = cookie(-name=>'ChrisCookie',
        -value=>\%txtValues,
        -path=>'/',
        -expire=>'+2h');

print header(-cookie=>$this_cookie);
print start_html('Creating A Cookie');
print h1('Creating A Cookie');
print end_html;

exit(0);
```

The expiry time can be set to an explicit date and time or to a relative time. In the example shown above the cookie will expire two hours after it was first set. If you leave the expiry time unset then the cookie will be deleted by the browser when it is closed down.

Each cookie can hold a set of values: you don't have to use one cookie per value. If you *did* then building many e-commerce applications such as shopping carts would be almost impossible. Using CGI.pm the values are saved in a hash using a unique name for each as the key and the text string as the value. These are written to the cookie.txt file in a single long string with items separated by ampersands:

```
name&Chris&ordernum&123&itemnum&34
```

The hash is then added to the cookie using the reference notation. Simply place a back-slash in front of the hash identifier and the module will handle the extraction and manipulation of the individual items.

Once a cookie has been created it can be amended by writing another cookie with the same name which contains different values. The new values overwrite the existing ones.

## 10.2.2 Reading a Cookie

If you are using cookies in e-commerce you will need to read the cookie back from the browser each time that the user makes some new selections. How do you get the cookie back? Again using CGI.pm this is very easy. Here's the code to read back a cookie and display all key:value pairs from the original values hash:

```
#!/usr/bin/perl -Tw

use CGI qw/:standard/;
use CGI::Carp(fatalsToBrowser);
use strict;
```

```perl
my %data = cookie('ChrisCookie');

print header;
print start_html('Reading Back A Cookie');
print h1('Reading Back A Cookie');

my @keys = keys %data;
my @values = values %data;

while(@keys){
    print("<p>");
    print(pop(@keys), " = ", pop(@values), "\n");
    print("</p>");
}

print end_html;

exit(0);
```

The cookie is read back by sending a request to the browser using just the name of the cookie. The returned data is then separated by the module into key:value pairs and stored in the hash:

```perl
my %data = cookie('ChrisCookie');
```

Do not expect intelligent processing from CGI.pm here. The first item is assumed to be a key, the second a value, and so on for the entire set of data. If you set the cookie using data in some other form then you'll get rubbish back at this stage. This is especially important where cookies were set using some mechanism other than CGI.pm. If any tidying up is needed then you'll have to do it once the data has been extracted into the hash.

In the example, I have written a trivial loop which extracts the keys and values into a pair of arrays. It then pops values off each array in turn until they are both empty and displays those values inside the HTML page:

```perl
my @keys = keys %data;
my @values = values %data;

while(@keys){
    print("<p>");
    print(pop(@keys), " = ", pop(@values), "\n");
    print("</p>");
}
```

which also shows you a different way of handling Perl hashes.

*10.2.2.1  **Deleting a Cookie***  To delete a cookie you need to rewrite it with a date/time string that was sometime in the past. The easiest way of doing this is to send an expiry time of `-1h`:

```perl
#!/usr/bin/perl -Tw

use strict;
use CGI qw/:standard/;
use CGI::Carp(fatalsToBrowser);

my %txtValues = ('Visit'=>'1');
my $this_cookie = cookie(-name=>'ChrisCookie',
        -value=>\%txtValues,
        -path=>'/',
        -expire=>'-1h');

print header(-cookie=>$this_cookie);
print start_html('Deleting A Cookie');
print h1('Deleting A Cookie');
print end_html;

exit(0);
```

## 10.3  TRACKING USERS WITH HIDDEN DATA

HTTP is a *stateless* protocol. When you go to a Web site, you request a page, the server sends it right back, or sends an appropriate error code if it can't. The server then forgets all about you. When you use a conventional desktop application, say a database input form, across a network, you log-on to a server. The server remembers you and is able to track and log all your actions until you log off. The database application contains some notion of a session simply because users will be interacting with it for a significant length of time. Interactions on the Web may only last for a single download. How can your CGI applications track users if the server doesn't provide any facilities? You might use cookies but some users don't like them. Instead try placing information about users inside the pages you send to them and the requests which they send back to you. That's exactly what I'm going to show you how to do in this section.

I've created a simple Web page containing an HTML form. It's basically a guestbook type application which returns a number of data items to the server. The CGI script processes the data and creates a new Web page with another form. Embedded in *that* form is some of the information returned the first time around.

Let's consider some uses for this idea. First, if you *have* used a cookie file on your site, you probably read it when a visitor first arrives. You then want to track that visitor through the site. This is most easily achieved by using a hidden value, possibly as the only item in a non-displaying form. To make the idea work you need to create every page dynamically and place the hidden value in each page. That's not difficult: in fact many large commercial sites do just such processing. However, it may put an unacceptable overhead on your server.

A second, similar, use might be to track registered users after they log on to the site. Sometimes cookie files are used so that repeat visitors don't have to log on; many sites make each visitor go through the logging on procedure then track them with hidden values taken from the log-on form.

Thirdly, many users who are worried about privacy, turn cookies off in their browser. The only way that you can track these people through your site is by hiding data inside the pages which you send to them. I'll extend this idea in Section 10.5 when I discuss the notion of a *session*, and how access can be restricted by ID and time.

> Note:
> If you do this, be careful about which values you choose to hide in subsequent pages: anyone can access the source code of a page from disk cache and you don't really want to be giving users e-mail addresses or site passwords!

## 10.3.1   The Initial HTML Page

```html
<html>
   <head>
      <title>The Initial Form</title>
   </head>
   <body>
      <form action="./test3.cgi" method="post">
         <p>Enter Your Name Here
         <input type="text" name="visitor" value="name"
                size="48" max length="48">
         <p>Enter Your Email Address Here (optional)
         <input type="text" name="email" size="48"
                maxlength="48" value="email">
         <p>Enter Your Comments Here
         <textarea name="msg" rows="20" cols="40"></textarea>
         <input type="submit" value="Submit The Form">
         <input type="reset" value="Clear The Form">
      </form>
```

```
        </body>
</html>
```

## 10.3.2  The CGI Script

The script doesn't have to do anything fancy here. I'm just going to create an HTML page which includes a form. On that form I've got a hidden field which has the value entered into the name field of the original form:

```perl
#!/usr/bin/perl -wT

# packages to be imported
use CGI qw/:standard/;
use strict;
use CGI::Carp(fatalsToBrowser);

# first quote the filehandle
use vars qw($GBOOK);

my $msg = new CGI;
my $name = $msg->param('visitor');
my $mail = $msg->param('email');
my $words = $msg->param('msg');

print $msg->header;
print $msg->start_html(-title=>"Maintain State With CGI.pm");

print<<EOT;
<h1>Maintaining State Through CGI.pm</h1>
<p>You Entered the following values in the form...
<table align=center border=1>
   <tr>
      <td>Name</td><td>$name</td>
   </tr>
   <tr>
      <td>Email Address</td><td>$mail</td>
   </tr>
   <tr>
      <td>Comments</td><td>$words</td>
   </tr>
 </table>
```

```
<h2>Next...</h2>
<p>Now select an item from the following list...
EOT

print $msg->start_form(-action=>'./proc.cgi');
print $msg->hidden(-name=>'user', -default=>$name);
print $msg->popup_menu('next', ['apples', 'oranges',
                                'pears', 'lemons']);
print $msg->end_form;

print $msg->end_html;
exit(0);
```

The hidden field doesn't display in the browser. If the user looks at the page source (Alt-U in Netscape), they'll be able to see this hidden field. It's not encrypted or treated in any fancy way, it simply doesn't get displayed. When this second form is submitted, the value in the hidden field comes right back with it. The second script is able to relate the two sets of input right back to the same user.

## 10.4  USING DATA FILES

The examples that I've demonstrated so far don't add much flexibility to your HTML development. You could do almost all of the things that I've shown without all of this effort. The problem with developing your site around CGI scripts is that you will end up using a lot of processing power to serve each page and yet the pay-offs are obvious. If you use any major Web sites such as search engines, on-line newspapers, or commercial sites such as Amazon.com, you'll spot a lot of pages that are created using CGI scripts.

The main use of automatically created pages comes when someone searches your database. You can create pages which return useful error messages which include the unsuccessful search string. Pages will often return search results formatted for easy use. Many sites return a series of pages, each of which contains a subset of the successful results to reduce download times.

In the following example I slightly modify the code from Section 9.4. This time I pass a string as a parameter which will be searched for in the database file shown below the code. I add a new subroutine which searches the database for the string that the user entered and either returns a table containing the data if found, or an error message.

The routines that were shown in Section 9.3 are stored in a file called common.pl and are used in this script.

```
require "./common.pl";
```

```perl
$search = @ARGV[0]; # pass the search string
                    # in as a parameter

# print to temporary file for debugging
$TARGET = ">./temp.html";
open(TARGET) || die("Unable to open output $TARGET\n
                    Program Aborting\n");

$SOURCE = "./page.dat"; # accept filename parameter
open(SOURCE) || die("Unable to open output $SOURCE\n
                    Program Aborting \n");

my $page = "";
my $title = "Building Simple HTML Pages";

# MIME type first - not needed when debugging
#   $page.= &Header; # only if run as a CGI script
$page .= &TopOfPage($title);
$page .= &SearchDB($search);
$page .= &Footer;
print TARGET $page;
exit(0);

sub BuildErrorPage {
  my $body = "";

  $body .= &Header;
  $body .= &TopOfPage("Script Error");
  $msg = ""
<p>The script was unable to complete your
request.
<p>IF you want further information please email
the Webmaster.";
  $body .= $msg;
  $body .= &Footer;

  return $body;

} # BuildErrorPage
```

```perl
sub SearchDB {
  $result = "";
  $found = 0;

  $DB = "./cakes.dat";
  open(DB) || die("Unable to open database file
                  $DB\nProgram Aborting\n");

  SEARCH:while($line = <DB>) {
    chomp $line;
    ($type, $filling, $style) =
                  split(/::/, $line);
    if( ($type = $search) || ($filling = $search)
                          || ($style = $search)){
      $found = 1;
      last SEARCH;
    }
  } # while

  if($found == 1) {
# have found the search string so return it
    return <<EOT;
<table border=2 cellpadding=3>
  <tr>
    <th>Type of Cake</th><th>Filling</th>
                        <th>Details</th>
  </tr>
  <tr>
    <td>$type</td><td>$filling</td>
                  <td>$style</td>
  </tr>
</table>
EOT

  } # if $found
  else {
    $result .= &BuildErrorPage();
    return $result;
  }
```

```
} # SearchDB
```

The database file used for the searches:

```
cookies::chocolate::grahams
cookies::fruit::raspberry chewies
cake::chocolate::black forest gateau
cookies::plain::grahams
```

Clearly the simple search routine can be modified to find every instance of a search pattern. This simple example stops once it finds a matching line. Try this for yourself. Hint: use arrays to hold the values as you find them.

## 10.5   RESTRICTING ACCESS WITH SESSION IDS

If you want to restrict access to your Web pages you have a limited range of options. If you want to track a user as they move through your pages, as you would with a shopping cart application, you are similarly restricted. The difficulty is that HTTP is a stateless protocol: when a Web surfer carries out an action there is no memory of previous actions that they have performed. If you want your applications to remember state information you have to build the code to do that.

Of course, you could use cookies to track users and to limit their access. That's not always possible, and of course it won't work when users have cookies switched off. There was a time when many users were becoming quite militant about the use of cookies, that attitude is less prevalent today. Even so, how many sales do you want to lose simply because your site is totally reliant on one approach?

The example that I am going to show here gives each person a unique ID tag each time that they visit the main page of the site. Every URL that they access includes the session ID which is checked by a Perl script. If they don't have a session ID they can't view the pages but instead receive an error message. The ID is made from a randomly generated text string and a timestamp. As a refinement, the timestamp could be separated off and used to limit the amount of time which users can spend at your site.

More complex applications can use the same techniques. To run a shopping cart you might create a temporary file, with its name based on the session ID, and as the customer orders items you write the order details into the temporary file. This gives a good record of orders which can later be copied into your main databases. If you have only a few users for your site you could give them each a session ID and log-on code, when they log on, their ID is validated. If they don't have a valid session ID then they have no access to any of your pages. What we want to do is to alter each URL from the first form shown below to the second:

```
<a href="../studlist.html">Student List</a>
```

```
<a href="./security.cgi?file=../studlist.html
        &session=35853c93120dd85d">Student List</a>
```

The simple application here has five stages:

- the user accesses the main page and is given a unique ID,
- every URL in every page has the ID appended,
- the session IDs are held in a file on the server,
- as each GET request arrives at the server the session ID is validated,
- if the user accesses the log-off page, their session ID is deleted from the file.

### 10.5.1   The Log-On Page

The first page of the site is a very simple piece of HTML. This page is required simply so that users will get sent to the CGI script which creates the ID:

```
<html>
    <head>
      <title>Welcome</title>
    </head>
    <body>
      <h1>Enter The Site Here</h1>
      <p>Click <a href="../cgi-bin/logon2.cgi">Here</a>
        To Enter</p>
    </body>
</html>
```

### 10.5.2   Creating a Session ID

A session ID has to be unique and remain so for as long as it is valid. You have to make sure that it will not be accidentally duplicated as to do so removes the limited security value that they have. Because of this you can't use a standard random number generator: these have to be seeded and if you get the seed wrong your random ID generator will produce a sequence in which every item is the same.

```
#!/usr/bin/perl -w

use CGI qw/:standard/;
use CGI::Carp(fatalsToBrowser);

$SESHID = ">>sessions.dat";
$in = new CGI;
$ID = &MakeID();
$stamp = &MakeStamp();
```

```
$ID .= ":$stamp";
&SaveID();

print $in->header(-expires=>'+2h');
print $in->start_html("Index Page");

print &MakePage();

print $in->end_html();
exit(0);


sub MakeID {
    # Seed the random generator
    srand($$|time);
    $session = int(rand(60000));

    # pack the time, process id, and random $session
    # into a hex number which will make up session id.
    $session = unpack("H*", pack("Nnn", time, $$, $session));
    return $session;

} # MakeID


sub MakeStamp {
    $yday = (localtime)[7];
    $hour = (localtime)[2];
    $stamp = "$yday.$hour";
    return $stamp;

} # MakeStamp


sub SaveID {
    flock(SESHID, 2);
    open (SESHID) || die "Unable to save session details";
    printf SESHID ("%s\n", $ID);
    close(SESHID);
    flock(SESHID, 8);
```

```
} # SaveID


sub MakePage {
    return <<EOD;
<h1>Bill Smiggins Inc.</h1>
<h3>Links</h3>

<ul>
  <li>
     <a href="validate.cgi?page=products.html&id=$ID">
        Products</a>
  </li>
  <li>
     <a href="validate.cgi?page=services.html&id=$ID">
        Services</a>
  </li>
  <li>
     <a href="validate.cgi?page=contact.html&id=$ID">
        Contacts</a>
  </li>
  <li>
     <a href="validate.cgi?page=ordering.html&id=$ID">
        Ordering</a>
  </li>
  <li>
     <a href="logoff.cgi?id=$ID">Log Off</a>
  </li>
</ul>
EOD

} # MakePage
```

The code for the *MakeID* function is adapted from an example given in *Instant Web Scripts* by Sol and Birzniecks, an outdated book which concentrates on version 4 of Perl.

```
sub MakeID {
    # Seed the random generator
    srand($$|time);
    $session = int(rand(60000));

    # pack the time, process id, and random $session
    # into a hex number which will make up session id.
```

```
    $session = unpack("H*", pack("Nnn", time, $$, $session));
    return $session;
```

```
} # MakeID
```

The first line of the function seeds the inbuilt Perl random number generator using the process ID bitwise ORed with the current time. Both the process ID and time are unique for any given session within a particular shell. This seed could not be guessed at by someone trying to hack your system. It is important that you only set the seed once in any interaction: I use this MakeID function only once with any given process ID.

A random integer between 0 and 60,000 is generated, which uses the seed we just set up. The time, process ID, and the random value just generated are packed into a sequence of a long integer and two short integers. The result of this operation is then unpacked into a sequence of hexadecimal values and returned.

The result of this process will be a 16-character sequence using a mixture of letters and numbers which could never be discovered accidentally. The session ID should be written into a file, along with the time at which it will expire: you only want IDs to be valid for a short time to reduce the security risk that would arise if people used the same ID for long periods. That is trivial code which is why I'm not showing it here. Just remember to append the ID to the file by opening it with the » operator.

Having created an ID, we want to create a timestamp. This example is very primitive: I simply concatenate the day of the year and the hour of the day into a string. I separate them with a dot so that I can split the two components and use them in comparison operations. For instance, I could refuse access to any page where the timestamp is more than four hours old. I'm not going to show you how to do that in this book, but such comparisons are very straightforward in Perl. Here's the function which creates the timestamp:

```
sub MakeStamp {
    $yday = (localtime)[7];
    $hour = (localtime)[2];
    $stamp = "$yday.$hour";
    return $stamp;
} # MakeStamp
```

The final stage is to save the session ID into a file. I'm going to append it onto the end of the file since that is fast and simple. I don't need the IDs in any particular order so appending them to the file will work nicely. On a busy Web site one user might be creating an ID whilst another is having their session validated. It's important that the two users don't conflict in their use of the sessions file. To prevent conflicts the file is locked before data is read out of it or written to it, with the lock released as soon as the file has been used:

```
sub SaveID {
    flock(SESHID, 2);
    open (SESHID) || die "Unable to save session details";
```

```
    printf SESHID ("%s\n", $ID);
    close(SESHID);
    flock(SESHID, 8);


} # SaveID
```

When all of that has finished an HTML page is sent back to the browser. The URLs inside the page are calls to a CGI script with attributes of a file name and the ID. These are created by simple textual substitutions:

```
<a href="validate.cgi?page=products.html&id=$ID">Products</a>
```

### 10.5.2.1  *The Output*  You probably wonder what the completed page contained when it arrived at a browser. It's included below, formatted so that it fits onto a book page:

```
<!DOCTYPE HTML PUBLIC "-//IETF//DTD HTML//EN">
<HTML><HEAD><TITLE>Index Page</TITLE>
</HEAD><BODY><h1>Bill Smiggins Inc.</h1>
<h3>Links</h3>

<ul>
  <li>
     <a href="validate.cgi?page=products.html&
        id=3af19af9448a45ac:122.18">Products</a>
  </li>
  <li>
     <a href="validate.cgi?page=services.html&
        id=3af19af9448a45ac:122.18">Services</a>
  </li>
  <li>
     <a href="validate.cgi?page=contact.html&
        id=3af19af9448a45ac:122.18">Contacts</a>
  </li>
  <li>
     <a href="validate.cgi?page=ordering.html&
        id=3af19af9448a45ac:122.18">Ordering</a>
  </li>
  <li>
     <a href="logoff.cgi?id=3af19af9448a45ac:122.18">
     Log Off</a>
  </li>
</ul>
</BODY></HTML>
```

### 10.5.3   Validating The Session ID

What happens when those hyperlinks are clicked? The browser sends an HTTP GET message to the server which has the session ID and the page that we're looking for as parameters. To validate the session, I search through the file of IDs, comparing each with the one received as a parameter. If I get to the end of the file without finding the ID, an error page is returned.

   If the ID is valid, the script reads in a partial HTML file. It adds in headers and footers and places the session ID into all URLs which are addresses of files on the local server. Any addresses for remote files, which start with http:// are unaltered. Here's the script:

```perl
#!/usr/bin/perl -w

use CGI qw/:standard/;
use CGI::Carp(fatalsToBrowser);

$SESHID = "sessions.dat";
$in = new CGI;
$p = $in->param('page');
$PAGE = "$p";
$ID = $in->param('id');
$found = 0;

flock(SESHID, 2);
open (SESHID) || die "Unable to open $SESHID";
DONE: while($line = <SESHID>) {
    chomp $line;
    if($line eq $ID) {
        $found = 1;
        last DONE;
    }
}
close(SESHID);
flock(SESHID, 8);

if($found == 1) {
    SendPage();
} else {
    SendError();
}

exit(0);
```

```
sub SendPage {
   open (PAGE) || die "Unable to open $PAGE";

   print $in->header(-expire=>'+2h');
   print $in->start_html("Bill Smiggins Inc.");

   while($line = <PAGE>) {
      $line =~ s/(\.\/[a-zA-Z\/0-9._-]+)/
         validate.cgi?page=$1&id=$ID/g;
      print $line;
   }

   print $in->end_html();
   close PAGE;

} # SendPage


sub SendError {
   print $in->header(-expire=>'+2h');
   print $in->start_html("Bill Smiggins Inc.");
   print <<EOD;
<h1>Access Error</h1>
<p>Unfortunately you do not have a valid ID and so cannot
access this page. Please go to <a href="./logon2.cgi">the
log-on page</a>.</p>
EOD
   print $in->end_html();

} # SendError
```

The alteration of URLs is done through a textual substitution. I'm assuming that a URL is ./ followed by a combination of letters, numbers and one or two other characters. When that pattern is found it is stored in a back reference which becomes part of the modified string:

```
while($line = <PAGE>) {
   $line =~ s/(\.\/[a-zA-Z\/0-9._-]+)/
            validate.cgi?page=$1&id=$ID/g;
   print $line;
}
```

The HTML files which I read through aren't actually complete HTML files. The validation script is adding in HTTP and HTML headers and finishing off the page. Therefore the page files only need to contain the material which will be displayed in the page body. Clearly, if you were using a scheme like this on a real site you would have to be sure that all of your files were going to be passed back by a script. This is as true of templating systems such as ASPs and PHP as it is of this application. Here's the content:

```
<h1>Bill Smiggins Inc</h1>
<h2>About our Company...</h2>

<p>This Web site provides clients, customers, interested
parties and our staff with all of the information that they
could want on our products, services, success and failures.

<hr>
<h3>Products</h3>

<p align="center">We are probably the largest supplier of
custom widgets, thingummybobs and bits and pieces in North
America.

<hr width="50%">
```

## 10.5.4  Logging Off

Finally here's the script which performs the log-off procedure. It's extremely simple. All that it does is read through the file of session IDs and copy into a temporary file any which *aren't* the one created for this user. The temporary file is then renamed so that it replaces the original file of session IDs. Notice that both files are locked whilst I'm using them so that access conflicts are avoided:

```
#!/usr/bin/perl -w

use CGI qw/:standard/;
use CGI::Carp(fatalsToBrowser);

$SESHID = "sessions.dat";
$TEMP = ">temp.dat";

$in = new CGI;
$ID = $in->param('id');

flock(SESHID, 2);
open (SESHID) || die "Unable to open $SESHID";
```

```
flock(TEMP, 2);
open (TEMP) || die "Unable to open $TEMP";

while($line = <SESHID>) {
    chomp $line;
    if($line ne $ID) {
        print TEMP $line."\n";
    }
}

close(TEMP);
flock(TEMP, 8);
close(SESHID);
flock(SESHID, 8);

rename("temp.dat", "sessions.dat");
exit(0);
```

## 10.6  EXERCISES

### Cookies

1. Consider whether the use of a custom security application or the use of Web cookies gives better access control to a site.

2. Add cookie handling to a guest book application. Can you use it to extract information from a form and then display that information back to the user some time later?

3. Why do *you* think that people sometimes worry about the use of cookies? Are they right to do so?

### Session IDs

1. If you haven't already done so, create a simple Web database application using CGI.pm. Use the database to hold details of your CD and MP3 collections.

2. Use session IDs to restrict access to your CD database to just two users.

3. Modify the access controls so that only one user can write data to the application and one other has read-only access.

### File Uploads

1. Create an on-line photo album to hold images of yourself, your family and friends.

2. Develop an HTML form through which pictures can be uploaded to the site. Information about the image such as its size, a suitable title and the name of the photographer should accompany the image.

3. Generate dynamic Web pages which automatically include new images as they are added to the album.

# 11
## Building Web Applications With Perl

Anyone who has done a lot of programming will tell you that many of the things that you want to do in your programs have been attempted before. Most people who teach, or theorize about, programming regard code reuse as vitally important to the software industry. Simply put, there's no point reinventing the wheel every time that you write a program. It's sensible to reuse code from previous projects wherever possible. Developers often build up large libraries of code that they will modify for new projects. Some people even write special code that can be used by anyone without modification. The Perl distributions come with varying amounts of such pre-written code.

In an interpreted language like Perl some mechanism is needed by which the namespaces of applications and library routines can be kept separate. If your application uses a variable name that has already been used in a library you are using, all sorts of unforeseen things[1] could happen. Perl provides the package mechanism to keep the namespace tidy. If you have to refer to a variable in a package then you use its fully qualified name:

```
$package::variable_name
```

A module is a special type of package. It's a package that is defined in a library file of the same name and in which the code is designed to be reusable. The reuse of code may be done by exporting symbols or by functioning as a class. The two packages that I'm concentrating on in this book (CGI.pm and Perl DBI) both operate as classes and allow the programmer to access their routines through method calls.

---

[1] These are called side effects.

When a module supports the object style of interaction you have to use a special notation to access its methods. You'll be familiar with this if you've seen or written any code in C or C++. An *instance*[2] of a class is created using the new keyword. The methods of that instance are then accessed by using an arrow . In practice it's fairly simple.

```
$instance = new PACKAGENAME;
$instance2 = new PACKAGENAME;


$instance->method_one; # execute method_one
$temp = $instance->method_two; # assign value
$instance2->method_two($temp); # method with
                               # parameter
```

Much useful documentation is available in perldoc perlmod, which you should read if you plan to write modules, and perldoc perltoot which gives an introduction to using OO ideas in Perl.

*Getting Modules*  If you run your own server, you'll be able to install pretty much what you want to. For a Perl developer this is really an ideal situation. Not all of the modules I'll discuss in this chapter are provided as part of a standard Perl distribution. Therefore you'll need to download and install them. If you run your Web site on a server provided by an ISP or by your employer or college, then you'll need to ask the System Administrator for help. You can't install these modules in your user space and then access them from your CGI scripts. They need to be installed properly. A second problem is that some of them rely upon other libraries and applications being present on the server. The graphics modules also need a variety of pieces of software whose facilities they use. Your friendly administrator could well have a few hours work ahead if they are going to set everything up for you.

If you run your scripts on a UNIX machine, everything should work properly. If your server is running NT, Windows 2000 or even MacOS you may have problems ahead. All of the software you need to complete this chapter was developed on UNIX boxes and ported to other systems. Installing and configuring some of these ports is, in my experience, fairly tricky. It can be done, but plenty of patience and coffee are definitely required.

The Perl code for hundreds of modules is available from CPAN and its myriad mirrors. You can access CPAN over the Web at http://www.cpan.org. Browse around the site to see what's available. The modules can be found listed by category and are generally provided in gzipped tar files. The following procedure is usually used to install modules on UNIX boxes, I'll demonstrate with the fictitious mymod.pm module:

- you'll need to be working as root or some other user who has administrative rights over the server and can install system software,

---

[2]More OO terminology. This means the named example of a class (or module) that gets manipulated by the program.

- download `mymod.tar.gz` from CPAN,
- create a temporary directory and uncompress the archive using:
  `gunzip mymod.tar.gz,`
- now extract the files from the archive with:
  `tar -xf mymod.tar,`
- that will create a directory below the current one called `mymod` which you should now change into,
- the archive will contain a file called `Makefile.PL` which is used to create a makefile using the command:
  `perl Makefile.PL,`
- now you can compile the module and documentation with:
  `make,`
- many modules come with test scripts, try this:
  `make test,`
- if the tests succeed you can install the module with:
  `make install,`
- finally delete the archive, `mymod.tar` and the `mymod` directory.

If the tests failed you don't necessarily have to worry. On my Debian GNU/Linux system they always fail due to a problem with the installation of Perl. The modules still work perfectly well. If the tests fail due to your set-up, ignore them. If they fail due to a problem with the module such as a missing file or library, then you'll need to do some digging to find a solution.

The module installation process should work under Windows but you will need to download `nmake.exe` from the Microsoft Web site and replace `make` with `nmake` in all of the instructions given above. You'll probably also need to buy a utility such as WinZip to handle the archive for you.

## 11.1  CARP

CGI scripts tend to leave a trail of error messages in the error logs of the server when they die or fall sick. These messages need to be neatly formatted and timestamped if they are to be of any use. The Carp module provided with the standard distribution of Perl is used to provide error messages in the same way as `warn()` and `die()`. The important difference is that the error is not reported at the line where it occurred but in the calling routine. This behavior is provided so that library modules can act more like core functions in their error reporting behavior.

The `CGI::Carp` module is an extension of `Carp()` especially for use with CGI scripts. Neatly formatted, usable error messages can be provided. Usually HTTP servers write errors to STDERR which is actually the server error log; CGI::Carp allows you to redirect your error messages to other open filehandles and store them locally. What if you want to send a CGI error back to the browser? Well you can do that too. Whatever method you choose to handle your error messages, CGI::Carp will generate something like:

```
[Fri Mar 12 09:37:06 1999] show.cgi: Use of
uninitialized value at ./show.cgi line 30,
<GBOOK> chunk 9.
```

That message is highly informative – the developer now knows what error they had, what module caused it, which line of code had the problem, and when the error happened. Very little additional debugging information could ever be provided.

To get a meaningful error message back to the browser you must use some of the additional functionality provided by CGI::Carp. At the top of your script where you are listing the modules it uses, simply include the line:

```
use CGI::Carp(fatalsToBrowser);
```

Your fully robust CGI script will now start off something like

```
#!/usr/bin/perl -Tw

# packages to be imported
use CGI qw/:standard/;
use strict;
use CGI::Carp(fatalsToBrowser);

my $in = new CGI;
```

## 11.2  COOKIES

Tracking visitors is important, especially to commercial Web sites. You may want to gather information about your users for use in demographic analysis, for instance. Many sites ask first-time visitors to fill in a form about themselves before they get access to the site. Two models are then available to developers for tracking users. Some sites ask a visitor to go through a simple log-in procedure each time that they arrive. Others use cookies.

A cookie is simply a piece of textual information which rather than being stored on the server is actually stored on the client machine. The mechanism was developed by Netscape as a way of overcoming the stateless nature of the HTTP protocol and first appeared in version 2 of Navigator. Cookies are a rather controversial topic among both Web surfers and developers. The controversy is basically about control, as indeed are most Internet controversies. Many people resent the fact that remote servers are able to write data to their hard drive without even having to ask. Often that data is encrypted and it's a rare site which says it's using a cookie.

From the developer's point of view cookies are excellent. They can be used to restrict access to whole areas, can be set to expire so that they provide a simple, and very insecure, form of access control, and they provide lots of information that businesses like. For example, without cookies you need to examine the server logs to see which parts of your site are popular. Do browsers simply ignore the catalogue for instance? How many people look at the page which contains all of your special offers? That information may not be available to you if your pages are hosted by an ISP. Use cookies though and you can find all of that and more. Let's say that your visitors all fill in an initial questionnaire. Using a cookie lets you find out which part of the site are used by all of the high earners and which parts by poor, starving students. You can then tailor content to the needs of different audiences within the same site.

If you, as a Web user, object to cookies then you can configure your browser so that the entire mechanism is switched off. This may restrict the number of commercial sites that you can visit but at least you'll keep your freedom intact. Although cookies are sent from the server they are stored by the browser. They are passed as part of the HTTP message header and hence can be safely ignored without corrupting the page content. For more information on the HTTP protocol turn to Chapter 17.

Developers don't have the luxury of choosing which mechanisms to implement. If a client wants to use cookies then you have to program them. It is easier than you might imagine.

## 11.2.1   Cookies in Detail

First let's see what all of the fuss is about. Netscape Navigator stores its cookies in a file called `cookies.txt`. Here's part of that file from one of my computers:

```
# Netscape HTTP Cookie File
# http://www.netscape.com/newsref/std/cookie_spec.html
# This is a generated file!  Do not edit

.amazon.com TRUE  /   FALSE 2082787201  ubid-main
     002-8015358-4455008
.yahoo.co.uk   TRUE  /   FALSE 1271361625  B
     97soiun7d3c42
www.homebuyers.co.uk FALSE /  FALSE 1293753600
     WEBTRENDS_ID 195.92.197.53-1125876848.29284862
```

Microsoft Internet Explorer stores each individual cookie as a separate file which makes manipulating them slightly harder for the user. At least with `cookies.txt` you can use a text editor to delete individual items if you don't want them in there. An Internet Explorer cookie file from the same machine looks like this:

```
ASGUID
1181408
```

```
activestate.com/
0
124316800
30056700
2387620512
29322478
*
```

Parts of these files are clear: they hold some domain names and some directory paths but a lot has meaning only to the server which created the cookie. Whilst we can't *reverse-engineer* other sites cookies, we can learn to create our own.

## 11.2.2    The Parts of a Cookie

A cookie has six parts. Before I describe them I would like to make a suggestion about their content. If you *are* going to write information to visitor's hard drives then you should be nice about it. A warning message somewhere on your site would be good, the option to turn cookies off would be very good but best of all make them expire within a reasonable time. Many sites create cookies which are designed to live for decades. This is ludicrous as most of them are only needed for a few minutes. It shows a lack of forethought on the part of the developers, and probably a lack of respect for their visitors. Finally don't pass encrypted data to your visitors. You are using *their* machines for *your* purposes. Get your cookies to write plain, legible text. I would even go so far as to suggest that this is an area where you could easily start to use XML within your sites.

But enough proselytizing, I hear you shout. Where's the code? Well, first let's see what the cookie is made from; then we'll see how to bake it for ourselves.

***11.2.2.1    Name***    Each cookie needs to have a name. The name doesn't have to be unique as browsers can store up to 300 cookies. Some common names such as `my_cookie` or `the_cookie` will be used many times. Any alphanumeric characters except white spaces[3] are valid inside a cookie. This field is compulsory.

***11.2.2.2    Value***    The point of cookies is to store data. The data is held in name:value pairs. If you are thinking about implementing these things in Perl, as we are, then that ought to be making you think about hashes straight away. A cookie can have as many of these name:value pairs as you want.

***11.2.2.3    Expiry Date***    Each cookie has a finite life after which the browser can safely delete it. The cookie can be returned to your scripts at any point during its life. The expiry time is set using a time and date string in Greenwich Mean Time format. If no expiry time is set the cookie will cease to be active when the browser is next shut down.

---

[3]Space, tab, newline, carriage return.

***11.2.2.4   Domain***   The cookie is only valid for one domain, or part of one domain. For instance if you want your cookie to be used through your whole site you might set the domain attribute to `.shu.ac.uk`. Here the browser will happily return the cookie to servers such as `www.shu.ac.uk` or `mybox.cms.shu.ac.uk` but not to other machines in the `.ac.uk` domain. If the domain were set to `www.shu.ac.uk` the cookie could not be accessed by `mybox.cms.shu.ac.uk` or any other machine in the `shu.ac.uk` hierarchy.

***11.2.2.5   Path***   The site further restricts the scripts which can access a cookie. By default it is set to `/` which means that all scripts in the domain may access the cookie. If you only wanted scripts in the directory `/cookie_handlers` to get at your cookie then the path would be set to `/cookie_handlers`. Scripts in directories like `/cgi-bin` would then not be able to use the cookie. This is a useful feature as it lets you create a variety of cookies for your site, each tailored to a slightly different set of needs.

***11.2.2.6   Secure***   If you only want your cookie used in secure communications, for instance when SSL is being used, then set the secure flag to 1. Otherwise the cookie will be passed through normal TCP/IP communications inside HTTP messages.

## 11.3   USING RELATIONAL DATABASES

For the developers of large commercial Web sites two issues override all others: security and data storage. The benefits of using the Web to conduct business disappear totally if you can't efficiently store, retrieve, and manipulate the data from customers. Web sites which don't handle data are little more than glorified advertising opportunities – although they have a rather larger potential audience. All of the CGI code that I've shown so far has written data to simple flat files. For many applications that is fine. However, if you're handling complex data, complex processing or need to keep your data secure then using a relational database is probably the best solution.

Whilst I'm not planning to show you how to program in SQL (the language used by most relational databases) I'm going to give a couple of examples that will convince you that using a database is so straightforward you ought to consider doing so.

### 11.3.1   Introducing DBI

There are many types of relational database available – some of them are even freely available on the Internet. The multiplicity of such platforms could present the end-developer with a problem of potentially insurmountable proportions. Imagine developing an application which could talk to an Oracle database, only for your ISP or company to decide that they were moving from Oracle to Ingres. If your application contained a lot of platform specific code then you would have to rewrite the whole thing. That is not only time-consuming and expensive but potentially dangerous. All of the debugging and incremental improvements that had been made to the original Oracle application would have to be repeated for the Ingres version. Fortunately, there is a database-neutral solution available in Perl 5.

## 11.3.2  RDBMS Neutral Database Applications

The Perl DBI module provides a neutral interface to many relational databases. It is an application programmer interface (API) which provides a library of functions, variables and conventions. According to the documentation with the modules these

"provide a consistent database interface independent of the actual database being used."

The DBI routines don't actually perform much of the processing of the application-database connection. That functionality comes from a driver module which must be specifically developed for the database being used. Database drivers are available for most of the commonly used relational databases. The drivers do the actual work while the DBI API provides a framework within which those drivers can operate. The relationship between the application, API, driver, and database engine is shown in Figure 11.1.

**Figure 11.1**  The Perl DBI

The great benefit for the application developer, of using the DBI module, is independence. If the database management system that you are using changes then you simply tell Perl DBI to use a different driver and leave the rest of your code totally unaltered. If the database driver has been developed properly, and those for the major databases have been around long enough now, then you should have no unexpected problems.

If you are working on UNIX systems then you have a wide range of RDBMS available. For the Web developer who uses Microsoft operating systems the choice is rather more restricted. However, once you've set up a working database under NT or Windows 98 it is just as easy to use as it would be under UNIX. In fact in one important aspect it is actually *easier* to use Windows. Microsoft has a technology called open database connectivity (ODBC) which provides a consistent interface to many relational database systems. A Perl DBI driver is available to talk to ODBC so that whatever back-end you use, once you have registered it with the ODBC manager you can access it through your Perl applications.

The implementation of DBI for each database system inherits and extends the methods of the generic Perl DBI package. You'll see when I talk about connecting to databases that, rather than use the generic package, you should use the package developed for your database management system.

Most applications that use DBI adhere to the cursor model. Again for detail look at any good relational database text. Briefly, though, a cursor lets applications access sets of data returned by SQL queries. A cursor reads the next tuple[4] returned and all operations are performed against that tuple.

---

Note:

In the following descriptions of the Perl DBI, $dbh is used as a generic value for a database handle. The value $sth is used to indicate a handle to a statement. Suitable names for both of these for your applications should be submitted as appropriate.

---

### 11.3.3  Perl DBI Methods

Perl DBI is a module so everything that was said in Section 9.5 when I described CGI.pm applies here too. I'm not going to go into too much detail about how the module works. Once you've seen it in action it's pretty straightforward and you can, as always, get lots of useful information from the documentation. In this case perldoc DBI should do the trick. What follows is, therefore, a brief skim across the surface that should get you started.

***11.3.3.1  Sessions*** Perl DBI doesn't really have sessions in the database sense. There isn't a continuous stream of operations from a specific, identifiable user to the database. Instead each connection into the database is identified by a handle[5] whose methods are called by Perl scripts. Relational databases can support many types of data. To simplify data handling in the driver all data is returned as string values. The application developer must manipulate those strings so that, for instance, numerical precision is not lost.

Often you will want to perform a number of operations on the same data set at the same time. Using Perl DBI you cannot perform more than one database operation at a time. If you want three consecutive operations then you must prepare and execute three statements. For more on using statements see Section 11.3.3.2.

As a final word of warning about Perl DBI, not all relational database systems support the same set of functions. For instance, the popular freeware database mySQL lacks both commit and rollback, so those operations are not supported by its driver. Therefore you need to read the documentation for the DBI driver that you are using before you start

---

[4]In effect a row from a set...
[5]Analogous to an object.

coding. And if you do have to port your application to a new database you may have to rewrite any non-generic code that you have used.

**$dbh = DBI->connect($data_source, $username, $password)**
**|| die $DBI::errstr**

When a connection is opened to the database it returns a handle. The handle will be used for all database operations in a similar way to a filehandle. If the connection cannot be opened the driver will set a DBI error which the application can then use to fail gracefully. This set-up lets each application program establish multiple connections to multiple databases and to manage each of those connections independently.

$data_source is actually a colon-separated set of values which identify the driver, database, and host. The driver is called through DBI:'driver name': with the driver name being case-sensitive. The following example establishes a connection to a mySQL database called webber running on the localhost.

```
$dbh = DBI->connect('DBI:mysql:webber:localhost',
        'webber','pwd')
    || die 'Unable to connect to database
        $dbh->errstr\n';
```

The driver name may, on occasion, require the port number at which the database is listening. For instance

```
DBI:mysql:webber:localhost:7000
```

It may be that for your database, particularly during testing, no user name or password is needed. Obviously this is unacceptable practice on a production system but during testing you can use empty strings for these values.

The interpretation and use of the parameters to $DBI->connect is driver dependent and not considered here. If you want more details then look in the perldoc for DBI and DBD.

Once a connection has been established the DBI methods are accessed through the filehandle. In object-oriented parlance the handle is an *instance* of DBI.

**$dbh->disconnect**

When you have finished using a connection to a database, that connection should be dropped by calling the disconnect method of the handle. Most systems restrict the number of connections that can be made. Although the limit is high, an intensively used CGI application may soon reach it if connections are not released after use.

Some database systems will automatically commit any remaining changes when you disconnect. This is not defined anywhere so it is important that you specify before disconnecting whether any remaining changes are to be committed or rolled back. Of course if your DBMS does not support commit and rollback of transactions, disconnecting is likely to lead to unspecified behavior. You must write code in your application to validate your changes rather then relying upon the integrity of the system.

Attempting to disconnect from a database that has uncommitted changes will raise a warning. To avoid this call the `finish` method before disconnecting.

`$sth->finish`

Is used to show that no more data will be returned from a statement handle. Calling this is a useful way of letting the database free resources.

### 11.3.3.2  *Preparing Statements*  You cannot simply write some SQL and run it against a database when using Perl DBI. Instead your SQL code must be prepared by the driver before execution.

`$sth = $dbh->prepare($statement)`
`|| die $dbh->errstr`

Prepares an SQL statement for execution and returns a handle to that statement to be held in `$sth`. The handle is then used in the `execute` statement. If the preparation fails an error string will be returned by the driver. The `prepare` method should not generally be used to execute SQL statements. Some drivers *will* execute some statements from the `prepare` method. You should consult the `perldoc` for your particular driver for more information on this.

Not all database systems support the concept of prepared queries. If a system doesn't use prepared queries then the `prepare` method simply stores the SQL in the handle for processing by `execute`.

The DBI `prepare` method does not parse SQL statements. They will be passed onto the database engine and any errors returned from there. Note that your SQL statements should not generally be terminated by a semicolon when run from DBI.

### 11.3.3.3  *Database Operations*

`$sth->execute || die $sth->errstr`

All processing needed to complete the (prepared) statement is performed. If the statement is executed successfully `true` will be returned.

> Note:
> In many circumstances, when querying a database, a successful execution may not return any data. In database operations an empty set does not imply failure of a query. For more details on this consult any good database text.

Select operations return the number of rows that the database will return to the application.

`$sth->fetchrow_array`

Returns the next row from the set of rows returned by the database. The row is returned as an array of values which is available for processing as a normal array.

`$dbh->selectrow_array($statement)`

Combines the `prepare`, `execute`, and `fetchrow_array` operations into a single

statement. If the SQL statement in the $statement parameter has already been pre-
pared, that step will not be repeated by selectrow_array.

**$sth->rows**

Returns the number of rows that a query is returning. Often this will be an indetermi-
nate value. A select operation simply returns rows until the set is empty; often even
the DBMS will not know how large the return set *is*.

**$dbh->commit || die $dbh->errstr**

If the database supports transaction operations, this will force it to make the most recent set of changes permanent.

**$dbh->rollback || die $dbh->errstr**

If the database that is being used supports transactions, this command will undo any
uncommitted changes that the application has made.

**$dbh->errstr, $dbh->err**

These are the database engine error string and error code, respectively. They corre-
spond to the most recent driver function call.

**$DBI::errstr, $DBI::err**

These are generic versions of the errors just described. They always refer to the last
handle used and so must be used with care if you have numerous handles open.

## 11.3.4   Using DBI and a Relational Database – An Example

This first example of using a database with Perl shows how to write a row of data to a
mySQL database. In this case the table being written into has five fields. Four of them are
text fields, the last one is a counter. The mySQL system supports an automatically incremented counter which always receives the value 0. The table being used in the examples
here is a simple Web guestbook with fields for the visitor name, visitor IP address, e-mail
address, and any comments that they may want to leave.

The second example reads data from the same table and prints it out to the screen. Notice
how the returned values are accessed from $row just like any other array values.

It is easy to see how these database examples could replace some of the file handling
code that I have shown throughout the CGI scripting chapters of this book.

### 11.3.4.1   Writing to a Database

```perl
#!/usr/bin/perl -w
use DBI;

$host = "DBI:mysql:webber:localhost";
$dbh = DBI->connect($host, 'webber','pwd')
  or die 'Unable to connect to database $dbh->errstr\n';

$insert = <<DONE;
```

```
insert into visitors values ('Bugs Bunny',
                             'carrots\@home',
                             '255.255.255.0',
                             'An updated Row',
                             0)
DONE

my $update = $dbh->prepare($insert);
$update->execute
    or die 'Unable to execute SQL command. $dbh->errstr';

$dbh->disconnect;
exit(0);
```

## 11.3.5   Reading from a Database

```
#!/usr/bin/perl -w

use DBI;
$host = "DBI:mysql:webber:localhost";
$dbh = DBI->connect($host, 'webber','pwd')
  or die 'Unable to connect to database $dbh->errstr\n';

$query = <<END;
select name, comments
  from visitors
  order by name
END

$cursor = $dbh->prepare($query);
$cursor->execute
    or die 'Unable to execute SQL command. $dbh->errstr';

my $row;
while($row = $cursor->fetchrow_arrayref) {
  printf("[%s] [%s]\n", $row->[0], $row->[1]);
  }

$cursor->finish;

$dbh->disconnect;
exit(0);
```

The following code fragments are typical pieces of SQL:

```
insert into visitors values ('Bugs Bunny',
        'carrots\@home',
        '255.255.255.0',
        'An updated Row', 0)
```

and

```
select name, comments
  from visitors
  order by name
```

## 11.4 USING LIBWWW

Sometimes you need to venture beyond the confines of your own Web site or databases. You need more data to provide more information on your site. Where are you going to get that data from? Why the Web, of course. Yes, strange as it may seem, there will be times when you want, or need, to create Web applications which can gather data from around the Web and incorporate that data into *your* pages. This seems like a strange concept, after all anything which surfs the Web is surely a Web client and I've been discussing and demonstrating the use of Perl in *server* applications. Didn't I even imply that Perl wasn't a language you could use inside a browser? Well, yes I have been concentrating solely on Perl as a server language and I'm *still* doing that. In this section I want to show how you can use Perl to build a script which can get information from other Web sites and then add that data to your pages.

You've probably seen this idea used around the Web. Many topical news sites are little more than dynamic lists of links to content on other sites. As the content changes, so the data those linked sites provide changes too. Even Web portals do this: Yahoo! provides endless links to news stories on sites run by organisations like CNN, the BBC and Reuters. Yahoo! goes even further by abstracting the first few sentences of the stories it's highlighting so that surfers can be selective about what they read. In the world of Open Source and Free Software, many Web sites list the latest updates to the Freshmeat archives[6] and to stories being run on every computer nerd's favorite site: Slashdot[7]. How are these things done? Well, in truth, I have no idea how large organisations like Yahoo! do this. For them it's really a trade secret, part of what makes them a distinctive brand. I do, though, know a way that you can get a foot in the door.

Perl has a set of modules which collectively are called libwww-perl. These are designed to be used when writing Web clients and replace low-level coding tasks involving things like sockets and ports with more high-level tasks involving URLs and whole Web

---

[6]http://www.freshmeat.net
[7]http://www.slashdot.org

pages. The best place to start with these modules is the documentation. Try `perldoc HTML::Simple`, to get an overview of what the modules can do, and to see some basic code.

I'm going to show you an application which uses a combination of CGI scripting, `libwww` and XML parsing just to build a small HTML table. I'm not going to explain the XML parsing here, you'll just have to trust me that this works. If you want to know *how* it works, leap ahead to Section 14.6 for all of the gory details. For now I'll concentrate on the networking aspects of building this client.

What does this client do? It incorporates a list of the current discussions at Slashdot into an HTML page. Sounds complicated doesn't it? Slashdot is a set of HTML pages, created using a whole load of Perl scripts. How can I find out what stories are running there and download the details of them into my own pages? A brute force solution to this problem might be to simply get hold of the HTML from the front page at Slashdot and strip out the bits I'm interested in. But what I want are the titles of the stories and their URLs. If you take a look at the site you'll see that it's got a very complex structure and finding the information that I want would be next to impossible. Fortunately the people who run Slashdot provide an XML file which contains all of the information that I need and more. Here's a sample of that file (reformatted slightly to fit on the printed page):

```
<story>
    <title>CD-R Prices Could Triple This Summer</title>
    <url>
        http://slashdot.org/article.pl?sid=01/05/09/0236235
    </url>
    <time>2001-05-09 03:03:03</time>
    <author>timothy</author>
    <department>stock-several-spindles</department>
    <topic>money</topic>
    <comments>168</comments>
    <section>articles</section>
    <image>topicmoney.gif</image>
</story>
```

All I have to do, therefore, is connect my script to the Slashdot Web server, download this file, which is called `slashdot.xml`, and process it in whatever way I need to. One final thing, before I get into the coding, the Slashdot site has an extremely high load. If you're going to practice writing a Web client using my code *please* download the `slashdot.xml` file just once, save it on your own Web server and work on that version. Once you've got a working script you can use the real file. Right, here's the code:

```
#!/usr/bin/perl -w

use CGI qw/:standard/;
use CGI::Carp('fatalsToBrowser');
```

```perl
use XML::Parser;
require LWP::UserAgent;

$ua = new LWP::UserAgent;
$rq = new HTTP::Request('GET',
    'http://www.slashdot.org/slashdot.xml');

$title = 0;
$url = 0;
@linktext = "";
@urls = "";
$j = $k = 0;

$response = $ua->request($rq);

if($response->is_success) {
    $parser = new XML::Parser;
    $parser->setHandlers(
                        Start => \&elStart,
                        End => \&elEnd,
                        Char => \&elChar);
    &makePage($response->content);
} else {
    print $response->error_as_HTML;
}

exit(0);

sub makePage {
    $parser->parse($_[0]);
    $page = new CGI;
    print $page->header;
    print $page->start_html("Slashdot.xml");
    print "<h1>Slashdot Stories</h1>\n";
    print qq(<table border="0">);

    for($i = 0; $i < $k-1; $i++) {
        print "<tr><td>";
        print "<a href=\"$urls[$i]\">$linktext[$i]</a>\n";
        print "</td></tr>";
    }
```

```perl
      print "</table>\n";
      print $page->end_html;
}


sub elStart {
   ($expat, $item, %atts) = @_;
   if($item eq "title"){
      $title = 1;
   } elsif($item eq "url"){
      $url = 1;
   }
}


sub elEnd {
   ($expat, $item, %atts) = @_;
   if($item eq "title"){
      $title = 0;
   } elsif($item eq "url"){
      $url = 0;
   }
}


sub elChar {
   ($expat, $item, %atts) = @_;
   if($title == 1){
      $linktext[$j] = $item;
      $j++;
   } elsif($url == 1){
      $urls[$k] = $item;
      $k++;
   }
}
```

The part of that script which creates the Web client, connects to the remote server and handles the response, is shown below:

```perl
#!/usr/bin/perl -w

require LWP::UserAgent;
```

```
$ua = new LWP::UserAgent;
$rq = new HTTP::Request('GET',
   'http://www.slashdot.org/slashdot.xml');
# variables cut here

$response = $ua->request($rq);

if($response->is_success) {
   # XML handling code removed from here
   &makePage($response->content);
} else {
   print $response->error_as_HTML;
}

exit(0);
```

Let's take that piece by piece and see what it's doing. The developers of libwww have taken an object-oriented approach to its development. The code has been broken down into a set of classes which each perform distinct functions. Each class can be used separately but most applications will use more than one of them. That's the case here, where I need to create an HTTP request, transmit it and handle the response from the Web server. Therefore I'm using a class called LWP::UserAgent which encapsulates[8] the HTTP::Request, HTTP::Response and LWP::Protocol classes. The script starts by creating an instance of the LWP::UserAgent which will perform most of the work for us.

**$agent = new LWP::UserAgent**
   constructs an instance of the UserAgent class and returns a reference to it.

   The next step is to create a request. As you might guess, an HTTP request consists of a request line, some headers and potentially some content.

**$rq = new HTTP::Request(method, URI [, header [, content]])**
**$rq = HTTP::Request->new(method, URI [, header [, content]])**
**$rq = HTTP::Request->new(method => URI [, header [, content]])**
   these constructors all work in the same way. Really the choice of which to use is down to personal preference. The request can handle either GET or POST forms as the method parameter. The URI parameter is the URI of the document which you want to retrieve. If you need to pass in any headers with your message these go as the third parameter. They should be wrapped inside an HTTP::Headers object. Next the request has to be processed.

---

[8] A term from object-orientation which means includes.

`request($request[, $arg[, size]])`
`simple_request($request[, $arg[, size]])`

LWP::UserAgent has two ways of submitting a request to a server. Actually, they work in the same way. The Request method can send more than one request and can handle operations such as redirections. The `simple_request` is much less complex and is used to submit just a single request. The first parameter should be a reference to an instance of the HTTP::Request class. The, optional, second argument, `$arg`, controls the way that the response from the server is to be handled. This must be either the name of a file in which you want the response stored, or a reference to a subroutine which will handle chunks of data as they arrive. If this parameter is missing, as in my example, the data is stored in the HTTP::Request object.

An HTTP request returns an error code alongside any data. These return codes can be used to control how your script operates. For instance if you get an error message back from the server then you won't want to show it on your page will you? These return codes become part of the HTTP::Response object and are accessed through its methods.

`$response = HTTP::Response->new(code[, message[, content[, header]]])`

constructs an HTTP::Response object with the specified code and, optionally a message, some content and a header. In the example script this object is created automatically when the request returns and then made available to us. The HTTP::response object has a number of attributes which we can access from our scripts.

`$response->code()`

returns the code which was sent from the server.

`$response->message()`

returns the message sent from the server.

`$response->base`

gives the base URI for the response. This actually returns a reference to a URI object.

`$response->is_success`
`$response->is_error`

return boolean values indicating the status of the request which was sent to the server.

`$response->error_as_HTML()`

returns a string which contains a complete HTML page giving details of which error occurred and why. Generally this method will only return anything useful if `is_error` has returned true. In the example this must have happened if the check of `is_success` failed.


## 11.5 TEMPLATE-BASED SITES WITH HTML::MASON

Dynamic Web sites usually have three elements. These are the HTML which the browser displays, the scripts which create the dynamic parts of the site and some form of data storage. By now you're familiar with all of those pieces. So far, in the scripting sections of the book, I've shown you how to place HTML inside Perl code. This seems sensible to experienced programmers, we tend to think in terms of algorithms and data structures.

But what if you're not a programmer, or if you are a Web designer? You'll probably think firstly about HTML files, page layout and site structure. You'll want to use scripting to support HTML, rather than using HTML to present the results of your scripts. A number of technologies are available which work like this. I cover PHP in some detail later and look at Microsoft's Active Server Pages and Sun Microsystems' Java Server Pages in Chapter 13. Most of these involve learning a new language. If you've worked your way through to here then you've already invested a significant amount of time in learning Perl, so finding that you now need to learn PHP could be more than a little irritating. Fortunately there is at least one solution which lets you use all of the facilities of Perl and, at the same time, get blistering levels of performance out of your Web server.

Mason is an open source Web engine which supports the development and delivery of large, complex sites. It is being developed by Jonathan Swartz and can be downloaded from http://www.masonhq.com where you'll also find HTML versions of the documentation, mailing lists to join and the beginnings of a useful FAQ. Mason is a Perl module with attitude. It's designed specifically to work with the Apache Web server and the mod_perl extension to it. The combination of Apache and mod_perl is vital since it provides extremely high throughput levels and extremely low response times. If you use those two pieces of software, the Perl interpreter lives in memory as do compiled versions of your scripts. There's little or no initiation time required when a script is called and performance levels approach those of native code[9].

Installing and configuring Mason is quite straightforward once you have Apache and mod_perl running. I'll leave the details to the supplied documentation. Take a look at:

```
perldoc HTML::Mason
perldoc HTML::Mason::Admin
perldoc HTML::Mason::Devel
```

the last of those being the documentation for developers.

I'm going to show you how to get a simple Mason page up and running, look at how you use the module to intertwine HTML and Perl, and finish by presenting a complex example. First, though, some more background. Mason is a sort of pre-processor which takes small pieces of code, called *components*, and joins them together to make a complete HTML page. Each component is stored in a separate file and may contain HTML, Perl or a combination of the two. When the pre-processor encounters Perl code inside a component it processes that code as if it were a script and uses the result in the page it's building. When it encounters HTML it places the code directly into the new page. The beauty of components is that they're easily re-used. If you create a menu based upon a dynamic search of your system, it can be included in every page on your site with a simple Mason

---

[9]And exceed anything you'll ever see from Visual Basic or Java.

statement. You get all of the flexibility of a frameset with none of the annoyance to your users. Life as a developer is also simplified. If you need to update part of your site, for instance to change a logo, you make the change once and it spreads through all your pages without you doing any work at all.

### 11.5.1 A Basic Application

I'm not going to show you the simplest of Mason pages, a *Hello World!* type application, since you can find examples of that in the perldoc supplied with the module. Instead I'll show you a more fully featured, yet still quite trivial, application.

You may remember from earlier that operating systems store details about the current system environment. This data can be accessed from Perl scripts using a builtin hash called %ENV. The following script displays those details in an HTML page. It also accepts a parameter from the browser, sent using either GET or POST, which controls the number of lines of data that are displayed. If you've got Mason installed try saving the script in your Mason directory as environ.html and running it using:

```
http://localhost/mason/environ.html?num_lines=12
```

although the exact path will change depending upon how you've configured your installation. Here's the code:

```
<& header, title=>' is now', bgcol=>'red' &>
<table border="1">
% foreach my $key (sort keys %ENV) {
<tr>
   <td>
      <b><% $key %></b>
   </td>
   <td>
      <% $ENV{$key} %>
   </td>
</tr>
%last if (--$num_lines <= 0);
% }
</table>

<& footer &>

<%args>
$num_lines=>10
</%args>
```

As well as the HTML file, you'll need to create and save two Mason components in the same directory. These are called `header` and `footer` and are shown below:

### header

```
<html>
<head>
<title>Current environment <% $title %></title>
</head>
<body bgcolor="<% $bgcol %>">
<h2>Current Environment <% $title %></h2>

<%args>
$title
$bgcol=>'yellow'
</%args>
```

### footer

```
<hr>
<p>This site &copy; 2001, Chris Bates.</p>
</body>
</html>
```

So how does that work? And, what's all the funny syntax about? Mason adds some more syntactic salt to the soup of symbols and meanings which is Perl. Fortunately there's only a couple more things to learn and they're pretty straightforward. Since Mason makes HTML pages from components it needs to be able to identify which component to include and where to place its content. This is done by placing the component name in this format:

```
<& footer &>
```

Sometimes you'll need to pass parameters to a component, the construct used is familiar from `CGI.pm` and numerous other Perl modules:

```
<& header, title=>' is now', bgcol=>'red' &>
```

where the parameters form a comma separated list of keys and values. The component receives its parameters by declaring them in a `<%args>` block:

```
<%args>
$title
$bgcol=>'yellow'
</%args>
```

The same approach is used by a *top-level* component to receive parameters from the browser. In the example, the browser can send a parameter called `num_lines` back to the script. This is accepted using this declaration:

```
<%args>
$num_lines=>10
</%args>
```

with the variable given a value in its declaration. This value will act as a default if the parameter isn't passed in. The arguments now need to be used in the component. This is done by placing them in `<% %>` tags:

```
<title>Current environment <% $title %></title>
```

with the current value held by the variable, `$title` in this case replacing the tag. When you want to execute lines of Perl, you place a % sign in the first column of the line. Don't leave any whitespace before the symbol though, as then the code won't be executed.

```
% foreach my $key (sort keys %ENV) {
%     last if(--$num_lines <= 0);
% }
```

### 11.5.2 Mason In Action

I decided I'd create a more complex application to show you some more of the features of Mason. I also wanted to demonstrate that a Mason page can be made from lots of components. Figure 11.2 shows the results of my efforts. I'm not going to take you through the whole set of code. It's included below so that you can find out how the page was created. I'll pick out one or two highlights along the way. Probably the best way of finding out how that page is made would be to recreate it for yourself then start changing bits. See what happens as it breaks and you'll soon learn how it all works.

*main.html*   The main page is a table and seven Mason components. Notice how components can be placed inside the table yet still work perfectly. This type of structure leads to really clean and readable code, once you've seen a couple of examples the structure of a page becomes obvious. Compared to this, CGI scripts are almost unreadable.

```
<& thetop &>
<table border="0" width="95%" cellpadding="2" align="center">
   <colgroup>
      <col width="100">
      <col>
      <col width="100">
   </colgroup>
   <tr valign="top">
      <!-- main header -->
      <td><& motd &></td>
      <td><& logo &></td>
   </tr>
```

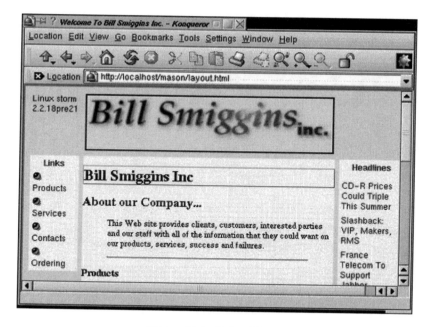

***Figure 11.2*** Using Mason

```
<tr valign="top">
   <!-- content -->
   <td><& links &></td>
   <td><& thebody &></td>
   <td><& headlines &></td>
</tr>
</table>
<& footer &>
```

***thetop*** I could have placed all the HTML which starts the page into the main file. I've deliberately split it out so that you can see that Mason components can be pure HTML.

```
<html>
   <head>
      <title>Welcome To Bill Smiggins Inc.</title>
      <link rel="stylesheet" type="text/css"
            href="../html/test.css" media="screen">
   </head>
<body bgcolor="#f0e68c">
```

***motd*** UNIX systems include a file called motd which contains a piece of text called *the message of the day*. This is sometimes used by system administrators to display a message to all users as they log-on to the system. In this component I read the contents of that file and show them on my page.

```
<table border="0" cellpadding="0" cellspacing="0" align="left">
       <tr><td><% $motd %></td></tr>
</table>

<%init>
my($MOTD, $motd, @tmp);

open MOTD, 'etc/motd' or die "Ooops";
while (<MOTD>) {
  @tmp = split /#/, $_;
  $motd = $tmp[0];
}
</%init>
```

The Perl code is placed inside `<%init>` tags. These create a special type of Mason element which is called as soon as the component is loaded. If you want to perform a lot of Perl processing inside a component, using `<%init>` is a very good idea. It lets you cleanly separate the HTML and Perl and makes the source much cleaner.

*logo*  More HTML, this time including a link to an image:

```
<table border="0" align="left">
  <tr>
    <td bgcolor="#000000">
        <img src="../html/logo.gif" height="80" width="352">
    </td>
  </tr>
</table>
```

*links*  This table of links is also used in Chapter 15:

```
<table border="0" align="left" cellpadding="0" bgcolor="#fff8dc">
<tr><th>Links</th></tr>
<tr><td><img src="../html/bullet.gif">  Products</td></tr>
<tr><td><img src="../html/bullet.gif">  Services</td></tr>
<tr><td><img src="../html/bullet.gif">  Contacts</td></tr>
<tr><td><img src="../html/bullet.gif">  Ordering</td></tr>
</table>
```

### *thebody*

```
<div style="background: #fff8dc">
<h1>Bill Smiggins Inc</h1>
```

```
<h2>About our Company...</h2>

<p>This Web site provides clients, customers,
interested parties and our staff with all of the
information that they could want on our
products, services, success and failures.

<hr>
<h3>Products</h3>

<p align="center">We are probably the largest
supplier of custom widgets, thingummybobs and
bits and pieces in North America.

<hr width="50%">
</div>
```

***headlines*** The most complicated component on the page is used to include headlines from Slashdot. I'm reusing a lot of the code from Section 11.4. I have, though, had to change the code which processes the XML file. In the Mason version I'm using regular expressions to pick out the rows of data which I'm interested in. I can do this because `slashdot.xml` is a well-defined and neat XML document. If I wanted to do this in anger I'd have to use proper XML processing code.

You're probably wondering why I went to the trouble of rewriting perfectly acceptable code which works well. Unfortunately I was faced with a limitation of Mason. You cannot place Perl functions inside Mason components and make calls to them. Mason converts each component into a Perl object and places code in such functions as *it* requires. If you create a function of your own, it may get wrapped inside Mason's function definition so that it no longer works. There are two solutions to this problem. First, as I've done here, write your code so that it doesn't require function calls. Mason lets you call builtin Perl functions and those in Perl objects and modules. This leads to alternative two, which is to define a class which encapsulates the functions you require. You then use that class inside your components. For large problems or industrial strength code, the latter alternative is by far the better approach. Since I haven't shown you how to implement object orientation in Perl I'm using the first alternative here.

```
<table border="0" align="left" bgcolor="#fff8dc">
<tr><th>Headlines</th></tr>
% for($i = 0; $i <= $k; $i++){
<tr>
  <td>
    <a href="<% $urls[$i] %>"><% $linktext[$i] %></a>
```

```
    </td>
  </tr>
% }
</table>

<%once>
my($ua, $rq, @linktext, @urls, $j, $k, $i);
my($response, $item, @lines);
</%once>

<%init>
require LWP::UserAgent;

$ua = new LWP::UserAgent;
$rq = new HTTP::Request('GET', 'http://www.slashdot.org/slashdot.xml');

@linktext = "";
@urls = "";
$j = $k = 0;
$response = $ua->request($rq);

if($response->is_success) {
  @lines = split /\n/, $response->content;
  foreach $item (@lines) {
    if($item =~ m/<title>(.+)<\/title>/) {
      push @linktext, $1;
      $k++;
    }
    if($item =~ m/<url>(.+)<\/url>/) {
      push @urls, $1;
    }
  }
}

</%init>
```

I've use a new Mason construct in there. The <%once>...</%once>, block is used to define code which is executed exactly once[10] when the component is loaded. Here I use it to scope the variables to the file and so avoid lots of error messages from the strict module.

---

[10] No surprise there, then.

*footer*   The final component on this page is the footer. It includes all of the HTML elements which are needed to complete a document and it displays the current time and date. I'm reusing the code from Section 8.8.3 to create these. However, because you can't easily place calls to functions within Mason components I need to slightly rearrange this code. Those parts of the script which do the work are removed from the GetTime function and placed inside an <%init> block instead:

```
<hr>
<p>The time is <% $time %> on <% $today %> </p>
<p>This site &copy; 2001, Chris Bates.</p>
<hr>
</body>
</html>

<%init>
 my ($sec, $min, $hour, $mday, $month, $year,
     $wday, $yday, $isdst, $day, $today, $time);

# put the time and date generation routine here

   $time = join ':', $hour, $min;
</%init>
```

## 11.6   CREATING AND MANIPULATING IMAGES

The Web is awash with graphics. The vast majority of pages include at least one static image, some include so many that waiting for their download to complete can be a nightmare. Images can be animated, used in navigation systems or included to provide vital information. Let's face it, the Web is a graphical medium. It wasn't always, in the early days the Web was purely text-based and a minority of users and developers would like to see a return to that era. In one respect, at least, many sites remain text-based. Most CGI scripts return a page of text to the browser, few programmers even bother to add decorative images. This isn't because the technologies don't exist, after all you can place hyperlinks which point to image files inside your CGI print statements. It's more likely that CGI programmers simply don't think about using images on their pages.

Since we're using Perl to develop our CGI scripts, we ought to investigate the facilities which it provides for graphics programming. If the language has any useful modules then we could try using them inside our Web pages. I hope you're already ahead of me here and have guessed that amongst the myriad things you can do with Perl, you can write programs which create and manipulate graphics. It's surprising at first glance that Perl, a text processing language, has graphical libraries. In fact if you look in the CPAN archive, you'll find that there are Perl modules for just about everything. The language has evolved. In so doing it has become a real general purpose language which can be used for many different classes of task.

What sort of image processing might you want, or need, to perform on your Web site? You might want to create images from scratch or you might want to alter existing images. Before writing any code you should be aware that this type of work can be extremely processor intensive. If you do a lot of graphical processing on your server you will place a high load on it and slow down other work. One good solution is to farm image processing out to another, dedicated, server. That's a great idea if you run your own servers, but generally it's not possible. You'll need to optimize your image processing code wherever you can and investigate profiling and performance enhancing tools before you do any serious work.

In my view, scripted image manipulation on Web sites can be used successfully in two areas. Firstly you can take existing images and alter them in some way. Creating image files can be difficult and time consuming. If you've gone to the effort of placing your digital photos onto your Web server, you probably don't want to have to edit each of those images in Adobe Photoshop to add a copyright message. You probably don't want to sort through and crop them all individually or add a sepia tint to each. You will probably want to preserve the image in its original state so that it can be used in different ways in different situations. It's important to remember that image files are just data files. When you alter the image you alter the data. Therefore if you change the color depth or file type you will be losing data from that file. Once that data has gone, it cannot be restored. Thus making those changes programmatically whilst preserving all of the image data is very appealing.

The second thing you can try is actually creating an image from scratch. The best use of this is probably the creation of graphs based upon data stored elsewhere. There are many situations in which you might need to present graphs of your data. You may want to demonstrate loading on your Web server, total sales over the last twelve months or absence rates amongst your coders on sunny days. Those data sets may be stored in plain text files on the Web server or inside proprietary software such as Excel spreadsheets or Oracle databases. If you can rely upon your users having the appropriate application, for instance the spreadsheet, on their machine then you might just as well use it. What if you need to present that data to sales staff who are on the road and have only a mobile phone and PDA with them? And what about download times? A spreadsheet is a large chunk of data to download, especially if you only need to scan a single graph. A small image, on the other hand, remains a small image however it's downloaded or viewed. The image can present exactly the same information as the spreadsheet graph so, why not use it?

Hundreds of different image formats are available. It sometimes seems that there's a rule somewhere stating that every single graphics package has to have a proprietary data format. Saving data in the native format of your graphics package ensures that you are saving the maximum amount of information possible about the image. Unfortunately it also means that the image is unlikely to be very portable. In fact, if you want to display an image in a Web browser you are really restricted to three data types: GIF, JPEG and PNG.

The GIF format was invented by Compuserve but uses a compression algorithm which Unisys had previously patented. This means that the developers of any software which can manipulate GIF files *must* pay royalties to Unisys. For a number of years the Unisys patent was widely ignored and many software applications were developed to manipulate GIFs. These included a number of Perl modules based around Thomas Boutell's GD library, which is written in C, and the ImageMagick library. Unisys has recently been much more assertive over its rights and these libraries no longer read or write GIF files.

> Note:
>
> The controversy over the Unisys patent doesn't mean that *you* can't use GIF files on your Web pages. It simply means that the *authors* of any software you use to create or manipulate those files must pay Unisys.

The loss of GIF as a format for the Web developer is important. GIFs have many advantages over other data types: they're nice and small and have just enough clarity to display well inside Web pages. GIF is a particularly nice format for logos, cartoons and graphs. JPEG, on the other hand, is designed for images of near photographic quality. A JPEG file will tend to be much larger than the same image stored as a GIF. The PNG format was developed as an open, patent-free replacement for GIF and is supported by version 3 and later of both Internet Explorer and Navigator. It's the format which I'm going to be using in the examples in this chapter.

I'm going to show you three different things you might want to try, and in doing so I hope to give you a brief introduction to the facilities in some of the Perl modules. I am *not* attempting to provide you with a user guide to those modules. Instead I'll give you enough information to get you started and to help you over some of the initial hurdles. Much more information can be found in the POD provided with the modules. If you want to go further, I'd also recommend checking out Shaun Wallace's book *Programming Web Graphics*. That was written when the modules still supported GIF files[11] but much of the detail remains appropriate and useful today.

Firstly I'll show you how to write some text onto an image using the GD.pm module. Secondly I'll show you how to create a simple graph with GD::Graph. Finally I'll demonstrate how you can filter and crop an existing image using ImageMagick.

## 11.6.1 Using GD

The GD module is a port to Perl of the GD library which was written by Thomas Boutell. The original version of the module was simply a wrapper around a set of calls to Boutell's C code. Later versions of the module include a complete port of the library to Perl. This

---

[11]It was published in spring 1999.

means that the library includes everything you need to draw and manipulate images. If you want to compile your own version then you'll need access to the header files and libraries from GD, if you're using a version someone else compiled, you won't. The module is available as a package for most Linux distributions and, from ActiveState, for Windows. By default, the GD.pm module produces PNG format images. Until recently the module could produce GIF files, older versions are available from its homepage. The port of GD was carried out by Lincoln Stein who also wrote CGI.pm.

**11.6.1.1  *Simple Applications***  I'll start by looking at a simple piece of code which writes a text string into a file as a PNG image. The process of creating an image has five stages:

- import the GD module into your script,
- create an image,
- create a color table which holds information about the colors that you'll use in the image,
- draw the image,
- output the image either to a file or to STDOUT for further processing elsewhere.

The following application shows those stages:

```
#!/usr/bin/perl -w

use GD;
use strict;

my ($newim, $red, $white, $OUT);

$newim = GD::Image->new(115, 20);
$white = $newim->colorAllocate(255, 255, 255);
$red = $newim->colorAllocate(190, 0, 0);
$newim->string(gdLargeFont, 0, 0, "This is a test", $red);

open(OUT, ">gdtest.png") || die ("Unable to open $OUT");
binmode OUT;
print OUT $newim->png;
close OUT;

exit(0);
```

Unlike many of the earlier examples, much of that won't make any sense at all without some explanation. I'll go through the code piece by piece and introduce the features of GD.pm along the way. The script starts with:

```
use GD;
use strict;
my ($newim, $red, $white, $OUT);
```

This tells the interpreter to use the GD module and to rigorously apply the rules of the language with the `strict` module. `GD.pm` includes three classes, each of which encapsulates a different set of functionality. These can be imported individually by writing, for instance:

```
use GD::Polygon;
```

or all of them can be included by using the statement shown in my script.

**GD::Image**

Used to read, store and write image data. This class provides access to many primitive graphics routines.

**GD::Font**

Holds information about fonts and is used when rendering text.

**GD::Polygon**

The polygon class is used to hold details of polygonal shapes. It stores a list of the vertices of the polygon which is rendered elsewhere.

```
$newim = new GD::Image(115, 20);
```

In graphics programming an image is a representation of a picture in memory. Before your scripts can perform any manipulations you need to create an image. This can be empty, as in the example, or based upon the contents of an existing file.

**$image = GD::Image->new([width, height])**

This creates a new image which contains no data. The `width` and `height` parameters are optional but if given they indicate the size of the image in pixels. If the parameters are omitted the image will be 64x64 pixels.

**$image = GD::Image(*FILEHANDLE)**

This creates an image based upon the contents of a filehandle. The filehandle must already be open.

**$image = GD::Image($filename)**

This creates an image based upon the contents of a file.

Once the image has been created the next stage is to allocate the colors:

```
$white = $newim->colorAllocate(255, 255, 255);
$red = $newim->colorAllocate(190, 0, 0);
```

This is done using the `colorAllocate()` method in the newly created image object. In the example I create two colors, the first one will be used for the background, the other for the foreground.

> **Note:**
> The first color that you create is *always* used as the background color for the image.

`$image->colorAllocate(red, green, blue)`
This function creates a color and returns its index in the color table. The parameters each take an integer value from 0 through to 255.

`$image->colorDeallocate($index)`
This marks the color at the given index as unused so that it can be reallocated.

`$image->colorClosest(red, green, blue)`
Will return the index of the allocated color which is closest to the one specified by the parameters. If no colors have been allocated the function will return -1.

`$image->transparent($index)`
All pixels which use the color at the supplied index are made transparent.

Now that the colors are allocated, it's time to create the image:

```
$newim->string(gdLargeFont, 0, 0, "This is a test", $red);
```

In this case I'm simply drawing a text string. I could have been using any of the dozens of drawing functions which the module provides.

`arc(cx, cy, width, height, start, end, $index)`
This draws an ellipse centered on position (`cx`, `cy`) with the specified height and width. The visible portion of the ellipse is given by the start and end positions. The arc is drawn in the color found at `$index` in the color table.

`fill(x, y, $index)`
This will fill a region starting at pixel (`x`, `y`) with the color found in the color table at the given index. The fill stops when it reaches any pixel which has a different color to the one at position (`x`, `y`).

`line(x1, y1, x2, y2, $index)`
This raws a line from the pixel at position (`x1`, `y1`) to the pixel at (`x2`, `y2`) in the color found at the given index.

`polygon($polygon, $index)`
This draws the polygon, which is described by the polygon object in the first parameter, in the color found at `$index`.

`rectangle(x1, y1, x2, y2, $index)`
This draws a rectangle whose top left corner is at (`x1`, `y1`) and whose bottom right corner is at (`x2`, `y2`). The rectangle is drawn in color `$index`.

`string($font, x1, y1, string, $index)`
This will draw a string starting at position (`x1`, `y1`) in the color at `$index`. The font can be any of:

- gdGiantFont
- gdLargeFont
- gdMediumBoldFont
- gdSmallFont
- gdTinyFont

**stringUp($font, x1, y1, string, $index)**

This works just like `string` but rotates the text through 90 degrees clockwise.

Finally the image is saved to a file:

```
open(OUT, ">gdtest.png") || die ("Unable to open $OUT");
binmode OUT;
print OUT $newim->png;
close OUT;
```

Writing to the file starts by opening it in a conventional way. Because some operating systems[12] distinguish between binary and text files, we need to set the filehandle to binary mode. This is done with:

```
binmode OUT;
```

Finally the data is written to the file using the `print` function and the filehandle closed.

### 11.6.1.2 *Working On The Web*
The previous example isn't very Web-aware. In fact the created image is saved to a file rather than being sent back to the browser. There's almost no point performing a manipulation like that on your Web site but not letting the user see the results instantly. In fact, getting the data back to the browser is very easy. You should remember that Web servers redirect STDOUT so that anything printed to it goes to the browser. The following code incorporates a couple of changes to get the output right:

```
#!/usr/bin/perl -w

use GD;
use strict;

my ($newim, $red, $white, $OUT);

$newim = GD::Image->new(115, 20);
$white = $newim->colorAllocate(255, 255, 255);
$red = $newim->colorAllocate(190, 0, 0);
$newim->string(gdLargeFont, 0, 0, "This is a test", $red);
```

---

[12]All variations of Microsoft Windows at the least.

```
print ("Content-type: image/png\r\n\r\n");
binmode STDOUT;
print $newim->png;
```

```
exit(0);
```

Notice that before running the `binmode` command I print a MIME type declaration:

```
print ("Content-type: image/png\r\n\r\n");
```

If I didn't do this, the browser would have no way of knowing that it was receiving an image file. Instead, it would attempt to show the characters inside the file as ASCII text. To avoid this, we need to warn the browser that it has to process the data as an image and display it properly.

If you comment out the printing of the MIME type, you can redirect the output of this script to a file or to another program so that you can check it's working. On a UNIX system[13] I can run the script and show its output in the ImageMagick `display` utility:

```
gdtest.cgi | display
```

or save the image in a file with:

```
gdtest.cgi > gdtest.png
```

### *11.6.1.3 Manipulating Existing Images*   The next situation which needs examining is the opening and alteration of an image which is stored in a file. The result may be written back to the file or sent to `STDOUT` from where it can be redirected. In the following example, I read in an existing file then draw a small blue triangle on top of it. Read the script then I'll explain it:

```
#!/usr/bin/perl -w

use strict;
use GD;

my ($IMGFILE, $im, $OUT, $triangle, $blue);

open(IMGFILE, "./logo.png")
    || die "Unable to open source file";
$im = newFromPng GD::Image(\*IMGFILE)
    || die "Unable to read image file";
close IMGFILE;
```

---

[13]So far as I know, you can't do this on a Windows box. You'll need to save the image in a file instead.

```
$triangle = new GD::Polygon;
$triangle->addPt(10, 5);
$triangle->addPt(50, 18);
$triangle->addPt(25, 4);

$blue = $im->colorAllocate(0, 0, 190);
$im->filledPolygon($triangle, $blue);

print ("Content-type: image/png\r\n\r\n");
binmode STDOUT;
print $im->png;
exit(0);
```

This script uses a different approach to creating an image. Rather than using the methods I outlined earlier, this time I use a specialized function:

```
$im = newFromPng GD::Image(\*IMGFILE)
```

**newFromPng GD::Image(FILEHANDLE)**

> This function creates a new image based upon the contents of a PNG file. A *reference* to a filehandle is passed in as the parameter. The function calls `binmode` when that is appropriate but does not automatically close the filehandle.

**newFromJpeg GD::Image(FILEHANDLE)**

> This will create a new image based upon the contents of a JPEG file. JPEG is a 24-bit format but GD uses 8-bit images so this method will lose data.

**newFromGd GD::Image(FILEHANDLE)**

> This creates an image based upon the contents of file in native GD format.

**newFromXpm GD::Image(FILEHANDLE)**

> Will create an image based on the contents of an XPM file. This method will not work in all versions of the GD module.

The next stage in the script is to create a triangle which I'll then draw on top of the image. The polygon object is an instance of the GD::Polygon class. Once created it is populated with a set of points. Each point represents one of the vertices of the polygon:

```
$triangle = new GD::Polygon;
$triangle->addPt(10, 5);
$triangle->addPt(50, 18);
$triangle->addPt(25, 4);
```

**addPt(x, y)**

> adds a point to the polygon,

**setPt(x, y)**
> changes the value of an existing vertex,

**deletePt(x, y)**
> deletes an existing vertex and returns the deleted value,

**length**
> returns the number of vertices in the polygon,

**vertices**
> returns a list in the polygon. Each item in the list is an array containing x and y co-ordinates.

The script concludes by writing the new image to STDOUT. Notice that this script leaves the original image in its original state.

## 11.6.2   Creating Graphs With GD::Graph

The GD module is clearly stocked with useful routines. These have been used by Martien Verbruggen in his creation of the GD::Graph module. This is a direct replacement for the earlier GIFgraph module. If you find that on your system, try to get an upgrade to the latest version of GD::Graph. Output formats mirror those of GD and, of course, data can be streamed back to a user so that the graph appears in their Web browser.

GD::Graph supports several types of graph and chart: line, point, area and bar graphs and pie charts. Individual data sets are displayed in different colors and you can supply titles, legends and titles for each axis. If you want a slightly different outcome there's also GD::Graph3D available which, you won't be surprised to learn, draws three-dimensional graphs.

### 11.6.2.1   *A Simple Application*   Again, I'm going to explain the module through a simple example. The following code draws a bar graph which contains two data sets. IT demonstrates the use of the key features of the module and should be enough to get you started:

```
#!/usr/bin/perl -w

use strict;
use GD::Graph::bars;

my (@data, @legend, $graph, $OUT, $drawn);

@data = ([qw(MON TUES WED THURS FRI SAT SUN)],
         [12, 356, 67, 346, 8, 0, 189],
         [45, 45, 45, 678, 45, 45, 5]
         );
```

```
@legend = ('Orders', 'Returns');
$graph = GD::Graph::bars->new();
$graph->set(x_label => 'Week Day',
            y_label => 'Volume',
            title => 'Returns and Orders (by day)');
$graph->set_legend(@legend);

my $format = $graph->export_format;

print STDOUT("Content-type: image/$format\r\n\r\n");
binmode STDOUT;
print STDOUT $graph->plot(\@data)->$format();

exit(0);
```

Let's look at some of the highlights.

I start of by deciding what type of graph I want to draw. The GD::Graph module supports several types, each implemented as a class. You must specify the type of graph you're going to create in your use statement:

```
use GD::Graph::bars;
```

**GD::Graph::area**
> is a graph which shows data as the area under a line,

**GD::Graph::bars**
> where data items are shown as bars,

**GD::Graph::lines**
> where data is represented by lines joining the data values,

**GD::Graph::linespoints**
> combines the features of a line and a point graph,

**GD::Graph::pie**
> in which data is represented as segments of a pie,

**GD::Graph::points**
> where data is represented by points.

The first stage in creating a graph must be the definition of the data set. Data is specified in an array which has to have a very particular format.

---

Note:
If you get the array structure wrong, GD::Graph will not be able to draw anything.

---

```
@data = ([qw(MON TUES WED THURS FRI SAT SUN)],
         [12, 356, 67, 346, 8, 0, 189],
         [45, 45, 45, 678, 45, 45, 5]
         );
```

The array consists of a series of arrays, each enclosed in square brackets. Each array *must* have the same number of items, if you don't have a value for one location use `undef`, don't leave a space. The next thing to do is to create a legend which is done using an array of strings, one for each data set that'll appear on the chart:

```
@legend = ('Orders', 'Returns');
```

Now we're ready to create the graph.

**`GD::Graph::type->new([width, height])`**
This creates a new graph object. Replace `type` in the definition with the class of graph which you want to create. The width and height parameters are optional, if you omit them the graph will be 400x300 pixels. The class of the graph will be one of lines, points, area, bars, linespoints or pie.

**`set(attribute => value...)`**
Once a graph object exists we can start to modify its default attributes. This is done using the `set` method which takes attribute/value pairs as parameters:

```
$graph->set(x_label => 'Week Day',
            y_label => 'Volume',
            title => 'Returns and Orders (by day)');
```

**`set_legend(@legend)`**
This sets the legend for your graph to the values in the array `@legend`,

**`$graph->export_format`**
The GD library defines a data type which it will use to export, that is to *output*, the finished graph. This function queries the library to find out what that format is and returns it, usually as a scalar,

**`plot(data)`**
This plots the graph and returns a `GD::Image` object,

Printing the graph is best done by combining the `plot()` and a call to the format object:

```
print STDOUT $graph->plot(\@data)->$format();
```

Of course, `GD::Graph` has many more options than I've shown you here. You can find out all about them in a command shell with:

```
perldoc GD::Graph
```

### 11.6.3    Using ImageMagick

Our final graphical application is included to show you the sort of thing which you can achieve if you use the correct module. ImageMagick is a set of tools which mostly run from the command line. These are truly industrial-strength tools, they can manipulate just about every graphics format that you can think of. They can perform conversions, filtering, help create animations and much more besides. Unlike GD, there's no direct Perl replacement for ImageMagick. Instead, there's a Perl wrapper which is used to call the native C code routines inside the ImageMagick tools. The Perl module you'll need is called `PerlMagick` At the time of writing, version 5.3 is available from CPAN.

The sample application I've created here takes an image in PNG format, inverts and crops it and filters it so that it looks like an oil painting. The two images are displayed inside a Web page. The result of all that processing is shown in Figure 11.3.

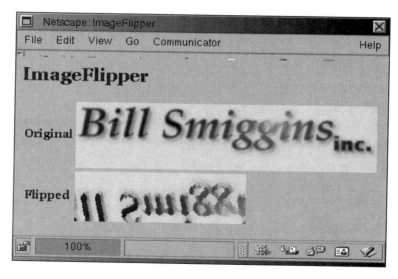

**Figure 11.3**   Using Image::Magick

### 11.6.3.1   *A Simple Application*   This little application has two pieces of code for us. An HTML page, and a CGI script.

### *The HTML Page*

```
<html>
   <head>
      <title>ImageFlipper</title>
   </head>
   <body>
      <h1>ImageFlipper</h1>
```

```
        <table border="0">
          <tr>
             <th>Original</th>
             <td><img src="./logo.gif"
                  height="80"
                  width="352"
                  alt="Logo"></td>
          </tr>
          <tr>
             <th>Flipped</th>
             <td><img src="../cgi-bin/flipper.cgi"></td>
          </tr>
        </table>
     </body>
</html>
```

There's nothing particularly new in that HTML. The important thing to notice is that the source of an image doesn't have to be a graphic file. In this example one of the sources is a CGI script:

```
<img src="../cgi-bin/flipper.cgi">
```

### The Script

```
#!/usr/bin/perl -w

use strict;
use Image::Magick;

my($image, $OUT, $blue);

$image = Image::Magick->new;
$image->Read('./logo.png');

$image->OilPaint(radius=>3);
$image->Crop('200x60+50+10');
$image->Flip();

print("Content-type: image/png\r\n\r\n");
$image->Write('png:-');
exit(0);
```

I've got absolutely no intention of going into any detail about that script. ImageMagick is extraordinarily complete and you really need to read its documentation before you attempt to use it. There's a Web site which has plenty of information, you can find it at:

`http://www.wizards.dupont.com/cristy/ImageMagick.html`

Only limited documentation is supplied with the PerlMagick distribution since it's effectively the same as ImageMagick. What you'll notice from the script I've given you is that reading, writing and manipulating images this way is pretty straightforward. Although ImageMagick itself is complicated, the API it offers is nice and clean.

## 11.7 EXERCISES

### Perl and Modules

1. What are the main features of the Perl module approach to library development?
2. Identify and describe the benefits which programmers get from the use of namespaces in programming languages.

### Relational Databases

1. List six benefits that arise from using relational databases in Web applications.
2. What is the Perl DBI module? How does it support database-independent applications development?
3. What is meant by the term session in conventional database usage? How does a DBI session differ from this?
4. Under what conditions would an application run more efficiently when using flat files rather than a database?
5. What is a prepared statement? Why must statements be prepared by DBI?
6. Alter your guestbook application so that it uses a relational database instead of flat files.
7. Write a database application using Perl DBI. How easy is it to build such an application so that it can be queried and updated from a Web page?

### `libwww`

1. If it isn't already available on your syste, install `libwww` and configure your system to use it.
2. Write a script to access the contents file at Slashdot. Display the contents of the file in your own Web page.
3. Write a script which will download an arbitrary Web page, extract its body section and display it inside a new Web page.
4. Modify your previous example so that the page contents are saved into a file.
5. Are there any legal or ethical objections to copying other sites in this way?

6. Write a script which measures the response times of various Web servers by seeing how long each takes to return the file `index.html`.

## HTML::Mason

1. Install and configre the `HTML::Mason` module. You may need to get hold of a copy of the Apache Web server before this works easily.

2. Create a simple page which uses two components: one for the header and one for the body. Check that a browser can access this page correctly via the Web server.

3. Create a guestbook which uses components to display comments from visitors.

4. Create an on-line photo album which is structured using Mason components.

## Manipulating Images

1. Download, install and configure the GD and PerlMagick modules. You may also need to install a version of ImageMagick.

2. Write a script which sepia tints the pictures in your on-line photo album.

3. Add a copyright message to each image as it is being downloaded from your site.

# 12
## An Introduction to PHP

Processing Web data using CGI has a relatively long history. Or at least as far as any Web technology can be said to have *history*, CGI has a long one. Simply because CGI was around first is no indication that it is any better than the alternatives, and there are plenty of those around just now. I'll take a look at two which are being pushed by big commercial players, Microsoft and Sun, in Chapter 13. Personally, I'm more interested in what the Free Software movement has to offer since excellent tools such as Perl and Apache come from that community.

Almost all non-CGI approaches to Web programming involve some form of *templating system*. Templates are outline HTML pages which have calls to scripts or programs embedded within them. When the page is requested the scripts are executed and the result of that execution replaces the original code. This is really the reverse of CGI. In CGI processing the script is called and it creates the HTML page. Why does it matter if the script or the markup come first? From a pure performance point of view the two approaches are really pretty similar. At runtime the server has to do quite a lot of work, but if you're using an Apache extension such as mod_perl you'll get great performance. The big difference really comes during development.

Large Web sites tend to be created by teams of people, each of whom brings their own specialized skills to the project. A really large site may need HTML authors, programmers to create scripts for both the server and the client, graphical designers and artists and, finally, content creators. If you're working for an organization like CNN or the BBC, you may only meet your collaborators at weekly team meetings, yet the work that each of you do is closely coupled to the work of everyone else. Consider the programmer and the HTML author. If a script is creating the HTML, who is leading the work? Is it the HTML author who decides what scripts are needed or the programmer who requests a particular HTML structure? And who does the design? Most programmers can create good code but their pages are likely to be poorly set out. HTML coders, on the other hand, may create great pages but lousy scripts.

This is where templating systems enter the picture. All of these systems place HTML and some scripting inside the same file but separate them so that they can be developed independently. The HTML author is able to write calls to scripted functions which a programmer can develop later. When the page is returned to a browser the script call is replaced by its result. That's enough introduction, this chapter is about PHP, so what is it?

## 12.1 PHP

The acronym PHP is one of the recursive kind favored by free software projects[1] and stands for *PHP Hypertext Processor*. The PHP project has a home on the Web at http://www.php.net where you can get source code, compiled binaries for systems like Microsoft Windows and a large, quite well written manual.

PHP is a development from a project called Personal Home Page Tools which was started by Rasmus Lerdorf in 1994. The original version consisted of a set of unique macros, a parser and some tools. The parser was rewritten in 1997 when a wider project was based around Lerdorf's original work. This parser was the basis of PHP3 which gained phenomenal popularity. Version 4 has another new parser and continues the growth in usage.

If you've never heard of PHP, you may be wondering just how popular it is. That is not a question which can be answered easily. It's possible to measure how many servers have PHP enabled and then calculate how many Web sites are hosted on those servers. In April 2001, the Netcraft Survey[2] said that PHP is available on over 1,000,000 servers and used in over 6,000,000 domains. Microsoft's ASP technology is more widely known but is actually used by fewer domains[3].

The reasons for the popularity of PHP are manifold:

- PHP is Web specific which makes it more attractive to many than, for instance, a more powerful tool like Perl,

- PHP is free software and has been ported to a vast range of operating systems.

- PHP works extremely well with many different Web servers, unlike the HTML::Mason Perl module which works best with Apache,

- PHP scripts can use many standard network protocols since libraries are supplied for IMAP, NNTP, SMTP and POP3 as well as HTTP,

- almost everything that Perl can do on the Web can be done by PHP including setting and reading cookies and image manipulation,

---

[1] After the example of GNU which stands for GNU is Not Unix.
[2] Which can be found at http://www.netcraft.com.
[3] Just 5,000,000 in January 2001.

- PHP is able to work with a vast range of database systems from UNIX DBM through relational systems such as MySQL to full size commercial solutions like Oracle.

The PHP language is described in its documentation as a mixture of Perl, C and Java. That sounds like a recipe for disaster but isn't, simply because you only have to use those facilities which you actually need. If you want to create classes and objects, you can. If you want to connect to a relational database on a remote server, you can. If you just want to parse data from a form and return an acknowledgement, you can do that too.

PHP is a large language but you can achieve a lot using just a small subset of it. I'm not planning to give you much more than an introductory overview in this book. I hope that I'll show you enough to enable you to get to grips with some quite complex scripting – you'll certainly see enough to help you to understand the documentation that is supplied with the PHP distribution. One important omission is the use of object-oriented development techniques. PHP can be used as a procedural language or it can be used to create complex object systems. I've not delved into the object-based features of Perl, and I plan not to look at those aspects of PHP. You'll find that a simple approach pays dividends when you're learning a new language, especially if you're not naturally inclined to be a programmer. If you do need to learn about PHP and objects, you'll find the discussion of object-orientation and JavaScript in Chapter 5 gives you a very useful primer.

## 12.2  USING PHP

Before I look at the PHP language, I'm going to show you how to use it. As ever you need some examples so that the explanation makes sense...but the examples won't make sense until you've read the explanation.

I don't want to spend time describing how to download, install and run PHP. You can get instructions from the project's homepage but you will find that configuring it to run with your particular Web server may be quite complex. Each Web server needs a different configuration – there's no such thing as a standard set-up on the Web. If you're using Apache, make sure that you also install the mod_php extension which will give greatly improved performance. In my experience, most systems seem to want developers to place their PHP files in the same directory tree as their HTML. Many of these same systems want CGI scripts in a special directory, usually called cgi-bin. This fits nicely with the PHP philosophy which places so much importance on HTML.

---

Note:
Unlike Perl's CGI.pm module, you can't normally run PHP as a standalone processor. If you want to use PHP you will need a running Web server.

---

Once you've got PHP installed on your Web server, you need to test it. Create a file called info.php and put this code in it:

```
<?php phpinfo() ?>
```

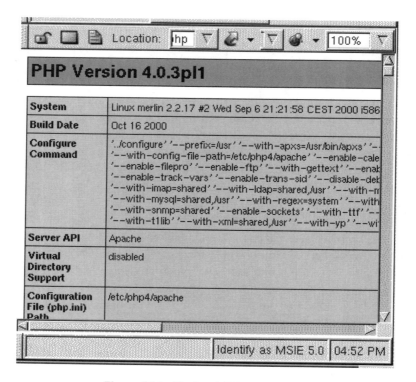

**Figure 12.1**   Testing A PHP Installation

Make sure that your Web server is up and running, then try to access the file through your Web browser. For instance on my desktop machine the address is:

```
http://localhost/html/info.php
```

Figure 12.1 shows part of the result on my system. If you don't get a similar result, you'll need to do some work on your configuration. If you've worked through some of the earlier programming examples in this book then you probably guessed that phpinfo() is some sort of function. It's one of many which are provided as part of the language. In this particular case it prints out vast amounts of information about your PHP installation, operating system and Web server. As an exercise try typing phpinfo into your favorite Web search engine. You'll find links to numerous of copies of the PHP documentation, you'll also see lots of people revealing fascinating things about their servers.

## 12.2.1   Including PHP In A Page

Once you've got PHP up and running, it's time to try creating a Web page. The following code is about the most simple you'll find anywhere. Save it in a file called simple.php and access it from the Web:

```
<html>
   <head>
      <title>Hello</title>
   </head>
   <body>
      <?php echo("<h1>Hello</h1>"); ?>
   </body>
</html>
```

The PHP instructions are placed inside special HTML tags. All PHP instructions have to be placed inside such tags, although you can place large blocks of code inside the same set. You do not have to use a new tag for each line of code. The inclusion of PHP within HTML files is called *escaping* in the PHP documentation. Four different methods are provided for escaping from HTML:

- `<?   echo("<h1>Hello</h1>"); ?>`
- `<?php echo("<h1>Hello</h1>"); ?>`
- ```
  <script language="php">
  echo("<h1>Hello</h1>");
  </script>
  ```
- `<% echo("<h1>Hello</h1>"); %>`

The first method is only available if your PHP installation has been configured to allow short tags. The second method is clear and is the one that I shall use in this book. The third method is useful if you find an environment which supports mixed scripting languages inside the same HTML file, most do not. The final method uses the ASP syntax and is also reliant upon server configuration.

When you want to display text in the browser the command you need is `echo()`. PHP shows its derivation from C and similar languages because lines of code are terminated using semi-colons and blocks of code are enclosed within braces[4]. Unlike JavaScript or Perl, PHP supports comments which span more than a single line of code:

```
<html>
   <head>
      <title>Comments</title>
   </head>
   <body>
      <?php echo("<h1>PHP Comments</h1>");
      // this comment only lasts for a single line
      /*
      * this comment spans more
```

---

[4]Which you can call curly brackets if you prefer.
```

```
        * than one line
        */
        ?>
    </body>
</html>
```

Comments are ignored by the interpreter when it parses your code. This means that you can use them in the *normal* way to describe your program, but you can also use them to *comment out* pieces of code which you do not want to execute.

Creating variables is also very easy. Variable names follow the same rules as Perl or JavaScript: alphanumeric characters are used plus the underscore and hyphen. Spaces are not allowed in variable names. There's one piece of syntax to note, variable names always start with the dollar sign:

```
$a_variable;
$name = "Chris";
$age = 36;
$height = 1.778;
```

## 12.2.2 Accessing HTTP Data

Creating Web pages which you can send back to the browser is pretty easy in PHP, what about getting hold of data that's been sent back from your Web forms? Again this is exceptionally straightforward. PHP automatically assigns data returned from a form to a variable which has the same name as the input element on the originating form. So, if you've got a text box on your form called address_line_1, you'll automatically get a variable called $address_line_1. You don't even have to declare or initialize it. Here's an HTML page containing a form, and a PHP script to process the return data:

```
<html>
    <head>
      <title>Web Forms in PHP</title>
    </head>
    <body>
      <h1>Web Forms in PHP</h1>

        <form action="http://localhost/html/guest.php"
              method="POST">

        <table border="0">
          <tr>
            <td>Your Name:</td>
            <td><input type="text"
                       maxlength="32"
```

```
                      size="20"
                      name="user"></td>
        </tr>
        <tr>
          <td>Your Email Address:</td>
          <td><input type="text"
                      maxlength="32"
                      size="20"
                      name="mail"></td>
        </tr>
        <tr>
          <td><input type="submit"
                      value="Submit Details"></td>
          <td><input type="reset"
                      value="Reset The Form"></td>
        </tr>
      </table>

    </form>
  </body>
</html>
```

Notice that the return data is going to be sent to a PHP script. Here that is:

```
<html>
    <head>
      <title>Your Data</title>
    </head>
    <body>
      <h1>Your Data Processed By PHP</h1>
      <table border="0">
      <tr>
          <th>Your Name:</th>
          <td><?php echo $user; ?></td>
      </tr>
      <tr>
          <th>Your Email Address:</th>
          <td><?php echo $mail; ?></td>
      </tr>
      </table>
    </body>
  </html>
```

## 12.3   VARIABLES

The use of variables is at the heart of all programming. Unlike Perl, where almost everything is either a scalar or an array, PHP variables have distinct types which means that they can be numbers, characters or strings. When PHP is interpreting your script it differentiates between these data types so that, for instance, you cannot generally add a string to a floating point number. Note, though, that you don't have to explicitly assign data types in your scripts. The PHP interpreter can work these things out for you. This means that a particular variable can hold numbers or strings or point to an array as the need arises.

Broadly speaking variables must have unique names which can contain a mixture of letters and numbers. Variable names are case-sensitive and cannot start with a digit. Case-sensitivity means that $fred is a different variable to $fRed.

### 12.3.1   Data Types

PHP variables are different from those found in languages like Java or C. They're much closer to the types of variable which we've encountered in JavaScript and Perl. Like those two, PHP is an interpreted language so nothing inside a script is really fixed until it runs.

*12.3.1.1   Numbers*   PHP supports two different numerical types. Most often you'll use *integers*. If you've not programmed before, the terminology may confuse you, but an integer is simply a whole number. They can be positive or negative values. The range[5] of integers in PHP is defined by the operating system and generally runs from approximately −2,000,000,000 up to 2,000,000,000. In computing terms that is $\pm 2^{32}$. PHP integers can be declared in base 10, base 8 (octel) or base 16 (hexadecimal):

```
$positiveInt = 14;
$negativeInt = -78;
$octelInt = 0421;
$hexadecimalInt = 0x1c;
```

The second numerical data type in PHP is the floating-point number. Floating point is a computer representation of positive and negative decimal numbers. They can be expressed as simple decimals or as exponential values. In PHP, floating point values are system dependent in the same way that integers are; however, the range is far larger. Floating points are 64 bit numbers with a range of approximately $\pm 1.8e38$. That's more than big enough for most Web scripts you'll ever write. Declaring floating point values is straightforward. The second example here uses the letter e to indicate that it's holding an exponential value:

```
$floater = 23.567;
$bigger = 4.6e7;
```

---

[5]The maximum and minimum values.

### 12.3.1.2 *Strings*

Most of the data that gets manipulated on the Web is text. In PHP, text is stored in strings. These must be surrounded with quotes so that the interpreter doesn't mistake them for commands. PHP lets you use either single or double quotes around a string. If you use double quotes, any PHP variables inside the string are replaced by their value. Here are a few strings:

```
$str = "A Simple String";
$str2 = 'Another String';
$str3 = "This is $str2";
$str4 = $str;
```

Like most programming languages, certain character sequences carry special meaning in PHP. For instance you need some way of telling the system to insert a newline inside the current piece of text. Such control characters must be replaced with *escape* sequences in your scripts. When the interpreter finds an escape sequence, those characters are replaced with the appropriate control code. Table 12.1 lists the possible escape codes in PHP.

***Table 12.1***  Escape Sequences in PHP

| Escape Sequence | Meaning |
| --- | --- |
| \n | Insert a newline character. |
| \r | Carriage return. |
| \t | Horizontal tab. |
| \\ | Backslash. |
| \$ | Dollar. |
| \" | Double quote. |

Joining strings together is done by the process of *concatenation*. PHP uses the dot operator to concatenate strings, as does Perl:

```
$str1 = "Have A Nice";
$str2 = "Day\n";
$str3 = $str1 . " ";
$str3 .= $str2;
```

Line three appends a string consisting of a single space onto the end of $str1 and stores the result in $str3. The operation uses $str1 but does not alter its value. In line four the value in $str2 is appended onto the value in $str3 and the result stored in $str3. PHP has a lot of operations which store their result in one of the original values, although most of these actually work with numbers not string.

### Here Documents

Often you will want to manipulate, especially display, a string which naturally spans more than one line of code. You can do this by placing a call to the echo () function before each line, but that is really pretty inefficient. Sending data to a browser like that may result in many calls to the interpreter and will certainly degrade performance. If the string is to be displayed pretty much *as is*, without any alteration, you are much better off using a *here* document. Unlike Perl, PHP will expand variables inside here documents. You're generally better off not doing this but instead keeping them in separate echo() statements to simplify code maintenance. In PHP a here document is delimited by « and a string token. The token is repeated at the end of the string to terminate printing. Again, unlike Perl, the terminating semi-colon appears after the terminating delimiter in PHP. The terminator must start in the first column of your code. Here's[6] an example:

```
<html>
   <head>
      <title>Using Here Docs</title>
   </head>
   <body>
echo <<<_DONE
<h1>Using Here Docs</h1>
<p> The string which is being displayed
in the browser can span
several lines.</p>
_DONE;
   </body>
</html>
```

As a refresher, the same here document in Perl would look like:

```
echo <<_DONE;
<h1>Using Here Docs</h1>
<p> The string which is being displayed
in the browser can span
several lines.</p>
_DONE
```

### 12.3.1.3 Arrays
When you need to store more than one data item in a list you'll need to use an array. An array is a structured list of data items which are accessed via an index value. PHP supplies two different array types: the basic array uses a numerical index to order its contents, the associative array uses a text string. The PHP associative array works exactly like the hash array in Perl, in fact it's the same thing[7]. You can actually mix and match the two array types in the same array in PHP so that some items are accessed by their index and others by a key value. I'm going to discuss them separately for clarity.

---

[6]D'oh!
[7]Strictly speaking, in Perl a hash is really called an associative array.

*The Basic Array*   Array operations are exactly the same as those found in JavaScript or Perl. Assignment to the array is done through index values. If you use empty brackets in an assignment operation, the new value is added onto the end of the array. PHP arrays can grow dynamically but if you want to remove items from the middle of an array you'll need to write your own function for doing so. Indexes in a PHP are placed in square brackets after the array name in exactly the same fashion as in Perl or JavaScript.

```
<html>
    <head>
        <title>Array Operations</title>
    </head>
    <body>
        <h1>Array Operations</h1>
        <ul>
        <?php
            $array[0] = "Fido";
            $array[1] = "Rover";
            echo "<li>".$array[1]."</li>";
            $mydog = $array[0];
            echo "<li>".$mydog."</li>";
            $array[] = $array[0].$array[1];
            echo "<li>".$array[2]."</li>";
        ?>
        </ul>
    </body>
</html>
```

*Associative Arrays*   In an associative array, each item is indexed with a key value. The key must be a unique string. Here's a simple example which can be dropped into the previous code:

```
<?php
    $array["pet"] = "Fido";
    $array["friend"] = "Rover";
    echo "<li>".$array["friend"]."</li>";
    $mydog = $array[0];
    echo "<li>".$mydog."</li>";
    $array[0] = $array["pet"].$array["friend"];
    echo "<li>".$array[0]."</li>";
?>
```

If you try running that code you'll find that the line

```
$mydog = $array[0];
```

doesn't produce any output. Although the two PHP array types can be mixed together, once you've created a key value for an array item you'll need to use that key to get at the data value. You can't assume that the data items are placed in the array in the order in which you supply them.

An associative array can be created using a syntax which will be familiar if you've worked through the Perl material:

```php
<?php
    $array = array(
        "pet" => "Fido",
        "friend" => "Rover");

    echo "<li>".$array["friend"]."</li>";
    $mydog = $array["pet"];
    echo "<li>".$mydog."</li>";
    $array[0] = $array["pet"].$array["friend"];
    echo "<li>".$array[0]."</li>";
?>
```

I'll look at the `array()` function in a while. What I want you to notice from that example is that key:value pairs can be passed to the array constructor using `=>` to link them. The key:value pairs are passed in as a comma separated list to the constructor.

*Multidimensional Arrays*   Sometimes data is nice and simple. For instance if you wanted to list all of the items sold by a grocer, you could use a simple array:

```php
<?php
    $veg[0] = "peas";
    $veg[] = "carrots";
    $veg[] = "purple sprouting broccoli";
```

but real data is often more complex than that. Consider the example of Fido and Rover. A dog's home might want to record more information about them such as their color, weight, or temperament. Possibly the easiest way of storing this data is to create a multidimensional array. This is really an array of arrays in which each item, for instance the dog's name, leads to more items, such as her details. In PHP both indexed arrays and associative arrays can be multidimensional. Here are examples of both in action down at the pound. First the associative array:

```html
<html>
    <head>
        <title>Pooches</title>
    </head>
    <body>
        <h1>At The Dog's Home Today</h1>
```

```
    <ul>
    <?php
    $array = array(
        "pen1" => array(
            "name" => "Fido",
            "color" => "brown",
            "temperament" => "quiet"),
        "pen2" => array(
            "name" => "Rover",
            "color" => "white",
            "temperament" => "noisy"),
        "pen3" => array(
            "name" => "Patch",
            "color" => "brown and white",
            "temperament" => "friendly"));

        echo "<li>".$array["pen2"]["name"];
        echo "<ul><li>".$array["pen2"]["color"]."</li>";
        echo "<li>".$array["pen2"]["temperament"]."</li>";
        echo "</ul>";
        echo "</li>";
    ?>
    </ul>
</body>
</html>
```

Next the PHP code from the indexed array:

```
<?php
    $array[0][0] = "Fido";
    $array[0][] = "brown";
    $array[0][] = "quiet";
    $array[1][0] = "Rover";
    $array[1][] = "white";
    $array[1][] = "noisy";
    $array[2][0] = "Path";
    $array[2][] = "brown and white";
    $array[2][] = "friendly";

    echo "<li>".$array[1][0];
    echo "<ul><li>".$array[1][1]."</li>";
    echo "<li>".$array[1][2]."</li>";
    echo "</ul>";
```

```
    echo "</li>";
?>
```

The associative array is much *cleaner* than the indexed version. That's partly a function of the data I'm using here. It's also because remembering that you want to access the color of the dog in pen2 is far easier than remembering that you want data item 1 of array item 1. Notice that when I was creating the associative array, I was able to nest calls to the `array` function. Each call was separated from the following one with a comma just as the data items were in the single dimensional associative array.

*Array Functions*    PHP supplies a rich set of builtin functions which can be used to operate on arrays. You'll find that using these builtin operations takes a lot of the pain out of the array data structure. In other languages, C for instance, handling arrays is fraught with difficulty. PHP is more like JavaScript in this respect: the language developers have done a lot of the hard work for you.

**array(var1[, var2[, varn]])**
Creates a new array which contains all of the values that are passed in as parameters.

**array_intersect(array1, array2[, arrayn])**
Returns a new array which contains all of the elements from `array1` which are also present in *all* of the other arrays. This function works best with associative arrays since it preserves the values of keys and the new array can be accessed via the key of `array1`. Here's an example:

```
<?php
    $pen1 = array("Fido" => "brown", "quiet");
    $pen2 = array("Rover" => "brown", "noisy");
    $new_array = array_intersect($pen1, $pen2);
    echo "<li>".$new_array["Fido"]."</li>";
?>
```

That code sets $new_array to the key:value pair "Fido" => "brown".

**array_keys(array)**
Returns an array containing all of the keys from the associative array which is given as the parameter.

**array_merge(arr1, arr2[, arrn])**
Merges all of the arrays which are given as parameters. If the arrays have common keys, the values from later arrays will override those from earlier ones.

**array_pop(array)**
Removes the last element from the array and returns it. This operation reduces the length of the array by 1.

**array_push(array, var1[, varn])**
Adds one or more elements onto the end of the array.

**array_reverse(array)**

Returns a new array which contains all the elements from the original array but now in reverse order.

**array_shift(array)**

Returns the first element in the array, removes it from the array and so shortens the array by one item.

**array_slice(array, offset[, length])**

Returns a subarray starting at the position indicated by the *offset* parameter. If no length is given, all elements to the end of the array are returned. If length is negative, the copy will stop that many elements from the end. Here's a small example which copies the last two elements from an array:

```php
<?php
    $fido = array("brown", "quiet", "small", "one-eyed");
    $tmp = array_slice($fido, 2);
    echo "<li>".count($tmp)."</li>";
    echo "<li>".$tmp[0]."</li>";
    echo "<li>".$tmp[1]."</li>";
?>
```

**array_unshift(array, var1[, varn])**

Pushes one or more elements onto the *start* of the array.

**asort(array)**

Sorts an associative array and in doing so preserves the association between each key and its value.

**count(var)**

Returns the number of items in the variable. Usually the variable will be an array, if it is not then count() will return 1. If the variable has not been set, count() will return 0.

**each(array)**

Returns the next key:value pair from an array.

**in_array($var, array)**

Returns TRUE if the variable, $var is present in the array.

**is_array(var)**

Returns TRUE of the variable is an array, FALSE if it is not.

**key(array)**

Returns the key value for the item at the current index.

**list(var1, var2[, varn])**

Assigns a set of values to variables as if they were an array.

**sizeof(var)**

Returns the number of elements in the array.

```
sort(array)
```

Sorts the items in an array into ascending order and returns the sorted list.

The following code shows a number of the array functions in action. The output is shown in Figure 12.2:

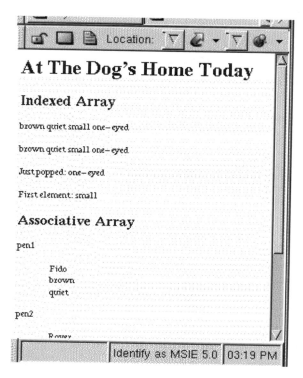

**Figure 12.2**   Converting Strings To Numbers

```
<html>
  <head>
    <title>Pooches</title>
  </head>
  <body>
    <h1>At The Dog's Home Today</h1>
    <h2>Indexed Array</h2>

    <?php
    $fido = array("brown", "quiet", "small", "one-eyed");

    echo "<p>";
    for($i = 0; $i < count($fido); $i++) {
```

```php
        echo $fido[$i]." ";
}

echo "</p><p>";
while(list($key, $val) = each($fido)){
    echo $val." ";
}
echo "</p>";

$tmp = array_pop($fido);
echo "<p>Just popped: ".$tmp."</p>";
$tmp = array_reverse($fido);
echo "<p>First element: $tmp[0]</p>";
?>
```

<h2>Associative Array</h2>

```php
<?php
$array = array(
    "pen1" => array(
        "name" => "Fido",
        "color" => "brown",
        "temperament" => "quiet"),
    "pen2" => array(
        "name" => "Rover",
        "color" => "white",
        "temperament" => "noisy"),
    "pen3" => array(
        "name" => "Patch",
        "color" => "brown and white",
        "temperament" => "friendly"));

echo "<dl>";
while(list($key, $val) = each($array)){
    echo "<dt>$key</dt><dl>";
    while(list($k, $v) = each($val)){
        echo "<dd>$v</dd>";
    }
    echo "</dl>";
}
echo "</dl>";
```

```
    ?>
   </body>
</html>
```

The code demonstrates the use of both array types. I start by displaying the indexed array in two different ways. Firstly I use a simple `for()` loop exactly as you'll have seen me do in JavaScript and Perl. The second variant uses some PHP functions:

```
while(list($key, $val) = each($fido)){
  echo $val." ";
}
```

This is a normal `while()` loop which uses some interesting functions to control iteration. The `each()` function is used to control movement across the array. When the end of the array is reached, this function will return FALSE and the loop will terminate. The function returns a key:value pair, in an indexed array it returns the array index and its associated value. I use the `list()` function to copy these into two variables. I'm not interested in the keys since I know that they are simply numerical values, so I ignore them in the print statement.

Printing out the contents of the associative array is slightly more complex. In part this is due to the nature of the data structure I've created.

```
while(list($key, $val) = each($array)){
  echo "<dt>$key</dt><dl>";
  while(list($k, $v) = each($val)){
    echo "<dd>$v</dd>";
}
```

This code has two loops. The outer one iterates across the main data structure, `$array`, copying the keys and values into two variables. Because the data structure I'm using is a multidimensional associative array, the values here are, themselves, arrays. I want to print out the values in these subarrays so I iterate across each of them. I extract the data values and finally display them.

### *12.3.1.4 Changing Data Type*
Strings can be evaluated as if they were numbers in the right circumstances. If a string contains only digits it can be used in mathematical expressions as if it were the equivalent number. For instance "12.561" automatically gets treated as 12.561. Optionally, such strings can start with '+' or '-' signs. If a string contains either 'e' or 'E' followed by one or more digits, it will be treated as an exponential value. Conversion of the string to a number stops when any characters are encountered which cannot normally be found in a number. Numbers, of course may be represented in base 10, 8 or 16. The following code shows some string conversions. The result is shown in Figure 12.3:

```
<html>
  <head>
```

```
    <title>Strings Into Numbers</title>
  </head>
  <body>
    <h1>Strings Into Numbers</h1>
    <ul>
    <?php
        $n = "0x237a";
        echo "<li>".$n."</li>";
        echo "<li>".($n * 3)."</li>";
        $n2 = "34re5";
        echo "<li>".($n2 + 2)."</li>";
        $n3 = "boo";
        echo "<li>".($n3 + 2)."</li>";
    ?>
    </ul>
  </body>
</html>
```

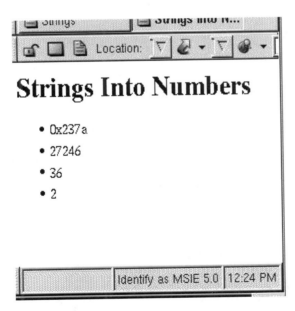

**Figure 12.3** Converting Strings To Numbers

PHP also supports *type casting*. This process involves dynamically changing the type of a data item. You might need to do this if your variable holds an integer but you want to use it in floating point arithmetic. These type casts can be automatic, for instance if you add a double to an integer, the result will be a double even if you are storing it in the original integer variable:

```php
<?php
   $int = 32;
   $float = 12.67;
   $int += $float;
   echo $int;
?>
```

But you can be explicit about type casts too. This is done by putting the type you want the variable to become in parentheses before the variable name:

```php
<?php
   $int = 32;
   $float = 12.67;
   $res = $float + (float)$int;
   echo $res;
?>
```

## 12.3.2   Regular Expression

A regular expression, which may also be called a regex or regexp, is a string which denotes a search pattern. The search pattern is applied to text strings inside your script. Regular expressions have been used for many, many years in computing but are still, in some ways, considered a bit of a black art. PHP regular expressions use identical syntax to those found in Perl, in fact they're based upon the Perl version. Since Perl regular expressions also heavily influenced the development of the JavaScript regex *engine*, the PHP and JavaScript versions work in the same way too. This happy coincidence means that I don't have to spend a lot of time here describing the syntax of the things since I've already done so elsewhere. Therefore, before reading this section I'd like to refer you back to Section 6.2 and Section 8.9.

Whilst the mechanism for creating the patterns which make up a regex are the same in all three languages, the way in which they're used differs. Having created the pattern, you'll need to use some PHP-specific functions if you want to apply it.

**preg_match(pattern, string[, matches])**

Hunts for strings which match the supplied pattern in the string subject. This match will stop once it has found a target. Optionally an array can be supplied as the third parameter. This will be used to store matches. The first item in the array, item 0, contains the text which matches. Any text matching patterns which are placed in parentheses[8] will be placed into subsequent array items. Here's an example:

```php
<?php
   $test = "This is a test";
```

---

[8]Compare this with backreferences in Perl.

```php
if (preg_match("/(\ws)\s(\ws)/", $test, $matches)) {
    echo "</h3>Matched<h3>";
    echo "$matches[0],<br>";
    echo "$matches[1],<br>";
    echo "$matches[2].<br>";
} else {
    echo "<h3>Did not match</h3>";
}
?>
```

the program outputs Matched is is, is, is., formatted suitably of course. The text his is contains the matched strings. It is stored in the first element of $matches. The two strings in parentheses in the regular expression describe the substrings that I want to store. The two matches are any single letter followed by the letter s, and must, themselves, be separated only by a single space. If the sample string $test were changed so that more than one space separated each word, it would not match the regular expression.

**preg_match_all(pattern, string)**
Works like preg_match() but matches *all* occurrences of the pattern in the string.

**preg_replace(pattern, replacement, string)**
If the regex pattern is found in the string, it is replaced by the string supplied as the second parameter.

**preg_split(pattern, string)**
Splits the string at all points which match the pattern. Returns an array of strings containing all of the substrings it creates.

Let's start by looking at a simple pattern match.

```html
<html>
    <head>
        <title>Regexes</title>
    </head>
    <body>
        <h1>Using Regexes in PHP</h1>
        <p>
        <?php
            $pattern = "/target/";
            $string = "Can you find the target?";
            if (preg_match($pattern, $string)) {
                echo "Found it";
            } else {
                echo "Didn't find it";
            }
```

```
    ?>
  </p>
 </body>
</html>
```

The pattern match could also have been written:

```
if(preg_match("/target/", "Can you find the target?"))
```

which is rather closer to the sort of thing you'll see in Perl. One thing about PHP which is slightly different to other languages, is that the pattern has to be inside quotes *and* it has to have delimiters. I've used slashes since by convention, they are used in most other pattern matching languages. Here's a match which stores its results:

```
<?php
    $pattern = "/([a-z]+\?)/";
    $string = "Can you find the target?";
    if(preg_match($pattern, $string, $matches)) {
        echo "Found $matches[0]";
    } else {
        echo "Didn't find it";
    }
?>
```

The pattern matches repeated lower-case characters followed by a question mark. Clearly this will only match `target?` in the string. The pattern is placed inside parentheses and gets stored in the first element of the array `$matches`. This example shows a simple replacement:

```
<?php
    $pattern = "/[a-z]+\?/";
    $string = "Can you find the target?";

    if($new = preg_replace($pattern, "replacement", $string)) {
        echo "$new";
    } else {
        echo "Didn't find it";
    }
?>
```

Again, I'm looking for the string `target?`. If the string is matched, it will be changed for `replacement`. This operation returns a new string and leaves the original, `$string` unaltered. Splitting strings work as you might expect. Here's one of the earlier Perl examples rewritten in PHP. Figure 12.4 shows the result:

```
<html>
    <head>
```

```
    <title>Regexes</title>
</head>
<body>
    <h1>Using Regexes in PHP</h1>

    <?php
        $test = "cookies::multipack::chocolate::brownies";
        $parts = preg_split("/::/", $test);

        echo "<ul>";
        while(list($key, $val) = each($parts)) {
            echo "<li>$val</li>";
        }
        echo "</ul>";
    ?>

</body>
</html>
```

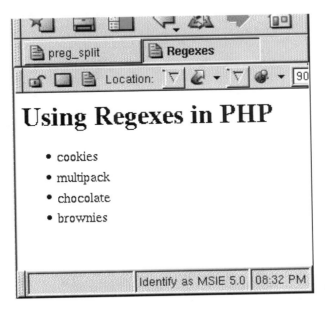

***Figure 12.4***  Splitting Strings

## 12.4  PROGRAM CONTROL

PHP scripts require structure in the same way that those written in JavaScript and Perl do. Like those two languages, PHP is structured in blocks of code with each block delimited by curly brackets. You've already seen this in the examples I've presented so far. Programs are much more than blocks and variables. Within a program you need to make choices about what will happen and decide how often things happen. You might want your program displaying an error message if a visitor fails to enter their email address in the appropriate field of your form. You may want to print out a list of items which a shopper has placed in their cart.

Program control is provided by a set of structures which let you make choices and decisions. Broadly, these program elements can be split into two sets: operators and control structures. Operators generally take two arguments and return a result. Most programming languages provide an addition operator which takes two numbers, adds them together and gives you back the answer. In PHP we also get operators which work on string data. I've already introduced you to the dot operator which is used to join strings together, for example. Table 12.2 lists the operators which PHP provides.

*Table 12.2*  Logical Operators (text and numerical)

| Op | Meaning | Op | Meaning |
|---|---|---|---|
| > | Greater than | >= | Greater than or equal to |
| < | Less than | <= | Less than or equal |
| == | Equal to | != | Not equal to |
| = | Assignment | + | Addition |
| / | Division | * | Multiplication |
| - | Subtraction | % | Modulus division |
| && | Logical AND | \|\| | Logical OR |
| ! | Logical NOT | += | Add two values then assign the result to the operand on the left |
| -= | Subtract then assign the result to the operand on the left | *= | Multiply then assign the result to the operand on the left |
| /= | Divide then assign the result to the operand on the left | .= | Concatenate two strings then assign the result to the operand on the left |
| %= | Modulus division then assign the result to the operand on the left | ++ | Increment a value by one |
| -- | Decrement a value by one | | |

Program control is provided through a set of branching and looping constructs. PHP provides the same set as many other languages.

## if...[ elseif...]   else

Many things inside programs are optional. As programs run they are continually having to make decisions about what to do. Generally these decisions are based upon the state of variables or the value of expressions. The program is being asked to evaluate expressions such as "if the value entered was greater than ten, do *A*, otherwise do *B*". In programming, such a statement is simplified to:

```
if(value > 10) {
    A
} else {
    B
}
```

The if...else structure makes choices based upon the value of the expression which follows if. Such expressions are called Boolean because they evaluate to either TRUE or FALSE. When the expression is TRUE, the code which follows if is executed. When the expression is FALSE, the code following the else clause executes.

If you have more than two choices, you'll need a slightly different construct. PHP provides an elseif clause which expands the number of choices you can make:

```
<html>
    <head>
        <title>Welcome</title>
    </head>
    <body>
        <h1>Welcome</h1>
        <p>
        <?php
            if($name == "Chris"){
                echo "Hi Chris!";
            } elseif($name != ""){
                echo "Hi $name";
            } else {
                echo "Please enter your name";
            }
        ?>
        </p>
    </body>
```

Save that code in a file called names.php in the directory where you normally keep your PHP/HTML files. Run it by typing the URL of the file and supplying a name as parameter. On my system I use:

```
http://localhost/html/names.php?name=Chris
```

You can have as many `elseif` clauses as you need in there. If you are making a lot of decisions in the same place, you'll probably find using `switch` instead makes your code much more readable.

> **Note:**
> In PHP we use `elseif`, in Perl we use `elsif` for the same thing. If you mix those up, you'll get syntax errors thrown up by the parser.

### while

The `while` loop is used when you want to perform a set of operations repeatedly until a condition becomes FALSE. Earlier you saw this code which repeats until there are no more items in the array:

```php
<?php
    $test = "cookies::multipack::chocolate::brownies";
    $parts = preg_split("/::/", $test);

    echo "<ul>";
    while(list($key, $val) = each($parts)) {
        echo "<li>$val</li>";
    }
    echo "</ul>";
?>
```

### for

The `for` loop also repeats. It's used in a more controlled fashion because we are explicit about the number of times that we want the loop to iterate:

```php
<?php
    for($i = 0; $i < 10; $i++) {
        echo "Hi $name";
    }
?>
```

### foreach

Looping over arrays can be done in a number of ways. I've already shown you how to use `each`, but that can lead to quite clumsy code. Using `foreach` leads to cleaner code. The basic syntax is:

```
foreach($array as $value)
```

which puts the next element of the array into `$value` on each loop. If you have an associative array, you'll need to extract both the key and the value:

```
foreach($array as $key => $value)
```

Here's the cookie example again:

```php
<?php
    $test = "cookies::multipack::chocolate::brownies";
    $parts = preg_split("/::/", $test);

    echo "<ul>";
    foreach($parts as $key => $val){
        echo "<li>$key => $val</li>";
    }
    echo "</ul>";
?>
```

## break

Not all loops need to run until their scheduled end. If you want to leap out of a loop, do so using break. The following code will print out the name which the user enters ten times unless that name is "Chris", that only gets printed once:

```php
<?php
    $count = 10;
    while($name) {
        echo "Hi $name";
        if(--$count == 0) {
            break;
        }
        if($name == "Chris") {
            break;
        }
    }
?>
```

## switch

When you need to select between lots of options, an if...elseif...else structure can become unwieldy. The switch statement is much more usable.

```
switch(expression) {
  case label:
      statement;
      [statement;]
      break;
  [case label:
      statement;
      [statement;]
      break;]
  [default:
      statement;]
}
```

A `switch` selects between a number of choices depending upon the value of the expression. The choices are identified by `case` statements, each has a `label` which equals one of the potential values of the expression. If none of the `cases` matches the expression, the optional `default` may be used instead.

*The Sieve Of Eratosthenes*    Here's a more comprehensive script which uses several different program control structures. The Sieve of Eratosthenes is an algorithm for calculating prime integers. Prime integers are whole numbers which are divisible only by themself and 1. This method uses an array to perform the calculation and is adapted from an exercise set by Deitel and Deitel in their *How To Program* books. The algorithm is:

- an array is created, the length set by a parameter passed to the script,
- all elements of the array are initialized to 1,
- starting at the third element of the array, the first two being 0 and 1,
  - the index is stored,
  - the array is looped through,
  - all elements whose index is a multiple of the stored value are set to 0,
- the index of each element whose value is 1 are displayed.

```
<html>
   <head>
      <title>Prime Numbers</title>
   </head>
   <body>
      <h1>Sieve of Erastothenes</h1>
      <ul>
      <?php
         if($len > 1000) {
            echo "<h2>Use only values up to 1000</h2>";
         } else {
            $counter = 1;
            $array[0] = 1;
            while($counter < $len){
               $array[] = 1;
               $counter ++;
            }
            for($i = 2; $i < $len; $i++) {
               if($array[$i] == 1) {
                  $inc = $i;
                  for($j = $i + $inc; $j < $len; $j += $inc){
                     $array[$j] = 0;
                  }
```

```
                }
            }
            for($i = 0; $i < $len; $i++) {
                if($array[$i] == 1) {
                    echo "<li>$i</li>";
                }
            }
        }
    ?>
    </ul>
    </body>
</html>
```

## 12.4.1  User Defined Functions

Large scripts tend to repeat the same operations as they run. When writing a script like
that you *could* repeat the same code in numerous places throughout the script. The difficulties with doing that have been well documented since the 1960s, broadly there are two
which need concern us here. Firstly, the repeated code will make your scripts larger, they
will take longer loading and being interpreted[9], put an increased load on your server and
reduce performance of your Web site. Secondly, whenever you repeat code you increase
the possibility of transcription and typing errors and of introducing errors of logic. These
lead to buggy code which takes longer to develop.

The solution is to extract the repeated code, place it into special blocks called *functions*
and place *calls* to those functions into the main body of your script. Functions can have
arguments, values which are passed to them, and can return the result of their processing.
Here's an example:

```
<html>
    <head>
        <title>Functions</title>
    </head>
    <body>
        <h1>Using Functions in PHP4</h1>
        <?php
        $array = array(
            "pen1" => array(
                "name" => "Fido",
                "color" => "brown",
                "temperament" => "quiet"),
```

---

[9]Yes, I know this must be offset against the cost of function calls.

```
            "pen2" => array(
                "name" => "Rover",
                "color" => "white",
                "temperament" => "noisy"),
            "pen3" => array(
                "name" => "Patch",
                "color" => "brown and white",
                "temperament" => "friendly"));

        foreach($array as $key => $val) {
            $name = showDog($val);
        }

        function showDog($dog) {
            foreach($dog as $key => $val) {
                if($key == "name") {
                    $ret = $val;
                }
                echo "$key -- $val<br>";
            } // foreach

            echo "<br>";
            return $ret;
        } // end of function

        ?>
    </body>
</html>
```

The function showDog() is passed an array and returns a string. I don't actually do anything with the string...it's there to show how return values work. Notice that in PHP4 you don't have to define a function before you call it. If you're still using PHP3 you'll need to find out how to define the function above the call in your code.

## 12.5   BUILTIN FUNCTIONS

PHP4 includes literally thousands of useful functions. I don't have the time or the space to describe them all in this book. Fortunately the PHP distribution includes a manual which outlines them all. I've attempted to show you some of the most useful PHP functions, but I've really tried to concentrate on those which have near-equivalents in Perl so that you can fairly compare the two languages.

In fact, one of the great things about developing using open source scripting languages is the shear volume of useful code that you have at your disposal. When you install PHP4 you're getting the basic language, an interpreter and copious libraries. Look around the Web for a short time and you'll find even more code – there's a large repository of libraries at the PHP Web site to get you started. In fact almost any programming task that you need to achieve on a Web site can be done with PHP.

One of the great benefits of PHP is said to be the ease with which your scripts can access relational databases. When you've used a few languages for the same task you find that PHP is nearly as good in this respect as more established languages like Perl and Python. It's facilities far exceed those of Java, C++ or Visual Basic. In fact you can get at virtually any database from inside a PHP script, all you need to do is use the right library. This is where one of the limitations of the language appears. In Perl there is a standard database interface for all relational systems which use SQL. Once you've learnt how to connect to Access on a PC, you can use exactly the same knowledge to connect to Oracle across a network. PHP is slightly less *developer friendly*, there's not the same common interface. None of the libraries are too complex though and much of your knowledge transfers pretty easily.

In this section I'm going to examine some of the facilities which the PHP libraries provide. I've tried to concentrate on those libraries which you can start using straight away. I'm *not*, though, looking at database access simply because of the variety of libraries available to you.

## 12.5.1   Math Functions

`abs(number)`
   Returns the absolute value of a number. If the argument is a floating point number, the return value will also be a float. Otherwise it will be an integer.

`acos(float)`
   Returns the arc cosine in radians.

`asin(float)`
   Returns the arc sine in radians.

`atan(float)`
   Returns the arc tangent in radians.

`ceil(float)`
   Returns the integer which is directly higher than the argument. `ceil(34.56)` would return 35.

`cos(float)`
   Returns the cosine in radians.

`exp(number)`
   Returns e raised to the power of the argument.

`floor(float)`
   Returns the integer directly lower than the argument.

`log(float)`

Returns the natural logarithm of the argument.

`log10(float)`

Returns the base 10 logarithm of the argument.

`max(arg1, arg2[, argn])`

Returns the largest of its arguments.

`min(arg1, arg2[, argn])`

Returns the smallest of its arguments.

`pi()`

Return the value of $\pi$.

`pow(arg1, arg2)`

Returns `arg1` raised to the power of `arg2`.

`rand([min[, max]])`

Returns a pseudo-random number. If `max` or `min` are set, they place limits upon the range in which the number will be generated. Before calling `rand()` you *must* call `srand()` to seed the random number generator.

`round(float[, precision])`

Rounds the floating point number. If no precision is specified, the number is rounded to the nearest whole number. For instance `round(3.6)` will return `4.0` and `round(3.2)` will return `3.0`. If the precision is provided, it sets the number of decimal places in the result.

`sin(float)`

Returns the sine in radians.

`sqrt(number)`

Returns the square root of its argument.

`srand(integer)`

Seed the random number generator using the supplied value. Random number generators are not really random. If left to their own devices and called repeatedly, they actually produce a sequence of values. At some point the sequence will repeat, the trick in writing a random number generator is to make the sequence before repetition very long. The sequence, and it's length, are determined by the *seed* value which is supplied. Therefore to get the appearance of a random sequence you must re-seed the generator each time that you use it.

`tan(float)`

Returns the tangent in radians.

## 12.5.2    Dates and Times

PHP has a decent set of functions for manipulating times and dates. Most often you'll want to get the current time and date to use as a timestamp either on a page or in a database. These functions are provided:

***Table 12.3***    Time and Date Formatting Characters

| Character | Meaning | Character | Meaning |
|---|---|---|---|
| a | Display am or pm | A | Display AM or PM |
| B | Swatch Internet time (invented by the Swiss watchmakers Swatch) | d | Day of the month as a pair of digits |
| D | Day of the week as three letters | F | Month as text |
| g | Hour in 12 hour format with no leading 0 | G | Hour in 24 hour format with no leading 0 |
| h | Hour in 12 hour format *with* leading 0 | H | Hour in 24 hour format with leading 0 |
| i | Minutes | j | Day of the month as integer |
| l | Day of the week in long text format | m | Month as integer |
| M | Month as three letters | n | Month as integer without leading 0 |
| r | Date formatted according to RFC 822 | s | Seconds |
| S | Ordinal suffix (such as "th" or "nd") | t | Number of days in the month |
| T | Timezone of the machine | U | Seconds since midnight on January 1st, 1970 |
| w | Day of the week as integer | Y | Year in four digit format |
| y | Year in two digit format | z | Day of the year as integer |

`date(format[, timestamp])`

Formats a timestamp as a date. If no timestamp is supplied, the current time is used. The format is defined by a string which uses the set of characters shown in Table 12.3. The following example displays a neatly formatted date:

```php
<?php
    echo(date("l dS F, Y"));
?>
```

The result of that code is shown in Figure 12.5. If you want formatting that is suitable for your locale, you should investigate the `strftime()` function.

# Time and Date

Tuesday 29th May, 2001

*Figure 12.5*  Formatted Date String

`getdate([timestamp])`

   Returns an associative array containing the elements of the date. If no timestamp is given, the current time is used. The keys for the array are:

- seconds,
- minutes,
- hours,
- mday (day of the month),
- wday (day of the week),
- mon (numeric month),
- year (numeric year),
- yday (day of the year as an integer),
- weekday (as text, using the full name of the day),
- month (as text using the full name).

`localtime([timestamp[, associative]])`

   Returns an array containing the elements of the timestamp. If no timestamp is given, the current time is used instead. If the Boolean value `associative` is TRUE the array will be returned as an associative array. The keys will be:

- tm_sec
- tm_min
- tm_hour
- tm_mday
- tm_mon
- tm_year
- tm_wday
- tm_yday

`mktime(hour, min, sec, month, day, year)`

   Returns a UNIX timestamp in seconds for the given date and time. All parameters are supplied as integers. The last day of a month can be expressed as day 0 of the *next* month.

`time()`

   Returns the a UNIX timestamp which represents the current time in seconds since midnight on January 1st 1970.

## 12.5.3   Using Files

Most of your scripts will need to store data at some point. You may only need to write data into a temporary file which gets deleted once the script has completed, or you may want to store many megabytes of data gathered from all the visitors to your site. Much of the literature and many of the tutorials which discuss PHP talk about storing all of this data in a relational database. If you surf the Web looking for PHP tutorials you'll see the same combination of PHP, Linux and MySQL described over and over again. For many applications a database is an irrelevance: they are designed to store and manipulate large volumes of data and many simultaneous connections. If you've got a low volume site with few connections and relatively little data you won't get any benefits from a database. Instead if you're creating a guestbook or an online diary, you're far better off saving your data in simple files.

PHP has many functions which handle files and directories. I'm going to show you just a few which you can use to open files, save data to them and read that data back. One really nice thing about the file routines in PHP is that they handle remote files as efficiently as they do local ones. From the point of view of a traditional programmer these might seem like weird ideas, but in the world of the Web they make perfect sense as you'll see.

A file is a collection of data stored on a disk and accessed via a unique name[10]. Generally when we talk about files we mean stored data on the local machine or on a machine which appears to be the local machine. On a Windows PC you may store all of your data on the C: drive and have a CD-ROM called drive D:. When you log on to a network at college or work, your PC may have access to a whole collection of servers around the organization. These servers will appear to be more drives and directories on the local system. For instance at work I get access to drives named F: through Z:. Providing they have the correct access permissions, your applications can open and read files from those drives as if they were stored on the C: drive of the machine.

What about files on other systems? If I have some files stored on a server which is run by my ISP rather than my employer, how can I get to those files? Generally the answer is that I need to use FTP to download a copy of each file and to upload the new version when I've finished with it. That's a well used and successful idea, but what happens if my Web application needs to alter the data in that file? Languages such as Perl can be used to automate an FTP connection but writing the code requires a certain amount of prior knowledge and experience. What if the file is residing on a Web server somewhere? Again, Perl has modules that can be used to automate that process. But what about PHP?

PHP is designed for the Web, it is supposed to work in a connected, Web world. Can it be used to manipulate files on remote servers? The answer to that is an emphatic *yes*, and what's more, the process is almost transparent. The fopen() function which is used to open files is described and demonstrated below. At this stage I'd just like to outline its Internet facilities.

---

[10]The full name of the file includes the path to it.

Opening a file is done with `fopen(filename)` which accepts a filename as the first of its parameters. If the `filename` is a standard directory/file combination such as these:

```
$data = c:\\MyFiles\\data\\guests.dat);
$data = fopen(/home/chris/data/guests.dat);
```

the file is assumed to be on the same machine that the script is on. Actually, and to be more rigorous, it's assumed to be *mounted* by the operating system and available as if it is on that machine.

---

**Note:**
On Windows machines, backslashes in the path to a file must be escaped or replaced with forward slashes.

---

If the filename starts with `http://`, the file is assumed to be on a remote Web server. A standard HTTP connection is opened to the server and the file is retrieved. When you access data like this you're not really working with the original file. The *open* file is really the data sent back by the HTTP response. You're actually going to be working on a copy of the data. This has important implications since the file might change whilst you're working on it. You can never assume that remote data is bang up to date; generally, though, this doesn't matter. Web data will give you a snapshot of the state of a system which is accurate enough 99 per cent of the time.

Filenames which start with `ftp://` are assumed to be on FTP servers. They can be accessed for reading and writing, although not at the same time. If the remote machine isn't running an FTP server you'll get an error if you try to use the FTP protocol to read or write a file on it. When you're using FTP you'll need to make *two* connections if you want to update a file: the first connection is made to download a *copy* of the file, the second to upload the amended version. During the period that your script is creating the amended file, the original is available to other users. As with HTTP access, you cannot assume that you've got the latest version. "Ah," you may say, "but I'm the only person who can access those files directly." That's fine, but how many copies of your script are executing concurrently? You've really no way of knowing. If concurrent access, especially to update the file, is likely to be important then you ought to consider using a database which enforces transactions and data integrity.

The files on FTP servers are protected by usernames and passwords. You may have downloaded files from FTP servers in the past via your Web browser without entering either a username or a password. Your Web browser will have done this for you automatically. Many file repositories around the Internet support *anonymous FTP* which lets anyone log on to the system as user *anonymous* provided they give their email address as a password. Files can then be downloaded from the server. If you're using remote files as part of a Web application, they won't be accessible via anonymous FTP, you'll need an account on the FTP server. The filename becomes a combination of username, password and file:

```
$data = fopen("ftp://chris:password@ftp.shu.ac.uk/guests.dat");
```

with the username and password separated by a colon.

The full set of PHP file functions is described in the supplied documentation. I'm only going to describe some of the more important functions and show you a simple example.

`copy($source, $dest)`

Copies the contents of $source into $dest. The two parameters are the names of the files. If the copy fails, the function returns FALSE, otherwise it returns TRUE.

`fclose($fp)`

Closes the file which is pointed to by $fp. The parameter $fp is a file handle, created using fopen() *not* the name of the file.

`feof($fp)`

Checks if the end of file has been reached. Returns TRUE if it has, otherwise it returns FALSE;

`fflush($fp)`

Writes all buffered output to the file which $fp points to. You should always call fflush() before you close a file because the operating system may buffer data without your knowledge. By calling this function you ensure that all data gets written out.

`fgets($fp, length)`

Reads up to length-1 bytes of data from $fp. The call to fgets() ends when a newline character or the end of file marker is reached. Newline characters are returned as part of the string.

`fgetss($fp, length)`

Works like fgets() but strips any HTML tags out of the data as it is read.

`file(filename)`

Reads the complete contents from the file and stores them in an array. Each line of data makes up a separate element in the array.

`file_exists(filename)`

Returns TRUE if the file exists and FALSE if it doesn't. This function will not work on remote files such as those you might try to access with FTP or HTTP.

`flock($fp, operation)`

Locks a file so that access to it can be controlled. This function works under most UNIX systems and Microsoft Windows. Many similar functions in other languages are unavailable on Windows. Operation takes one of the following values:

- LOCK_SH denotes a shared lock – used for reading a file,
- LOCK_EX denotes an exclusive lock – for writing to a file,
- LOCK_UN releases a file lock.

`fopen(filename, mode)`

Opens the file. Works on local and remote files as described above.The modes are listed in Table 12.4.

***Table 12.4***   File Modes

| File Mode | Meaning |
|---|---|
| r | Opens the file for reading. Reading starts at the beginning of the file. |
| r+ | Opens the file for reading and writing. The file pointer starts at the beginning of the file. |
| w | Opens the file for writing. Places the pointer at the start of the file and sets the file length to zero. This means that all data previously in the file will be deleted unless you have previously copied it elsewhere. If the file does not exist, it will be created. |
| w+ | Opens the file for reading and writing. Places the pointer at the start of the file and sets the file length to zero. This means that all data previously in the file will be deleted unless you have previously copied it elsewhere. If the file does not exist, it will be created. |
| a | Opens the file for writing. The file pointer is placed at the end of the file. If the file does not exist, it is created. |
| a+ | Opens the file for reading and writing. The file pointer is placed at the end of the file. If the file does not exist, it is created. |

**fputs($fp, string[, length])**

Writes the string to the file pointed to by $fp. If the optional length is given, that many bytes are written. Otherwise the entire string is written.

**fread($fp, length)**

Reads up to length bytes from $fp. This operation is suitable for reading either text or ASCII data on systems such as Windows which distinguish between the two.

**tmpfile()**

Creates a temporary file which is ready to be written to. The function returns a file-handle to the new file. The file is deleted when fclose() is called on it.

**unlink(filename)**

Deletes the file whose name is given as parameter. Return FALSE if there is an error.

The following code operates on the simple cookie database that I created in Section 8.10 for use with small Perl applications. This code reads through the database and echoes the contents out to the browser:

```
<html>
  <head>
```

```
        <title>Biscuit Database</title>
    </head>
    <body>
        <h1>The Biscuit Database</h1>
        <?php
            makeContent();
        ?>
    </body>
</html>

<?php
    function makeContent() {
        $fp = fopen("cookies.dat", "r");
        if($fp) {
            while(!feof($fp)){
                $row = fgets($fp, 1024);
                $bicks = preg_split("/::/", $row);
                echo "<h3>Next Row</h3><ul>";
                for($i = 0; $i < count($bicks); $i++) {
                    echo "<li>";
                    echo $bicks[$i];
                    echo "</li>";
                }
                echo "</ul>";
            }
            fclose($fp);
        }
    } // makeContent
?>
```

### 12.5.4  Cookies

A cookie is a text string which is stored in your visitor's PC by *your* script. Cookies are both useful and controversial. If you're running a large site or doing e-commerce, then cookies are an excellent way of tracking users or of managing transactions. Most shopping cart applications are based around cookies, using them to track the items that a shopper has ordered. Users, especially those concerned with civil liberties in cyberspace, are worried about the wide-spread use of cookies. They're often used by advertisers, especially those selling banner advertising, to track users through sites. Whilst the advertiser won't know who is viewing their banners, they will be able to build a picture of the type of viewer they're attracting. I guess that whether this offends you or not depends upon your philosophical outlook. The important consideration for a developer is that if you use cookies too widely, you may drive potential customers away – or worse yet, make it impossible for them to do business with you.

Creating cookies in PHP is easy. Simply place a call to the `setcookie()` function before the HTML tag at the top of your page. It needs to go there since cookies are sent as part of the HTTP header message which is sent *before* the HTML page.

```
setcookie(name[, value[, expiry]])
```

Each cookie has to have a name. Generally all cookies from each area of your site will have the same name so that you can retrieve them and track your visitors. If you don't pass a name to the function, you'll get an error. If the only parameter that you give to the function is the name, the cookie will be deleted.

Cookies are designed to expire after a preset length of time. That expiry time is set using the third parameter which is an integer value. This should be created using the PHP `mktime()` or `time()` functions. If you use a time that has already passed, the cookie will be deleted.

Cookies are automatically returned and can be accessed using a variable which is the same as their name. This code reads in and displays a cookie, and sets it with a new value which was passed to the script as a parameter. The cookie will expire after 20 minutes:

```php
<?php
    setcookie("CookieTest", $val, time()+1200);
?>
<html>
    <head>
        <title>Functions</title>
    </head>
    <body>
        <h1>Using Cookies</h1>
<?php
    echo "<h2>The cookie is: $CookieTest</h2>"
?>
    </body>
</html>
```

Try saving that as a file called `cookie.php`. Run it using:

```
http://localhost/html/cookie.php?val=Julie
```

Run it a few more times, changing the parameter string from `Julie` each time. You will have to force the browser to perform a reload to see the new value since the cookie is returned to the script before it is set to a new value.

### 12.5.5   Other Useful Functions

Here are a few more functions that you need to use the language in productions code:

```
is_array(var)
```
   Returns TRUE if the variable is an array,

```
is_double(var)
```
   Returns TRUE if the variable is a double,

```
is_float(var)
```
   Returns TRUE if the variable is a floating point number,

```
is_int(var)
```
   Returns TRUE if the variable is an integer,

```
is_string(var)
```
   Returns TRUE if the variable is a string,

```
is_object(var)
```
   Returns TRUE if the variable is an object.

## 12.5.6  Bringing It All Together

In Section 11.4 I showed how Perl could be used to download the index file from Slashdot and display its XML contents inside an HTML page. I reused the idea in Section 11.5.2 although with a more *rough and ready* attempt at extracting content from the XML file. This section shows you how to do the same thing, using that same rough and ready approach in PHP. The resulting page, displayed in Mozilla version m18 is shown in Figure 12.6.

```
<html>
    <head>
        <title>Slashdot.xml</title>
    </head>
    <body>
        <h1>Slashdot</h1>
        <p>News from Slashdot at <?php echo date("h:ia") ?> on
        <?php echo date("l jS F, Y"); ?>.</p>
        <?php
            makeIndex();
        ?>
    </body>
</html>

function makeIndex() {
    $fp = fopen("http://www.slashdot.org/slashdot.xml", "r");
    echo "<table>";

    while(!feof($fp)){
        $line = fgets($fp, 1024);
```

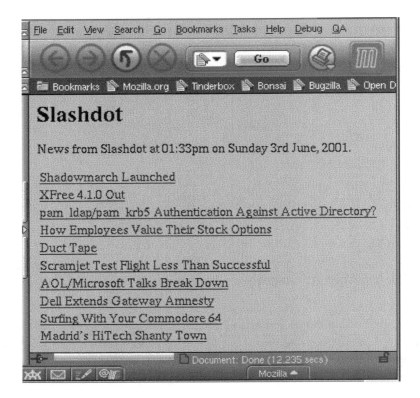

**Figure 12.6**   Viewing Slashdot

```php
    if(preg_match("/<title>(.+)<\/title>/", $line, $match)){
        $linktext = $match[1];
    }
    if(preg_match("/<url>(.+)<\/url>/", $line, $matches)) {
        echo "<tr><td>";
        echo "<a href=\"$matches[1]\">$linktext</a>";
        echo "</td></tr>";
    }
  }
  echo "</table>";
}
?>
```

I'm not going to explain that code, you'll find it all described either earlier in this chapter or by looking back at the Perl chapters. What you almost certainly will notice if you compare the samples is that this version is very *clean* compared to the Perl version. It's smaller and more legible which ought to mean that it's also easier to maintain in the future.

## 12.6 EXERCISES

1. Install PHP 4 and configure your Web server to use it. Test the installation by using `<? phpinfo() ?>`.

2. Write a guestbook in PHP. Your page should accept input from users through a form and return a message to them.

3. Modify your guestbook so that all messages are saved in a file.

4. Write a script which reads the guestbook data back out of the storage file and displays it, neatly formatted, in a new page.

5. Add a search facility to your guestbook so that visitors can search for messages left by other people whose names they know.

6. Add a stylesheet to format your guestbook.

7. Use PHP to display the current time of day at the server within a Web page.

8. Write PHP routines which validate all data entered into your guestbook.

9. Implement the Sieve of Eratosthenes method for discovering prime numbers in PHP.

# 13
## *Active Server Pages and Java*

Whilst CGI scripting has proven to be an extremely adaptable and useful technology it does not meet the needs of every developer. In some cases CGI scripting is too complex; often a large effort is required to create simple solutions. Many developers find themselves using Web servers which do not have good support for CGI. Other developers find that they actually want *more* power or flexibility than they find in their CGI scripting languages. It seems unlikely that a single technology could satisfy all of these needs but that is exactly what some claim for both Active Server Pages and Java.

## 13.1  ACTIVE SERVER PAGES

Active Server Pages (ASP) was developed by Microsoft to run alongside its Web server, Internet Information Server (IIS). Both IIS and ASP are designed to tightly integrate into the Windows operating system. IIS is so easy to install and configure that almost anyone can have a Web server up and running in minutes. Whilst the same is true of servers such as Apache, IIS enjoys the benefits of the Microsoft brand name. People who would shy away from difficult tasks such as configuring a Web server are reassured and willing to make the effort if the software comes from Microsoft.

If you plan to run a Web server on a specific operating system then making as much use as possible of the facilities of that system is a good idea. ASP lets you do just that. Scripts are run through dynamic link libraries (DLL). Each DLL loads into memory and can service requests repeatedly until unloaded. This makes ASPs very efficient at run-time when compared to traditional CGI scripting.[1] Even more useful, though, is the ability of ASP scripts to access any DCOM, ActiveX, object on the system. Therefore ASP can be easily included in organization-sized distributed systems which involve numerous components and which may move far beyond the HTTP/CGI model of computing.

That's all very well but you are probably asking yourselves exactly *what* ASP is. Put simply, ASP extends the HTML pages by embedding *server-side* scripting into the HTML. These scripts are processed by a suitable Web server and the *processed* page sent to the browser. The Web browser never gets to see the scripts even though they started off inside the page.

Clearly the ASP model has a lot to recommend it. If you are handling static pages which include dynamic *elements* then you can greatly reduce the processing requirements by first building those static elements. Using CGI the whole page must be built each time that it is required, which may lead to excessive effort when only a few data items are changing.

Because ASP is a Microsoft technology you might expect to have to use one of its languages for the scripting parts of each page. In fact the technology supports any scripting language although most ASP developers will use either JScript or VBScript. Most texts that you read about ASP use VBScript for their examples but that is purely an illustrative choice. You can write ASP in any scripting language which provides a suitable ActiveX scripting engine to link the Perl interpreter to the IIS Web server. Fortunately the ActiveState distribution of Perl includes just such an engine so we can use Perl to create ASP scripts. That means that not only can you continue to use the same server-side language as for your CGI scripts, but you can compare the technologies and make informed decisions about the merits of each for your projects.

---

[1] The optional `mod_perl` module does much the same job for Perl scripts with the Apache server on *any* platform.

### 13.1.1 ASP – an example

This simple example shows how to create a page with ASP which the server will return to the browser. I'll show you the code first, then quickly explain what it does before discussing how ASP works from server to browser and back again.

```
<%@ LANGUAGE="Perlscript">
<! DOCTYPE  html public
          "-//w3c//dtd html 4.0//en"
          "http://www.w3c.org/TR/PR-html4.0/loose.dtd">
<html>
   <head>
      <title>My First ASP</title>
   </head>
   <body>
   <h1>My First ASP</h1>
   <p>This page contains some PerlScript. It's embedded
   in the

   <%
      $Response->write(qq(<font color="DarkGreen">
   ASP</font>));
   %>
   <hr>

   <%
      my @words = qw(first second mickey mouse);
      $i = 0;
      $len = $words;
      $msg = "<p>Yet More Text ";
      $Response->write("<p>Hi Mom");
   %>
   <%= $msg %>

   <table border=1 align="center">
      <tr><th>The Words are</th></tr>

      <%
      foreach(@words){
         $Response->write("<tr><td>".$words[$i++].
   "</td></tr>\n");
      }
      %>
```

```
      </table>
      </body>
</html>
```

There's obviously some code in that sample that makes sense. There is also going to be some which doesn't – but not too much! Let's get the code that you should understand out of the way first. You'll be very familiar with most of the HTML tags in there and by now you ought to recognize the fact that there's some Perl in there too.

The new pieces of the code are all easy to pick out. Another pair of HTML-style tags has been created: <% and %>. These are used to delimit sections of code written in a scripting language. These scripts are passed by the IIS Web server to the appropriate ActiveX engine which executes them and returns the results to the server. IIS is then able to substitute the result for the script and send the complete page back to the browser.

You might be wondering how IIS knows which scripting engine to call. ASP uses any available language, although VBScript and JScript are most common. The choice of language is governed by the line

```
<%@ LANGUAGE="Perlscript">
```

where Perlscript is replaced with the name of the language that you wish to use.[2] This language selection line can be placed anywhere in your HTML page provided that it occurs *before* the first piece of scripting. It makes sense to me to put the declaration at the top of the page before any HTML. You may prefer to place it just before it is used.

> **Note:**
> You can only use one language in any single ASP page.

Did you notice that in the example the script code was littered throughout the HTML document? This is one of the clear benefits of technologies like ASP. Unlike JavaScript in which the code tends to be written in the file head and then called from the body of the page, with ASP the code is written at the point at which it is used.

Because Perlscript is a cut-down version of Perl, many of the usual conventions continue to apply. You can use modules and libraries, and put your own code into files which you use from within your scripts. What you can't do is to use the CGI.pm module to handle data from users or to create new pages. This is what ASP is doing. In Section 13.1.2 I will look at how requests and responses are handled and at the same time clarify the role of $Response in the listing shown above.

The final part of the sample ASP that might be confusing you is:

```
<%= $msg %>
```

The <%= %> syntax is used to direct the output from a function to STDOUT . In this case the *function* is a scalar value which is printed out; however, any piece of Perl which returns a

---

[2]Although you will, of course, prefer to use Perlscript, won't you?

single value could be used here instead. Passing a hash or an array into the call is probably not a good idea as you will want to format larger amounts of data so that they are neatly displayed by the browser.

What else can Perlscript do for you as an ASP developer? Well, how about *easy* connection to relational databases just as an example. The next piece of code shows a guestbook-style application. In this case a user has supplied a name and e-mail address to a Web form. A connection is established to an ODBC database such as Microsoft Access which is searched for the name and address:

```
<%@ LANGUAGE="Perlscript" %>
<html>
   <head>
      <title>Your Search Results</title>
   </head>
   <body>
      <h1>Your Search Results</h1>

   <%
   use DBI;

   my $name = $Request->QueryString('input_name')->Item(1);
   my $ad = $Request->QueryString('input_address')->Item(1);
   my $dbh = ""; # database connection handle
   my $sth; # statement handle
   my @row; # hold data from database

   $dbh = DBI->connect('dbi:ODBC:guestbook', '', '')
      || die $dbh->errstr;

   $sth = $dbh->prepare("select * from guests where name=$name
      and email=$ad");

   $sth->execute;

   # now check for a submission
   if(@row = $sth->fetchrow_array) {
      $Response->write(
         "<p>$name <b>has</b> made a submission to
   our database");
      }
   %>
```

```
    </body>
</html>
```

## 13.1.2   The ASP Objects

Using Perlscript to program ASP looks pretty simple. Indeed it really is just as easy as using conventional CGI approaches. Most of the page can be created statically by a dedicated Web designer which leaves the programmer free to concentrate on getting the scripts working properly. There is a clear separation in the code between the HTML and the script, which makes the pages much more readable, but there is a layer of complexity associated with the idea. The complexity all comes from something called the Object Model. Just when you were getting to grips with the client-side Document Object Model, Microsoft comes along with another one – this time a server-side model which has nothing at all in common with the DHTML DOM.

Objects are *things* which have defined boundaries and whose internals[3] are usually hidden from the world. Objects provide services for other parts of an application through their *methods*. A method is just like a function but, again usually, objects only let the world use some of their methods. Others are hidden away for internal use. Objects are a real boon to the developers of complex systems. These developers can now write really complex code which can be easily added to other applications or easily used by other developers.

ASP technology defines five objects which you can use in your scripts. I'll briefly outline all five before describing the two you'll meet most often in more detail. The Perlscript objects all have names which start with a capital letter. You *have* to follow this convention in your scripts as these objects are created automatically. If you use lower-case letters then you'll be using a different object which will probably not exist, leading to run-time errors.

### 13.1.2.1   *The Request Object*   ASP uses its built-in functions to take a lot of the hard work out of handling form data. In the traditional CGI model of Web development each programmer must handle requests from users in their own way. This has given us useful code libraries such as CGI.pm, created by experienced programmers who have distilled the knowledge of the community and created something useful.

Microsoft has done the same with ASP. Like all Web servers, IIS has its own functionality for extracting data from client requests whether sent with the POST or GET method. Whilst in CGI scripting the data is passed to the application for processing *directly from the server*, in ASP scripting the script receives pre-processed data.

Data sent by a user is packaged as a request object which Perlscript calls $Request. The request object may contain a number of different data items but the most important ones are data about cookies, data sent via POST, and data sent via GET. I'll give examples of using all of these in Section 13.1.3.

---

[3]How they work.

### 13.1.2.2 The Response Object

In the ASP scripts I have shown so far in this chapter, you'll have seen a Perl variable called `$Response`. After reading the description of request objects you might be able to guess what this particular variable is.

The response object controls the transmission of data from the server to the Web browser. Any type of data can be sent back, although obviously you'll normally be sending HTML. You can also configure the HTTP header by handing things such as cookies to it directly from your ASP scripts.

You'll mostly be using the `$Response->Write()` property of this object to dynamically create HTML but there are a few others which you should know about. The response object has a cookies value which you'll see in action in Section 13.1.3. When setting a cookie for a page you must write it before sending any other output to the page otherwise the browser will simply ignore it.

To make sure that everything happens in the correct order, the response object has a `$Response->Buffer` property which you can set to *on* to cache the page before sending it. Caching is important when you are generating lots of data and want the user to see the whole page rather than just part of it.

HTML pages can have an expiry time. This can be set from the ASP script and is measured in minutes from the time that the browser receives the page. The expiry time is set through the `$Response->Expires` property. Finally, browsers can be automatically redirected to another site by using `$Response->Redirect($url)`.

### 13.1.2.3 The Server Object

The server object holds information about the Web server itself and lets you use some of its functionality. For instance you can set the maximum time that a script will execute before generating an error. This is especially useful if you are accessing databases which may not be present on the system or which may be very busy. It avoids the situation where a single script hogs the server for an inordinate, or even indefinite, length of time.

A method called `$Server->HTMLEncode` will convert characters such as < into their HTML equivalent such as `&lt;` automatically – obviously useful when you are processing data from databases for inclusion in Web pages.

### 13.1.2.4 The Session Object

HTTP is stateless and has no concept of a *session*. I've already shown you two ways of artificially creating Web sessions by adding hidden fields to forms and by using cookies. ASP provides a third option called a **Session**. This uses cookies but they are set by the server itself, not by the programmer and are valid only for a limited time. Using `$Session` the following sequence happens:

1. The user requests a page. Any cookies which are valid for the server are returned along with the page.

2. If no cookies are sent a new session is created and a cookie is set on the browser.

3. If cookies were sent they are checked to see if one is an ASP session ID. If a session ID is returned then it is checked to see if it has timed out yet.

4. If the cookie has timed out a new session is created and a new cookie set.

5. If the cookie is valid and not timed out the existing session is restored from memory.

Obviously there are a great many applications where this sort of background session control is very useful. As with all of these ASP ideas, if you want to know more read the documentation which comes with your Web server and with ActiveState Perl.

### 13.1.2.5   *The Application Object*   Finally we have the application object. This is used to share data within a Web application. The idea of an application is rather nebulous but is basically a developer-assigned set of pages within a site, or set of sites, on one server. In the vast majority of cases you won't ever need to use this object so I don't plan to discuss it any further.

## 13.1.3   Using ASP to Handle a Guestbook

If you start to use ASP then you'll spend a lot of time either processing data from forms or creating HTML pages. I'm going to show you a simple example which demonstrates how you might use ASP effectively. This simple application is yet another Web guestbook. The advantage of the guestbook as an educational tool is that it lets me demonstrate lots of functionality within a simple context. It is also a very adaptable application: you should be able to see fairly quickly how this can adapted to make a simple stock control system for instance.

The guestbook has four separate pieces:

- A database.[4]

- An HTML page which acts as a front-end and lets the user choose to add data or to view existing data.

- An appropriate page in response to the selection. I'll use the user's name as a cookie here. The page will have a form to allow data addition or querying of the database.

- A page which includes a response to the previous action. This will use two different scripts: one to add data, the other to display data.

That's the plan, let's look at how to implement it.

### 13.1.3.1   *The Database*   This code is going to use the ODBC driver because we're working with a Windows-based system. You can implement the database using any ODBC-compliant database software that you have. If you want to use a database which does not support ODBC then simply use the appropriate driver. However, ODBC is so easy and convenient that it's well worth investigating.

The database for this guestbook couldn't be simpler. It only has one table, and that only has two fields. I'm not trying to show you how to create a leading-edge e-commerce site in

---

[4]You can modify this code to use a plain text file if that better meets your needs.

this chapter. What I am trying to do is to present some of the capabilities of the available technologies so that you have at least a foot in the door when you try to use them in your own applications.

Create a new database and give it a name which will be unique on your system. If you haven't yet tried to create and run a database powered guestbook then call it guestbook. The database needs to have just a single table called guests which has two columns: name and email. Both columns should be of type text. Save the database then you are ready to configure an ODBC driver for your database. This is really very simple:

- Open up the Windows Control Panel[5] and select 32bit ODBC.

- Choose the Add button to create a new ODBC data source.

- Choose the driver for your database. This should have been configured automatically when you installed the database software.

- Next you'll be asked to configure the driver for your new guestbook database:

    - Set the Windows DNS name to guestbook.

    - Set the Server to the IP address of your machine. If you are testing this on a machine which doesn't have its own IP address (such as your home machine) then set this to the loopback address 127.0.0.1

    - The Database Name should be set to the name that you gave your database when you created it. This needs to be a unique name, of course, for your system.

    - If you are password protecting your database, as you *must* for a production system, then enter the details of the User and Password.

    - Select OK to save this configuration.

> Important:
> If you want your ODBC-enabled database available to the whole of your system then all this happens under the System DNS tab. If you only want the database accessible under a specific user log-on then configure ODBC under the User DNS tab.

### 13.1.3.2 *The First Page*

Once your database is up and running you can start to write the HTML and ASP pages. The system has an HTML front page which is static. All other pages are going to be created dynamically through ASP scripts. You'll need to put the scripts in a directory which IIS can find. I'm going for the simplest option here and putting everything in the same directory. To learn why this is not the safest thing to do on a production system read Chapter 9 and Section 17.4. Here's the code for the front page.[6] Save this in a file called gbook.html.

---

[5]This lives under My Computer on the Windows desktop.
[6]Notice that I use a table to make the form layout look better.

```html
<html>
  <head>
    <title>An ASP Guestbook</title>
  </head>
  <body>
    <h1>An ASP Guestbook</h1>
    <form method="post" action="./selection.asp">
    <table border=0>
      <tr>
        <td colspan=3>Choose one of these Options</td>
      </tr>
      <tr>
        <td><select name="option" size=1>
          <option value="new" selected>Add New Data
          </option>
          <option value="view">View Existing Data
          </option>
        </select></td>
        <td>
          <input type="submit" value="Submit The Query">
        </td>
        <td>
          <input type="cancel" value="Cancel">
        </td>
      </tr>
    </table>
    </form>
    </hr>
  </body>
</html>
```

### 13.1.3.3 *Responding to the Selection*   The response to the introductory page will contain one option from the choice of two. We're going to return another page which holds either the existing contents of the database or a form for new data. This code is rather long but ought to be quite clear. Save the code in a file called `selection.asp`.

```perl
<%@ LANGUAGE="Perlscript" %>
<%
# cache the page so it holds all data when returned
# to browser
$Response->{Buffer} = 1
%>
```

```
<html>
<head><title></title></head>
<body>
    <h1>Testing ASPs</h1>
<%

# get the parameter
my $choice = $Request->Form('option')->Item(1);

# set a cookie
$Response->Cookie('ASPTest')->{Expires} = "+1h";
$Response->Cookie('ASPTest')->{Path} = "/";
$Response->Cookie('ASPTest')->{Domain} =
      ".your.domain.here";

if($choice eq "new")
    { addNewData; }
else
    { viewExistingData; }


# use a Perl heredoc to write out the rest
sub addNewData {
    $Response->Write(<<EOT);
<form method="post" action="./addtodb.asp">
<table border=0>
    <tr>
      <td colspan=4>Enter your data in these fields
      </td>
    </tr>
    <tr>
      <td>Name</td>
      <td><input type="text" name="name"></td>
      <td>Email Address</td>
      <td><input type="text" name="add"></td>
    </tr>
    <tr>
      <td colspan=2>
        <input type="submit" value="Submit Data">
      </td>
```

```
        <td colspan=2>
          <input type="cancel" value="Cancel">
        </td>
      </tr>
</table>
</form>
EOT


} # addNewData


sub viewExistingData {
    $Response->Write(<<EOT);
<table border=1>
<tr>
  <th>Visitor Name</th>
  <th>Email Address</th>
</tr>
EOT

my $dbh = ""; # database connection handle
my $sth; # statement handle
my @row; # hold data from database

$dbh = DBI->connect('dbi:ODBC:guestbook', '', '')
  || die $dbh->errstr;

$sth = $dbh->prepare("select * from guests");
$sth->execute;
while(@row = $sth->fetchrow_array){
    $Response->Write("<tr>");
    $Response->Write("<td>$row[0]</td><td>$row[1]</td>"
    $Response->Write("</tr>");
}

$Response-Write("</table>");

} # viewExistingData
%>
```

```
<hr>
</body></html>
```

### 13.1.3.4 *Adding New Data*

Almost done now. The final stage is to add the new data into the database and send an acknowledgment back to the browser. If you plan to try this out save the code in addtodb.asp. I start by checking for a cookie. If I don't get one back then I redirect the user to the first page. This provides a very simple form of access control but I could have done this automatically by using an ASP Session Object.

```
<%@ LANGUAGE="Perlscript" %>
<%
# cache the page so it holds all data when returned
# to browser
$Response->{Buffer} = 1;
my $mycookie = $Request->Cookie('ASPTest')->{Item};
%>

<html>
<head><title></title></head>
<body>
    <h1>Testing ASPs</h1>
<%
# get the parameters
$new_name = $Request->Form('name')->Item(1);
$new_add = $Request->Form('add')->Item(1);

# if we didn't get a cookie then send them an error
if($mycookie eq "")
    { sendError; }
else
    { upData; }


sub sendError {
    $Response->Write(<<EOT);
<h2>Warning</h2>
<p>I notice that you've not visited my front page in
the last hour. I always like my guests to come in through
the front door.

<p>Please go to <a href="./gbook.html">the front door</a>
before I'll accept your submission.
```

```
EOT

} # sendError


sub upData {
my $dbh = ""; # database connection handle
my $sth; # statement handle

$dbh = DBI->connect('dbi:ODBC:guestbook', '', '')
   || die $dbh->errstr;

$sth = $dbh->prepare("insert into gbook values $new_name,
      $new_add");
$sth->execute
   || die($Response->Write("<p>Unable to add to the
      database");

$Response->Write(<<EOT);
<p>Thanks for your details. I've now added them to
<em>The Database</em>.
EOT

}
%>


<hr>
</body></html>
```

Whilst there is a lot of code in those examples, what you now have is a skeleton for many Web applications. Try it out then tailor it to your needs. You'll need to add lots of error handling code to make it a robust application.

## 13.2 JAVA

If you've been around the Web and computing for any significant amount of time in the last five years you must have heard of Java. Depending upon your point of view Java is either the most exciting development in programming languages for a decade, an interesting but immature technology, or a load of hype, and hot air. I am not here to convince you one way or another on this one. Personally I like Java. A lot. Most of my teaching and programming uses it and I think it's one of the most productive and usable languages I have tried.

### 13.2.1 A Brief History Lesson

Java is a product of Sun Microsystems. They developed it, they own it, and they control it. It's widely available because Sun decided to give away binary implementations[7] – probably before they realized what they had created. In fact Sun has a history of giving away successful and useful products, they did just the same with Tcl/Tk for instance.

Java started life in the early 1990s as a language called Oak. Oak was intended to be used to develop programmable domestic appliances such as intelligent microwaves and sophisticated remote controllers. In fact the market for such devices never took off and Sun retargeted Oak. In 1995 Oak was branded as Java and released upon an unsuspecting world. Java had new features which meant it was ideal for programming networked applications with a particular emphasis on writing for the Web.

Since its release Java has altered in a number of ways. The underlying language was slightly modified for the release of Java 1.1 in 1997. Since then the main changes have been in the provision of APIs to meet different needs. A new set of interface classes called Swing, packages for writing 2D and 3D graphics applications, a CORBA ORB, JavaBeans technology for developing component software, database connectivity, and more have been added. Java is now a complete language which can be used to develop almost any type of application. It continues to attract developers with millions downloading free software development kits from companies such as Sun and IBM.

### 13.2.2 About Java

Each programming language has things at which it is good, and things at which it is bad. Perl is an excellent choice if you want to process textual data or administer a network. It's a lousy choice if you want to build software with a nice interface. Prolog is great for logic systems, COBOL fine for producing text reports and invoices but neither is much use if you need to develop a Web browser. 'What about C++?' I hear you cry. Well through the late 1980s and into the 1990s C++ became the *de facto* standard development language in the computer industry. If a technology is that widely used it ought to be good at something and I'm sure C++ is, but no one remembered to tell me just what. The problem with C++

---

[7]Executable implementations not source code.

is that it is large, has a steep learning curve, and using it requires lots of programming knowledge from the outset. Which, strangely, brings me to Java.

Java is C++ for the rest of us. It uses a C++ style syntax but has been designed to be much, much easier to use. The core language is quite small and is extended by myriad packages of useful routines. In fact most of the time programming in Java involves finding the right routine in the right package to do the job. Other possible advantages of Java include:

- object-orientation,
- platform independence,
- excellent networking capabilities,
- no pointers, so it is easier to program and debug than C++,
- lots of support available in books and on the Web,
- wide variety of Application Programmer Interfaces (APIs),
- implementations are available free of charge for many popular platforms.

Of those virtues the most well known, and possibly most important, is platform independence. Java, like JavaScript and Perl, can run on any system which has the right set-up. Of course programs written in many languages will run on a wide number of platforms under the right circumstances. Most UNIX programs are written in C or C++ and run across many different flavours of UNIX on a variety of hardware types. This is achieved by recompiling the source code for each platform. UNIX systems usually have a compiler installed alongside the operating system so that any user can compile programs. PC systems running Microsoft Windows or Apple MacOS rarely include compilers. Programs for these systems are always distributed in a ready-compiled form called a *binary*. The holy grail of systems development is to create application programs which will run on any architecture without recompilation. This is only really achievable when developers use an *interpreted language*.

### 13.2.2.1 *Interpretation*  Programs written in an interpreted language such as Perl are distributed as source code – plain text. This is read by the interpreter and executed. Some interpreters, including Perl, convert the plain text into an intermediate form called *bytecode* and then execute the bytecode. The great advantage of using a bytecode intermediate is that the program can be executed far more quickly than if it were plain text yet the distributed application can run anywhere that has an interpreter. This seems so obvious that it sometimes comes as a surprise that anyone would go to the trouble of compiling programs. Well, converting text to bytecode then executing the bytecode instructions all takes time. A lot of time. Compiled programs just have to be loaded into memory and then executed. They start up more quickly and run more quickly than interpreted ones. There is no way that an interpreted program can complete its execution as quickly as a compiled one so for most developers there is a trade-off between speed of execution and ease of distribution.

What does all of this have to do with Java? Well Java is an interpreted language *and* a compiled language. When someone writes a Java program they run the source code through a utility called `javac` which converts the text into bytecode. The bytecode is then distributed to users. Therefore the first, and most time-consuming, phase of interpretation happens only once when the programmer creates the bytecode.

When the program executes it runs on something called a *virtual machine*. This provides a sort of abstraction between the hardware and the bytecode. Virtual machines need to be written specially for each combination of hardware and operating system but they all execute the same code and produce the same result. On some systems a second compilation phase happens at run-time. The bytecode can be converted to optimized native code by a just-in-time bytecode compiler. This happens as the program executes and vastly improves performance. For example if a program is passing through a loop 100 times, on the first time it is interpreted as bytecode and also compiled to native code. This iteration will be slow. On the other 99 iterations the native code executes and these are quick.

Of course all of the above assumes that the run-time system has a suitable version of the virtual machine and the runtime libraries. This is quite a large assumption and one that is rarely borne out by experience. Sun has released three major versions of Java: 1.0.2, 1.1 and now 1.2.[8] Each version provides backward compatibility but that doesn't work in reverse. A 1.0.2 virtual machine cannot run code written in Java 1.1 due to major changes in the core language. Even within versions there are inconsistencies.

Sun releases *reference* compilers and libraries with the hope that third party developers will create commercial versions. The Sun products are not intended to be the last word in Java systems, nor are they supposed to be the fastest available. Sun also release standards which detail what a run-time system needs to do to be Java-compliant. This should mean that code which runs on one Java 1.1 virtual machine will run on them all. It won't. Unlike Perl, Tcl or Python where great efforts are put into ensuring compatibility across platforms, Java implementors constantly seem to mess this up. The worst of this situation occurs with Web browsers. Many Web browsers include their own virtual machines to run client-side Java programs called *applets* which can be created as parts of Web pages. Browsers never seem to have virtual machines which work with the kinds of applet users actually find on the Web.

### 13.2.2.2  *Why Use Java on the Web?*  Java has better support for networking than almost any other programming language. Java networking is totally based around the Internet suite of protocols (See Chapter 17) but many leading-edge techniques have been incorporated. Remote Method Invocation (RMI) lets an object run methods which are part of other objects *on other machines*. Technologies such as Object Request Brokers (ORB) can be used to connect entire corporate networks together including older systems such as mainframe computers. Java applications can run on servers and client workstations,

---

[8]Which, confusingly, is also called Java 2.

and be distributed across machines without users being aware that anything unusual is happening.

The commonest reason for getting into Java is probably to develop Java applets. These are small programs which can be embedded into Web pages and executed automatically when the page is loaded by a browser. Applets extend the functionality of the browser in a variety of ways. Word processors can be developed which run entirely inside a browser and which save files on remote servers, networked 3D games can be created, remote sensing devices can be viewed on-line in near real time. The uses to which applets can be put are limited only by the imagination, and desire, of their developers.

Running code inside a Web browser is a massive potential security hole in any system. Someone could write an applet which runs invisibly in the background while the user reads a page but which returns vital system configuration data back to its server. Applets could be used to introduce viruses onto systems as Trojan horses[9], or to tie up processing in denial of service attacks. A language like Java is potentially very dangerous without a good security model. Java has such a model. Java applets run inside a sandbox which restricts what they are allowed to do with and to the system on which they are running. Although the level of restriction can be varied the default settings mean that Java applets cannot:

- access files on the local system,
- open network connections other than to their home server.

> Java on the Web:
> Java covers the whole application from server to client and back again, it provides many powerful technologies, it can be used to extend the browser, and it provides a good, if far from perfect, security system.

If Java is so good why do developers still use languages such as Perl and JavaScript?

- Java performance is not great. CGI scripts written in Perl, run by Apache using `mod_perl`, will outperform Java servlets on many machines.
- JavaScript lets you manipulate the elements of an HTML page and create fun DHTML effects.
- HTML plus JavaScript downloads and initializes far faster than HTML plus Java.
- Learning Java takes time. It is much harder than learning JavaScript for example.
- Java support may be limited or non-existent on devices such as mobile phones or WebTV sets.

## 13.2.3 Programming in Java

I'm not going to show you how to program in Java. There's far too much complexity in the language. I don't even have the space here to give more than a trivial overview of what it

---

[9]Malicious code which is passed around disguised as another application.

can do. My main reason for talking about Java at all is to demonstrate *servlets*. A servlet is a Java program which runs on a Web server and provides exactly the same functionality as a CGI script. Sun presents servlet technology as being full of benefits to the developer but it does not actually add anything new to the CGI model. Performance may be slightly better than using Perl but Java has fewer facilities for handling complex textual manipulation.

A more complex and interesting technology is provided by Java Server Pages (JSP). These combine the full power of the Java language with a developmental model which is very similar to ASPs. Calls to Java programs are embedded inside HTML pages and processed by the server before the page is sent to the user. Understanding JSP requires a good working knowledge of Java which is why I've not included any examples in this book. If you want more information then I have listed a few useful Web sites at the end of the book.

### 13.2.3.1 *Acquiring and Using Java*

If you want to use Java then you need to get hold of a Java Development Kit (JDK). You almost certainly have a set of Java packages and a virtual machine installed on your computer if you run version 4 or later of Internet Explorer or Netscape Navigator but I'm afraid that isn't going to be any help at all. The run-time system of packages and virtual machine will happily run applets within the browser but it doesn't include facilities for compiling and building applets or applications. You can get a commercial JDK from any decent software supplier. Free versions are available for download from the Internet and occasionally they are given away with computer magazines.

There is little difference between the commercial and free JDKs. Most of the commercial systems come with an Integrated Development Environment which includes an editor, compiler, and debugger. Usually these systems also include a drag and drop system for building interfaces which greatly simplifies that process for beginners. Figure 13.1 shows a typical example: Borland JBuilder version 2.

**Figure 13.1**  Borland JBuilder

Any JDK which is available for free download from a manufacturer's Web site will lack the IDE. Instead you'll get a compiler, a virtual machine and a way of running applets, all of which run from a command line. This is much more like the way that we have written and developed Perl scripts. In addition the IDEs usually include copious documentation on the various packages. If you use a free JDK you'll have to download the documentation for yourself as well.

The choice of free or commercial software is totally up to each individual. All can be used to create exactly the same products and all require a certain amount of adaptation from users. I don't like using IDEs in any language so I use a command line system but many of my students find the IDE much easier to handle. My current JDK is version 1.1.8 from IBM which has been benchmarked as one of the fastest systems available. I also use an add-on compiler, again from IBM, called Jikes. This is the fastest Java compiler that you can get.

If you are using an IDE to develop your Java code you will need to read the supplied documentation to find out how to compile and test your programs. The command-line tools use a compiler called `javac` and a run-time virtual machine simply called `java`. All Java compilers insist that source code files contain a class which has the same name as the file. There can be other classes in the file too, but one must follow this rule. If I create a class called `Test` and save it in a file called `Test.java` I compile it using:

```
javac Test.java
```

which will produce a bytecode file called `Test.class`. To execute the program I would then use:

```
java Test
```

Notice that when running the file I miss off the file extension. All Java run-time systems understand that bytecode files have the `.class` extension .

The easiest way of understanding *why* so many developers have started using Java is to look at some code. Because there isn't time or space in this book to take a serious look at Java I'm going to show just a few simple examples of the language. I'll start with the classic *Hello World* as a command-line program, add a simple interface to it, and then convert the whole thing into an applet which will run inside a Web page.

### 13.2.3.2  A Simple Application   This little application introduces some of the key features of Java. After you have seen, and possibly tried, the code I'll talk you through them. What you will see during the discussion is that many of the ideas used in Perl also apply here. Basically all programming languages require a similar set of tasks from the programmer. The programmer just has to go about those tasks in different ways.

Here's the code. If you are going to try the program then you need to save it in a file called `Simple.java` *with* an upper-case S. Compile it using `javac Simple.java` and run it with `java Simple`.

```java
import java.io.*;
import java.lang.*;

class Simple {
    public static void main(String argv[]) {
        Simple obj = new Simple();
```

```
        }

    Simple() {
        System.out.println("Hello World\n");
        }

    } // class Simple
```

So what does `Simple.java` do? It prints a line of text on a terminal window such as a DOS box or UNIX xterm. Let's look at the program in more depth.

The first thing that you need to do in Java is declare all of the packages which your program needs. These are the libraries of routines which were written by other developers and which provide functionality you need and aren't going to write yourself. In this case I'm using a package called `java.lang` which holds many of the low-level facilities of the language, and one called `java.io` which is used to perform input and output operations. In Perl libraries are included in programs through the use of either `use` or `require`, in Java packages are `imported`. Package names are a form of URI[10] with dot-separated paths. The asterix at the end of the `import` statement indicates that all routines in the package are to be imported for use.

Java is a properly object-oriented language in which everything is a class.[11] In the example `Simple` is therefore a class. Despite using classes Java programs need a starting point. Perl scripts basically start executing from the top of the source code. Compiled languages don't work like that. Instead each program must provide a starting point from where execution will begin. In Java, as in C and C++, this is done through a function called `main`.

```
public static void main(String argv[ ])
```

The code declares a `main` routine and makes it `public` so that any other program can use it to start our application. The `main` function has to be `static` which simply means that only one instance of it can exist within the running program. It is also `void` which means it doesn't return any data to the operating system when it terminates. Some applications return integer values to operating systems so that the OS can tell if they have terminated normally. Finally `main` has a parameter which is an array of strings called `argv`. Do you remember that Perl also takes its parameters into an array of strings called `argv`? They are both showing their heritage here as the same thing happens in C.

Next it is time to create an object. In fact that's all that the `main` method in this program does:

```
Simple obj = new Simple();
```

There's now an object called `obj` living in the system. The construction of this object used the keyword `new` which we have met before in both JavaScript and in Perl when

---

[10]Uniform resource indicator
[11]Except for primitive data types such as integers.

handling modules. When `obj` is constructed it just does one thing which is to print out a message:

```
System.out.println("Hello World\n");
```

`System.out` is a stream which points to the screen. This uses some low-level routines to actually send the text to the screen buffer for drawing. A stream is an object-oriented way of getting data to travel from one place to another. Usually streams are used to direct input from files or keyboard to programs or to send output to files or screen. Java takes the concept further by using the same model to send data across networks. Once you can print to the screen and read from the keyboard in Java you can (almost) send data right across the universe.

### 13.2.3.3   *A Graphical Application*   Writing to a terminal is all very well but most users want applications with interfaces. Java provides two different sorts of interface as standard: the Abstract Windowing Toolkit (AWT) and Java Foundation Classes (JFC). For some reason the JFC system is also known as Swing and you'll see the two names used interchangeably if you read anything about Java.

The simple 'Hello World' application becomes a lot more complex when an interface is added. I'm going to add a simple AWT surround to the text which produces a little application as shown in Figure 13.2.

**Figure 13.2**   A Simple Application

The code for the application has grown somewhat from its command-line origins:

```
import java.io.*;
import java.lang.*;
import java.awt.*;

class SimpleAWT extends Frame {
    static TextArea ta;
    static String newline;
    static Dimension win_size;

    public static void main(String argv[]) {
        newline = System.getProperty("line.separator");
        win_size = new Dimension(200, 50);
        SimpleAWT sawt = new SimpleAWT();
```

```
        }

    SimpleAWT() {
        super();
        this.setSize(win_size);
        this.setTitle("SimpleAWT");
        ta = new TextArea(2, 30);
        ta.appendText("Hello World" + newline);
        this.add("Center", ta);
        this.pack();
        this.show();
        } // constructor

    public boolean handleEvent(Event e) {
        if (e.id == Event.WINDOW_DESTROY) {
            System.exit(0);
            }
        return super.handleEvent(e);
        }

    } // SimpleAWT
```

If you want to see the application run you need to copy the code into a file called `SimpleAWT.java`, compile it using `javac SimpleAWT.java` and run it using `java SimpleAWT`. The program will work with any JDK of version 1.1 or later and may work with version 1.0.2 although I don't have access to that for testing.

The very first line after the package import statements contains an important new piece of Java:

```
class SimpleAWT extends Frame
```

This says that a new class is being created but that it extends another class called `Frame`. `Frame` is part of the AWT and this application is going to use many of its facilities as defined in the package, but it is also going to implement one of them in a different way. By extending a class we create a new class with new facilities which *automatically* includes the facilities of the existing class. Java's extension mechanism is one of the ways in which it implements the object-oriented idea of *inheritance* which you may have read about elsewhere.

Before any of the methods in the SimpleAWT class I declare three variables:

```
static TextArea ta;
static String newline;
static Dimension win_size;
```

These are class variables and because they are `static` only one instance of each of them can exist in the system. The `TextArea` is a graphical component which holds text strings. The use of the string `newline` is important as it shows one way in which the much hyped platform independence of Java can be used. Every type of operating system uses a different character, or set of characters, to represent the end of a line. In many programming languages, include Perl and JavaScript, this character is represented as \n but the actual system may use something different. Java doesn't take the risk of using an incorrect character Instead the command:

```
newline = System.getProperty("line.separator");
```

finds the correct newline character for the system and stores it as a string which can be used in all print operations. As well as getting the newline character the `main` routine also sets the size that the window is going to be:

```
win_size = new Dimension(200, 50);
```

which in this case is 200 pixels wide and 50 pixels high. The constructor does most of the work for this class. It starts by calling a method called `super`:

```
SimpleAWT() {
    super();
    this.setSize(win_size);
    this.setTitle("SimpleAWT");
```

When a class inherits  properties from another it has to call the constructor of *that* class from within its own constructor. In fact this call has to be the first line of the constructor. The new facilities can then be added onto those of the *super class*. In this case the super class is `Frame` which creates a window and handles a lot of communication with operating system devices such as mouse and keyboard. Once an object has been created it can refer to itself and set its own properties and configuration values by using the keyword `this`. All objects have names which can be used by the rest of the system but all object call *themselves* `this`.

The constructor finishes by creating a `TextArea`, adding some text to it, and then adding the `TextArea` to the window:

```
ta = new TextArea(2, 30);
ta.appendText("Hello World" + newline);
this.add("Center", ta);
this.pack();
this.show();
} // constructor
```

Our simple application has one final method: `handleEvent`. Java is yet another event-driven language. The `Frame` class responds to certain types of event such as users clicking the close icon of the window. Whilst `Frame` objects notice the event, the actual action taken in response has to be written by each developer. In this case we want the application to close down when the frame receives a `WINDOW_DESTROY` event but to ignore all other events:

```
public boolean handleEvent(Event e) {
    if (e.id == Event.WINDOW_DESTROY) {
        System.exit(0);
        }
    return super.handleEvent(e);
    }
```

### 13.2.3.4 A First Applet

Converting even a simple application into an applet needs some fairly drastic surgery to the code. Applets exist inside HTML pages and so don't need some of the furniture which applications have. In particular they have no need for frames. Much of the code in the "Hello World" application is related to the frame. By removing this we can create much cleaner and simpler code:

```
import java.io.*;
import java.lang.*;
import java.awt.*;
import java.applet.Applet;

class SimpleAWTApplet extends Applet {
    TextArea ta;
    String newline;

    public void init() {
        newline = System.getProperty("line.separator");
        ta = new TextArea(2, 30);
        ta.appendText("Hello World" + newline);
        add(ta);
        validate();
        }

    } // SimpleAWTApplet
```

This program creates a `TextArea`, adds some text to it, and then forces the browser to display the applet. This is done through the `validate()` command issued once the applet has been created in memory. Applets cannot be created outside of an HTML page. They don't need a `main()` method. Instead, applets have a method called `init()`. This is called by the browser each time that it wants to start the applet. In very simple applets `init()` is able to take the place of both `main()` and of the class constructor. The HTML page is as simple as the applet, consisting of an `object` tag. You may see some texts still using the `applet` tag but that is only included in HTML 4 for backwards compatibility. You'll also see that in this example I use an XHTML[12] formulation by ending an empty element with a forward slash. Our basic applet is shown in Figure 13.3.

```html
<html>
   <head>
     <title>A Simple Applet</title>
   </head>
   <body>

   <p>Here is the SimpleAWTApplet</p>
   <p align="center">
      <object code="SimpleAWTApplet.class" width="200"
      height="50" />
   </p>

   </body>
</html>
```

**Figure 13.3**   A Simple Applet

Applets only execute while their parent HTML page is being viewed. Once the browser moves off to another page the applet is removed from memory. When applets are no longer active they are automatically deleted by the garbage collector which means that they don't take up lots of system memory.

---

[12]See Section 3.5 for information on XHTML.

## 13.2.4  Java Servlets

So far you have seen that Java can be used to build applications and to provide additional client-side functionality on the Web. It can also be used to write a wide range of different server applications. The most attractive features of Java actually lie in its server-side abilities. Java technologies can be used to link together many different types of server so that mainframes, databases, and mini-servers can all work together seamlessly within one application. Often such complex *heterogeneous* systems are built as part of an intranet system.

Intranets use standard Web technologies such as TCP/IP, HTTP and CGI to link applications which run inside browsers to corporate information stores. In such a system if you use Java to glue the servers together and Java on the client, why not use Java to process CGI requests? For a few years now Sun Microsystems has provided the technologies which are needed to do just that. This technology is called the Java Servlet.

Before you can develop and run servlets you need to install a servlet server. At the moment the servlet technology is not built into any production Web server but is provided as an extra download from the Java Web site at Sun. The standard Java servlet software is now being produced by the Apache group[13] in cooperation with Sun and again can be downloaded for free. This software, called Tomcat, acts as both a servlet and JSP server but is still very much in development. Installing and running Tomcat is really very easy. It is written in Java and will therefore run on any platform. Simply follow the installation instructions and you are ready to try using servlets.

The Tomcat server runs from the command line like any other Java program. If you normally develop and run your Java applications from within an IDE you will need to find out how to make them work from a terminal. Once you have the server running it will listen for messages on port `8080` of your machine. To connect to it locally you use the address:

```
http://localhost:8080/
```

Writing a servlet is really like writing any other Java program except that servlets use a special API. I'm going to show you two simple servlet examples based upon the sample applications supplied with the Tomcat server. First I'll show how to echo a Web page back to the browser, in this case printing the message "Hello World", second, I'll demonstrate how to set and retrieve cookies. Once you've seen the two examples I'll conclude by defining some of the key parts of the Java servlets API.

### 13.2.4.1  *Hello World*  All server-side Web technologies work in basically the same way when interacting with the browser. The normal input and output routes, `STDIN` and `STDOUT`, are redirected so that data passes between browser and server application. The Java servlets server redefines the streams automatically to pass data between the browser and the servlet application.

---

[13]Responsible for the Apache Web server.

Servlets are ordinary Java source code files which are compiled into `.class` files using any standard Java compiler. The API files are supplied with the Apache Tomcat server so that no extra downloads are required before you start work. Once you've created a servlet it is referred to by browsers using the full path to the class file but *without* the file extension:

```
http://localhost:8080/servlets/Hello
```

If you have downloaded the server and API files and want to try servlets for yourself then save the following code in a file called `HelloWorld.java`. In the case of my particular Tomcat installation I place source and class files in the same directory as the sample applications:

```
jakarta-tomcat\webapps\examples\Web-inf\classes
```

Here is the code:

```java
import java.io.*;
import java.util.*;
import javax.servlet.*;
import javax.servlet.http.*;

public class HelloWorld extends HttpServlet {
    public void doGet(HttpServletRequest request,
                      HttpServletResponse response)
        throws IOException, ServletException {

        String title = "Hello World";
        response.setContentType("text/html");
        PrintWriter out = response.getWriter();

        out.println("<html>");
        out.println("<body bgcolor=\"white\">");
        out.println("<head>");
        out.println("<title>" + title + "</title>");
        out.println("</head>");
        out.println("<body>");
        out.println("<h1>" + title + "</h1>");
        out.println("</body>");
        out.println("</html>");
    }

} // class HelloWorld
```

Compile the program using:

```
javac HelloWorld.java
```

and access it via your browser. The address of the file will be:

```
http://localhost:8080/examples/servlet/HelloWorld
```

If everything compiles and runs you should see a message in your browser. The code itself might look different to anything that you've seen before in this book but the logic is the same. The `HelloWorld` class is a subclass of `HttpServlet` which simply means it extends the functionality which that class provides. This program imports four packages, plus `java.lang.*` which is always imported by default:

```
import java.io.*;
import java.util.*;
import javax.servlet.*;
import javax.servlet.http.*;
```

Just like applets, servlets cannot be run independently. They are always started by the servlet server and so do not need a `main()` method. This example contains just one method called `doGet()` which is an implementation of a method that is defined in `HttpServletRequest`. `doGet()` has two parameters which, just like in ASP, are both objects. The first is an object which encapsulates the request that was sent from the browser. The second object encapsulates the response that will be sent back to the browser. All of the work necessary to perform the communication such as extracting data from HTTP `post` or `get` messages has been done in the creation of the `request` object, which massively simplifies the use of servlets. If problems arise while `doGet` is operating it will create an error, called an exception in OO terminology, which `GET` returned to the browser.

The response object has to be told that the content it will handle is going to be HTML so the MIME type is set:

```
response.setContentType("text/html");
```

The `response` object sends messages to the browser via a data stream of type `PrintWriter`. A local reference is created to this stream and data printed on the stream.

```
PrintWriter out = response.getWriter();
out.println("<html>");
```

All of the different server-side Web technologies work in basically the same way. The biggest difficulty in using them is choosing an implementation language with which you are happy. Once that is done the processes are almost identical.

### 13.2.4.2 *Cookies*  My second Java servlet example shows you how to set and retrieve cookies. Whilst the caveats about cookies and privacy still apply here, they do provide a very simple mechanism for tracking your users. In fact servlet cookies are so simple that over using them would be a temptation. If you don't want to offend at least some of your visitors then you should be moderate and restrained with cookies.

If you want to try this cookie example you should save the code in a file called `aCookie.java`. To access it from your Web browser on your desktop PC the address, if you used the same directory as before, is:

```
http://localhost:8080/examples/servlet/aCookie
```

Here is the code:

```java
import java.io.*;
import java.util.*;
import javax.servlet.*;
import javax.servlet.http.*;
import javax.servlet.http.Cookie;

public class aCookie extends HttpServlet {
    static int cnt;

    public void doGet(HttpServletRequest request,
                      HttpServletResponse response)
        throws IOException, ServletException {
      Cookie[] cookies;
      Cookie cookie;

      response.setContentType("text/html");
      PrintWriter out = response.getWriter();
      out.println("<html>");
      out.println("<body bgcolor=\"white\">");
      out.println("<head>");

      String title = "Using Cookies";
      out.println("<title>" + title + "</title>");
      out.println("</head>");
      out.println("<body>");
      out.println("<h3>" + title + "</h3>");

      cookies = request.getCookies();
      if (cookies.length > 0) {
         out.println("<p>Your Browser holds these
         cookies:");
         for (int i = 0; i < cookies.length; i++) {
            cookie = cookies[i];
            out.print("<br>Cookie Name: "
                  + cookie.getName());
```

```
        out.println("  Cookie Value: "
              + cookie.getValue());
      }
   } else {
      out.println("<p>You don't have any cookies
      set");
      }

  String cookieName = "Another Cookie";
  String cookieValue = "Holding This Value";
  cookie = new Cookie(cookieName, cookieValue);
  response.addCookie(cookie);
  out.println("<P>");
  out.println("Your Cookies are: <br>");
  out.print("Name   " + cookieName);
  out.print(" Value   " + cookieValue);

  out.println("</body>");
  out.println("</html>");
  }

} // class Cookies
```

When the cookie example is run it produces output like that shown in Figure 13.4.

**Figure 13.4**  Servlet Cookies

The code uses a new package called `javax.servlet.http.Cookie` which contains all of the code needed to create and use cookies. In this program I create an array of cookies and an individual cookie:

```
Cookie[] cookies;
Cookie cookie;
```

The cookie handling code is broken into two parts. The program starts by reading the existing cookies on the browser. Remember it will only read those cookies set by this program from this server. The code for that is:

```
cookies = request.getCookies();
if (cookies.length > 0) {
   out.println("<p>Your Browser holds these cookies:");
   for (int i = 0; i < cookies.length; i++) {
      cookie = cookies[i];
      out.print("<br>Cookie Name: " + cookie.getName());
      out.println("Cookie Value: " + cookie.getValue());
      }
   } else {
   out.println("<p>You don't have any cookies set");
   }
```

The `getCookies` method of the request object is used to return an array of cookies. If the array is empty nothing else is done here. If the array contains some cookies the program prints them out one at a time. Again, printing is redirected to the `PrintWriter` stream of the `response` object. Data is extracted from the cookie before printing using its `getName` and `getValue` methods.

Setting a cookie is just as simple:

```
String cookieName = "Another Cookie";
String cookieValue = "Holding This Value";
cookie = new Cookie(cookieName, cookieValue);
response.addCookie(cookie);
```

The cookie constructor takes two strings as parameters. One is used to set the name and the other the value of the cookie. The cookie is then sent to the browser using the `addCookie` method of the `response` object.

### 13.2.4.3 *The Servlet API*
Full documentation for the servlet API is provided with the Tomcat server. As I haven't described Java in any great detail I don't think that a full description of the servlet API would be very useful at this point. However I will point out some of the methods in the `javax.servlet.http` and `javax.servlet.http.Cookie` classes that you might find useful. You can then compare the functionality available here with that provided by Active Server Pages and Perl/CGI.

### 13.2.4.4   Class javax.servlet.http.HttpServlet
This is an abstract class which has to be subclassed to be used. The subclass will have all of the functionality required to use HTTP servlets. The servlet server is multithreaded so production implementations must be able to handle concurrent requests.[14]

Servlet classes must implement at least one of these methods:

**HttpServlet()**
> This class is abstract and so objects of this class cannot be created. Hence this constructor does nothing. If you want to use the methods of the `HttpServlet` class then you must create a subclass which contains the implementation of its methods.

**doGet**
> This method lets the servlet handle `get` requests. As with all HTTP communications you must make sure that you send headers such as MIME types before you send the response page. If you get this wrong the browser will display an error message instead of your page.

**doPost**
> Handles data sent using the `post` request. The functionality you supply here can be identical to that supplied in `doGet` if you wish.

**doPut**
> Used when handling the `put` request which browsers can use to place files on the server. The `put` request is similar in intent to using FTP.

**doDelete**
> Used to delete files from the server.

**getServletInfo**
> Lets the servlet return information about itself to another process.

### 13.2.4.5   Class javax.servlet.http.Cookie

**Cookie(String name, String val)**
> Creates a new cookie with the name and value which were supplied as parameters.

**getComment**
> Returns the comment string within the cookie if that has been set.

**getDomain**
> Returns the domain to which the cookie applies.

**getName**
> Returns the name of the cookie.

**getPath**
> Returns the file path on the server to which the cookie applies.

---

[14]For evaluation and demonstration purposes don't worry about this.

`getValue`
> Returns the value of the cookie.

`setComment(String val)`
> Sets the comment value of the cookie to the string `val`.

`setDomain(String val)`
> Sets the domain for which the cookie applies to `val`.

`setName(String val)`
> Sets the name of the cookie to `val`.

`setPath(String URI)`
> Sets the server file path over which the cookie operates to `URI`.

`setValue(String val)`
> Sets the value of the cookie to `val`.

## 13.3  EXERCISES

### Active Server Pages

If you have access to Internet Information Server try out the following exercises.

1. Read the Active Server Page documentation which is supplied with IIS.

2. Follow this procedure to write and test an ASP script:

    (a) Create a simple ASP script which returns an HTML page to a browser.

    (b) Create a directory under the `inetpub` tree called `scripts`.

    (c) Place your ASP script in the new directory and name it `first.asp`.

    (d) Test your script by accessing it through a Web server and browser. The address of the script will be
    `http://127.0.0.1/scripts/first.asp`.

3. Write a second ASP script which processes data sent from a Web form using the `GET` method.

4. Rewrite your form and associated script to use the `POST` method.

5. Now try out the guestbook application from this chapter.

### Java

1. If you have not yet done so, download and install a Java Development Kit for your platform.

2. Download and install the API documentation.

3. Try to compile and run some of the sample applications and applets which came with your JDK.

4. Download and install the Tomcat server.

5. Try running some of the sample servlets which are supplied with Tomcat.

6. If you are comfortable with Java try implementing some of the CGI and ASP examples using servlets.

# 14
# *XML: Defining Data for Web Applications*

Over the years many technologies have excited the computer industry. Artificial intelligence, structured programming, databases, interfaces, networks have all had an impact beyond their designer's expectations. The current big thing on the Web is not some fancy multimedia application or new access technology, it's a way of describing data. Why does the Web need *another* way of describing data? Isn't that what HTML is for? Read on and I hope that I can clarify the situation and excite you to the possibilities that the Extensible Markup Language (XML) presents.

Data can easily be saved and presented as plain text and for many applications nothing else is needed. For instance configuration files such as Windows .bat files are rarely viewed by systems users, they provide control information for applications, and plain text is the perfect way of handling them. A word-processed document on the other hand is meant to be displayed, edited, and printed *and* to look good in each of those situations. Data often only has structure which must be recognized and remembered such as those Windows .bat files. In some situations applications need to present just the raw data while in others they are showing formatted data. The difficulty for developers is to combine all of these requirements into a single file type. Fortunately there is a standardized way of doing exactly that.

Back in the 1970s organizations were already suffering from large volumes of data which could not be shared between applications. Each program used its own proprietary format and those formats had a worrying tendency to change with new versions of the software. IBM developed a *markup*language which could be used to add structural and formatting information to data and which was designed to be simple enough to be included in any application. That markup language was adapted to be suitable for general use and in 1986 the Standard Generalized Markup Language was adopted as standard 8879 by the International Organization for Standardization (ISO).

So what is a markup language? Well, a markup is a set of instructions, often called *tags*, which can be added to text files. When the file is processed by a suitable application the tags are used to control the structure or presentation of the data contained in the file. Most commonly tags are used by applications when presenting data. There are many, many different types of presentational markup such as Microsoft Rich Text Format (RTF), Adobe Portable Document Format (PDF), and HTML. Each of these is a useful powerful solution to the problem of displaying information but all have the same limitation: they describe how the data *looks* but give no information about *what* it is.

This is the point at which XML enters the picture. XML is a subset of SGML, which simply means that it is composed of parts of the SGML specification. The designers of XML chose to include only those parts of SGML which are used most often and which can help to structure data and documents. This means that any valid[1] XML document is also a valid SGML document which is useful as lots of tools have been written over the years to create and manipulate SGML. SGML tools are often far more sophisticated than HTML editors. They include facilities for validating data, for creating tags, and for describing documents. Such tools can use data written by any other SGML editor and some can even be embedded into other applications.

Whilst markup systems such as HTML set out a standard set of rules which are applied to all documents, XML and SGML are a little different. XML is a sort of *meta-markup*: a grammar for creating other markup languages. By applying the rules of XML to a particular need, developers can create their own markup languages which conform to an international standard and can be manipulated by many applications but which are exactly tailored to a specific set of needs.

> Rule:
> XML is used to describe the structure of a document *not* the way that it is presented.

XML is a *recommendation*[2] of the World Wide Web Consortium (W3C). The current version of the standard is 1.0 but this is a fast moving area so expect new versions in the near future. A large number of other technologies and ideas are closely related to work on XML. Therefore anything written about the topic will soon be superseded. For the most accurate and up-to-date information on all of the technologies that I discuss in this chapter see http://www.w3c.org.

Although XML is a very young technology it has caught the imagination of many developers. Two areas in which XML appears to have potential are structuring data for storage where a relational database is inappropriate, and structuring data for presentation on Web

---

[1] Here valid means that the document conforms to its specification. I'll look at this in more detail later.
[2] Their version of a standard.

pages. If a system is handling small quantities of data or if the data lacks a *relational* structure[3] programmers have usually resorted to creating their own data formats. For example,
configuration files on many systems take a form like the following, which comes from the
Ghostview PostScript viewer on a PC running Windows NT:

```
[Devices]
bit=72,96
bitcmyk=72,96
bitrgb=72,96
bj10e=360x360,360x180,180x360,180x180
bj200=360x360,360x180,180x360,180x180
bjc600=360x360,360x180,180x360,180x180
bjc800=360x360,360x180,180x360,180x180

[cdj500]
dBitsPerPixel=24
dBlackCorrect=4
dShingling=2
dDepletion=1
```

In Section 10.4 I created a simple database which used pairs of colons to separate the
parts of each data item and newlines to separate items themselves:

```
cookies::chocolate::grahams
cookies::fruit::raspberry chewies
cake::chocolate::black forest gateau
cookies::plain::grahams
```

Many programmers use characters such as the vertical bar, |, instead of colons. The
important point is that none of these characters used as separators appear in the actual
data. Manipulating any of these data files needs the facilities which are provided by languages like Perl: regular expression parsing, string matching and replacement, and iteration through repetitive structures. XML is used to create structured data and hence it is
also very suitable for manipulation with Perl.

Through the rest of this chapter I am going to talk about the individual pieces which
make up the XML jigsaw, describing each and showing how they fit together. I'll be demonstrating XML with a simple application: a recipe book. I will show how to build the necessary data structures, how to create a grammar in XML to describe those structures, and
how to use styles to Web enable the recipe book. In Section 14.6 I'll take the recipe book
further and show how you can start to build a dynamic application to handle searching
and displaying of recipe data using XML and Perl.

---

[3]See any introductory database text for a description of relational structures.

## 14.1   BASIC XML

You've already seen a lot of markup in this book so you probably have a good idea what XML is going to look like. If that idea is that XML closely resembles HTML then you are correct. Here's the start of a structure for our recipe book:

```
<?xml version="1.0"?>

<recipes>
  <category type="loaf">
    <name>Basic Farmhouse</name>
    <ingredient></ingredient>
    <cooking>
      <time></time>
      <setting></setting>
    </cooking>
    <serves></serves>
    <instructions>
      <item></item>
    </instructions>
  </category>
</recipes>
```

That's not too complicated – but does it work? Is it *really* XML? Well Microsoft ships an XML parser as part of Internet Explorer 4 and 5, so we can find out.[4] All that you have to do to display your XML files is to open them with one of those browsers. Figure 14.1 shows what my recipe book looks like. The formatting there isn't too special and some funny things have happened to the XML but it all seems to be there. Notice the small hyphens before some of the items? Those items are containers which hold other XML elements. IE5 lets you hide or display the contents of container elements by clicking those hyphens with your mouse.

Look back at the code and in particular the first line. This is a *Processing Instruction* which tells applications how to handle the XML. In this case it also serves as a version declaration and says that the file is XML which should adhere to the rules for XML version 1.0. All of your XML applications *must* include a similar declaration, formatted in the same way:

```
<?xml version="1.0"?>
```

What happens if you break the rules? How do parsers cope? The rules state that the parser must halt when it finds an error and that it may return a message back to the calling application. Let's make a change in the recipe book so that it is no longer well formed. Change the line

---

[4]Netscape are going to be providing the same sort of functionality as part of Navigator 6.

**Figure 14.1** Internet Explorer 5 Displaying XML

```
<serves></serves>
```

into

```
<serves></servs>
```

and run the file through the browser once more. This time Internet Explorer displays the message shown in Figure 14.2.

## 14.1.1 Valid or Well Formed?

XML documents may be either valid or well formed. These terms imply different levels of conformance between the document, the DTD, and the XML standard. A well formed document is one which follows all of the rules of XML. Tags are matched and do not overlap, empty elements are ended properly, and the document contains an XML declaration. There are many such rules which are available in the XML recommendation document. A valid XML document has its own DTD. The document is well formed but also conforms to the rules set out in the DTD.

**Figure 14.2** Internet Explorer 5 Displaying an XML Error

Many XML parsers and libraries have been written in the last few years. A few of these are *validating*. They check that the document and its DTD are in agreement. Others such as Microsoft Internet Explorer 5 simply check that the document is well formed. The parser or library that you choose to use depends upon your needs. Although in this book I use non-validating parsers simply because they are what I have available, all of the XML *is* actually valid.

## 14.1.2  XML elements

XML documents are composed of just three things: elements, control information, and entities. Let's look at each of those in turn. Most of the markup in an XML document is element markup. Elements are surrounded by tags much as they are in HTML. The content of the document has a structure imposed by the rules of XML although this structure is quite loose. Each document has a single *root* element which contains all of the other markup. You have already met this idea in HTML where all documents are enclosed inside `<html></html>` tags. The document is then composed of a number of *sections*, each of which is enclosed between tags. The sections themselves are also elements, of course.

***14.1.2.1 Nesting Tags*** Even the simplest XML document has nested tags.[5] Unlike HTML these *must* be nested properly and closed in the reverse of the order in which they were opened. The following code is invalid XML because the order of the tags has become confused, with tags overlapping:

```
<category type="loaf">
   <name>Basic Farmhouse</name>
   <ingredient></ingredient>
   <cooking></cooking>
   <serves>
   <instructions></serves>
   </instructions>
</loaf>
```

Each XML tag has to have a closing tag, again unlike HTML.[6] There is no way that a parser can extract control information from the structure of the document. In HTML a parser will, for instance, assume that a `<td>` tag has been closed if it reads a `<tr>` tag. That's only possible because the parser is working within the context of HTML. It's not a general principle to be applied elsewhere.

***14.1.2.2 Case Sensitive*** HTML lets you use mixed upper- and lower-case letters inside markup. XML is case sensitive and you must use lower case for your markup. You'll use some upper-case letters inside control information but not inside your tags.

***14.1.2.3 Empty Tags*** Elements usually have content. A recipe without ingredients would make no sense after all and there would be no point in including empty `<ingredient></ingredient>` pairs in a recipe book. Elements may be empty though if you are formatting data retrieved from a database or entered by a user. Where the content of the element is missing the tag becomes:

```
<ingredient />
```

Look back at Figure 14.1 and you'll see that is how Internet Explorer displayed the empty tags in my skeleton document.

***14.1.2.4 Attributes*** Sometimes it is important that elements have information associated with them without that information becoming a separate element. Again this is an idea you've met before:

```
<img src="../images/uncle_fred.png" height=120
     width=34 alt="Uncle Fred">
```

---

[5]Tags inside tags.
[6]See Section 3.5 for a description of the way that HTML parsing is moving.

The markup would be very messy if all of those *attributes* and *values* were pulled out into individual tags:

```
<img>
    <src>../images/uncle_fred.png</src>
    <height>120</height>
    <width>34</width>
    <alt>Uncle Fred</alt>
</img>
```

Isn't that awful? Making the img element into a *container* adds nothing to our understanding of the data and may actually make handling it more complex.

The next piece of code adds some attributes to the ingredient tag of the recipe book:

```
<ingredient amount="200" unit="ml">milk</ingredient>
```

Notice that the values associated with each attribute are in quotes? Again that's an XML rule that doesn't apply in HTML. Attributes are actually not as easy to use as you might think. You need to spend some time thinking about whether an item really *is* an attribute or if it should be an element itself. Consider how you are going to be processing the item, how it might be stored and if it can stand alone. For instance if I wanted my recipe book to find all occasions on which 200 ml of a liquid was used then I would make amount an element rather than an attribute. Searching on an element rather than an attribute of element is logical and simple to me. Elements have more context and meaning than attributes. Attributes simply describe properties of elements. Unfortunately these design decisions cannot be resolved through a set of simple rules so you are on your own when it comes to designing your structures.

## 14.1.3  Control Information

Although you won't know this yet, you have already seen all of the XML control information. There are three control structures: comments, processing instructions, and document type declarations.

### *14.1.3.1  Comments*  XML comments are exactly the same as their HTML cousins. They may span several lines or be contained on just a single line of the page. All take the form:

```
<!-- comment text here -->
```

The same type of comment is used in both XML source files and in Document Type Definition (DTD) files, which we'll look at in Section 14.2. It is important that you thoroughly comment XML and DTD to aid in development and maintenance. Whilst your carefully crafted ingredient attribute might be obvious when you first create a document it may not be so clear when you come to edit that data in 10 years' time!

### 14.1.3.2 *Processing Instructions*  Processing Instructions (PI) are used to control applications. In this book I'm only scratching the surface of XML and I'm only going to use one PI. We met this earlier:

```
<?xml version="1.0"?>
```

Remember? That instruction tells the application that the data in the file follows the rules of XML version 1.0. Whether the file is being parsed or validated it must obey the XML 1.0 rules. This instruction must be the first instruction in your XML file because if it isn't, the parser won't have any rules to work with and will simply return an error to you. Some parsers such as the Microsoft one make assumptions if you omit the version information and assume that you are using version 1.0. It is far safer to force this behavior than to leave it to chance.

### 14.1.3.3 *Document Type Declarations*  Each XML document has an associated Document Type Definition. The DTD is usually held in a separate file so that it can be used with many documents. You *can*, though, place a DTD inside the XML file. I'll show you how to do that in a while but for now I'll concentrate upon the more useful external DTDs.

The DTD file holds the rules of the grammar for a particular XML data structure. Those rules are used by validating parsers to check that not only is the file valid XML, but that it also obeys its own internal rules. HTML has a set of DTDs which it can be validated against. Here's how you use them in XML:

```
<!DOCTYPE Recipes SYSTEM "recipe.dtd">
```

This declaration tells the parser that the XML file is of type `Recipes` and that it uses a DTD which is stored in a file called `recipe.dtd`. Furthermore the location is actually a URL[7] so the application knows that it should retrieve the DTD from the current directory.

The keyword `SYSTEM` is quite important in there. Some DTDs are available as International *standards*, such as those recommendations of W3C which relate to HTML. Other DTDs are developed by individuals and organizations for their own use. Each of these has a different effect on the application processing the document. Internationally agreed DTDs are denoted by the use of the keyword `PUBLIC`; any DTD which you develop yourself or have developed for you is denoted by the keyword `SYSTEM`.

## 14.1.4  Entities

The final part of an XML document *may* be one or more entities. An entity is a *thing* which is to be used as part of the document but which is not a simple element. An example of an entity is something like an image or an encrypted signature which you wish to use frequently. Rather than having to create some XML each time that the signature is used, the

---

[7]Strictly the W3C uses the term Uniform Resource Indicator (URI) when discussing XML. A URL is a *type* of URI. In this chapter I shall use the more familiar URL so as to avoid confusing readers too much.

entity itself can be included in the XML. The processing application is then able to handle the inclusion of the entity in an appropriate way.

## 14.1.5 Putting it All Together

Here is a rather more complete recipe book. If you try this code for yourself, you'll find that you get an error unless you also create and save the DTD described in Section 14.2.

```xml
<?xml version="1.0"?>
<!DOCTYPE Cookbook SYSTEM "recipe.dtd">

<cookbook>
<category type="loaf">
  <recipe>
    <name>The Basic Loaf</name>
    <ingredient>
       <qty amount="825" unit="ml"/>
       <item>Warm water</item>
    </ingredient>
    <ingredient>
       <qty amount="20" unit="g"/>
       <item>Granulated Dried Yeast</item>
    </ingredient>
    <ingredient>
       <qty amount="20"/>
       <item>Sugar</item>
    </ingredient>
    <ingredient>
       <qty amount="450"/>
       <item>Stoneground wholemeal flour</item>
    </ingredient>
    <ingredient>
       <qty amount="900"/>
       <item>Strong white bread flour</item>
    </ingredient>
    <ingredient><qty amount="20"/>
       <item>Salt</item>
    </ingredient>
    <ingredient>
       <qty amount="55"/>
       <item>Fresh Lard</item>
    </ingredient>
```

```xml
<cooking>
   <time>15</time>
   <gas>8</gas>
   <electric>230c</electric>
</cooking>
<cooking>
   <time unit="minutes">30</time>
   <gas>6</gas>
   <electric>200c</electric>
</cooking>
<serves />
<instruction>
   <ins>Add the yeast and sugar to the warm water and
   leave to activate</ins>
</instruction>
<instruction>
   <ins>Sieve the flour and salt into a large bowl</ins>
</instruction>
<instruction>
   <ins>Crumble the lard into the flour until it has a
   "breadcrumb" texture</ins>
</instruction>
<instruction>
   <ins>Mix the liquid into the flour</ins>
</instruction>
<instruction>
   <ins>Turn onto floured surface and knead for 300
   strokes</ins>
</instruction>
<instruction>
   <ins>Form into a ball, place in a warm place until
   doubled in size</ins>
</instruction>
<instruction>
   <ins>Knead for another 100 strokes</ins>
</instruction>
<instruction>
   <ins>Form into a ball, place in a warm place until
   doubled in size</ins>
</instruction>
<instruction>
```

```
            <ins>Form into five loaves and leave to rise for 30
            minutes</ins>
        </instruction>
        <instruction>
            <ins>Bake!</ins>
        </instruction>

    </recipe>
    <recipe>
        <name>Wheatgerm Bread</name>
        <!--
            NOTE that this recipe is incomplete. I included it
            so that you will see how the processing works with
            multiple data items
        -->
    </recipe>
</category>
</cookbook>
```

I must admit that I'm not totally satisfied with that XML structure. Where I've used:

```
<cooking>
    <time unit="minutes">30</time>
    <gas>6</gas>
    <electric>200c</electric>
</cooking>
<instruction>
<ins>Form into a ball, place in a warm place until doubled in
size</ins>
</instruction>
```

I would have preferred something like:

```
<cooking>
    <time unit="minutes">30</time>
    <setting type="gas" value="6"/>
    <setting type="electric" value="200c"/>
</cooking>
<instruction>
Form into a ball, place in a warm place until doubled in size
</instruction>
```

which also happens to be valid XML. The reason that I've used the former version is [8] XSL. When I came to write a stylesheet for the original version I discovered either the limitations of XSL or of my XSL programming abilities. Whatever the reason, I took a pragmatic decision to write working code rather than elegant code. You'll make many similar decisions as *you* work with these infant technologies.

## 14.2 DOCUMENT TYPE DEFINITION

Writing the XML is only half the story. The XML has neither meaning nor context without a grammar against which it can be validated. The grammar is called a Document Type Definition (DTD). The DTD has quite a complex structure which makes sense given the difficult and important nature of its role. Writing a good DTD is probably the most difficult aspect of using XML in your applications. Before I look at the details here's a DTD for my recipe book:

```
<!ELEMENT cookbook (category+)>
  <!ELEMENT category (recipe+)>
  <!ATTLIST category
    type CDATA #REQUIRED>

  <!ELEMENT recipe (name, ingredient+, cooking+, serves?,
instruction*)>
    <!ELEMENT name (#PCDATA)>

    <!ELEMENT ingredient (qty, item)>
      <!ELEMENT qty (#PCDATA)>
        <!ATTLIST qty
          amount CDATA #REQUIRED
          unit CDATA "g">
      <!ELEMENT item (#PCDATA)>

    <!ELEMENT cooking (time*, gas*, electric*)>
      <!ELEMENT time (#PCDATA)>
        <!ATTLIST time
        unit CDATA "minutes">
      <!ELEMENT gas (#PCDATA)>
      <!ELEMENT electric (#PCDATA)>

    <!ELEMENT serves (#PCDATA)>
```

---

[8]Extensible Stylesheet Language. See Section 14.5 for more details.

```
<!ELEMENT instruction (ins*)>
  <!ELEMENT ins (#PCDATA)>
```

Looking at that DTD there is quite a lot to explain – and I haven't used all of the possibilities which XML provides. Before I start the explanation, if you have access to a copy of Internet Explorer try saving the recipe book source (as `recipes.xml`) and DTD file (as `recipe.dtd`). View the XML by opening `recipe.xml` in the browser. It should all work nicely. You can even omit all attributes which say (exactly) `unit="g"` or `unit="minutes"` and the file will still display as intended. Figure 14.3 shows what you might get.

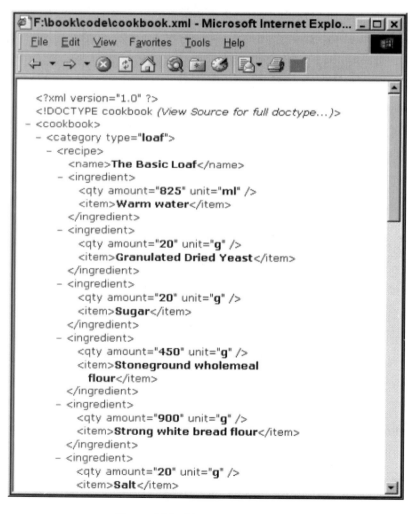

***Figure 14.3***   The XML Recipe Book

Just like the XML source the DTD actually only has a few components, it is the way that those components are assembled which leads to complex structures like the recipe book.

DTDs can be included in the XML file. The XML source file will then look like the next example:

```
<?xml version="1.0"?>

<!DOCTYPE recipe[
  <!ELEMENT cookbook (category+)>
  <!-- Rest of DTD here -->
]>

<cookbook>
  <!-- Rest of XML here -->
</cookbook>
```

The DTD is all placed inside a single DOCTYPE tag and is surrounded by square brackets [...].

## 14.2.1  Elements

The XML document is composed of a number of elements. Each of those elements may itself be made from other elements and some of the elements in the document may contain attributes. This structure is reflected in the DTD. The first *node* of the XML document is called the *root node*. It contains all other nodes of the document and each XML document must have exactly one root node. In the recipe book, the root node is called *cookbook* and all of the nodes which it holds are called *category*. Defining that in XML is straightforward:

```
<!ELEMENT cookbook (category+)>
```

All elements are declared using the same format. The element tag starts with an exclamation mark and the word ELEMENT in upper-case letters. This is followed by the name of the element. The element ends with some information in parentheses. Each element can either be a container which holds further elements or it can define data. In the case of container nodes, the parentheses hold a comma-separated list of sub-elements. Each sub-element can also be associated with a control character indicating how often it appears. These control characters are listed in Table 14.1.

The root node contains at least one other element definition with that element appearing at least once in the XML document. In the recipe book I've defined just one node, category, appearing below the root but that node is itself quite complex. Concentrating on the ELEMENT tags for now, the category element is defined as:

```
<!ELEMENT recipe (name, ingredient+, cooking+,
    serves?, instruction*)>
```

***Table 14.1***   DTD Elements which Control Repetition

| Symbol | Example | Meaning |
|---|---|---|
| Asterix | item* | The item appears zero or more times. |
| Comma | (item1, item2, item3) | Separates items in a sequence in the order in which they appear. |
| None | item | Item appears exactly once. |
| Parentheses | (item1, item2) | Encloses a group of items. |
| Pipe | (item1 \| item2) | Separates a set of alternatives. Only one may appear. |
| Plus | item+ | Item appears at least once. |
| Question mark | item? | The item appears once or not at all. |

which is a list of elements. The `name` appears just once, at least one `ingredient` and one `cooking` elements are required, only a single `serves` element is allowed but as many `instructions` as the recipe requires can be used.

Elements which contain data items are declared using the format:

```
<!ELEMENT name (#PCDATA)>
```

In this case the parentheses contain the data type of the element. The data type must be preceded by a # symbol. Although XML documents can contain many data types, the more complex such as `gif` are included as entities. Elements basically hold one of two data types: PCDATA and CDATA. CDATA is plain text character data which is not passed through the engine of the XML parser. PCDATA is parsed character data which may contain XML markup and hence has to be handled by the parser. The default data type for elements is PCDATA but CDATA can be very useful. If the content of the element contains any of the characters which are used for markup such as < or > you will not want the parser to handle these. If they are parsed then you may get errors about the structure of your document.[9] The use of CDATA lets you avoid parsing.

### *14.2.1.1 Attributes*   So far we've seen that an XML element can contain other elements or data items. Some elements are more complex than this and have attributes which may be optional. This idea is well established in HTML where tags such as

```
<a href="http://www.shu.ac.uk">A hyperlink</a>
```

have important information inside the tag. In the case of the HTML address tag the content of the element is the text or image which the user selects with the mouse. The address which the tag points to is an attribute of the element.

---

[9] As in HTML these characters can be replaced with entities such as &lt;.

Attributes are important and useful when you are handling complexity. Some XML elements need to hold more than one piece of information. Some of that information will be displayed or handled by applications but other pieces are used to control the behavior of the application. The latter types are best included as attributes. In the recipe for bread the ingredients all have attributes:

```
<qty amount="825" unit="ml">Warm water</qty>
```

The most important information about an ingredient is *what* it is. If we wanted to search the recipe book to find all recipes which need, for instance, onions then we need onion to be the content of the ingredient. It is unlikely that we would want to search for all recipes which contained a pinch of something or which use grams as a unit of weight. The amount of onions in a recipe is an attribute; as information it is less important than the fact of using onions.

Once you have decided that some of your XML elements have attributes, then you need to include this information in the DTD. Associated with the element declaration is an ATTLIST which may contain:

- the name of the element,
- the name of each attribute,
- the data type of the attribute,
- any value which will be used as a default if the attribute is omitted from the XML source,
- control information about the use of the element.

```
<!ATTLIST qty
    amount CDATA #REQUIRED
    unit CDATA "g">
```

This attribute declaration shows an element with two attributes. The first one is called amount. This element is of type CDATA which means that it holds plain text which will not be passed through XML parsers. The attribute is REQUIRED which means that it *must* be included when the element is used. Failure to do so will result in the parser raising an error. The second attribute, unit is also of type CDATA. This element is optional but a default value, "g", is shown. If the attribute is omitted from the XML the default will be used instead.

As well as the REQUIRED and default controls, attributes may be FIXED, in which case, as with default, a specific value will be used if the attribute is not included. Finally, attributes can be IMPLIED. These are optional and can be safely ignored if no value is given.

## 14.2.2 Entities

You have already seen, in HTML, that some markup elements can contain complex data. These elements are called entities. Think of an entity as a container which will be filled with some form of content. The content may be included in the XML file, an *internal* entity, or stored in another file, an *external* entity. As with attributes and elements, entities may be either parsed or non-parsed. All complex data items which do not need to pass through the XML parser should be defined as non-parsed.

### 14.2.2.1 Internal Entities

Internal entities are used to create small pieces of data which you want to use repeatedly throughout your schema. For instance in the recipe book it may reduce the size of the source files if we declare an entity like this:

```
<!ENTITY POS "Pinch of salt">
```

which could then be used in an `instruction` like this:

```
<item>Finally add the &POS;</item>
```

When an entity is included the name is preceded by an ampersand and followed by a semicolon. That's also the way that HTML control characters such as < (`&lt;`) or ©(`&copy;`) are included in documents. In fact this is the same idea but with user-defined entities.

### 14.2.2.2 External Entities

Almost anything which is data can be included in your XML as an external entity. Here's a quick example which shows how to create a container for a Portable Network Graphic (png) image in an XML schema.

```
<!ENTITY myimage SYSTEM "unclefred.png" NDATA PNG>
```

You may remember from the discussion of XML that the SYSTEM keyword shows that we have created the data for our local application. This picture of Uncle Fred is not part of some internationally agreed standard. The address of the image is given in URL format so that the processor knows where to find the data object. The end of the entity declaration is NDATA PNG. NDATA tells the processor that we have created a `notation` for this type of data. Notations are important because the XML parser and most XML applications will only handle a limited range of data types. Where an application uses a data type which the XML parser does not understand a *helper application* must be specified. The data will then be passed to this helper for processing.[10] Declaring the helper looks like this:

```
<!NOTATION PNG SYSTEM "xv">
```

That passes the image to a paint program for viewing (the standard UNIX xv application in this case).

---

[10]The same model is, of course, used by Web browsers with multimedia data.

## 14.2.3 Namespaces

If everything in your XML document is an element then how does the parser identify items? It uses the element name to create an internal representation as described in Section 14.4. No problem so far, but what happens if two different elements which represent different types of object have the same name? Look at this example:

```
<staff>
  <name>Chris Bates</name>
  <dept>
    <name>School of CMS</name>
  </dept>
  <room>2323</room>
</staff>
```

Here I've got two elements called name but they each represent different things and have different meanings. Applications could confuse these two items, thus rendering the whole XML document useless. In a small document that isn't a problem as you can simply invent a new name for one of the elements. What happens in a large organization where, potentially, there are hundreds of different XML schemas? The answer is to use *namespaces*.

A namespace is a way of keeping the names used by applications separate from each other. Within a particular namespace no duplication of names can exist. Applications may use many different namespaces at the same time. The implementation of namespaces is system dependent. Scripting languages such as Perl create internal data structures to manage these. Compiled languages rely upon the compiler to alias names statically as the program is compiled. XML developers can specify their own namespaces which can be used in many applications. A namespace is included in the XML in the same way as a DTD:

```
<?xml version="1.0"?>
<!DOCTYPE Recipes SYSTEM "recipes.dtd">
<!xml:namespace ns="http://URL/namespaces/breads"
      prefix="bread">
<!xml:namespace ns="http://URL/namespaces/meats"
      prefix="lamb">
<recipes>
  <category>
    <bread:name>Basic Loaf</bread:name>
  </category>
  <category>
    <lamb:name>Roast Lamb</lamb:name>
  </category>
</recipes>
```

Each `category` of recipe has a `name` element. However, because the namespaces have been declared there is no chance of an application confusing the two names.

You won't need to use namespaces until your XML documents become quite large or your applications are processing many different schemas at the same time. More information is available from the W3C Web site (`http://www.w3c.org`).

## 14.3   XML SCHEMA

Document Type Definitions have been successfully used in SGML applications for many years. From the XML view, though, they appear to have a number of limitations. The most important objection to DTDs is that they are too document-centric. As the name implies a DTD is created to describe the structure of a text document, which is what SGML files are. XML, on the other hand is not intended as a way of describing text documents. Instead XML is used to define any form of structured information, which may range from a love letter through to the interface of an application. Secondly, and related to the first point, DTDs assume that the content of an element will be either text or a child element. That's not the case in some XML applications where elements may hold binary data, for instance. Finally, writing DTDs is not easy. They use a grammar and syntax all of their own. If you're planning to use XML plus DTD you'll have to learn more and deal with more complexity.

So what are the benefits, if any, of DTDs? Primarily they are successful because they are well-understood. You'll find a wealth of information on the Web and in textbooks and magazines describing how to use and create a DTD. You'll also find plenty of tools which support their creation and use, all serious SGML and XML editors support DTD editing as well. Many tools require a DTD if they're going to validate your documents. Given these benefits, anything which comes along to replace DTDs has a hard job. It's going to have to provide all of the facilities of a DTD yet be easier to author. At the same time the replacement must be easy to build into existing tools. If it doesn't get support from the tools manufacturers, technical excellence will count for nothing since it just won't be used.

A number of candidates have been proposed over recent years with a clear winner emerging recently. The W3C developed a technology called XML Schema which they accepted as a recommendation in Spring 2001. XML Schema is itself an XML application which means when you use it you only need a single grammar and can use your normal XML editor to create it. At the time of writing few tools are available which can use XML Schema to validate XML documents. Automated support is sure to start to appear soon. XML Schema is a complicated language and since it can't easily be used at the moment I'm not going to describe it in too much detail. Instead, I shall reformulate the recipe book DTD and point out one or two useful features.

## 14.3.1 Schema For The Recipe Book

The complete XML Schema definition of the recipe book is a very long piece of text. I'm only going to include a partial schema in this book to save space. Writing the remainder is, as they say, left as an exercise for the reader.

```
<?xml version="1.0" encoding="utf-8" ?>
<xsd:schema xmlns:xsd="http://www.w3.org/2001/XMLSchema">
  <xsd:element name="cookbook">
    <xsd:complexType>
      <xsd:sequence>
        <xsd:element name="recipe">
          <xsd:complexType>
            <xsd:sequence>
              <xsd:element name="name" type="xsd:string"/>

              <xsd:element name="ingredient">
                <xsd:complexType>
                  <xsd:sequence>

                    <xsd:element name="qty">
                      <xsd:complexType>
                        <xsd:attribute name="amount"
                        type="xsd:decimal" />
                          <xsd:attribute name="unit"
                        type="xsd:string" />
                      </xsd:complexType>
                    </xsd:element>

                    <xsd:element name="item"
                            type="xsd:string"/>
                  </xsd:sequence>
                </xsd:complexType>
              </xsd:element>

            </xsd:sequence>
          </xsd:complexType>
        </xsd:element>

      </xsd:sequence>
    </xsd:complexType>
  </xsd:element>
</xsd:schema>
```

This schema defines a namespace for its elements. Elements and some attributes, those which define data types, all exist in that namespace. XML elements are defined within XML Schema as being either simple types or complex types. A complex type contains other elements or has attributes. Notice that when you define the attributes of a complex element, these definitions must follow those of any child elements which it may have.

A simple type defines an element which is a container for data. Within a complex type the individual components form a sequence which must be defined in the schema document. Elements and attributes may have a data type which is defined as an attribute of the element definition, although if the element is designed to be empty, this will be omitted. The XML Schema recommendation lists a range of data types from traditional integers and strings through to day, month and XML types such as NMTOKEN. Although my example doesn't show this, you can restrict the number of times which an element must appear in a valid document. Such restriction is done by setting two attribute, minOccurs and maxOccurs in the schema.

XML Schema looks like it will be an important tool for XML developers. It won't replace the DTD since they continue to be used by SGML authors, but you'll see more of them used as tool support appears. You can find lots of useful documentation, including a comprehensive primer, on the W3C Web site at http://www.w3c.org.

## 14.4 DOCUMENT OBJECT MODEL

XML parsers can handle documents in any way that their developers choose – up to a point. The W3C recommendations for XML specify the *external* behavior that parsers must have. That simply means that a parser has to structure its output in a specific way, has to pass certain messages to applications, and has to handle specified types of input. However the *internal* behavior of the parser such as the data structures which it uses or the types of algorithm used to handle XML parsing, are not specified. This is important because it means that developers can use whatever language they want, or need to, when implementing a parser, but that parser will have standard behavior.

Two models are commonly used for parsers: SAX and DOM. SAX parsers are used when dealing with *streams* of data. The data, XML documents, is passing from one place to another with the parser acting as an intermediate way-point. Typically this model is used when passing XML data across a network between applications and is widely used by Java programmers. SAX-based parsers do not have to build large static models of the document in memory and are intended to run quickly.

The SAX model is, though, unsuited to use on Web sites where repeated querying and updating of the XML document is required. Here it is sensible to build some sort of representation which can be held in memory for the duration of the use of the application. In such cases a DOM-based parser is the better route.[11] So what is DOM? The acronym stands for the Document Object Model which is a concept which you should be pretty familiar with by now.

The DOM is an Application Program Interface (API) for XML documents. If you're not a programmer you may well be wondering what an API is supposed to be. Basically an API is a set of data items and operations which can be used by developers of application programs. The Microsoft Windows environment has a very rich API which is used by developers when creating Windows programs. Rather than create their own functionality for buttons, for instance, they use the functionality which Microsoft has already created. However, access to that functionality is restricted by the API: if the API doesn't let something happen then it can't be done, even if technically it is a good idea.

How does the idea of an API work with XML? Well the DOM API specifies the *logical* structure of XML documents and the ways in which they can be accessed and manipulated. If you write an application which uses a DOM-compliant XML parser[12] then your application will function in a certain way. Changing the parser you use for another DOM-compliant parser, possibly written in a different language, will leave the operation of your application totally unaffected. That sounds fanciful and optimistic but really does work in practice. It's possible to swap a parser made by Sun, for example, with one made by IBM and to rebuild and run the application without changing any code.

The DOM API is just a specification. There isn't a single reference piece of software associated with it which everyone must use. This is unlike Microsoft Windows where all developers use a standard set of libraries which contain the Windows code. Anyone can write an XML parser in any language. All of those parsers can be implemented in different ways. What is important is that they all present the same interface to other applications.

DOM-compliant applications include all of the functionality needed to handle XML documents. They can build static documents, navigate and search through them, add new elements, delete elements, and modify the content of existing elements. The DOM views XML documents as *trees* like that shown in Figure 14.4, but this is very much a *logical* view of the document. There is no requirement that parsers include a tree as a data structure. What is important is that each node of the tree, each XML element, is modeled as an object. This means that the node encompasses both data and behavior and that the whole document can be seen as a single complex object.

Object-oriented theory lets each object have a unique identity which means that some very useful options are open to the DOM processor. If each node has a unique identity then the tree can be searched for individual nodes. To an application the document then becomes simply a structured set of data items which it may manipulate. That may not be very beneficial when handling a Web page but it certainly *is* when your XML contains a database.

---

[11]This is the way that the Microsoft parser (`msxml.dll`) in Internet Explorer works.
[12]One which sticks to the standard API.

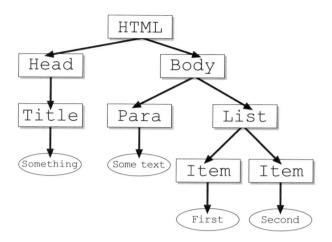

**Figure 14.4** Sample Document Object Model

The DOM *exposes* the whole of the document to applications. It is also *scriptable* so applications can manipulate the individual nodes. If you worked through the JavaScript and Dynamic HTML chapters, you've used this idea before. HTML documents can also be viewed as XML documents and accessed through a DOM structure. Languages such as JavaScript can easily be used within Web clients to manipulate the components of a Web page. XML takes the same sort of idea much further but the DOM is *not* DHTML. The current version of the DOM specification makes no inclusion of events. It is the ability to respond to events which gives DHTML its power; hopefully this ability will be included in later versions of the DOM.

## 14.5 PRESENTING XML

All of the Web presentation technologies are moving towards an implementation-independent paradigm. There is an increasing tendency to keep the data and formatting information separate from each other. We have seen this in the Web development sphere where formatting information is kept in styles, often stored in stylesheet files which may optionally be applied to the HTML text by the browser. The importance of using styles cannot be overstated: the same data can be formatted differently for any number of devices and, importantly, that formatting can be appropriate for the device and its user.

Stylesheets are an attractive and seductive idea which the specifiers of XML have been keen to adopt. The *Extensible Stylesheet* is a language used to express stylesheets which are then used to present XML documents.

XSL stylesheets are *not* the same as HTML Cascading Stylesheets. Rather than create a style for a specific XML element or class of elements, with XSL a template is created. This template is used to format XML elements which match a specified pattern. Usually the template is a page design *or* the design of part of a page. The application simply substitutes the template for a marker in the formatted page. It's a seductive idea which is actually rather complicated in practice.

I want you to be able to actually *use* some of the ideas from this chapter. To that end I'm going to be working with Internet Explorer. The XML parser in IE5 was developed to output HTML from a combination of XML and XSL. I'll show you how to take the XML recipe book and make it look more like a conventional Web page.

---

**Note:**

Although these examples produce HTML output, XSL could be used to produce any type of markup from LaTeX through to Rich Text Format.

---

I'll start by showing you some code and then discuss it bit by bit. XSL is pretty complex and I don't have the space here to show you everything that it can do. What I'm going to concentrate on is a *transformation* from XML to HTML. Basically what XSL does is transform one data structure into another. You start out with some XML code and then by applying the rules from the XSL you output something else. If you read the documentation from the W3C Web site you'll see that these transformations involve tree-based data structures. Remember from the discussion of XML that these are *logical* trees and that applications can implement them in any way that they need to. So let's look at the code, which takes a perfectly acceptable XML cookbook and converts it for display within a Web page.

We need to start by altering the XML so that the parser knows that it needs to use a stylesheet. I'll be using the XML code from Section 14.1.5 and the DTD from Section 14.2. The DTD doesn't need to change. Here is the change that the XML requires:

```
<?xml version="1.0"?>
<!DOCTYPE Recipes SYSTEM "recipe.dtd">
<?xml:stylesheet type="text/xsl" href="recipe.xsl"?>

<cookbook>
<category type="loaf">
```

I've added a single line of code which is a reference to a stylesheet called `recipe.xsl`. Notice that the reference is actually a URL even though the stylesheet is, in this case, on the same drive as the XML file. Now for the stylesheet itself:

```
<?xml version="1.0"?>

<xsl:stylesheet xmlns:xsl="uri:xsl">
<xsl:template match="/">
<html>
  <body>
    <h1>The Cookbook</h1>
    <xsl:for-each select="cookbook/category">
```

```
<table border="1">
  <xsl:for-each select="recipe">
  <tr>
     <th colspan="3" style="font-size:25;color: purple">
     <xsl:value-of select="name"/></th>
  </tr>
  <tr><th colspan="3">Ingredients</th></tr>
  <tr style="color:red; font-style:italic;
  text-align:center">
     <td colspan="2">Item</td><td>Amount</td>
  </tr>

  <xsl:for-each select="ingredient" order-by=
  "ingredient/item">
  <tr>
     <td colspan="2"><xsl:value-of select="item"/></td>
     <td>
     <xsl:value-of select="qty/@amount"/>
     <xsl:value-of select="qty/@unit"/>
     </td>
  </tr>
  </xsl:for-each>

  <tr><th colspan="3">Instructions</th></tr>

  <xsl:for-each select="instruction">
  <tr>
     <td colspan="3"><xsl:value-of select="ins"/></td>
  </tr>
  </xsl:for-each>

  <tr><th colspan="3">Cooking Instructions</th></tr>
  <tr style="color:red; font-style:italic;
  text-align:center">
     <td colspan="2">Setting</td><td>Time</td>
  </tr>
  <tr style="color:blue">
    <td>Gas</td>
    <td>Electric</td>
    <td></td>
```

```
      </tr>

      <xsl:for-each select="cooking">
      <tr>
         <td><xsl:value-of select="gas"/></td>
         <td><xsl:value-of select="electric"/></td>
         <td>
           <xsl:value-of select="time"/>
           <xsl:value-of select="time/@unit"/>
         </td>
      </tr>

      </xsl:for-each>
      </xsl:for-each>
   </table>
   </xsl:for-each>
</body></html>
</xsl:template>
</xsl:stylesheet>
```

Even if you've followed everything so far I imagine that is pretty cryptic. Certainly my first experience of reading an XML stylesheet left me wondering just what I was seeing. When the XML file `recipe.xml` is loaded into Internet Explorer 5 the browser produces some very reasonable output. If you have access to IE5 try saving the DTD, XSL, and XML then loading the XML file into the browser. If you don't have IE5 take a look at Figure 14.5 to see what you're missing.

Remember when you look at the sample output that I'm using IE5 because it handles XML *now*. I don't have to write any code of my own and I don't have to wait for other developers to create XML handling applications. Microsoft is there already.

Before I dive into some of the intricacy of the recipe stylesheet I'll just make a couple of points about using XML and XSL. First, where I've declared default values for attributes within the DTD I have to use those attributes in the XML. When the application processes the XML it automatically includes the default if no alternative value is given. That's standard XML, but it's nice to see it working as specified even when using XSL. Second, I have found XSL to be an awkward technology. XSL *seems* to include normal programming techniques such as repetition and selection, but if the XML isn't structured in a way that XSL likes, incompatibilities start to appear. It is *much* easier to rewrite the XML than get XSL to do what you want. In addition you can't easily debug XSL. If the stylesheet includes an error then the browser will probably display a blank screen. Finding the error can sometimes become a nightmare.

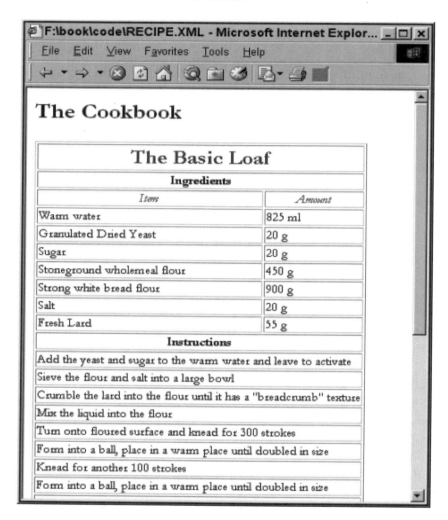

**Figure 14.5** The XML Recipe Book Formatted with XSL

## 14.5.1 The Recipe Book XSL Explained

The stylesheet begins with a declaration which tells the application exactly what it is handling. Right at the top the application needs to know that this file is a stylesheet. It can't rely upon the link from the XML file to *know* that these instructions form a stylesheet. In the XML file we have a line like

```
<?xml:stylesheet type="text/xsl" href="recipe.xsl"?>
```

which is an instruction telling the application to fetch a specific file and to use that file as a stylesheet. If the link is wrong then the application has no way of knowing. Instead it may start parsing the file and give parser errors. Much better, surely, if the application looks for a stylesheet declaration inside the linked file and returns a sensible error if it can't find one.

```
<xsl:stylesheet xmlns:xsl="uri:xsl">
```

The declaration not only says that the file is a stylesheet, it also creates a namespace. Stylesheets are valid XML documents and may contain markup which is also present in the XML document. To avoid this problem all XSL elements are contained within one namespace. In the case of our example the namespace is called `xsl`.

```
<xsl:template match="/">
```

The next element declares an XML template. To briefly recap, a template acts as a set of instructions to transform an XML document into a particular output document. A stylesheet may contain many templates for use in different situations. Where multiple templates are found inside one stylesheet, XSL can be used to select between them.

In the recipe book I only declare a single template which I apply to the whole XML file. This is done through the attribute `match="/"`. This is a pattern matching command. Whenever you need to select XML elements within your template a pattern is created. Any elements which match the pattern will be subject to the transformations which it includes. Think of the XML document as a hierarchy of these patterns, each separated by a slash. For instance:

```
/cookbook/category/ingredient/item
```

Once the whole document has been selected for transformation, the actual work can begin. I am transforming the recipe book into an HTML document. To do this I create the framework of an HTML page with empty spaces in which I will place my XSL elements. Here is part of that framework:

```
<html>
  <body>
    <h1>The Cookbook</h1>
    <!-- for each category -->

    <table border="1">
      <!-- for every recipe -->

      <tr>
        <th colspan="3" style="font-size:25; color: purple">
          <!-- display the name of the recipe -->
        </th>
      </tr>
```

```
    <!-- end every recipe -->
  </table>

  <!-- end each category -->

 </body>
</html>
```

The plan is that I will display the whole recipe book within an HTML table. I will start by moving through all of the recipes in one category, then move onto the next category. I am making no assumptions about the structure of the data: the structure is closely controlled by the DTD so I *know* that I have categories which contain recipes. I do not attempt to check that a recipe is in the correct category: that type of processing requires more powerful code than XSL can provide.

Once inside a category I will move in turn through the recipes. Notice that as well as indicating where the XSL processing happens I include an HTML comment showing where a piece of processing ends. Finally I will display the name of the recipe inside the table as an HTML `<th>` element.

Moving through all elements of one type is easy. The XSL namespace that I'm using here has an `xsl:for-each` element which does exactly that. Processing occurs inside this element and looping terminates once the pattern no longer matches. The first pattern match I need is to find categories inside the cookbook:

```
<xsl:for-each select="cookbook/category">
```

Once this pattern matches, processing moves inside the HTML table. Here I look for all recipe elements and loop through those which I find:

```
<xsl:for-each select="recipe">
```

Finally I need to look for recipe names and display them. The display happens automatically whenever I find a name. The search is also straightforward. Again it happens through a pattern match:

```
<xsl:value-of select="name"/>
```

This time the text string which the XML element holds will be returned *if* the name of the element matches the pattern name. That's confusing at first. Let's break it into pieces.

1. Find the next unprocessed recipe.

2. Read each element in turn.

3. If the element name does not match the pattern name ignore the element.

4. When an element such as `<name>Wheatgerm Bread</name>` matches the pattern, extract and return the content of the element. In this example the content is the text string `Wheatgerm Bread`.

The xsl:value-of element is an empty element. It is not a container for markup or data. Instead the value which it returns is substituted for it in the output document. In the example shown above, the text string Wheatgerm Bread is placed into the th element of the HTML document. Searches can hunt attributes as easily as elements. The xsl:value-of element includes the name of the element which contains the attribute we are interested in. The names are split by a slash and an ampersand:

```
<xsl:value-of select="qty/@amount"/>
```

XSL transformations use this simple algorithm:

- The parser searches for a pattern,
- If it finds the pattern it either processes further instructions or returns the text held in an XML element,
- Where text is returned that is placed into the output document at the same point that the XSL element occupies in the template.

## 14.5.2 XSL Elements

I have used a few XSL elements in this chapter. These are commands which the XSL processor understands. More commands will undoubtedly be added as the technology matures. Here are definitions of those which are currently supported. Most of these elements select data from the XML document although a few are used to control the processor. Where data must be selected the XSL element takes the form:

```
xsl:element select=value
```

The value is usually a pattern which matches a node or set of nodes within the XML structure.

**xsl:apply-templates**
A stylesheet can contain a number of templates. Each of these can be directed toward a different output format. This command directs the processor towards the most appropriate template for the situation.

**xsl:attribute**
Creates an attribute node. The attribute is then applied to the output element. Usually the attribute is based upon an attribute value from an XML element.

**xsl:cdata**
A CDATA section is added to the output document.

**xsl:choose**
The condition of an element can be tested. The result of this test can then be used by commands such as xsl:when.

**xsl:comment**
Copies the target node from the input source to the output.

`xsl:copy`

A comment is added to the output document. The application will usually not display these.

`xsl:define-template-set`

A set of templates is defined. These can be given *scope*.

`xsl:element`

Creates an element in the output.

`xsl:entity-ref`

Creates an entity reference in the output.

`xsl:eval`

Evaluates a piece of text. This element means that scripts can be embedded into the template adding plenty of flexibility to the processing.

`xsl:for-each`

A single template is applied to a set of XML elements.

`xsl:if`

Boolean conditions can be tested. For instance you may choose to produce output only when an attribute takes a specific value.

`xsl:node-name`

The name of the current node (XML element) is inserted into the output.

`xsl:otherwise`

Used for conditional testing of element or attribute values.

`xsl:pi`

A processing instruction is inserted into the output.

`xsl:script`

Global variables and functions can be declared within a template.

`xsl:stylesheet`

Defines a set of templates.

`xsl:template`

Defines a single template for output based on a specific pattern.

`xsl:value-of`

Evaluates an XSL element. The element is specified in the `select=` attribute of the command.

`xsl:when`

Used in conditional testing.

### 14.5.3   Styling XML With Cascading Stylesheets

Formatting XML using XSL means that you need a complex processor to get any meaningful output. Generally, at the moment, authors are converting their XML into either HTML or PDF for display. Some Web browsers are able to parse XML, although those parsing capabilities may quite limited in practice. If you want to display your XML in a Web browser there's an alternative which has a very low overhead. XML files can be combined with cascading stylesheets such as those described in Chapter 4. When displayed in a browser the XML file will display just as if it were HTML.

Of course all this assumes that you have a browser which can handle CSS and XML properly. Your choice of browser is quite limited at the moment. At the time of writing I've successfully used these techniques with Opera version 5 on Windows NT and Linux and Mozilla 0.9. I've been less successful using Internet Explorer 5.5 which may have been due to problems in either my XML or CSS files. There's no point trying any of this with Netscape 4 since it doesn't support XML. Netscape 6 is said to provide limited support and since it's based around a version of Mozilla which is older than 0.9, it should be OK.

In the following example I'm going to style the index file from Slashdot which I used in Section 11.4. The resultant output is shown being displayed by Opera 5 in Figure 14.6. All of the processing was performed by the Web browser which received both the XML and stylesheet files from the server.

**Figure 14.6** Opera Displaying CSS Formatted XML

Before I show you the stylesheet, you need to know how to include it in your XML file. The following line of code will be familiar from the XSL examples that you saw earlier:

```
<?xml-stylesheet type="text/css" href="slash.css"?>
```

but notice that the MIME type has been changed to reflect the correct data type. The stylesheet is pretty straightforward:

```
story{
   font-family: "arial", "helvetica", "sans-serif";
   font-size: 4pt;
}

title{
   font-family: "times", "times new roman", "serif";
   font-size: 24pt;
   padding-top: 15pt;
   color: #002312;
   background: #fffff0;
   display: block;
}

url {
   font-family: "Courier";
   font-size: 14pt;
   color: #ab0000;
   background: #fffff0;
}

author {
   font-size: 18pt;
   font-variant: small-caps;
   text-decoration: underline;
   display: block;
}

time {
   font-size: 10pt;
   font-style: italic;
}

department {
   font-size: 16pt;
   color: #0000ce;
   display: block;
}
```

   Instead of creating styles for individual HTML elements such as td or h1, I create styles for the individual elements inside the XML file. All of the attributes which could be used when creating styles in HTML can be used here. The best way of finding out what works is to try the example for yourself and then modify parts of it. The only thing that you may not have seen before is the use of the display attribute.

**display: block|inline**

> XML elements are not automatically mapped into paragraphs when the browser displays the file. In fact all of the elements inside the file are strung together into a single very long line. Clearly, though, by displaying the file inside a browser you are envisaging some sort of hierarchy of information. This necessarily involves the placing of some elements on new lines, whilst others may be displayed next to each other.
>
> If you want an element to appear on a line by itself you must make that element a block. In HTML elements such as headings and paragraphs are regarded as blocks. When the end tag of the element is encountered, a blank line is drawn. The same thing happens with XML blocks.
>
> By default, XML elements are treated as inline elements. These are displayed within the flow of the text without new lines. An inline element is really analogous to an HTML span element.

Cascading stylesheets provide limited formatting of XML. You can't use them to create lists or tables. If you need those more complicated elements then you should seriously consider using XSL. If you only need a simple way to view an XML file on the Web, CSS looks like a good alternative.

## 14.6 HANDLING XML WITH PERL

Perl and XML go so naturally together that a large number of modules have already been made available which perform many of the most fundamental XML tasks. The list of modules stored on CPAN is large and growing. Here is a selection of the latest versions in early 2000. Because these modules are created by volunteers their rates of development will vary but it is clear that a lot of work is being done.

```
Index of /modules/by-module/XMLIndex
  Name                        Last modified        Size

  Parent Directory            25-Jan-2000 10:07       -
  XML-Catalog-0.01.tar.gz     10-Jun-1999 22:37      3k
  XML-DOM-1.25.tar.gz         24-Aug-1999 09:46    120k
  XML-DT-0.11.tar.gz          30-Jul-1999 06:04     18k
  XML-Dumper-0.4.tar.gz       19-Jun-1999 23:50      5k
  XML-Edifact-0.40.tar.gz     26-Feb-2000 00:34    297k
  XML-Encoding-1.01.ta..>     27-Dec-1998 01:22    185k
  XML-Filter-Hekeln-0...>     01-Mar-2000 19:18      8k
  XML-Generator-0.5.ta..>     08-Sep-1999 20:14      4k
  XML-Grove-0.46alpha...>     09-Sep-1999 16:06     27k
```

```
XML-Handler-YAWriter..>  01-Mar-2000 19:18      23k
XML-Node-0.09.tar.gz     15-Nov-1999 12:23       7k
XML-Parser-2.27.tar.gz   25-Sep-1999 15:43     380k
XML-QL-0.07.tar.gz       26-May-1999 13:43       8k
XML-RSS-0.8.tar.gz       27-Dec-1999 01:09      19k
XML-Registry-0.02.ta..>  25-Oct-1998 23:09      47k
XML-Simple-1.03.tar.gz   05-Mar-2000 12:58      25k
XML-Stream-0.1b.tar.gz   16-Feb-2000 12:42       8k
XML-Template-1.0.3.t..>  24-Feb-2000 21:00      10k
XML-Twig-1.9.tar.gz      17-Feb-2000 16:39      21k
XML-Writer-0.3.tar.gz    09-Dec-1999 10:09      11k
XML-XPath-0.16.tar.gz    28-Feb-2000 02:42      21k
XML-XQL-0.61.tar.gz      02-Aug-1999 16:08     106k
XML-XSLT-0.19.tar.gz     09-Feb-2000 08:26      92k
XML-miniXQL-0.04.tar.gz  16-Jun-1999 03:46      11k
libxml-perl-0.07.tar.gz  22-Feb-2000 14:31      52k
xslt-parser-0.14.tar.gz  16-Dec-1999 07:14      79k
```

I am going to show you just two ways that you can marry XML and Perl. First, I'll use a simple parser to move through the XML recipe book; second, I'll use a DOM parser to achieve the same results. It will, hopefully, be clear how the XML structures created by these parsers can be transformed into HTML documents.

Transforming XML into HTML is only one thing that can be done with Perl. Whilst the same can be achieved with XSL, using Perl means that you can add querying and updating capabilities. Perl also has significant performance benefits over XSL. Most importantly, if you use Perl for these tasks then most of the work is done by the server.

- Where the *client* is doing the work, as with XSL, more data may be sent. This adds to the load on the network and reduces security because you must reveal all of your data before the client-side parser can start to work on it.

- If the transformation from XML to HTML is complex then it may take quite a while on lower powered PCs. On a powerful server the same transformation could be very fast. Users do not like waiting for data but they *really* dislike waiting while their PC processes data.

- If many of the visitors to your site will use the same data then you will want a persistent data structure on the server. Combining Perl, mod_perl, Apache and XML lets you build a structure based upon passing the data through the parser just once. Accessing this persistent data structure will be fast but will also lend itself to further optimisation.

## 14.6.1 Parsing XML with Perl

Earlier I made the claim that Perl and XML are well suited to each other. Perl is a text manipulating language, XML is data expressed in a textual form. Using one to program the other seems fairly natural, and indeed it is. This does not mean that manipulating XML is in any way *easy*. In fact the Perl scripts I use in this section are the most complex in this book. Each introduces new ways of working and new features of the language that I've not previously shown you. When you are learning a new programming language, adding new features gradually is important. It is also sensible to learn those new features only when you actually *need* to. There's no point confusing yourself right from the start. If you have struggled with Perl so far, take your time over these programs. I've tried to explain their key features but you will still need to use the online documentation.[13]

### 14.6.1.1  *Parsing*

The process of taking a file and breaking it into its components is called *parsing*. The components are defined by a grammar, the rules of the language, although this may be implied by the file structure rather than formally specified. Parsing is one of the commonest activities carried out by software. Whether an application is reading in configuration information from a text file, manipulating simple databases or reading in a complex formatted document, it must perform parsing.

In Section 10.4, I demonstrated the use of text databases. A simple file structure in which data items were separated by pairs of colons was parsed like this:

```
SEARCH:while($line = <DB>) {
  chomp $line;
  ($type, $filling, $style) =
                 split(/::/, $line);
  if( ($type = $search) || ($filling = $search)
                        || ($style = $search)){
     $found = 1;
     last SEARCH;
  }
} # while
```

### 14.6.1.2  *Parsing XML*

Instinctively a brute-force approach seems like it will be successful when parsing XML documents. After all they are just structured data files with items separated by `<tag>...</tag>` pairs. Why not use regular expressions to find start and end tags and take the parsing from there? The reality is that you are definitely better off *not* handling the parsing yourself. XML is not a simple data structure and cannot be handled with regular expressions for these reasons:

- White space and newlines have no meaning in XML. They are used to make handling the markup easier for humans but are ignored by parsers.

- XML elements will often span a number of lines of text.

---

[13]`perldoc` man pages, HTML files from ActiveState.

- Perl regular expressions cannot handle arbitrary nesting.

- XML documents can contain external entities which the parser must include in its operation.

- Matching pairs of tags is not straightforward in complex documents.

- XML elements may contain optional parameters and your parser must be equally adept at handling their presence and absence.

The most important reason for avoiding XML parsing is that Perl already has a very functional XML parser module available for free. Why spend time writing a parser when you can use the work of other people? Your time will be better spent working on your own application which uses the parser. This doesn't mean that you shouldn't try to write an XML parser, just that if you have a job to do you should use the existing tools rather than try to reinvent them.

### 14.6.1.3 XML Parsers

There are four parameters which can be used to categorize parsers. They may be validating, non-validating, stream-based, or tree-based. A validating parser uses both an XML file and a DTD to check that the XML adheres to the rules of the application. If the XML breaks the rules by straying from the DTD then the parser will create an error and stop processing the files. Non-validating parsers are much more tolerant. They only use the XML document and are quite content if it is *well formed*. A well formed document is one which sticks to the general rules for XML such as having only one top-level element and no overlapping tags. At the moment all available Perl-based parsers are non-validating.

The parser can operate using either a stream or a tree of data. Stream-based parsers must read the entire document each time that an operation is requested and send a message to the controlling application when specific events occur. I'll show you how to do this in Section 14.7. A tree-based parser builds a static representation of the document which corresponds to the structure of the original XML. This tree may be updated by adding, removing, or modifying the *nodes*[14] at run-time. You may read elsewhere about SAX and DOM parsers. SAX is an informal specification for stream-based parsers which was primarily written for use with Java programs. DOM is a recommendation of W3C for use with tree-based parsers. In Section 14.8 I'll use a DOM-compliant parser to manipulate the XML recipe book.

## 14.7   USING XML::PARSER

The basic components of each XML document *may* include

- elements,

---

[14]The internal representations of XML elements.

- a list of attributes and their values for each element,

- processing instructions,

- comments.

I'm going to show you simple applications which concentrate on extracting elements, attributes, and values and reformatting them as plain text.

The first example uses the XML::Parser module. This comes as standard with the ActiveState distributions and the latest versions are always available for download from CPAN. XML::Parser can of course be added to any up-to-date Perl installation which lacks it. Although I only have enough space to provide a quick overview of the module and its facilities you can get comprehensive documentation by using perldoc XML::Parser. ActiveState provides the same information in both POD[15] and HTML formats.

XML::Parser was originally written by Larry Wall,[16] and is now maintained by Clark Cooper. It is based upon a module called XML::Parser::Expat which provides a low-level interface to the Expat library, which in turn was written by James Clark. Expat was written in C and is widely used as the foundation of XML parsers. Fortunately the underlying complexity is hidden from applications developers. You may choose to find out how XML::Parser works its magic if you want to. On the other hand you may just want to use its facilities without knowing how it does what it does.

XML::Parser implements a number of methods and *event handlers*. I discussed methods and events when introducing JavaScript, although JavaScript calls methods *functions*. Look back at Chapter 5 for more information. The important thing to remember when using XML::Parser is that it is event-driven. The parser will read through your XML file and when it reaches certain pieces of markup it will signal your application. The parser is generating a message in response to an event; you may have built your application to respond to that type of message, in which case the code that you write inside an *event handler* will now be executed. If you have not written an event handler for a given event, the parser will continue working through the XML document.

## 14.7.1   XML::Parser Methods

**new(OPTION=>VALUE)**

The constructor method which creates a new, named parser. With all of these methods, lists of optional parameters are allowed. Each parameter is passed as a keyword=>value pair and items are separated by commas. The following options are the most useful of those allowed:

**style=>debug|subs|tree|object|stream**

The parser can operate in a number of ways. Each has a different effect.

---

[15]Plain Old Documentation: the platform-neutral system for documenting Perl modules and libraries.
[16]The man responsible for creating Perl in the first place.

**debug**

Displays the document in outline form.

**subs**

At the start of elements a subroutine from an external package is called. At the end tags of elements another subroutine is called. This routine has an underscore appended to its name. The external package is included through the Pkg option.

**tree**

A parse tree is returned to the application.

**object**

Works like the tree style but creates a hash object for each element.

**stream**

Uses routines from Pkg. It looks for routines called StartDocument, StartTag, EndTag, Text, PI, and EndDocument.

**Handlers**

This option takes an anonymous hash as its value. The hash contains the names of events as keys and the names of subroutines as values. The subroutine will be called if the named event occurs. Each handler gets passed a reference to the underlying Expat parser as its first parameter.
For instance in:

```
$p = new XML::Parser(Handlers =>(Start=>\&getStart))
```

the parser will call the getStart subroutine each time that the Start event occurs.

**Pkg**

Include a package of subroutines. These are used instead of event handlers if the subs style has been set.

**ErrorContext**

If this is set then errors will be reported in context. This option accepts an integer value which sets the number of lines of code to display on either side of the line which contains the error.

**ProtocolEncoding**

Selects one of the following protocol encodings: UTF-8, UTF-16, ISO-8859-1, or US_ASCII

**Namespaces**

If this is set to true the parser will process namespaces.

**setHandlers(TYPE, HANDLER)**

Event handlers can be registered using this method rather than as parameters to the new method. Handlers which are set by setHandlers override handlers set earlier in the program.

**parse(SOURCE [option=>value])**

Runs the source through the parser. The source is either a string containing the XML document or an open IO::Handle to a file containing it. Any of the constructor options which pass to Expat may be specified here. They will only apply for the duration of this method.

**parsefile(FILE [option=>value])**

This opens FILE for reading, parses, and then closes it. Again Expat options may be specified for the duration of this method call.

## 14.7.2 XML::Parser Event Handlers

The module has many event handlers. Each handler accepts a reference to the Expat parser being used as the first parameter. Usually your code will ignore this parameter. Most of the handlers are listed below:

**Start(Expat, element[attr, val])**

Created when a start tag has been found. element is the name of the XML element; attribute:value pairs are created for each attribute of the element.

**End(Expat, Element)**

Generated when an XML end tag is found. Calls to empty elements will generate both start and end events.

**Char(Expat, string)**

Non-markup has been recognized. The text is passed in as the string parameter. This handler may be called on more than one occasion by the same piece of non-markup.

**Proc(Expat, target, data)**

A processing instruction(PI) has been found.

**Comment(Expat, data)**

An XML comment is found in the source.

**CdataStart(Expat)**

Called at the start of a CDATA section.

**CdataEnd(Expat)**

Called at the end of the CDATA.

**Default(Expat, string)**

Called for all characters which do not have a specified handler either because they are not part of the markup or because no handler has been registered for them.

**ExternEnt(Expat, base, sysid, pubid)**

An external entity is referenced by the source, the base URI is used when resolving relative addresses, sysid is the system ID, and pubid the public ID.

**Entity(Expat, name, val, sysid, pubid, ndata)**
Called when an entity is declared. For internal entities `val` contains the value of the entity with the last three parameters undeclared. If `ndata` has a value it contains the notation used by the entity.

**Element(Expat, name, model)**
Called when an element declaration occurs.

**Doctype(Expat, name, sysid, pubid, internal)**
Called if a DOCTYPE declaration is found. If an internal subset was declared it will be in the `internal` parameter. Otherwise this parameter will be undefined.

### 14.7.3  XML::Parser and the Recipe Book

To demonstrate the use of `XML::Parser` I have created a simple application which reads through the recipe book and displays its contents. The primitive output from the application is in the form:

```
Element=>ingredient
Element=>qty
        Attributes: (unit=>ml) (amount=>825)
End=>qty
```

You will find the later discussion of the code much more straightforward if you first enter it into an editor and then run it. Save the code in a file called `parser.pl` and execute it from a command line using:

```
parser.pl recipe.xml
```

Try running other XML files through this application. You should find that it works for all well formed XML files. Here is the complete code:

```perl
#! /usr/bin/perl -w

# include the modules etc. that we need
use strict;
use XML::Parser;

# create a globally scoped parser
my $parser = new XML::Parser;

# and define what it's going to do
$parser->setHandlers(
        Doctype => \&getDoctype,
        Start => \&getStart,
        End => \&getEnd,
```

```perl
               Char => \&getChar);

# now get the file name from the command line. This is
# the data to actually parse
$file = $ARGV[0];

# parse the XML file
$parser->parsefile($file);

# and look for a specific string - change the parameter
# if you use a different XML file
$parser->parse('<name>Wheatgerm Bread</name>');

# for details of the parameters passed into these handler
# functions see perldoc XML::Parser
sub getDoctype {
    printf("DTD => %s : file => %s\n", $_[1], $_[2]);
}

sub getStart {
    my $key = "";
    my $value = "";
# put the attributes & values into a hash. They will pair
# up nicely and correctly if they are correct in the
# original XML file
    my ($expat, $item, %atts) = @_;

    print "Element=>$item\n";

# now extract the attribute=>value pairs and display them
    if (%atts) {
        print "\tAttributes: ";
        foreach $key (keys %atts) {
            $value = $atts{$key};
            print "($key=>$value) ";
        }
        print "\n";
    }

} # getStart
```

```perl
sub getChar {
   my $str = $_[1];
# need to handle repeated calls to the handler with empty
# strings so: find repeated word characters at the start
# of the string
   if ($str =~ /^\w+/) {
      print "\tValue $str\n";
   }
}

sub getEnd
   { print "End=>$_[1]\n"; }

exit(0);
```

Read carefully through the code and much of it will make sense to you. I'll just discuss the pieces which you may be finding difficult. If you want to be sure that your ideas are correct put some debugging information into the code. Adding `print` statements liberally throughout the source is a useful way of finding out exactly what is happening under the hood.

Having created a new parser I give it some work by adding handlers:

```perl
$parser->setHandlers(
        Doctype => \&getDoctype,
        Start => \&getStart,
        End => \&getEnd,
        Char => \&getChar);
```

When the parser encounters doctype elements, start and end tags, or character data, processing passes to a subroutine. The subroutines are declared in the `parser.pl` file but the `setHandler` method is using a new notation to access them. Unfortunately the explanation of this notation will get rather complicated. If you have never been exposed to object-oriented techniques before you may have to read through this a few times before it makes sense.

The parser object `$parser` was created by using the new method of the `XML::Parser` class. Once the object has been created[17] Perl code can access it by name. Think of the object as a distinct and unique thing within the system. I have written some subroutines which are going to handle processing of the XML in response to events from the parser. The easiest way to implement this is to let the parser know the identity of those routines so that it can use them itself. The alternative might be to write a handler routine which receives notification of all events from the parser and selects the appropriate routine. Such an

---

[17]The OO term for this is *instantiation*.

approach would be extremely messy and would run counter to object-based programming techniques.

I've written the routines, the parser has been created, and now I need to tell the parser that the routines exist. This is done by creating a *reference* to each routine and passing the reference to the parser object. A reference is, as the name suggests, a data item which refers to another thing. It's rather like a unique name for an item but has a slightly different effect. In most programming languages if the name of anything is passed around then the whole of the *thing* goes with it. The processor performs lots of memory management to manipulate such data movements. A reference is a small data item which is easily manipulated.

To create a reference to an item a backslash is placed in front of the name of the item. References can be created to any scalar, array, or hash, and to subroutines. For lots of information on using references and accessing the data which they point to see:

```
perldoc perlref
```

The code `Doctype => \&getDoctype` creates a reference to a subroutine called `getDoctype`. This reference is associated with a key called `Doctype` within the parser. Now when the parser finds a doctype element in the XML it knows the name and (memory) address of a routine which can further process the element.

The parser can operate on any XML file as it does nothing that might be considered application specific. The name of the file is passed as a command-line parameter when the parser is invoked. Command-line parameters get stored in an array called `ARGV` and are extracted using:

```
$file = $ARGV[0];
```

Once the parser has been created and the name of the XML document extracted it is time to do some parsing. I get the parser to run through the whole of the document using:

```
$parser->parsefile($file);
```

which displays the whole of the document. But `XML::Parser` can be used for other purposes too. To search for a specific element within the document I use:

```
$parser->parse('<name>Wheatgerm Bread</name>');
```

The `getStart` subroutine starts by extracting all parameter values:

```
my ($expat, $item, %atts) = @_;
```

The `$expat` scalar is not used in the example program. `$item` holds the name of the element and the hash `%atts` holds the attributes – if there are any. Extraction of the attributes uses a technique which should be familiar from earlier Perl chapters:

```
foreach $key (keys %atts) {
    $value = $atts{$key};
    print "($key=>$value) ";
}
```

The final piece of cryptic coding occurs in the getChar routine. This routine displays character data and ought to be pretty straightforward. It gets two parameters: a reference to the instance of Expat and a string. It ignores the first and displays the second. Easy. Except there's a problem. XML::Parser calls this subroutine a lot. A single piece of character data in the XML document may lead to many Char events and hence to many calls to their handler, which in this case is getChar. Again surely there's no problem? But there is: many of those calls consist of empty strings. If they are all printed out then the program ends up printing lots of blank lines.

There is no way of knowing in advance how many empty strings will be passed for each piece of character data so we can't write code which, for example, prints the third string while ignoring all others. Instead we need to check if the string passed in is empty. If it is then ignore it, otherwise use it. Remember that XML parsers ignore white space at the start and end of lines – it's only use in source files is to make them legible. Therefore we know that the string passed into getChar must start with a character so let's use a regular expression to find it. If the string is empty the code passes on by:

```
if ($str =~ /^\w+/) {
    print "\tValue $str\n";
}
```

Even this simple application is capable of a lot of work. For instance, it is easy to see how the print statements might be altered to output HTML code which could be streamed to a browser. More querying capabilities might easily be added; the data could be reformatted on its way to (or from) a database. The only problem is that the whole source file has to be read through each time you need to perform an operation. That's a big performance hit on a Web server handling large XML files. Fortunately DOM parsers let you build static data structures which are often more useful.

## 14.8   HANDLING THE DOM WITH PERL

The XML::DOM module is a DOM level 1 compliant parser which extends the XML::Parser module. The DOM parser creates a tree-style data structure composed of *nodes*. Each node may, depending upon its type, contain other nodes and subtrees. Nodes which represent documents and elements can contain other nodes; nodes representing attributes, text, comments, CDATA, etc. cannot. XML::DOM extends the facilities specified for DOM level 1 but I do not intend to discuss any of those extensions here.

The module is composed of a great many methods which are subdivided into categories. Methods are available to handle any situation that may arise while manipulating XML, but because the module is so complex I will not be listing all of the methods available in each subclass here. In fact I'm only going to look at a very small subset. This subset will be enough to help me explain a simple example and should serve to whet your appetite for discovering more.

The XML::DOM module is not provided as standard in Perl distributions. It can be downloaded from CPAN or installed in an ActiveState Perl distribution using the Perl Package manager (ppm). Complete documentation is supplied with the code and can be viewed by using perldoc XML::DOM. ActiveState supply the same documentation in HTML format; if you install the module using PPM it will automatically be added to the documentation index.

### 14.8.1 XML::DOM

Constant integer values are used to identify the type of each node. Table 14.2 shows the constants, hopefully their meanings are self-explanatory!

***Table 14.2*** Constants Used in XML::DOM

| Name | Value |
|------|-------|
| UNKNOWN_NODE | 0 |
| ELEMENT_NODE | 1 |
| ATTRIBUTE_NODE | 2 |
| TEXT_NODE | 3 |
| CDATA_SECTION_NODE | 4 |
| ENTITY_REFERENCE_NODE | 5 |
| ENTITY_NODE | 6 |
| PROCESSING_INSTRUCTION_NODE | 7 |
| COMMENT_NODE | 8 |
| DOCUMENT_NODE | 9 |
| DOCUMENT_TYPE_NODE | 10 |
| DOCUMENT_FRAGMENT_NODE | 11 |
| NOTATION_NODE | 12 |
| ELEMENT_DECL_NODE | 13 |
| ATT_DEF_NODE | 14 |
| XML_DECL_NODE | 15 |
| ATTLIST_DECL_NODE | 16 |

Typically these values are used in Boolean operations to control processing.

```
if ($elem->getNodeType == ELEMENT_NODE) {
   $nodename = $elem->getTagName;
}
```

The XML::DOM class has the following subclasses and interfaces:

- XML::DOM::NodeList (interface)
- XML::DOM::NamedNodeMap (interface)

- XML::DOM::DOMImplementation (subclass)
- XML::DOM::XMLDecl (subclass)
- XML::DOM::ElementDecl (subclass)
- XML::DOM::AttlistDecl (subclass)
- XML::DOM::AttDef (subclass)
- XML::DOM::Node (subclass). This class is further extended by
    - XML::DOM::Attr (subclass)
    - XML::DOM::Element (subclass)
    - XML::DOM::ProcessingInstruction (subclass)
    - XML::DOM::Notation (subclass)
    - XML::DOM::Entity (subclass)
    - XML::DOM::DocumentType (subclass)
    - XML::DOM::DocumentFragment (subclass)
    - XML::DOM::Document (subclass)
    - XML::DOM::CharacterData (interface). This class is extended by
        * XML::DOM::Text (subclass)
        * XML::DOM::Comment (subclass)
        * XML::DOM::CDATASection (subclass)

## 14.8.2   XML::DOM::Node

The node class provides a range of methods which can be used to process any type of node. In the standard object-oriented fashion, when methods apply only to a specific type of node they are provided by subclasses. For instance, only XML elements have unique names. These names are accessed through the getTagName method of XML::DOM::Element.

Methods of the Node class are mostly concerned with manipulating the document tree. Working with the document tree involves moving from node to node. If the current node is a document or an element then it may have further nodes below it forming a subtree. This subtree is manipulated through the methods of the XML::DOM::Node class. When a method has no data to return it will return the Perl value undef, which for the purposes of XML::DOM acts as a null value.

The methods available through XML::DOM::Node include:

**getNodeType**

Returns an integer indicating the type of the current node. The list of available types is shown in Table 14.2.

**getNodeName**

Returns the name of the node. This may be a property of the node or hard-coded in. The name is found by calling a method belonging to one of the subclasses of XML::DOM::Node.

**getParentNode, setParentNode(parentnode)**

These manipulate the node immediately above the current one in the tree. If the node is new and has not yet been added to the tree then `setParentNode()` method adds it as a child of the named node. Until a node is actually added to the tree its parent will be `undef`.

**getChildNodes**

Returns a list of all of the children of the current node. This is returned as a `NodeList` object which has its own methods.

**getFirstChild**

Returns the first child of the current node.

**getLastChild**

Returns the last child of the current node.

**getPreviousSibling**

Returns the node immediately before the current node.

**getNextSibling**

Returns the node immediately after the current node.

**getAttributes**

Returns a `NamedNodeMap` containing the attributes of the current node.

**insertBefore(newnode, refnode)**

Inserts the new node immediately before the current node which is passed as the `refnode` parameter.

**replaceNode(newnode, oldnode)**

Replaces the node in its second parameter with that in its first.

**removeChild(child)**

Removes the child node from the tree.

**appendNode(child)**

Appends the child to the end of the list of children of the current node.

**hasChildNodes**

Returns `true` if the current node has children.

**getElementsByTagName("tag")**

Returns all elements which have the name supplied as a parameter. To return all of the elements in a tree, use the parameter `"*"`. The parameter is a string which must be quoted.

### 14.8.3 XML::DOM::NodeList

A `NodeList` is a collection of nodes. The class does not specify how the nodes are collected together but they are stored in the order in which they appear in the XML document.

`item(int)`

The contents of the list are accessed by the index of their position in the list. These indexes start from 0. If you try to access an item which is greater than the size of the list `undef` is returned.

`getLength`

Returns the number of items in the list. Because the indexes start from zero, this will be one greater than the index of the final item.

### 14.8.4  XML::DOM::NamedNodeMap

The `NamedNodeMap` is a collection of nodes which can be accessed directly via their name. Nodes in the collection are unordered.

`getNamedItem(name)`

Returns the item named in `arg` or `undef` if it is not found.

`setNamedItem(name)`

Adds a node to the collection. The `nodeName` is passed as the parameter and used the as key within the collection.

### 14.8.5  XML::DOM::Element

The majority of items within a DOM tree will be elements. `XML::DOM::Element` class inherits from `XML::DOM::Node` and so can use its methods. For instance `getAttributes` can be used to return all of the attributes associated with a particular element.

`getTagName`

Returns the name of the element. This is the value used inside the XML tag: the element `<cookbook>` has the name cookbook.

`getAttribute(name)`

Returns the value of a named attribute.

`setAttribute(name, value)`

Creates a new attribute with the specified name and value. If the element already has an attribute of that name its stored value is changed to the value of the parameter.

`removeAttribute(name)`

Deletes the named attribute.

`getAttributeNode`

Returns an `Attribute` node associated with this element.

`setTagName(name)`

Changes the name of the element.

## 14.8.6   XML::DOM::Text

If the majority of items in the tree are elements, then second most numerous are text items. Objects of type XML::DOM::Text represent character data. Any markup found inside the text will be used to create a subtree below the current node.

## 14.8.7   XML::DOM and the Recipe Book

The DOM approach to handling XML is far more flexible than the stream approach and this is reflected in the XML::DOM module, which provides a comprehensive feature set. Developers are helped through these features by the excellent structure of the module. At any time it is obvious where you need to look for help. If you are handling a node, then the methods available to you come from the node class or one of its superclasses. If you use the strict directive and the -w flag when running your programs you will get useful messages. For instance, if you try to use a method which a class does not provide, the interpreter will tell you exactly what you are doing wrong.[18]

I've written a small DOM program which, like the previous example, reads through an XML document and displays its contents. Before reading the discussion of the code, I recommend that you try it out. Save the script in a file called domparse.pl and run it using:

```
domparse.pl recipe.xml instruction
```

Now change instruction to fred. What happens this time?

```perl
#!/usr/bin/perl -w

# include the modules etc. that we need
use strict;
use XML::DOM;

# create a parser
my $parser = new XML::DOM::Parser;

# parse the file and create the DOM tree
my $doc = $parser->parsefile($ARGV[0])
    or die ("Unable to parse $ARGV[0]\n");

my $nodes = $doc->getElementsByTagName("*");

# start by parsing the whole file
```

---

[18]Although it may find a cryptic way of doing so.

```perl
&parseCookbook;

# find a specific element supplied at the command line
my $found = 0;
&searchCookbook($ARGV[1]);
if ($found == 1)
   { print "$ARGV[1] found in file $ARGV[0]\n"; }
else
   { print "$ARGV[1] NOT found in file $ARGV[0]\n"; }

exit(0);

# ------------ ## ------------ #
# ------------ ## ------------ #

sub parseCookbook {
   # declare some vars
   my ($i, $j, $l);
   my ($elem, $kids, $child, $val, $nodename, $attrs);
   my ($nodevals, $attval);

   # first find the elements
   for $j (0 .. ($nodes->getLength - 1)){
      $nodevals = "";
      $attval = "";
      $elem = $nodes->item($j);
      if ($elem->getNodeType == ELEMENT_NODE) {
         $nodename = $elem->getTagName;
      }

      # then find their children
      if ($elem->hasChildNodes){
         $kids = $elem->getChildNodes($i);
         for $i (0 .. ($kids->getLength - 1)){
            $child = $kids->item($i);
            if ($child->getNodeType == TEXT_NODE){
               $val = $child->getNodeValue;
               # only print this if not an empty string
               if (($val) && ($val =~ /^\w/m)) {
                  $nodevals .= "$val ";
               }
```

```perl
            }
            $attrs = $child->getAttributes;
            if ($attrs){
                for $l (0 .. ($attrs->getLength - 1)) {
                    $val = $attrs->item($l)->getNodeValue;
                    # only print if not an empty string
                    if (($val) && ($val =~ /^\w/m)) {
                        $attval .= "$val ";
                    }
                }
            }
        }
    }
    if (($nodevals ne "") || ($attval ne "")){
        print "$attval $nodevals\n";
    }
  }
} # parseCookbook

sub searchCookbook {
    my ($i, $elem, $nodename);
    my $hunt = $_[0];

    for $i (0 .. ($nodes->getLength - 1)){
        $elem = $nodes->item($i);
        if ($elem->getNodeType == ELEMENT_NODE) {
            $nodename = $elem->getTagName;
            if ($nodename eq $hunt){
                $found = 1;
            }
        }
    }
} # searchCookbook
```

The DOM application takes two parameters: the name of an XML document and an XML element which the program will attempt to find in the document. The program begins by creating a new parser. This parser then runs through the XML document and creates a tree. This is done through the `parsefile` method of the underlying XML::Parser class.

```perl
my $doc = $parser->parsefile($ARGV[0])
```

The result which `parsefile` returns is a representation of the XML document in a format which the XML::DOM methods can manipulate. The first operation is to extract nodes from the tree. Remember you can extract just a subset of the tree if that is all that you need. In this case I'm going to extract all of the nodes as I want to work with the whole document:

```
my $nodes = $doc->getElementsByTagName("*");
```

I now have a list of nodes stored in the imaginatively named $nodes which I can start to work on. I'm going to work through the entire document printing out the names of the XML elements, the contents of those elements; and their attributes. The first step is to find out how many nodes the document contains using getLength. The program then iterates through that list using the index value as a controller. Iteration stops after position (getLength - 1) as this is the last item in the list:

```
for $j (0 .. ($nodes->getLength - 1))
```

If the node is an element node then its name is saved for later use. The node type is compared to one of the global constants from XML::DOM:

```
if ($elem->getNodeType == ELEMENT_NODE) {
    $nodename = $elem->getTagName;
}
```

Next I check to see if the node has children. If it *does* then I'll work down the tree:

```
if ($elem->hasChildNodes){
    $kids = $elem->getChildNodes($i);
```

If a child node exists and it is a text node then the content is extracted. If the content is anything other than an empty string it is saved:

```
if ($child->getNodeType == TEXT_NODE){
    $val = $child->getNodeValue;
    # only print this if it's not an empty string
    if (($val) && ($val =~ /^\w/m)) {
        $nodevals .= "$val ";
    }
}
```

Next, I extract any attributes that the node has and save them. I use the extraction on all nodes. If the node does not have children the extraction operation will return undef, which I check for:

```
$attrs = $child->getAttributes;
if ($attrs){
    for $l (0 .. ($attrs->getLength - 1)) {
        $val = $attrs->item($l)->getNodeValue;
        # only print this if it's not an empty string
        if (($val) && ($val =~ /^\w/m)) {
```

```
        $attval .= "$val ";
    }
  }
}
```

## 14.9 EXERCISES

### XML and XSL

1. What are the practical differences between general markup schemes such as XML and proprietary systems such as Rich Text Format?

2. Create an XML document which holds a diary of appointments. You should include day, date and time of events, and details of each event and of other people who may be involved. Load the XML file into a parser such as Microsoft Internet Explorer 5 to check if it is well formed.

3. Create a Document Type Definition for your diary.

4. Why do applications use a DTD when the XML document follows the same structure?

5. Can you list three benefits of the Extensible Stylesheet (XSL) mechanism?

6. Complete the XSL framework from Section 14.5.1 on page 485.

7. Write an XSL stylesheet to transform your diary into an HTML page.

### 14.9.1 Parsing XML

1. Why does XML use both streaming and tree-based parsing?

2. List three benefits of using Perl to manipulate XML.

3. If you have not yet installed the XML::DOM module do so now either by downloading it from CPAN or by using ppm if you have the ActiveState installation.

4. Modify the parser shown in Section 14.7.3 to output HTML rather than plain text.

5. Modify the DOM application from Section 14.8.7 so that it outputs formatted HTML.

# 15
## Good Design

The technical aspects of HTML are relatively straightforward. It is not difficult to program, and in fact many tools let you create Web pages as easily as you might word process a letter. What separates the good Web sites from the bad is the way that they have been designed.

Web design is complex and subjective. Few good resources exist to help the neophyte designer and I'm not about to write one. I do, though, think that having written a bit of HTML I am in a position to give some general guidelines. I'm also willing to look for advice from higher authorities. In this case the guru of Web design and usability is Jakob Nielsen, I'll be referring to some of his ideas in this discussion. Nielsen fights hard against the trend towards multimedia content all over the Web. He does this not because he disapproves of the use of sound, animated images or Java applets, but because the widespread use of these technologies restricts the use that can be made of the Web. I'll discuss more of these ideas in Sections 15.3 and 15.4. For now I'll just mention a couple of things.

Firstly, there's the discipline of *usability*. This is the study of how using technology can be made easier, what's sometimes called *user-friendliness*. Large media companies such as the BBC, http://www.bbc.co.uk, and software houses such as Microsoft spend millions of dollars annually on their Web sites. If the site is difficult to navigate or doesn't work as a visitor expects, that money has been wasted. To get best value from their Web sites, many companies perform the same sort of testing and evaluation as is done for pieces of software like word processors. This testing comes under the general heading of usability. I'm not suggesting that you should do a lot of testing on your personal Web sites, but if you're developing sites for clients or expecting lots of visitors, such testing is definitely something which you should investigate. A good place to start your investigation is Jakob Nielsen's site which can be found at http://www.useit.com. You might also consult his books, especially *Designing Web Usability* which as well as presenting many good ideas, shows some examples of both good and bad practice.

The second important consideration is the technology which your potential users have available to them. The entry bar is being raised all the time on the Web. The modern generation of browser is a large and complex piece of software. Running these beasts requires a relatively fast processor and plenty of memory. If on top of that you expect your users to have a PDF viewer, a Java virtual machine and Shockwave installed, you shouldn't be too surprised if few people actually enter your site. You might argue that *everyone* has a powerful PC these days, and anyway the modern PC is an incredibly cheap commodity device. That's true in Western Europe and North America, but what about the rest of the World? Web designers need to start preparing now for the massive potential audience they have in Asia and South America. It's possible that as these markets grow, people there will be acquiring fast machines because that's what is being made. They may even get higher bandwidth connections than we have in Europe or North America. Equally, though, these areas may grow through use of technologies which are three or four years behind the leading edge. Do you want to lose visitors simply because the expectations you have of them are too high?

You may have a target audience in mind when you write your pages. This is particularly true if you're writing for a corporate Intranet or writing for a few people. For instance, if you are writing for an audience of scientists who use the same software then you can target your design towards them and their platforms. For example, if your audience is going to be using UNIX workstations it is unlikely that they'll have access to a QuickTime viewer so there would be no point in using QuickTime movies. Similarly many Web users continue to use platforms which don't support Java. If you want to attract business from the casual passer-by then avoid using too much Java for the moment.

Download times matter. If your pages take a long time to download over a 33.6 Kbps modem line people will go elsewhere. Several famous examples leap to mind. Boo.com, for instance, was created to sell designer clothing on-line. Their site was heavily dependent upon use of Macromedia Flash animations which took an eternity to download. The site was rendered unusable on a home PC, even if customers existed for the Boo.com concept, the site was so slow they went elsewhere.

Images are important. They offer information and decoration which is why designers like them. Images also take a long time to download. If someone is paying for their access to the Web they will not enjoy downloading your *small* 200K JPEG.

Sound can brighten a Web page. It can also annoy the reader and their colleagues. Don't rely upon sound to get information across as anyone browsing from an office or Internet café may not be able to hear it. Music is similarly difficult to get right. You might find a piece of music relaxing, it may remind a potential customer of the death of a loved one. Sound files are included in pages using the `object` tag.

Use colors, use background images but be careful. Make sure that your text remains clear and legible when viewed with 256 colors. Remember that many PC users set their screen resolution to 800 by 600 pixels and use 16,000 or fewer colors.

## 15.1 STRUCTURE

It is important that your site is structured sensibly. Remember the purpose of any Web site is to impart information or to get a reaction which will hopefully be sales if it's a commercial site. If the structure of the site isn't clear users won't be able to navigate to the information in which they are interested. Unlike a book or paper catalogue you can't flick though a Web site to find something. There are a number of commonly used techniques for aiding navigation. Most commonly an index is given at the top of the page, or a set of buttons is provided at the top and bottom. Remembering that this is hypertext, you should provide copious links from the body of your documents, although too many can make them crowded. When you provide a hyperlink make sure that you design a way in which the reader can get back.

One popular navigational aid is called a breadcrumb trail. The idea is that each page has a line of hyperlinks along the top which refer back to previous pages in the hierarchy. The user is able to quickly move back to previous sections without going near the back button of the browser. A breadcrumb trail works best on sites which have large amounts of well-structured pages. They are particularly popular with on-line magazine sites such as http://www.zdnet.com. Figure 15.1 gives a small example.

**Figure 15.1** A Breadcrumb Trail

The easiest way to navigate is probably the use of frames or tables. Using a table is an interesting approach to page layout that is commonly found on classy Web sites. Using frames makes moving through the site even easier. With a frame you can make sure that links to pages are always available on the screen. Using well-designed navigation tools means that the visitor never has to get lost within your pages.

Whichever navigational scheme you use, you should be aware of the difficulties which visually-impaired users might have with your site. Of all the groups which can struggle on the Web, the visually-impaired probably suffer more difficulties than just about anyone else. The browsers which these people use can have problems with framed sites and those which use lots of tables. The sites which seem to be least usable are those which have lots of images acting as hyperlinks. Whenever you use an image, especially if it provides meaningful content, you should use the `alt` parameter:

```
<a href="./history.html">
<img src="../images/history.png" alt="Link to history.html">
</a>
```

so that even if the browser can't handle the image, it can get useful information from the tag.

## 15.2 TABLES VERSUS FRAMES VERSUS. . .

Frames are simple, provide excellent navigation, and ought to be highly popular. In fact many Web surfers hate using frame-based sites. The reasons for this are not difficult to discover. Sites over-use frames, each frame takes up space on the visitor's screen for borders and scrollbars: more frames equals less space for information. More importantly, though, if you are not careful you can easily create a situation in which other Web sites appear inside one of your frames. If a visitor selects a link to an external site from one of your frames that site will appear inside your frame. Often the only way that a user can rectify this is to restart the browser. I'll show one solution to this problem in Section 15.2.2.

The problem with using a table to provide the structure of the page is that it makes the design of the page much more complex. If you decide to use a table then you have to be sure to get it right – if you make a mistake the page will look really terrible.

Well, that's the controversy. How do you go about writing a Web page based inside a table? To demonstrate the techniques I'll build the same page in a table and in a set of frames and you can make your own mind up about which is preferable.

### 15.2.1 The Code

#### 15.2.1.1 *Using a Table*

```
<html>
  <head>
    <title>Bill Smiggins Inc</title>
  </head>
  <body bgcolor="#ffffff" text="#362e00">
  <! -- start of the table>

  <table>
     <! -- first of all the logo >
     <tr>
```

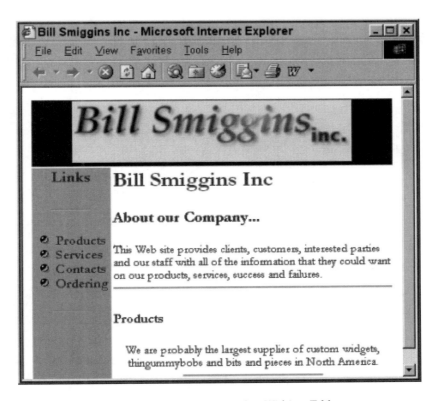

**Figure 15.2** Formatting a Site Within a Table

```
   <td colspan=2 align="center" bgcolor="#000000">
      <img src="./logo.gif">
   </td>
</tr>
<tr>
   <td bgcolor="#7cb98b" width="20%" valign="top">
   <! -- and then the links >
   <h2 align="center">Links</h2>
   <hr width="50%">
   <h3>
     <img src="./bullet.gif">   Products
   <br>  <img src="./bullet.gif">  Services
   <br>  <img src="./bullet.gif">  Contacts
   <br>  <img src="./bullet.gif">  Ordering
   <br><hr width="50%">
   </h3>
   </td>
```

```
        <td width="70%">
        <! -- and finally the information >
        <h1>Bill Smiggins Inc</h1>
        <h2>About our Company...</h2>
        <p>
        This Web site provides clients, customers, interested
        parties and our staff with all of the information
        that they could want on our products, services, success
        and failures.
        <hr>
        <h3>Products</h3>
        <p align="center">We are probably the largest supplier
        of custom widgets, thingummybobs and bits and
        pieces in North America.
        <hr width="50%">
        </td>
    </tr>
    </table>
    </body>
</html>
```

### 15.2.1.2  *Using Frames*  File One containing frame definitions

```
<html>
    <head>
        <title>Bill Smiggins Ltd</title>
    </head>

    <frameset rows="25%,75%">
        <frame name="TOP" src="./banner.html" scrolling="no">

        <frameset cols="15%,75%">
            <frame name="A" src="./links.html" scrolling="no">
            <frame name="B" src="./headers.html">
        </frameset>

    </frameset>

</html>
```

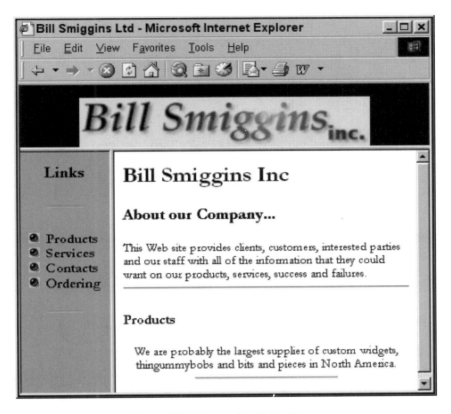

**Figure 15.3** Formatting Using Frames

### File Two containing contents for frame TOP

```
<html>
   <head>
      <title>Banner</title>
   </head>
   <body bgcolor="#000000">
      <p align="center">
      <img src="./logo.gif">
   </body>
</html>
```

### File Three containing contents for frame A

```
<html>
   <head>
      <title>Links</title>
   </head>
```

```
  <body bgcolor="#7cb98b">
      <h2 align="center">Links</h2>
      <hr width="50%">
      <h3>
          <img src="./bullet.gif">  Products
          <br><img src="./bullet.gif">  Services
          <br><img src="./bullet.gif">  Contacts
          <br><img src="./bullet.gif">  Ordering
          <br><hr width="50%">
      </h3>
  </body>
</html>
```

**File Four containing contents for frame B**

```
<html>
    <head>
        <title>Bill Smiggins Inc</title>
    </head>
    <body>

        <h1>Bill Smiggins Inc</h1>
        <h2>About our Company...</h2>

        <p>This Web site provides clients, customers,
        interested parties and our staff with all of the
        information that they could want on our products,
        services, success and failures.

        <hr>
        <h3>Products</h3>

        <p align="center">We are probably the largest
        supplier of custom widgets, thingummybobs and bits
        and pieces in North America.

        <hr width="50%">
    </body>
</html>
```

*Table 15.1* Contrasting Frames and Tables

| Frames | Tables |
|---|---|
| Need multiple source files. | A single source file. |
| Code is easy to read and it is clear where any piece should go. | The code can be confusing, especially when you are putting data tables inside your formatting table. |
| Writing the code is time consuming, but not too difficult. | Coding for tables like this can be very difficult, the code is not easily maintained. |
| It's easy to add new pages or new sections to your site. | Changing the structure of the site can involve a major re-write of the code for the table. |
| Each frame can be scrolled independently | You have to scroll the whole page to move around |
| Borders, if used, can look messy. | No borders are used, but you have to be careful with padding cells which can waste screen space. |
| Users can get stuck inside your frameset if you are not careful. | Tables behave like any non-formatted page. |
| The screen can look cluttered. | A very clean look. |

## 15.2.2 Escaping From Framesets

If you've ever been trapped inside a frameset you'll know how irritating it can be. When users leave your site you should try to be nice to them. If you are not careful they will be viewing the new site inside just one of your frames. It's easy to avoid this problem. On every link to an external page simply put _TOP as the target. When the link is clicked it will open up in a new window. Easy!

```
<a href="some URL" target="_TOP">Click here</a>
```

## 15.2.3 Discussion

First of all I should issue a caveat about those images: to get everything usefully legible I've shrunk the browser down and then put *life-size* screen captures in. Therefore not everything in the images is arranged as nicely as it would be in a full-screen browser window. I mention this so that I can discuss the relative merits of the techniques without having to get sidetracked into discussing the placement of the bullet point GIFs and the text. What are the issues that matter here? Table 15.1 neatly summarizes the differences between the approaches.

Ultimately frame-based Web sites are a straightforward extension of *conventional* sites. Table-based sites require a lot of input into the design process and are more likely to be static. The Web should be dynamic – content should be updated regularly. Frames make this simple and therefore ought to be the better solution. The fact that Web designers can debate the merits of the approaches suggests that nothing is as simple as it could be. This debate will continue.

## 15.3 ACCESSIBILITY

As I mentioned earlier, blind or partially sighted Web surfers can find the Web an extremely unfriendly and unusable place. Too much information is contained in images when it could easily have been expressed as text. Too often, images are used as the source of hyperlinks yet no alternative text is provided. One might, rightly, ask how disabled users are supposed to use these sites. Conversely, developers may argue that it is not *their* job to provide access to everyone and that better software might provided solutions to many of these difficulties.

If you are developing a private Web site for your own interests that last point is perfectly valid. If you are creating a commercial Web site then it isn't. Legislators throughout Europe and North America have passed a series of laws which give disabled people the right to equal access to computer systems. Whilst these laws are most likely to be applied to corporate Intranet systems, customers visiting any commercial Web site can surely expect equality of treatment. If you are using the Web to generate sales, for customer support or to provide information about your products you really *ought* to take on-board the equal access message.

Developers, especially those with a design background, sometimes worry that creating an accessible site means creating an ugly one. That isn't the case at all, there are many things which you can do to make your site work for all users whilst keeping all of those nice design flourishes. The basic rules for accessible Web design are:

- Use markup to express meaning, not to control appearance.

- When HTML elements have attributes such as `alt` which can add meaning, use those attributes.

Detailed guidance on all of these issues is available from the Web Accessibility Initiative. Their Web site can be found at:

```
http://www.w3c.org/WAI
```

My two rules for Web design are based upon the requirements and abilities of the assistive software which visually impaired users in particular, have available to them. Browsers have been available for a few years now which *read* Web pages out loud. Screen readers have been used for a number of years, but they are general purpose and can read many different applications. The Web is, obviously, very different to a word processor. The requirements which it places on software are much greater, using a dedicated application is the best choice. If you want to implement accessible design, try this guidance:

- Set a high contrast between the background color and the colors which you use for your text.

- If you *must* use a background image, make it pale and simple.

- Make sensible use of headings to add structure and meaning. Use <h1> for the main title of the page and <h2> and <h3> for sections and subsections.

- If you have along page, provide an index at the top and hyperlinks to allow movement within the page. Don't make users scroll needlessly.

- Place all formatting information in stylesheets, users may then choose not to load these.

- Use relative font sizes rather than absolute ones. Users can then make text as large as *they* need.

- Test your pages with very large font sizes, 24 point for instance.

- Test your pages with *Bobby* from the Center for Applied Special Technology. This excellent application can be found at `http://www.cast.org/bobby`.

- Test your pages with a range of users including someone who is red-green colorblind.

I haven't considered access for those with physical disabilities in this section. That's quite deliberate. Most physical disabilities lead to difficulties using input devices such as mice or keyboards. A range of alternative control devices are available and Web browsers such as Internet Explorer are relatively easy to configure and control. In general, at the moment the physically disabled are well catered for and can use most Web sites, even those which rely on Java applets or ActiveX.

## 15.4  INTERNATIONALIZATION

The Web is an international phenomenon. Where ever you go in the World you can access the Web. I wouldn't be surprised to find that astronauts on the International Space Station spend those long evenings between space walks surfing for cheap holidays and on-line dates. Sure, at the moment most Web users are American and most of the rest speak English as either their first or second language. At the moment. As the growth in the number of Web users peaks in North America, it starts to take off elsewhere. The next surge in numbers is likely to come from Eastern Europe, South America or China. Those users will have Spanish, Chinese and German as their common languages. Pretty soon the Web will cease to be the sole preserve of English speakers, actually they'll be in the minority before too long.

How you react to the changing nature of the Web depends upon what you want to use it for. If your Web site is based around your hobby and you're only ever going to be visited by fellow enthusiasts, you can use any language that you like. If your business is in Idaho and all of your potential customers live within 200 miles then English is probably the ideal language for your Web catalog. If, on the other hand, you aspire to rival Amazon.com then your Web site had better be available in a variety of languages.

You need to use the widest possible set of characters on your pages. Web browsers support the Unicode character set which uses 16 bits per character for an alphabet with thousands of letters. You also need to think about things like formatting dates, times and numbers. State locations alongside times, for instance: 3:00 p.m. New York time. Be aware that 1,500 and 1.500 can mean the same or radically different things depending on who is reading the number.

Having an international Web site involves more than simply translating the page content. If you want visitors, and their business, from Birmingham to Bahrain and Bali you need to be sensitive to their cultures. This obviously applies to the main textual content of your pages. It also means that any icons or other images you use should avoid giving offense. Don't expect you customers to make the effort of *not* being offended. If you want their business, *you* need to be the one making the effort.

## 15.5 EXERCISES

### Web Design

1. Make a list of factors that affect the design of a Web page.

2. Convert the list you've just made into a series of guidelines that encompass *best practice* in Web site design.

3. Is HTML development a process which encourages good design, or does the relatively simple nature of the process mean that developers are more likely to simply throw a site together?

4. Think about Web sites that you have visited. Do you prefer a table-based or frame-based layout? Try to give three reasons for your choice.

5. Take a page that you've already developed and recreate it based firstly around a table and then around a frameset. From a developer's perspective which is preferable?

6. Run your Web pages through a validator such as Bobby (http://www.bobby.org).

# 16
## *Useful Software*

You can write HTML without using any special software. In fact I do just that. I use a freeware editor called Programmer's File Editor[1] when working on Windows systems, and emacs when using UNIX.[2] Once I've created some code I want to know that it looks good, or if it's a CGI script then I want to test it out, therefore I need a number of applications on my computer to help me author Web pages. If you are going to work your way through this whole book then two pieces of software are essential: a Web browser and a Perl interpreter. Two further programs are useful but definitely optional: a Web server and a relational database that can communicate both with Perl and with the Web server. In the rest of this chapter I will discuss each of these types of software before finishing off by describing ways in which you can access remote servers provided by an ISP.

---

[1] available for download from http://www.lancs.ac.uk/people/cpaap/pfe.
[2] Much of the code in this book was tested on Linux which is a clone of UNIX.

## 16.1 WEB BROWSERS

If you want to write Web pages then the chances are that you've surfed the Internet and have access to a Web browser. Good, because you will need one to preview your HTML pages as you create them. There are numerous Web browsers available and I am not going to discuss the merits of all of the different ones. Most browsers are free or available as shareware, where you get to evaluate the program for free but must pay a relatively nominal fee for continued use.

The market for Web browsers is dominated by two companies: Netscape and Microsoft. Netscape produce the Navigator browser as part of the Communicator suite, while Microsoft ships versions of Internet Explorer as part of both NT and Windows 98. Microsoft has released version 5 of Internet Explorer and it should not be too long before Netscape releases its next version of Navigator. These are graphical browsers which by default display all images they come across. Some people, notably those with visual handicaps, use a browser called Lynx which is totally text-based and will not display images.

Navigator and Explorer go beyond simple Web browsing. Both include fully functional e-mail clients and Usenet news readers. In the case of IE these are supplied as Outlook Express which, although a separate program, is fully integrated with the browser. Browsers are becoming very powerful pieces of software. Internet Explorer is now regarded by Microsoft as an integral part of its desktop operating systems. Each is continually developing new capabilities and some of these, such as the ability to handle XML data, will be very important in the near future. For most users it's important to have the latest version of a browser but how do you really make the choice?

### 16.1.1 Choosing a Browser

The choice of which browser you use may depend upon a number of factors but if you are looking to upgrade then you need to think about some of these:

- Does the browser run on my operating system?
- Does the browser support the use of Cascading Style Sheets?
- Does the browser support the use of plug-ins for most popular Web data types? (real audio and video, compressed files, Shockwave, QuickTime, MIDI, MPEG audio and video)
- Does the browser support Java applets (using at least version 1.1 of Java)? And do you want to *use* Java applets anyway?[3]
- Does the browser support the use of JavaScript? If so which version?
- How large is the download? Or can you get the software from a CD-ROM on a magazine?

---

[3]I'm not going to discuss Java applets here but while I would argue that they are a good thing, many people would disagree. Browse the Web for different points of view.

- Does the manufacturer regularly upgrade the product as standards change?

- How much hard disk space will the installed browser need?

- How much memory will the browser need?

- Will I need an ultra-fast processor to use the browser?

Unfortunately the choice of browser is not restricted by that extensive list. For instance, if you want to use or develop sites which use JavaScript then you might not be able to use IE. Microsoft has its own implementation of JavaScript which it calls JScript. Microsoft developed this by reverse engineering JavaScript, which means that the two languages are not guaranteed to be 100 per cent compatible. The same problem arises with Java with different versions from different companies. The differences between products are also reflected across operating systems where MacOS[4] users tend to be particularly poorly served.

It's likely that browser incompatibilities will continue to plague the World Wide Web and are something that we are all going to have to learn to live with.

## 16.1.2   Using Your Browser During Development Work

It's not immediately clear to everyone that a Web browser can be used during the development process to preview Web pages. It's all very well knowing what the different HTML tags are, and how they work, but even the most experienced author needs to look at displayed pages to verify that their design is correct.

Many novice Web authors believe that they have to put their pages on a Web server and access them across the Internet. In fact this isn't so. When you access an HTML page from a Web server it is simply streaming the HTML and text back to the client browser. The client is doing all of the work in the interaction by formatting the text and images and making sure that they display properly on the screen.

If a file is opened by the browser directly from the local hard disk, the browser will still be able to format and display its contents. You can't access CGI scripts in this way but we'll look at potential solutions to *that* problem later. To open files in your browser simply set it to work offline and then use the `file open` dialogue from the `file` menu to search for the file. If you use relative links, as explained in Section 2.4.1, in your pages you'll be able to follow all internal hyperlinks too.

## 16.2   PERL

CGI scripts can be developed in most programming languages, the only restriction being that the Web server must be able to execute the script. Perhaps the most popular languages for CGI development are Perl, Visual Basic, and, increasingly, Java. Of these, Perl is the

---

[4]The operating system developed by Apple.

dominant language; in many ways it's the standard for this type of work. What makes Perl so popular?

- CGI scripts tend to be relatively simple, often only having a dozen or so simple procedures.

- Most CGI work involves the manipulation of text strings. Perl was specifically developed to handle text.

- Perl is freely, and widely, available. You can get Perl interpreters and associated libraries for most operating systems.

- Perl has evolved into the CGI niche; the language has grown new features to help ease CGI development.

- Many useful packages of code have been written by others to help *you* write better CGI scripts.

- There is a mass of helpful information available from World Wide Web sites and Usenet newsgroups.

I'm not going to pretend that Perl is an easy language to learn or use. It is highly idiosyncratic, and code written by other people can often be both complete gibberish and wonderfully optimized and efficient at the same time. Writing CGI scripts doesn't begin to test the full facilities of the language. As CGI developers we only need to use a small subset and, fortunately, that subset is pretty straightforward.

### 16.2.1 Acquiring and Using Perl

The current version of Perl is 5, which was a major rewrite from version 4. Anything that you do with Perl should use version 5.[5] Writing, debugging and testing CGI scripts on remote servers can be a massively frustrating experience. If you aren't the system administrator then it's unlikely that you'll be able to get any useful error messages back if your scripts fail. How is it possible to build good quality software without error messages? Frankly it isn't. If you want to write CGI scripts then you need to start by having a copy of the language available that you can run from your command line.

Before trying to install your own copy of Perl, check that you haven't already got one available. If you use the UNIX operating system on an institutional machine, or if you use a PC running Linux then the chances are that you already have Perl. To find out, simply open up a terminal session and type the command:

```
perl -v
```

If you have Perl, then a few lines of version information will be displayed. If it's version 4 then you need to investigate how to get an upgrade at your site.

---

[5]Assuming, of course that it's available on your server.

If you're not using UNIX then it's more than likely that you won't have access to a copy of Perl. If you want to install your own version of Perl or upgrade the version on a UNIX machine you'll need to download a copy from the Internet. Perl can be downloaded for free from a number of Internet sites. The most efficient download may be from a site that is geographically close to you. To find your nearest local mirror[6] point a Web browser at:

```
http://www.perl.com/CPAN
```

### 16.2.1.1 *Perl On Windows Systems*

The preceding section really assumes that you are using a UNIX-type operating system. In fact Perl 5 is available for just about any operating system that you can think of. You need to install the correct version for your platform. The standard version for Microsoft Windows users has become the ActiveState[7] version. This comes as a self-installing executable, although prior to installing it, Windows 95 users will need to get hold of a copy of DCOM from Microsoft's Web site. Running this version of Perl needs a 486 processor, 8 MBytes of RAM, and about 20 MBytes of hard drive space for the installation.

As well as the basic Perl system the ActiveState release includes comprehensive documentation in HTML format, an ActiveX scripting engine and a plug-in for use with Microsoft's IIS (Internet Information Server) Web server. You'll see the latter in action in Section 13.1 which discusses using Perl when writing Active Server Pages.

As with UNIX you can find out which version of Perl you have from the command line. Figure 16.1 shows a screenshot of the output my current installation gives when I type `perl -v` at a command prompt.

### 16.2.1.2 *Useful Modules*

Whatever version of Perl you install will inevitably be incomplete. Perl coders all over the world write useful pieces of code which they then donate to the wider community of developers. Much of this code is available from the CPAN mirrors.[8] If you use ActiveState Perl, as I do, then you have a built-in utility called the Perl Package Manager (PPM). This provides a pain-free way of installing modules and of upgrading those that you have. You can find much more about PPM from the documentation that you get with the ActiveState install.

## 16.3 WEB SERVERS

Did you know that your PC can be a Web server? Most of the popular Web servers are freely available; in fact, there may be one bundled with your operating system. The *de facto* standard for Web servers is Apache which is used by well over 50 per cent of all Web providers and which is available for most varieties of UNIX and for Win32 systems. Popu-

---

[6]Servers which copy the contents of others are usually called *mirrors*.
[7]Visit them on the Web at http://www.activestate.com.
[8]Start looking for these from http://www.perl.com/cpan.

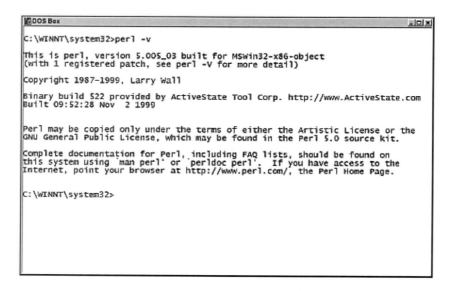

**Figure 16.1**   Output from perl -v under DOS

lar among Windows users is Microsoft Personal Web Server, which can be found bundled in the Windows NT client software.

Even if you don't want to make your PC available on the Internet, a local copy of a Web server can be very useful during the development process, especially when working on CGI scripts.

Most Web servers need a TCP/IP stack if they are going to work. If you use a modem then you already have this installed and working. Your PC will have an IP address of 127.0.0.1 and a domain name of localhost. If you install a Web server you can access your HTML pages through it by using those addresses. The browser will act just as if it had loaded the pages across the Internet. The same thing happens if you try to run a CGI script from one of your Web pages: the Web server software will hunt around for the script and the Perl interpreter and execute the script for you.

A local Web server isn't essential, and may be a security risk if you are connected to a LAN and don't configure it properly. However, using your PC as both client and server can save you from a lot of frustration with your CGI scripts.

## 16.4   MOD_PERL

CGI scripts are slow and resource hungry. They tie up a lot of server time, often to little effect. Add a little database access to a script or try creating a graphic on-the-fly and you'll have ridiculously long response times. If you are running a commercial Web site then response times matter. For users there is little that is more annoying than waiting for a server to respond. Look at the server logs at your site and see how many people surf away if a page isn't loaded within 10 seconds. The most important words in Web development must be *security* and *performance*. Security is a complex topic which I'll leave for others. Performance is a much easier thing to get right.

When you write a Perl script for a CGI server you don't have to compile it, unlike in languages such as C. When a user requests your script the Web server starts the Perl interpreter which loads your script and internally compiles it to *bytecode*. Only then can it execute the script. There is a phenomenal overhead in operating that way. Various solutions have been developed over the years including Active Server Pages (Section 13.1) and Java Servlets, (Section13.2). The advocates of each of these say the same things. Basically it is claimed that ASP and Servlets radically outperform CGI scripts written in Perl. That *was* true but it certainly isn't any longer.

The developers and users of the Apache Web server have provide a number of optional modules which can be used to extend and improve the capabilities of that server. One of these extensions is called `mod_perl`. The `mod_perl` module works by loading the Perl interpreter into memory just once and then keeping it there. As each script is required it is compiled and also loaded into memory, where it remains. Later calls to that same script use the compiled version from memory.

Clearly Perl code runs slower than C code. That's a fact of life when you use an interpreted language but the same is true for Java or VBScript inside Active Server Pages. If we compare like with like we see that Perl on Apache and using `mod_perl` can outdrag Java Servlets and easily outperform VBScript ASPs. Unlike Java, Perl is a *truly* platform-independent solution and has been for years. ASP technology runs only on IIS and *that* requires Windows. If you want speed, scalability, and platform independence then Apache, `mod_perl`, and Perl is the best way to develop server-side Web solutions.

## 16.5 DATABASES

Consider this scenario on a typical commercial Web site. You create a Web site with some forms and CGI scripts to process the data that you're getting back. Customers are placing orders and checking up on the processing of those orders. How do you store and manipulate your customer and order data? If this was an ordinary application you would use a database, so why not use one on the Web? There's really no reason *not* to use a database on a commercial Web site. If you're building an intranet you can even link the organizational databases into your Web front-end via CGI scripts.

Yes, that's right, Perl scripts can talk to databases using SQL. There are a number of free databases for UNIX systems, and many PCs have a relational database installed with an office package.

On the other hand, if you don't want all the hassle of installing and managing a database then the alternative is to use flat files. For the vast majority of Web applications flat files of data are perfect. We can use use them to develop guestbooks and to count the number of visitors to the site, and even to provide restricted access to Web pages.

---

Note:
Don't feel that you *have* to use a database: on small sites you often don't!

---

## 16.6   ACCESSING YOUR ISP

Most Web developers have to use an Internet service provider. Even most businesses use someone else to host their Web site. It might have the company name but it isn't running on their servers. ISPs have all of the technical know-how and security expertise that you need.

### 16.6.1   Software

When you sign-up with an ISP they *may* provide you with the software to manage your site. They also may not. Basically you need two things: a telnet program and an FTP program. FTP and telnet are usually available from the command-line of your operating system; however, this can be rather unfriendly. Many graphical programs are available which take a lot of the sweat out of using FTP, in particular. You might find one of these on a magazine cover disk, or hidden in your operating system. If you don't then you can use your Web browser to download suitable software from one of the many shareware or freeware repositories on the Web.

### 16.6.2   FTP

FTP stands for File Transfer Protocol. As the name suggests it's used to transfer files around. FTP is used to *download* applications or data from servers onto your local drive or to *upload* onto a remote server. Having uploaded data you may need to change permissions on files or change file names so that your site works. Many graphical FTP programs let you do this, but command-line utilities often don't. In addition a graphical FTP program makes the creation of remote directories simple. This is something that you'll often find yourself repeating as you develop your site.

***16.6.2.1   The Command-line***   Using FTP from the command-line is not difficult but it can be time-consuming. Whereas graphical utilities allow you to *drag and drop* groups of files (or even entire directory structures), command-line FTP means moving one file at a time. The command-line approach is more efficient if you only want to move a couple of files, or if you need to fetch a file back from the server for further editing. Read the help pages that your operating system has, to find out how to use command-line FTP.

***16.6.2.2  Anonymous FTP***  Many servers support anonymous FTP. This service lets anyone log on to the machine and access the files there. The service is usually configured so that only a restricted subset of files is available for download. By convention these files are kept under the /pub hierarchy. You've probably used this service without realizing. Ever downloaded software using a Web browser? You were almost certainly using anonymous FTP. Performing FTP with a Web browser is straightforward but isn't the most efficient method that you could employ. For that you need to use a dedicated FTP program.

To use anonymous FTP, users must log on to the remote server as a default user named anonymous. The next step is to give a full e-mail address as a password. This can be done using the command-line or through any of the graphical FTP programs that are now available. The benefit of using this rather than your Web browser is that downloads tend to be *much* faster and are much less likely to corrupt the data.

Here is a transcript of an FTP session in which I access my Web site at work from my desktop PC:

```
Connected to apple.shu.ac.uk.
220 apple FTP server (SunOS 5.7) ready.
Name (www.shu.ac.uk:chris): chris
331 Password required for chris.
Password:
230 User chris logged in.
Remote system type is UNIX.
Using binary mode to transfer files.
ftp> ls
200 PORT command successful.
150 ASCII data connection for /bin/ls (143.52.51.214,1026)
(0 bytes).
total 88
drwxr-xr-x  13 cmscrb    www     512 Feb 22 11:34 .
drwxr-xr-x 231 www       www    3072 Feb 17 16:04 ..
-rwxr-xr-x   1 cmscrb    100    1870 Sep 23 15:45 advice.html
drwxr-xr-x  10 cmscrb    100     512 Feb 22 11:33 book
drwx---rwx   2 cmscrb    100     512 Nov  1 10:27 cgi-bin
-rwxr-xr-x   1 cmscrb    100    3822 Sep 23 15:45 choice.html
drwxrwxrwx   5 cmscrb    100     512 Sep 23 15:45 cm128
drwx--x--x   5 cmscrb    100     512 Nov  1 11:41 cm202
drwxr-xr-x   2 cmscrb    100     512 Sep 23 15:46 convert
drwxr-xr-x   6 cmscrb    100     512 Jan 19 14:43 dist_obj
drwxrwxrwx   2 cmscrb    100     512 Feb 22 11:33 download
drwxrwxrwx   2 cmscrb    100     512 Sep 14  1998 images
-rwxr-xr-x   1 cmscrb    100    2663 Sep 23 15:56 index.html
drwxr-xr-x   2 cmscrb    100     512 Jan 19 14:46 javadocs
```

```
-rw-rw-rw-    1 cmscrb    100    1515 Sep 20 11:34 main.css
drwxr-xr-x    3 cmscrb    100     512 Oct  1 14:03 ola
-rw-r--r--    1 cmscrb    100    2185 Sep 23 15:45 template.html
drwxrwxrwx    3 cmscrb    100     512 Feb 23  1999 test
-rwxr-xr-x    1 cmscrb    100    1476 Sep 23 15:45 welcome.html
-rw-rw-r--    1 cmscrb    100 12800 Jan 27  1998 work.dot
226 ASCII Transfer complete.
ftp> cd cm128
250 CWD command successful.
ftp> mget books.html
mget books.html? y
200 PORT command successful.
150 Binary data connection for books.html (143.52.51.214,1029)
(2336 bytes).
226 Binary Transfer complete.
2336 bytes received in 0.00212 secs (1.1e+03 Kbytes/sec)
ftp> bye
221 Goodbye.
[chris@cms-2323]
```

### 16.6.3   Telnet

Telnet is a way of opening a shell on a remote machine. It's usually done from the command-line, and even the best graphical telnet utilities add very little extra functionality. Telnet is useful if you want to access files, create directory structures, change permissions, test CGI scripts, or perform simple edits which don't require a download of the complete file. To telnet to a server simply type:

```
 telnet server_address
```

at the command prompt. You'll be asked to log on and then you will be in your directory structure. From here you can usually manipulate files, but you can only use the command-line of the server. This means that if you need to edit a file you'll probably be restricted to using a command-line editor such as vi.

   If you want to know what a telnet session looks like, it is similar to FTP – especially if this is the first time you've ever seen either of them. Here's an example:

```
[chris@cms-2323] telnet www.shu.ac.uk
Trying 143.52.2.89...
Connected to apple.shu.ac.uk.
Escape character is '^]'.
```

SunOS 5.7

```
login: chris
Password:
Last login: Tue Feb 22 14:48:20 from teak.shu.ac.uk
Sun Microsystems Inc.    SunOS 5.7      Generic October 1998
apple% pwd
/u2/WWW/htdocs/schools/cms/teaching/crb
apple% ls
advice.html     cm202           index.html      test
book            convert         javadocs        welcome.html
cgi-bin         dist_obj        main.css        work.dot
choice.html     download        ola
cm128           images          template.html
apple% cd cm128
apple% ls -l
total 78
-rw-r--r--    1 cmscrb    100      6869 Oct 18 11:08 assign.html
-rw-rw-rw-    1 cmscrb    100      2336 Sep 23 15:45 books.html
drwxr-xr-x    2 cmscrb    100       512 Mar 11  1999 gbook
-rw-rw-rw-    1 cmscrb    100      3129 Oct 15 14:54 index.html
-rw-rw-rw-    1 cmscrb    100      4240 Feb 16 10:30 lects.html
drwxrwxrwx    3 cmscrb    100       512 Feb 16 10:28 lectures
-rw-r--r--    1 cmscrb    100      4748 Sep 23 15:45 tut1.html
-rw-r--r--    1 cmscrb    100      4638 Sep 23 15:45 tut2.html
drwxrwxrwx    2 cmscrb    100       512 Feb 13 21:01 tutorials
-rw-rw-rw-    1 cmscrb    100      2660 Feb 13 21:02 tuts.html
-rw-rw-rw-    1 cmscrb    100      3571 Sep 23 15:45 web.html
apple% exit
apple% logout
Connection closed by foreign host.
[chris@cms-2323]
```

---

**Restrictions:**
Few ISPs let their customers run CGI scripts or databases. There are many good reasons for this but the most important is security. CGI scripts represent a massive security hole and the ISP has no way of knowing that yours have been developed properly. They don't have the time to check through your code, debugging and improving it. Before you start designing a CGI-intensive site make sure that you will be able to host it with your ISP.

## 16.7 EXERCISES

1. What factors need to be considered when choosing a Web browser?

2. Outline some of the advantages of using Perl for CGI scripting compared to, for example, C++.

3. How can you run your own Web server at home? Is this a realistic alternative to using an Internet Service Provider either during development, or for hosting your completed Web site?

4. What are the FTP and telnet protocols for?

# *17*
## *Protocols*

Web development is all about making use of networks. Networking lies at the heart of everything that I have written about in this book but most people, even most software developers, know little about the subject. In this chapter I'll try to fill in some of those gaps. This is not meant to be a comprehensive guide to networking just a discussion of a few relevant technologies.

Most computer users are familiar with the idea of a network. It is simply a set of computers which are connected together in some way, often so that some resource can be shared between them. What is a resource? Well it can be many things, usually though it will be something like a printer or a scanner, or a server which holds a whole load of applications. In the latter case the applications will be available for use by anyone who is authorized to log on to the network. If you've worked in a modern computerized business or studied almost anywhere in the last five years you'll have used these types of *network resource*. Commonly they are found on small networks within a single department or building. Such networks are called Local Area Networks, LANs for short. A large organization such as a university may have a great many LANs but they all work in the same way, and they can even be interconnected so that resources can be accessed from anywhere in the organization.

Access to LANs has to be controlled. Network security, and the security of the data on those networks, is big business today. Users are typically given a *log-on code* which allows them to access some, or all, of the facilities provided by the network. Organizational networks have their own operating systems which provide many of the facilities needed to administer[1] the network. Popular examples in wide usage today include UNIX, NetWare from Novell, and Microsoft NT. Each of these systems was developed independently and

---

[1]Control and manage hardware, software, and users.

they all work in different ways, leading to employment opportunities for many highly trained specialist engineers.

You are more likely to be familiar with using networks to share data. The World Wide Web is an application which allows data sharing across interconnected Wide Area Networks, WANs. Most home users, and many business users too, store all of their applications on the hard disk of their desktop PC. Most data will also be stored on PCs, but there are times when we all need to share data with colleagues who are physically distant from us. In such cases data must pass from our local machine across other networks to our remote collaborator. We may access the Web from home via a modem and the local telephone network. Both of these are examples of using the Internet, which is just a nice name for the global interconnection of smaller networks. This raises two problems:

- How can machines which use different operating systems, applications, and hardware communicate?

- How can applications find individual machines when many millions are connected together?

In Section 17.2 I'll look at the problem of finding a specific machine but first, communication protocols.

## 17.1 PROTOCOLS

If you read anything about networks you'll find yourself reading about *protocols* at some point. They seem important, vital even, as they're mentioned so often, but what is a protocol? Put simply, a protocol is a set of rules which govern how computers can communicate. The protocol dictates the way that addresses are assigned to machines, the formats in which they will pass data, the amount of data which can be sent in one go[2]. Think of a protocol as a common language. Without it each application must be able to translate into, and out of, the formats of any machine which it talks to. With the protocol everyone is talking the same language.

Here's an analogy which might be useful. At inter-governmental bodies like the United Nations each government brings along some of its translators. As each speech is made, the appropriate translator renders the words legible. But there's a problem. The world has many hundreds of languages and there aren't enough well-trained translators for all of them. In fact, for some languages finding anyone who could do the translation might prove impossible. Think how much easier life at the UN would be if everyone spoke French or Japanese or Esperanto. Of course using a common language would bring problems too. Not everyone would be fluent in the chosen standard language, and if they were, there might still be difficulties over exact meanings,[3] and someone would be certain to stick to

---

[2]Data is sent as *packets* which have set minimum and maximum sizes.
[3]English speakers can't even agree on how we should spell many common words, such as colour/color!

their own mother tongue. The ideas that could be expressed in this way would be simpler yet less clear than those under the current system.

That simplicity is *just* like computer communications. Everyone uses certain common standards. These may not be the best technical solutions but each manufacturer is able to implement them efficiently . Where a network uses only a single product such as Microsoft NT, the supplier is free to implement the best technical solution that they can. Where networks interconnect, manufacturers use the agreed format. This sounds like a recipe for disaster but in fact it works *extremely* well. The whole of the Internet is underpinned by just two protocols: the Internet Protocol (IP) and the Transmission Control Protocol (TCP). The World Wide Web adds a couple more into the mix: Hypertext Transfer Protocol (HTTP) and the Common Gateway Interface (CGI). And that's pretty much that. Let's look at those protocols and see why they are so important.

## 17.2   IP AND TCP

The two protocols upon which the whole Internet runs are Internet Protocol and Transmission Control Protocol. Between them these provide all of the requirements to transmit and receive data across complex WANS. Networks are made of layers with each layer providing a different type of functionality. Each layer *abstracts* the layer below it, adding functionality while hiding complexity. Figure 17.1 shows how some of the most important of these layers fit together.

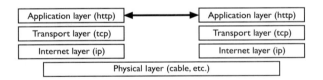

**Figure 17.1**   Layers of a Network Protocol

The physical layer  is made from the actual hardware (cables, network interface cards, etc.) and the drivers which are required to run that hardware. For our purposes we can ignore this. The networks which interest us run across many types of physical layer. The application layer  represents, as its name suggests, the application which we are running. In our case this application is the Web and the application layer is  HTTP. I'll examine HTTP in Section 17.3.

Figure 17.1 shows the data path between applications. This path is *logical*: there isn't a real permanent connection between the two applications. Clearly data passes between the applications but the data is sent as a series of packets. Each packet is free to find its own way across the network. When transmitting across complex networks such as the telephone system, packets may be routed along many different paths.

A useful analogy here is to consider postal systems. If you wanted to send 20 large items to an individual you might package them all into a single box and send them with the postal service. However, if the items are really large it might be better to send each one individually. Once you've sent them you have no way of knowing how the postal service handles them. They may all travel together in the same truck, but equally they may travel in a number of trucks whose drivers all take different routes to the destination. The route taken doesn't matter to you or to the person who is receiving the parcels. All that matters is that the are sent safely and that they arrive safely.

When we say that a connection is logical we therefore mean that, to the applications there is a real connection, but at the physical layer that connection is not present. The multi-layer model means that application developers, for instance, can concentrate on developing their own programs without having to consider the complexities of getting data from one machine to another.

### 17.2.1 Internet Protocol

In the Internet layer of a sending machine the data is split into packets which also contain addressing information about the recipient. Implementations of the Internet Protocol[4] are probably the most common way of generating and addressing data packets in widespread use today. IP packets have between 20 and 60 bytes of header information and up to 65,515 bytes of data. Figure 17.2 shows the structure of the header, which as you can see contains all of the information that might be needed to get a packet from point A to point B.

| IP version 4 bits | Header length 4 bits | Service type 8 bits | Message length 16 bits | Fragment ID 16 bits | |
|---|---|---|---|---|---|
| Fragment control 16 bits | Time to live 8 bits | Protocol 8 bits | Checksum 16 bits | Source address 32 bits | |
| Destination address 32 bits | Options padding 32 bits | Message data | | | |

**Figure 17.2** The Internet Protocol Packet Header

Why don't all IP packets take the same route? When most people encounter these ideas for the first time they tend to think that opening a physical connection between the machines and funneling all of the data through that connection would be the most efficient approach. Well it might,[5] but the designers of IP had other criteria to satisfy. IP was one of the many useful computing ideas which grew out of the Cold War years. IP was designed to be used in military networks which had the ability to survive catastrophic failures of

---

[4]In discussing protocols we usually refer to the protocol even if we really mean *implementations* of it.
[5]Although sending lots of data across a busy network like this is pretty inefficient.

some nodes. If you built a network in which all data passed through a single point in, for instance, Sheffield and that point was terminally damaged in some way then your whole network would be rendered useless. IP doesn't work like that. If Sheffield was destroyed, data would simply find a way to its destination which didn't involve passing through there. Of course data intended *for* Sheffield would still experience problems.

IP has relatively limited functionality. The protocol makes no guarantee of delivery: just because a packet of data is sent, there is no reason to expect that it will arrive. Large messages, which means any over 65,515 bytes, must be sent as a series of packets. Because these packets may be sent along different routes they can arrive in a different order from that in which they were sent. Further functionality is needed to provide sequencing and guaranteed delivery. These functions, and more, are supplied in most Internet systems by the Transmission Control Protocol.

### 17.2.2 Transmission Control Protocol

Abstraction means only having to deal with complexity when you need to. When a system is receiving data across a network it has no reason to spend time preparing that data for use by applications. IP gets the data onto and off the network but on its own it provides no support for applications. The data packets are not sequenced. TCP fills in some of the gaps left by IP. A packet sent from a system which uses TCP has another set of headers in addition to the IP headers. These provide control information for use by TCP. A typical structure is shown in Figure 17.3.

**Figure 17.3**  The Transmission Control Protocol Header

When a host receives a data packet the IP code removes the IP header and passes the packet onto TCP code. If only one packet was sent the TCP headers are removed and the packet is passed onto the application. If several packets were sent, TCP must store them as they arrive until the whole data set is stored. As each packet is stored, TCP sends an acknowledgment message back to the sending machine indicating which packet it now has. If an acknowledgment is not received by the server for a specific packet it will transmit that packet once more.

Using TCP places a significant processing load on both sender and recipient. Each must buffer[6] the outgoing message until all packets are received and acknowledged. The recipient must then strip the headers from the packets and reassemble the original message. TCP is, frankly, slow. It is very widely used because the benefits massively outweigh the costs. Large volumes of data can be sent and their safe arrival is guaranteed.[7]

### 17.2.3   Internet Addresses

Networking only happens if machines can identify each other and so send data to the correct place. All machines connected to the Internet and using IP have a unique address. Some machines, such as those on organizational LANs have fixed addresses. Others, such as home users who have a dial-up connection with and Internet Service Provider,  are dynamically assigned addresses each time they log on to the Internet.

The addressing system used by the Internet Protocol gives each machine a unique four-byte numerical address. These addresses are usually written in the form `127.0.0.1`.[8] Each of the four bytes in the addressed is represented by an integer in the range 0 to 255. As you've already seen in this section the IP packet header includes the address of the sending machine and of the recipient. As the packet is routed through the network, each router chooses the *best* route to the destination address.

Whilst computers have few problems handling numbers (basically that's *all* that they do), human users prefer textual addresses. A system called the Domain Name System, DNS, is used to address hosts. Each numerical address has a textual equivalent, for instance `www.shu.ac.uk` maps onto `143.52.2.89`. When you enter a text format address into your browser a dedicated machine called a DNS server converts it into the numerical form before the packets are sent.

A further refinement lets a server run a number of Internet connected applications at the same time. Each application is assigned a *port number*. This is simply an area of memory which the application will use for its network connections. Ports can be numbered anywhere from 0 to 65,535 with each one potentially assigned to a different application. HTTP servers usually run on port  80 and FTP servers use port 20 for data transfer and port 21 to receive commands. If you want to know more about ports any introductory networking text should help.

## 17.3   HYPERTEXT TRANSFER PROTOCOL

If you look back at Figure 17.1, you'll see that the top level of the diagram shows the application layer. Logically, data transfer happens between applications and uses services from

---

[6]Store in local memory.
[7]As far as is technically possible.
[8]This is the loopback address: the address of the PC when it wants to talk to itself.

the other layers. The World Wide Web has its own special protocol which applications like browsers and Web servers use to talk to each other. This protocol is the Hypertext Transfer Protocol (HTTP).

HTTP runs on top of TCP but changes some of the ways that TCP works. In particular TCP is *session-oriented*, the server and client maintain a (logical) connection for the duration of a data exchange. HTTP has no concept of a session. Once a message has been sent and received the two machines forget about each other. This presents application developers with problems. It's very useful to be able to remember who is visiting your site if, for instance, you are running a commercial site and must track transactions through a number of screens. Sections 10.5 and 11.2 show two ways of circumventing this particular limitation.

## 17.3.1   HTTP Sessions

Under HTTP there are four steps to communicating across the Web:

- make the connection,
- request a document,
- respond to a request,
- close the connection.

I'll briefly look at each of these steps in more detail.

**17.3.1.1   *Connection Setup***   The browser opens a standard TCP connection to the server. Port 80 is used by default but any port which is not required by another application *can* be used. If a non-standard port is used, both client and server must be aware that this will happen. In fact as the Web has become more and more popular the use of non-standard ports has almost disappeared. Where ports other than 80 are used, the port number is added to the URL as in this example: `http://www.some.server.com:8080`.

Any software application may be developed to use HTTP. There's nothing special about the way that Web browsers work and there is no reason why a network-aware word processor, for instance, could not communication using HTTP.

**17.3.1.2   *Browser Request***   Once the TCP connection is established, the browser requests a given document using its URL. The message will be in the format:

```
GET /first.html HTTP/1.1
```

The command `GET` tells the server that the browser is attempting to retrieve a document. The document is assumed to be stored on the server and so the fully qualified address which includes the DNS name of the server is not needed. The request ends with the version of the HTTP protocol to be used. The request message is terminated by repeating the characters carriage return and linefeed:

```
\r\r\n\n
```

Browsers can send a variety of other commands including POST which sends form data to the server, HEAD, which gets only the page header and not the data, and PUT, which is used to transmit a data file to the server.

The request can be refined by the addition of more commands. Typically the browser appends an Accept command which indicates the data types it can handle. The name of the application may also be appended using the command User-Agent. Combining all of this into a complete request gives

```
GET /first.html HTTP/1.1
Accept: text/html
Accept: text/plain
User-Agent: Mozilla/4.7[en](win95;i)4
```

with two blank lines appended to the message.

### 17.3.1.3 *Server Response*

The httpd (Web server) process can automatically insert information into the header of a response. Often this is the MIME type of the document which is based upon the file type. Unfortunately CGI scripts which create HTML documents cannot use this mechanism and must explicitly include this information. The following headers may be returned by your CGI scripts:

- Content-Type: tells the browser how to process the document. This field is required: as you saw in Section 9.4.
- Location: used to automatically redirect the browser to another URL.
- Set-cookie: set a Netscape cookie.

The server response begins with a response code. The details of some of these are shown in Section 17.3.2. A typical response in which the file has been successfully found and returned looks like:

```
HTTP/1.1 200 OK
Server: Apache/1.3
MIME-Version: 1.0
Content-Type: text/html
Content-length: 53
```

```
<html>
<head></head>
<body>
<h1>Title</h1>
</body>
</html>
```

**17.3.1.4 Closing the Connection** The client and server can both close the connection. This uses the standard TCP approach. If another document is required a new connection must be opened.

## 17.3.2 HTTP Server Response Codes

*Table 17.1* HTTP Server Response Codes

| Response Code | Meaning |
|---|---|
| 200 OK | This is the commonest code. It indicates that the message contains the requested data including all necessary headers. |
| 201 Created | The server has created a file which the browser should now attempt to load. This code is only used as a reply to POST requests. |
| 204 No Content | The request was processed successfully but there was no data to return to the browser. |
| 301 Moved Permanently | The page has moved to a new URL which the browser should automatically load. |
| 400 Bad Request | The request from the client used invalid syntax and could not be processed. |
| 401 Unauthorized | Some form of authorization information is needed before this resource can be accessed. This authorization was not supplied. |
| 404 Not Found | This is the commonest error response. It indicates that while the request was valid, the server could not find the document. |
| 500 Internal Server Error | The server generated an error which it cannot handle. |
| 501 Not Implemented | The server is unable to process the request due to some missing or unimplemented feature. |
| 503 Service Unavailable | The server is temporarily unable to handle requests. |

Web servers can send *many* different codes to the browser. Some of these get displayed by the browser but users rarely know what they actually mean. The codes are grouped together logically with codes in the 200–299 range indicating a successful request, 300–399 indicating that a page may have moved, 400–499 showing client errors and 500–599 showing server errors. The main codes are listed in Table 17.1.

## 17.4 COMMON GATEWAY INTERFACE

When the browser submits data to the server (usually from a Web form) the server is unable to fully process that data. The data must be passed onto a dedicated application for processing. As part of the processing an HTML page may be dynamically generated and returned to the browser. The format in which the server passes data to the appropriate program is defined by the Common Gateway Interface protocol.

CGI applications can be written in any language. Chapter 9 demonstrated how to write these in Perl. Each time that the server gets data for a script it initiates the script as a separate process. This places a significant processing load on the server and is the main reason that Active Server Pages *can* run more quickly than CGI scripts, even when written in the same language. There is a big benefit in this model. If the script crashes, the server is unaffected, assuming that a suitable operating system is being used. Additionally the script can only access a limited set of facilities on the machine and hence the model is relatively secure.

### 17.4.1 The Dangers of Using CGI

If you decide to write a CGI script then you are inevitably going to run a serious security risk.[9] Each CGI script that you write presents its own opportunities for malicious misuse and for accidental bugs. Two basic types of security hole exist:

- scripts may present information about the host system to hackers,
- scripts which execute commands from remote users, for instance search scripts, are vulnerable to hackers who attempt to trick them into executing system commands.

On UNIX systems the Web server is never run as user nobody. Instead a special user is created, often called something like www. A special user group is also created to hold www and any ordinary users who want to set up Web pages. The user nobody has minimal privileges but it must still be able to run some commands. These can be used for instance to mail the /etc/passwd file back to a hacker. Application developers will tend to want to keep the CGI scripts somewhere in their own directory tree. This is not inherently dangerous but presents problems from the sys-admin point of view. If you are going to let users develop scripts which are themselves potential security holes then you want to be able to minimize the risk that those scripts present. By making developers store their scripts in cgi-bin the system administrator can track which scripts are installed and what they do. The cgi-bin directory can have its access permissions set to further reduce the risk.

In Chapter 8 I suggested that scripting languages are preferable to compiled languages for the development of CGI applications. From a security point of view the compiled script is definitely safer. The source code of interpreted scripts is freely available for any user. If hackers can get to your code then they can examine it for holes which they can exploit; if

[9]See also The World Wide Web security FAQ written by Lincoln D. Stein and widely available on the Web.

your application is compiled then no one can get at the source code. When configured properly Web servers should prevent access to any executable program but there are situations in which you can accidentally make source code available. If you edit your script file in the `cgi-bin` directory most editors will create a backup copy containing the original source before you edited it. This will be renamed slightly: in Programmers File Editor, backups usually have $$$ appended to the file name; in Emacs, backups have tilde appended. This situation is very easy to avoid by removing editing rights from the `cgi-bin` directory so that you have to edit your files elsewhere and copy them to that directory, overwriting the previous version.

You should be careful when you download a script from the Internet for use on your own site. Always read the code, make sure it does what the author claims. If you don't understand the code then don't use the script. Follow this rule wherever you get the code from, even Perl code on CPAN sites may have bugs: just because a program is widely used doesn't mean it's perfect. Look at the number of security holes being found in Microsoft and Netscape browsers. Check these aspects of each script:

- How large is it? Big scripts are more likely to have bugs.
- Does it read or write to the host file system? Check that your own access restrictions are not breached and that sensitive files are not touched.
- If the script downloads further files from the authors own site *do not use it*. This is a sure way to get *Trojan horse* programs onto a server.
- If the script uses other programs on your system such as `sendmail`[10] does it do so safely?
- Does the script need suid (set-user-ID) privileges? This is very dangerous. Never run CGI scripts like this.
- If the script validates data received from HTML forms the author has thought about security issues. No guarantee that they got the right solution, of course.
- Does the script rely on the PATH environment variable? This is dangerous and should be avoided.

### 17.4.2 Environment Variables

Table 17.2 lists some of the environment variables that can be accessed and used by CGI scripts. The script shows how these variables might be used.

The following Perl script prints all of the environment variables for your system. Try running it from your command line. Once you know how to write and set up CGI scripts alter the script so that it prints an HTML page containing the values:

```
#! /usr/bin/perl -w
$ENV = "";
```

---

[10]A powerful e-mail delivery mechanism for UNIX systems.

***Table 17.2***   CGI-related Environment Variables

| | |
|---|---|
| SERVER_PROTOCOL | Name and revision of the protocol used to send the request. |
| REQUEST_METHOD | For HTTP requests valid methods are HEAD, GET and POST. |
| PATH_INFO | Clients can append path information onto a URL. The server will decode this information before passing parameters to the CGI script. |
| PATH_TRANSLATED | A physical mapping of PATH_INFO provided by the server. |
| QUERY_STRING | Information following ? in the URL. Not decoded by the server. |
| SCRIPT_NAME | Logical path to the current script. |
| REMOTE_HOST | Hostname making the request. If this information is not available the server leaves the variable unset. |
| REMOTE_ADDR | IP address of the requesting host. |
| CONTENT_TYPE | Where information is attached via a POST request this gives the MIME type. |
| CONTENT_LENGTH | Length of content data in bytes. |

```
$ENV{REQUEST_METHOD}="GET";
$ENV{QUERY_STRING}="name=Chris+Bates&email=Chris%40home";

foreach $key (keys %ENV) {
  $val = $ENV{$key};
  printf("Environment variable:\t%s %s\n",$key,$val);
  }
```

## 17.4.3   The GET and POST Methods

Why are there two methods for getting information from the client to the server? Well first, the HTTP protocol specifies different uses for the two methods, and second, you use them to return different types of information, and hence they trigger different types of response from the CGI application.

GET requests are not supposed to change the state of the server more than once. If a user responds through GET and some file on the server such as guestbook is altered, pressing reload on the browser which triggers a new request should not lead to a change in the guestbook. POST requests do not automatically have this effect but a browser will usually prompt the user before resubmitting a POST.

A further difference is the amount of data that can be returned with the two methods. The GET returns its data as command-line parameters. Some UNIX systems have a limitation of 256 characters on the command line so, if the length of the URL plus parameters is likely to exceed this, POST should be used. Because POST data is enclosed within the body of the HTTP response it is safer than GET data: it is not displayed as part of the URL and hence less open to snooping.

Finally, the two methods pass data into your script in different ways. POST data arrives from STDIN, the number of bytes is given by the CONTENT_LENGTH variable (see Section 17.4.2). GET data is passed into the QUERY_STRING environment variable.

A sample GET request as you might see it at the browser is shown below:

```
http://myserver.ac.uk/cgi-bin/
query.cgi?page=request&keywords=cgi+scripting+perl
```

### 17.4.4    Using CGI Scripts

CGI scripts usually perform three tasks, although only one is actually required. Your CGI script must parse the input, whether it comes from GET or POST. You may then have to perform some processing such as reading or writing data files. You will probably want to return an HTML page to the user either because that's what they requested or as a confirmation after a transaction.

#### *17.4.4.1  Configuring Scripts On The Server*    Firstly you need to check some information with the system administrator on your Web server. You need to know which directories you can use for your CGI scripts, what Perl version, module and libraries they have, what extension you should give to your scripts and what operating system they're using. Typically the CGI scripts will go somewhere like ~/cgi-bin, a subdirectory of your home directory. If the server runs Microsoft NT you may have to run your CGI scripts as windows batch files using the WinCGI protocol. Because this is both non-standard and proprietary, and not used even by all NT servers, it is not covered here. Microsoft Internet Information Server is just one NT Web server which easily runs Perl scripts.

> Note:
> If you're in any doubt, consult the documentation that came with your server software. In fact, because Web servers are *very* susceptible to attack, you should always read this whether installing or upgrading. If you have a Web server out on the Internet it *will* be attacked. The only questions are: how often will attacks happen; and how serious will they be.

Put your CGI script on the server using FTP, or whatever tool your ISP provides, and in the appropriate directory. The directory and all scripts that it contains must be executable by any user. That is you have to set the access permissions so that anyone can run your programs. To do this leave the directory by moving to its parent and type:

```
chmod 755 <directory_name>
```

Enter the directory and, assuming your scripts are called `<name>.cgi`, type:

```
chmod 755 *.cgi
```

Using your Web browser access your Web pages and check that everything works as you expected. Make sure that you create error conditions as well as running successful operations to fully check your software.

### 17.4.4.2 Running Scripts from the Command-line
When creating and debugging scripts you need to run them locally so that you can access all error messages and really see what is happening. This technique assumes that your CGI script is just another Perl script. Anything that can be done as CGI, can be done as a normal Perl program, with two caveats. Firstly rather than reading the data in from the server we must actually supply the data in the script or in an input file[11], secondly CGI scripts direct output to STDOUT and error messages to STDERR, we'll be directing the output to a temporary file instead.

Once you have a working script you simply edit it to remove the references to temporary files and it will work perfectly as a CGI script.

## 17.5 THE DOCUMENT OBJECT MODEL

Dynamic Web pages are a combination of three things:

- formatted page content,
- executable scripts embedded within the page,
- an interface which lets scripts operate on the elements within the document.

You've met, and used, languages which meet the first two requirements in that list in this book. Those languages are *usually* HTML to format the content and JavaScript to manipulate it. In the near future we may see more *exotic* combinations such as XML and VBScript become widespread. Whatever technologies we use when authoring our pages, one thing is not going to change. The scripts that we develop need to be able to access the elements which make up the document. How do they do this? The simplest answer is that they use an *application programming interface*, API, which is provided by the Web browser itself.

---

[11]CGI.pm provides a mechanism by which we can supply data from the command-line.

An API is a set of hooks into a library of routines which developers can use from within their own programs. There are APIs for all sorts of things. The computer system you use probably has some sort of window-based interface. The functionality which is required to draw and manipulate those windows is encapsulated in a library which is made available to developers when they write code. The developer simply uses the functions which the library provides so that, for instance, each programmer can draw buttons or menus in the same way. HTML and XML documents are made of objects such as headings or paragraphs which we want to be able to manipulate in our programs.

This is where the Document Object Model, DOM, enters our lives. The DOM is an API for HTML and XML documents. In fact, it is probably one of the key things that you need to understand if you're going to develop DHTML. Because the DOM makes everything on the page into an object, it provides a mechanism through which those elements can be manipulated by programmed scripts. The DOM does not specify any event handling, yet that is a key aspect of any interactive application. According to the W3C Web site, event handling *may* appear in a future version of the DOM.

So what does the DOM provide? Well it describes the *logical* structure of documents formatted with HTML[12], how those documents can be accessed and how they can be manipulated. Because the DOM exists, developers can create documents, manipulate their structure and modify, delete or add elements within them. Best of all, the DOM is language and system neutral so you should be able to apply the same *ideas* to scripts written in JavaScript for Netscape browsers on Linux, and VBScript for use in Internet Explorer.

Of course, life is never clean cut. In reality the DOM is implemented by the browser manufacturers and as an applications developer you can only access those parts of the API which they provide. All manufacturers seem to implement different parts of the DOM and, worse, to implement parts of it in different ways. That's why you can write some perfect, standards compliant, JavaScript which runs really well in Netscape but does nothing useful in Internet Explorer or Opera or some other browser. There's a further complication with Internet Explorer: it is *very* closely tied to the Windows operating system. The DOM as implemented by Microsoft has been radically extended to include lots of IE-specific functionality. It's not all bad news though, some of those Microsoft extensions make accessing the elements inside a page far easier, others are being widely adopted. Netscape 6, for instance, includes `innerText` and other useful Microsoft developments. In the rest of this chapter I want to look at the DOM, describe some of the API as defined by W3C and delve into some of the features that you'll find in Internet Explorer.

---

[12]I'm going to concentrate on HTML in this discussion. In fact the DOM applies equally to XML documents and applications.

## 17.6 INTRODUCING THE DOCUMENT OBJECT MODEL

The DOM model of an HTML document is a hierarchical structure which might reasonably be represented as a tree. However, this structure does not imply that DOM-compliant software must manipulate the document in a hierarchical manner; it is simply a representation. The relationship between some HTML code and the DOM is shown in Figure 17.4.

**Figure 17.4**  Sample Document Object Model

```
<html>
    <head>
        <title>Something...</title>
    </head>
    <body>
        <p>Some text...</p>
        <ul>
            <li>First
            <li>Second
        </ul>
    </body>
</html>
```

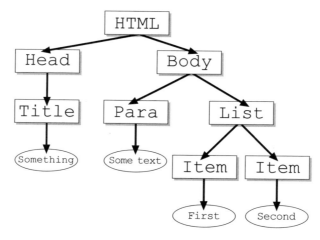

One benefit of establishing the DOM is that any two implementations of the same document will arrive at the same structure. The sets of objects and relationships between those objects will be compatible. In turn this means that a script associated with the document which is used to manipulate those objects should perform consistently in both cases. There is no suggestion that the visual representation of the document will be identical in both cases as implementation is left to the browser developers.

The DOM models, but does not implement:

- the objects that comprise a document;
- the semantics, behavior, and attributes of those objects;
- the relationships between those objects.

Although the DOM is now central to the development of DHTML, its development was actually preceded by that of DHTML. The specification for the DOM came from the need to create an independent set of objects that could be used by JavaScript programmers as they develop dynamic Web pages.

Unfortunately, the standardization of the DOM has not fed back into a standard approach to object implementation from Microsoft and Netscape. They both lag behind the standard. The single biggest difficulty that JavaScript and JScript developers face is the inconsistencies that Netscape Navigator and Microsoft Internet Explorer exhibit in their approaches to the DOM. For the foreseeable future these differences will remain. Scripts can be developed which work under both browsers but this is difficult and leads to lots of redundant code. Alternatively, developers may decide that as most of the users of a site have a particular browser, they will use just the DOM for that system. If you are developing for a corporate Intranet or other relatively closed system then this is the best choice to make. If you develop for the world at large then you have little choice but to struggle with these complexities or adopt a minimal approach to scripting and use only that subset of objects which both browsers support in the same way.

## 17.7 EXERCISES

1. Why are protocols necessary when different types of system try to communicate?

2. What is the relationship between the Internet Protocol and the Transmission Control Protocol?

3. Can you think of a reason why the IP header contains the addresses of both the sender and the recipient?

4. What is the CGI protocol?

5. What is meant by the terms CGI script and CGI scripting?

6. How do CGI scripts differ from other types of application program?

7. List five dangers that are inherent to CGI scripts.

8. What are the GET and POST methods of the HTTP protocol?

9. Why is it generally thought better to use POST than GET in Web applications?

10. List six of the environment variables that you can use in your CGI scripts.

# 18
## *Case Study*

The SweatHut Fitness and Sporting Club (SFASC) has decided that it requires a presence on the World Wide Web. SFASC is a medium-sized members-only club which caters to individuals, families, and block memberships for companies. The club currently has 12,000 members with approximately 250 people leaving and joining each year.

Having decided to develop a Web site, the committee which runs SFASC has realized that they totally lack the necessary skills and experience in-house. After a series of acrimonious meetings they have decided to engage a contractor to design and build their site. You are that contractor.

The committee members are hesitant about the Web. Some remain unsure that SFASC has any use for the Web or that it has anything to offer to them. Consequently, prudently and sensibly they have decided to start off slowly and to gradually build a more complex site if the need arises. A friend of the club secretary has suggested a work plan which is similar to one successfully used by her company.

## 18.1 THE PLAN

You are instructed to follow the plan step-by-step.

*Step One*  Create a simple homepage which gives contact details for the club and lists the activities which they run. Suitable images may be included and an appropriate logo designed. The page should be nicely formatted using colors and fonts of your choice. It is felt important that the homepage is in no way garish or startling.

***Step Two*** The homepage having been successful, you are to move on to creating a more comprehensive Web site. The pages on this site should all have a small logo in the top right-hand corner of the page and copyright and contact information at the foot of each page. The latter information should be in a 9-point monospaced font such as Courier and must be centered on the page. Your site needs a front page which provides a welcome to the site and has links to these other pages:

- the names of the committee members and their roles,
- contact information,
- activities which the club runs,
- membership information: how to join, the levels of fees etc.
- links to useful external sites.

All pages should use consistent formatting styles.

***Step Three*** If you have not done so before, you should move all formatting information into styles.

***Step Four*** Add meta tags to the head section which can be used by search engines.

***Step Five*** To make the site slightly more dynamic you should create JavaScript powered rollover buttons for all of the main links.

***Step Six*** The time has come to add some interactivity using CGI scripts and Perl. The first scripts will let people apply for membership on-line and then check the status of their application. To achieve this you will need to create a simple HTML form which has the following fields:

- name,
- type of membership (annual, lifetime, family),
- address,
- e-mail address,
- forms of exercise undertaken (running, weight training, cycling, swimming, tennis, badminton, aerobics, other, none),
- frequency of exercise,
- proficiency (expert, proficient, beginner).

When the form is submitted, the content of all fields should be checked using JavaScript. This check will ensure that all fields are completed. On the server, data should be converted to XML and written to a text file. You will need to create your own XML DTD for this.

*Step Seven*   Club members should be able to book activities on-line. Your site needs to display a weekly schedule for each activity which includes the number of places available and the instructor at each session. Users should enter their name into a form along with details of time and activity. Again data needs to be saved in a suitable XML file. The format of all screens and data structures is left to your discretion.

## 18.2   THE DATA

The committee has provided you with some information about the club. As always, when working in a dynamic medium such as the Web, this data is very fluid. You will want to store it in files which can be easily manipulated. You have not been provided with information about the club accounts but everything else which you need should be here. *As this is an exercise in prototype development you should invent further data if you need it.*

**Address**
The SweatHut Fitness and Sporting Club,
345 Greengage Lane,
Small Town, Florida.
   **Email**
secretary@sfasc.com

   **Telephone**
555 123 1234

   **Committee Members and Officials**

| Role | Name |
| --- | --- |
| Chair | Mrs Emiline Tibbins |
| Secretary | Mr Jonathon Sneer |
| Treasurer | Mr Roger Thornton |
| Restaurant Manager | Mrs Jane Greer |
| Chef | Mr Anthony T. Jones |
| Chief Instructor | Miss Amy Baxter |
| Gardener | Mr Walsh |

### Membership Information

| Type | Duration | Price |
|---|---|---|
| Individual | Annual | $ 90 |
| Individual | 5 Years | $ 350 |
| Individual | Lifetime | $ 500 |
| Child | Annual | $ 25 |
| Child | Five Years | $ 100 |
| Family | Annual | $ 200 |
| Family | Five Years | $ 750 |
| Corporate | Annual | $ 500 (per 10 memberships) |

### Activities

| Activity | Instructor | Price (non-members) |
|---|---|---|
| Squash | Mr E. Forsyth | $ 5.00 |
| Running (treadmill) | Mrs G. Harrison | $ 2 per hour |
| Aerobics | Miss A. Baxter | $ 2.50 |
| Aerobics (Women Only) | Miss A. Baxter | $ 2.50 |
| Aerobics (Under 15s) | Miss A. Baxter | $ 1.00 |
| Swimming | Mr F. Williams | $ 1.20 |
| Swimming (Children) | Mr F. Williams | $ 0.60 |
| Swimming (Women Only) | Miss A. Baxter | $ 1.20 |
| Swimming (Families) | Mr F. Williams | $ 5.00 |
| Weight Training | Mr E. Forsyth | $ 5.00 |
| Weight Training (Women Only) | Mrs G. Harrison | $ 5.00 |
| Circuit Training | Mr E. Forsyth | $ 2.50 |
| Circuit Training (Women Only) | Mrs G. Harrison | $ 2.50 |

### Background

The SweatHut Fitness and Sporting Club was founded in 1983 as a small members-only fitness club. The club founder was Mrs Jenny Abraham who funded the initial development using a legacy left by her late father. She purchased an area of land on the edge of the city which was ripe for development. A Sports Center and Restaurant complex was designed and built by 1984. The first members enrolled in February of that year. Part of the land was sold in 1990 for a housing development providing sufficient income to enlarge the existing club facilities so as to allow more members. By the late 1980s the Committee which runs the club had decided that more members were required. As a consequence membership was open to any individual or family who wished to join. Two years later a simple form of corporate membership was created. This caused trouble on the committee which only ended when Mrs Abraham resigned. Since then the club has continued to grow due to its combination of good facilities and low fees.

### Facilities

The Club owns its own spacious facilities. The purpose-built center stands in 15 spacious acres of land on the edge of the city. Within the sports center the accommodation is luxurious. The club has its own 25 meter swimming pool, 4 squash courts, a large gymnasium which accommodates badminton, netball, and basketball matches and can also be used for circuit training. The well-appointed weight training room has modern equipment, treadmills, rowing machines, and static bikes for spinning sessions.

For the less energetic two sauna rooms are provided alongside a jacuzzi and tanning room which has four sunbeds. The center also has separate spacious changing rooms for men and women which are equipped with secure lockers for personal possessions. Showering, washing and toilet facilities complete the changing room accommodation.

No members club would be complete without a restaurant, and SFASC is no exception here. A very highly praised restaurant provides healthy eating at lunchtimes and in the evening. Lunches are typically light meals such as salads while in the evening the Chef provides a range of quality three-course meals. The restaurant is licensed to sell alcohol and a large selection of wines is available.

The grounds have been landscaped. Relaxing walks among their seasonal planting schemes are a popular activity with members. It is hoped that the gardener, Mr. Walsh, will soon be able to offer classes in plant care for those who are interested.

# *References*

1. The ActiveState Web Site. `http://www.activestate.com`.

2. The Apache Group. `http://www.apache.org`.

3. Doug Bell and Mike Parr. *Java For Students*. Prentice Hall, 1999.

4. Don Box, Aaro Skonnard, and John Lam. *Essential XML Beyond Markup*. Addison-Wesley, 2000.

5. Mary Campione and Kathy Walrath. *The Java Tutorial*. Addison Wesley Longman, 1998.

6. Nigel Chapman. *Perl The Programmer's Companion*. John Wiley and Sons, 1998.

7. Tom Christiansen and Nathan Torkington. *Perl Cookbook*. O'Reilly and Associates, 1999.

8. Dave Cintron. *Fast Track Web Programming*. John Wiley and Sons, 1999.

9. The Comprehensive Perl Archive Network. `http://www.perl.com/CPAN`.

10. Arman Danesh. *Teach Yourself Javascript in a Week*. Sams.net, 1996.

11. Harvey Deitel, Paul Deitel, and Tem Neito. *E-business And E-commerce How To Program*. Prentice Hall, 2001.

12. Harvey Deitel, Paul Deitel, Tem Neito, Ted Lin, and Praveen Sadhu. *XML How To Program*. Prentice Hall, 2001.

13. Microsoft DHTML, HTML and CSS Site. `http://msdn.microsoft.com/workshop/author/dhtml/dhtmlovw.asp`.

14. Netscape DHTML Site. `http://developer.netscape.com/tech/dynhtml/index.html`.

15. David Flanagan. *JavaScript: The Definitive Guide*. O'Reilly and Associates, 1998.

16. Jeffrey E. F. Friedl. *Mastering Regular Expressions*. O'Reilly and Associates, 1998.

17. The Free Software Foundation. `http://www.fsf.org`.

18. Danny Goodman. *Javascript Bible*. IDG Books, 1998.

19. Sun Microsystems Java Site. `http://www.java.sun.com`.

20. The JavaScript FAQ. `http://www.javascripter.net/faq/index.htm`.

21. Microsoft JScript Site. `http://msdn.microsoft.com/scripting.jscript/default.htm`.

22. JavaScript Faqts. `http://javascript.faqts.com`.

23. HTML::Mason Homepage. `http://www.masonhq.com`.

24. Dave Mercer. *ASP3.0 A Beginner's Guide*. Osborne/McGraw-Hill, 2001.

25. Microsoft XML Site. `http://msdn.microsoft.com/xml/default.asp`.

26. Jakob Nielsen. Jakob Nielsen's Homepage. `http://www.useit.com`.

27. Jakob Nielsen. *Designing Web Usability*. New Riders, 1999.

28. Netscape JavaScript Site. `http://developer.netscape.com/tech/javascript/index.html`.

29. William J. Pardi. *XML in Action*. Microsoft Press, 1999.

30. Perl Faqts. `http://perl.faqts.com`.

31. The PerlMagick Homepage. `http://www.imagemagick.org/www/perl.html`.

32. Programmer's File Editor. `http://www.lancs.ac.uk/people/cpaap/pfe`.

33. The PHP Homepage. `http://www.php.net`.

34. Official PHP Documentation. `http://www.php.net/docs.php`.

35. PHP Faqts. `http://php.faqts.com`.

36. Randal L. Schwartz. *Learning Perl*. O'Reilly and Associates, 1997.

37. Randal L. Schwartz, Eric Olsen, and Tom Christiansen. *Learning Perl on Win32 Systems*. O'Reilly and Associates, 1997.

38. Sun Microsystems Servlet Page. `http://www.java.sun.com/products/servlet/index.html`.

39. Slashdot. `http://slashdot.org`.

40. Selena Sol and Gunther Birzniecks. *Instant Web Scripts With CGI Perl*. M and T, 1996.

41. Sriram Srinivasan. *Advanced Perl Programming*. O'Reilly and Associates, 1997.

42. The Apache Tomcat Server. `http://jakarta.apache.org/tomcat/index.html`.

43. World Wide Web Consortium (W3C). `http://www.w3c.org`.

44. Larry Wall, Tom Christiansen, and Jon Orwant. *Programming Perl*. O'Reilly and Associates, 3 edition, 2000.

45. Shawn P. Wallace. *Programming Web Graphics With Perl and GNU Software*. O'Reilly and Associates, 1999.

46. Joseph Webber. *Special Edition Using Java 1.1*. Que, 1997.

47. Aaron Weiss. *The Complete Idiots Guide To Javascript*. Que, 1997.

48. A. Keyton Weissinger. *ASP in a Nutshell*. O'Reilly and Associates, 1999.

49. Russell Winder and Graham Roberts. *Developing Java Software*. John Wiley and Sons, 1999.

50. The XHTML Recommendation. `http://www.w3c.org/TR/2000/REC-xhtml1-2000126`.

# *Glossary*

**%ENV**  A Perl hash which holds details of the environment in which a script is being executed.

**$_**  Array of parameters passed into a Perl subroutine.

**$ARGV**  Array of values passed into a Perl script from the command line.

**Applet**  A Java program which executes inside a Web browser. Applets usually have restricted functionality.

**Array**  A data structure in which items are stored sequentially.

**ASP**  Active Server Pages is a Microsoft Web server technology in which scripting commands can be embedded within HTML files.

**Browser**  A piece of software used to view HTML documents. Internet Explorer from Microsoft and Netscape Navigator are the two most popular examples.

**CGI**  Common Gateway Interface described the format of data when it is passed from a Web server to a server-side script.

**CGI Script**  Application which processes data passed from Web servers using the CGI protocol.

**Client**  A system usually running on a desktop PC which accesses services and data from other machines on a network.

**Command Shell**  A text-only interface to an operating system.

**Cookie**  A piece of text which Web servers may store on users PCs so that those surfers can be tracked through a Web site.

**DHTML**    Dynamic HTML: a combination of scripts and HTML which executes inside a Web browser. Used to build complex and dynamic Web pages.

**DOM**    Document Object Model is the set of elements which make up an HTML or XML document.

**DOS**    The underlying operating system on many Microsoft Windows products. DOS can be accessed through a primitive command shell.

**ECMAScript**    International standard for a particular scripting language. Implemented as Javascript by Netscape and as JScript by Microsoft.

**Environment Variable**    A variable which can be assigned in a command shell to change the way that operating systems or applications operate. Examples include the PATH which is a set of directories the operating system searches when trying to find an application.

**Event**    Something which triggers a response from a program. May be initiated by a user of by another application.

**FTP**    File Transfer Protocol is the standard way of tramsferring files between servers which use IP.

**Function**    A piece of program code which achieves a single task. These code fragments are called functions in Perl. See also *subroutine* and *method*.

**Hash**    A Perl data structure in which values are associated with unique keys. The data value can be accessed via the key.

**HTML**    Hypertext Markup Language is the language used to format documents for use on the World Wide Web.

**Hypertext**    Documents can be linked together based upon context and meaning.

**Internet**    The collection of servers around the world which can share data. These servers all use the Internet suite of protocols.

**IP**    Internet Protocol defines the basic network functionality which the Internet uses.

**Java**    An object-oriented programming language developed by Sun Microsystems. Java is very useful when building applications which operate across networks.

**JavaScript**    The Netscape implementation of ECMAScript.

**JScript**    The Microsoft implementation of ECMAScript.

**Linux**    A freely available (and free) operating system for PCs. Works very much like UNIX.

**Markup**    Commands placed within text documents to define how they are structured or presented.

**Method**    A piece of program code which achieves a single task. These code fragments are called methods in object-oriented languages. See also *subroutine* and *function*.

**Microsoft**    The largest comapny in the world. Manufacturers of the Windows family of operating systems.

**MIME**   Multipurpose Internet Mail Extensions let email systems exchange application data such as spreadsheets.

**Object**   Data structure within a running programming which encapsulates the functionality of a real-world item.

**Object Orientation**   A software development technique in which programs are based around objects.

**ODBC**   Object Database Connectivity is a technology which connects PC applications to relational databases running on those systems.

**Perl**   A programming language which is most commonly used for systems administration and Web scripting.

**Perldoc**   Documentation system which comes with Perl.

**PHP**   Popular server-side scripting languages used to create dynamic Web pages.

**POD**   Plain Old Documentation is the standard documentation format for Perl.

**Script**   A small program which is usually written in an interpreted language such as Perl or VBScript.

**Scalar**   Simple Perl variable which can be either a number or a text string.

**Server**   A system which provides services to other machines on a network.

**Servlet**   A Java application which interacts with a Web server through the CGI protocol.

**SGML**   Standard Generalized Markup Language is a complicated markup scheme which can be used to format any document.

**Subroutine**   A piece of program code which achieves a single task. These code fragments are called subroutines in Javascript. See also *function* and *method*.

**Sun Microsystems**   Californian networking company who developed the Java programming language.

**Tag**   An individual piece of HTML or XML.

**TCP**   Networking protocol which provides session oriented services to applications. Runs on top of IP.

**Telnet**   A protocl which allows access to remote computers through authenticated logons.

**UNIX**   A powerful operating system which was developed in the mid 1970s. Still widely used on servers.

**Variable**   A anmed data item in a program.

**VBScript**   A cut down version of Visual Basic which can be used to add scripting to applications including Web pages.

**W3C**   The World Wide Web Consortium is a voluntary group which creates and approves standards for Web applications.

**World Wide Web**   A hypertext system which links documents on millions of servers around the globe.

**WYSIWYG**    What You See Is What You Get editors display documents whilst you edit them in the same as they will appear when finished.

**XHTML**    The latest W3C recommendation for HTML. Applies the rules of XML to HTML pages.

**XML**    Extensible Markup Language is a subset of XML. It is designed to create grammars which describe documents so that they can be used over networks such as the Internet.

# Appendix A
# HTML Color Codes

| Name | Red | Green | Blue | Hex Value |
|---|---|---|---|---|
| aliceblue | 240 | 248 | 245 | f0f8ff |
| antiquewhite | 250 | 235 | 215 | faebd7 |
| aqua | 0 | 255 | 255 | 00ffff |
| aquamarine | 127 | 255 | 212 | 7fffd4 |
| azure | 240 | 255 | 255 | f0ffff |
| beige | 245 | 245 | 220 | f5f5dc |
| bisque | 255 | 228 | 196 | ffe4c4 |
| black | 0 | 0 | 0 | 000000 |
| blanchedalmond | 255 | 235 | 205 | ffebcd |
| blue | 0 | 0 | 255 | 0000ff |
| blueviolet | 138 | 43 | 226 | 8a2be2 |
| brown | 165 | 42 | 42 | a52a2a |
| burlywood | 222 | 184 | 135 | deb887 |
| cadetblue | 95 | 158 | 160 | 5f9ea0 |
| chartreuse | 127 | 255 | 0 | 7fff00 |
| chocolate | 210 | 105 | 30 | d2691e |
| coral | 255 | 127 | 80 | ff7f50 |

| Name | Red | Green | Blue | Hex Value |
|------|-----|-------|------|-----------|
| conflowerblue | 100 | 149 | 237 | 6495ed |
| cornsilk | 255 | 248 | 220 | fff8dc |
| crimson | 220 | 20 | 60 | dc143c |
| cyan | 0 | 255 | 255 | 00ffff |
| darkblue | 0 | 0 | 139 | 00008b |
| darkcyan | 0 | 139 | 139 | 008b8b |
| darkgoldenrod | 184 | 134 | 11 | b8860b |
| darkgray | 169 | 169 | 169 | a9a9a9 |
| darkgreen | 0 | 100 | 0 | 006400 |
| darkkhaki | 189 | 183 | 107 | bdb76b |
| darkmagenta | 139 | 0 | 0 | 8b008b |
| darkolivegreen | 85 | 107 | 47 | 55662f |
| darkorange | 255 | 140 | 0 | ff8c00 |
| darkorchid | 153 | 50 | 204 | 9932cc |
| darkred | 139 | 0 | 0 | 8b0000 |
| darksalmon | 233 | 150 | 122 | e9967a |
| darkseagreen | 143 | 188 | 143 | 8fbc8f |
| darkslateblue | 72 | 61 | 139 | 483d8b |
| darkslategray | 47 | 79 | 79 | 2f4f4f |
| darkturquoise | 0 | 206 | 209 | 00ced1 |
| darkviolet | 148 | 0 | 211 | 9400d3 |
| deeppink | 255 | 20 | 147 | ff1493 |
| deepskyblue | 0 | 191 | 255 | 00bfff |
| dimgray | 105 | 105 | 105 | 696969 |
| dodgerblue | 30 | 144 | 255 | 1e90ff |
| firebrick | 178 | 34 | 34 | b22222 |
| floralwhite | 255 | 250 | 240 | fffaf0 |
| forestgreen | 34 | 139 | 34 | 228b22 |
| fuchsia | 255 | 0 | 255 | ff00ff |
| gainsboro | 220 | 220 | 220 | dcdcdc |
| ghostwhite | 248 | 248 | 255 | f8f8ff |
| gold | 255 | 215 | 0 | ffd700 |
| goldenrod | 218 | 165 | 32 | daa520 |
| gray | 128 | 128 | 128 | 808080 |
| green | 0 | 128 | 0 | 008000 |
| greenyellow | 173 | 255 | 47 | adff2f |
| honeydew | 240 | 255 | 240 | f0fff0 |
| hotpink | 255 | 105 | 180 | ff69b4 |

| Name | Red | Green | Blue | Hex Value |
|------|-----|-------|------|-----------|
| indianred | 205 | 92 | 92 | cd5c5c |
| indigo | 75 | 0 | 130 | 4b0082 |
| ivory | 255 | 255 | 240 | fffff0 |
| khaki | 240 | 230 | 140 | f0e68c |
| lavender | 230 | 230 | 250 | e6e6fa |
| lavenderblush | 255 | 240 | 245 | fff0f5 |
| lawngreen | 124 | 252 | 000 | 7cfc00 |
| lemochiffon | 255 | 250 | 205 | fffacd |
| lightblue | 173 | 216 | 230 | add8e6 |
| lightcoral | 240 | 128 | 128 | f08080 |
| lightcyan | 224 | 255 | 255 | e0ffff |
| lightgoldenrodyellow | 250 | 250 | 210 | fafad2 |
| lightgray | 211 | 211 | 211 | d3d3d3 |
| lightgreen | 144 | 238 | 144 | 90ee90 |
| lightpink | 255 | 182 | 193 | ffb6c1 |
| lightsalmon | 255 | 160 | 122 | ffa07a |
| lightseagreen | 32 | 178 | 170 | 20b2aa |
| lightskyblue | 135 | 206 | 250 | 87cefa |
| lightslategray | 119 | 136 | 153 | 778899 |
| lightsteelblue | 176 | 196 | 222 | b0c4de |
| lightyellow | 255 | 255 | 224 | ffffe0 |
| lime | 0 | 255 | 0 | 00ff00 |
| limegreen | 50 | 205 | 50 | 32cd32 |
| linen | 250 | 240 | 230 | faf0e6 |
| magenta | 255 | 0 | 255 | ff00ff |
| maroon | 128 | 0 | 0 | 800000 |
| mediumaquamarine | 102 | 205 | 170 | 66cdaa |
| mediumblue | 0 | 0 | 205 | 0000cd |
| mediumorchid | 186 | 85 | 211 | ba55d3 |
| mediumpurple | 147 | 211 | 219 | 9370db |
| mediumseagreen | 60 | 179 | 113 | 3cb371 |
| mediumslateblue | 123 | 104 | 238 | 7b68ee |
| mediumspringgreen | 0 | 250 | 154 | 00fa9a |
| mediumturquoise | 72 | 209 | 204 | 48d1cc |
| mediumvioletred | 199 | 21 | 133 | c71585 |
| midnightblue | 25 | 25 | 122 | 191970 |
| mintcream | 245 | 255 | 250 | f5fffa |
| mistyrose | 255 | 228 | 225 | ffe4e1 |

| Name | Red | Green | Blue | Hex Value |
|------|-----|-------|------|-----------|
| mocassin | 255 | 228 | 181 | ffe4b5 |
| navajowhite | 255 | 222 | 173 | ffdead |
| navy | 0 | 0 | 128 | 000080 |
| oldlace | 253 | 245 | 230 | fdf5e6 |
| olive | 128 | 128 | 0 | 808000 |
| olivedrab | 107 | 142 | 35 | 6b8e23 |
| orange | 255 | 265 | 0 | ffa500 |
| orangered | 255 | 69 | 0 | ff4500 |
| orchid | 218 | 112 | 214 | da70d6 |
| palegoldenrod | 238 | 232 | 170 | eee8aa |
| palegreen | 152 | 251 | 152 | 98fb98 |
| paleturquoise | 175 | 238 | 238 | afeeee |
| palevioletred | 219 | 112 | 147 | db7093 |
| papayawhip | 255 | 239 | 213 | ffefd5 |
| peachpuff | 255 | 218 | 185 | ffda69 |
| peru | 205 | 133 | 63 | cd853f |
| pink | 255 | 192 | 203 | ffc0cb |
| plum | 221 | 160 | 221 | dda0dd |
| powderblue | 176 | 224 | 230 | b0e0e6 |
| purple | 128 | 0 | 128 | 800080 |
| red | 255 | 0 | 0 | ff0000 |
| rosybrown | 188 | 143 | 143 | bc8f8f |
| royalblue | 65 | 105 | 225 | 4169e1 |
| saddlebrown | 139 | 69 | 19 | 8b4513 |
| salmon | 250 | 128 | 114 | fa8072 |
| sandybrown | 244 | 164 | 96 | f4a460 |
| seagreen | 46 | 139 | 87 | 2e8b57 |
| seashell | 255 | 245 | 238 | fff5ee |
| sienna | 160 | 82 | 45 | a0522d |
| silver | 192 | 192 | 192 | c0c0c0 |
| skyblue | 135 | 206 | 235 | 87ceeb |
| slateblue | 106 | 90 | 205 | 6a5acd |
| slategray | 112 | 128 | 144 | 708090 |
| snow | 255 | 250 | 250 | fffafa |
| springgreen | 0 | 255 | 127 | 00ff7f |
| steelblue | 70 | 130 | 180 | 4682b4 |
| tan | 210 | 180 | 140 | d2b48c |
| teal | 0 | 128 | 128 | 008080 |

| Name | Red | Green | Blue | Hex Value |
|------|-----|-------|------|-----------|
| thistle | 216 | 191 | 216 | d8bfd8 |
| tomato | 255 | 99 | 71 | 006347 |
| turquoise | 64 | 224 | 208 | 40e0d0 |
| violet | 238 | 130 | 238 | ee82ee |
| wheat | 245 | 222 | 179 | f5deb3 |
| white | 255 | 255 | 255 | ffffff |
| whitesmoke | 245 | 245 | 245 | f5f5f5 |
| yellow | 255 | 255 | 0 | ffff00 |
| yellowgreen | 154 | 205 | 50 | 9acd32 |

# Appendix B
# JavaScript Keywords and Methods

## B.1 THE WINDOW OBJECT

**Properties**

`frames[ ]`
  array of frames stored in the order in which they are defined in the document.

`frames.length`
  number of frames.

`self`
  current window.

`opener`
  the window (if any) which opened the current window.

`parent`
  parent of current window if using a frameset.

`top`
  main window which creates all frames.

`status`
  message in the status bar.

**defaultStatus**
default message for the status bar.

**name**
the name of the window if it was created using the open() method and a name was specified.

### Methods

**alert("*string*")**
open a box containing the message.

**blur()**
remove focus from current window.

**confirm("*string*")**
display a message box with OK and Cancel buttons.

**focus()**
give focus to current window.

**prompt("*string*")**
display a prompt window with field for the user to enter a text string.

**scroll(*int,y*)**
move the current window to the chosen x, y location.

**open("URL", "*name*", '*options string*')**
open new window showing the page at URL. The window is given the name of parameter two and its appearance may be controlled by the options list. See section 7.2 for more details.

**close()**
close the current window.


## B.2   THE DOCUMENT OBJECT

### Properties

**title**
title of current document.

**location**
URL of the current page.

**lastModified**
A *date* object.

**referrer**
URL of the page from which the user came.

**bgColor**
hexadecimal representation of the page colour.

**fgColor**
> hexadecimal representation of the text colour for the current page.

**linkColor**

**vlinkColor**

**alinkColor**
> hexadecimal representation of the colours used for links.

**forms[]**
> array of forms on the current page.

**forms.length**
> the number of form objects on the page.

**links[]**
> array of links from the current page in the order in which they appear in the document.

**links.length**
> the number of hyperlinks on the page.

**anchors[]**
> an array of named anchors (internal links).

**anchors.length**
> number of anchors in the document.

**images[]**

**applets[]**

**embeds[]**
> arrays of images, Java applets and plug-in objects on the current page.

### Methods

**write("*string*")**
> write an arbitrary string to the HTML document.

**writeln("*string*")**
> write a string to the HTML document and terminate it with a newline character.

**clear()**
> clear the current document.

**close()**
> close the document.

## B.3  THE FORM OBJECT

### Properties

**name**
> the (unique) name of the form.

**method**
> submission method in numeric form. 0 = GET, 1 = POST.

`action`

the action attribute of the form.

`target`

if specified this is the target window for responses to the submission of the form.

`elements[]`

an array containing the form elements in the order in which they are declared in the document.

`length`

the number of elements in the form.

### Methods

`submit()`

submits the form.

`reset()`

resets the form.

### Event Handlers

`onSubmit(method)`

actions to be performed as the form is submitted.

`onReset(method)`

any actions to perform as the form is reset.

## B.4   THE NAVIGATOR OBJECT

### Properties

`appCodeName`

the internal codename of the browser.

`appName`

the real name of the browser.

`appVersion`

the browser version, includes major and minor version numbers.

`userAgent`

a complex object which comprises the appCodeName, appVersion details and the operating system being used.

`plugins[]`

array of plugins installed on the user's machine.

`mimeType[]`

array of MIME types supported by the user's browser.

### Methods

`javaEnabled()`
>   returns `true` if the browser has Java support switched on.

## B.5   THE STRING OBJECT

**Properties**

`length`
>   the number of characters in the string.

### Methods

`big()`
`blink()`
`bold()`
`fixed()`
`italics()`
`small()`
`sub()`
`strike()`
`sup()`
>   these methods surround the string with their respective HTML tag.

`fontColor(hex)`

`fontSize(int)`
>   add respective HTML tags into the string to change font colour and size.

`charAt(int)`
>   returns the character at the indicated position.

`indexOf(string), [int]`
>   searches for the first instance of the string given as parameter 1 in the string. Optionally a start position for the search can be given.

`lastIndexOf(string), [int]`
>   find the last instance of parameter 1 in the string.

`substring(int, int)`
>   return the substring starting at position 1 and ending at position 2.

`toLowerCase()`

`toUpperCase()`
>   change the case of the whole string.

## B.6   THE DATE OBJECT

**Methods**

`getDay()`

`getDate()`

`getHours()`

`getMinutes()`

`getMonth()`

`getSeconds()`

`getTime()`

`getTimeZoneOffset()`

`getYear()`
    return the respective value as an integer.

`setDate()`

`setHours()`

`setMinutes()`

`setMonth()`

`setSeconds()`

`setTime()`

`setYear()`
    set the respective value.

`toGMTString()`

    return current date in GMT format.

`toLocaleString()`

    return date in appropriate format for the locale of the client.

`parse(date)`

    convert a date string into millisecond format.


## B.7   THE MATH OBJECT

**Methods**
`abs(x)`

`acos(x)`

`asin(x)`

`atan(x)`

`cos(x)`

`log(x)`

`round(x)`

`sin(x)`

`sqrt(x)`

`tan(x)`
    apply the appropriate function to x.

`ceil(x)`

    return the lowest integer that is equal to or greater than x.

`exp(x)`
> return e to the power x.

`floor(x)`
> return the largest integer that is lower than or equal to x.

`max(x,y)`
> return the greater of x and y.

`min(x,y)`
> return the lesser of x and y.

`pow(x,y)`
> return x to the power y.

`random()`
> returns a random real number between 0 and 1.

## B.8 THE ARRAY OBJECT

**Properties**

`length`
> the number of elements in the array.

**Methods**

`join(character)`
> join all elements from the array into a single string. The elements are separated by the character passed as parameter. The default separator is the comma.

`reverse()`
> reverse the array.

`sort()`
> sort the elements of the array into ascending lexographical order.

## B.9 THE IMAGE OBJECT

**Properties**

`border`
> the border of the object.

`complete`
> value is `true` if the image has been fully loaded by the browser.

`height`
> the height of the image in pixels.

**length**
> the number of images in the image array.

**name**
> the name of the image.

**src**
> the URL for the image.

**width**
> the width of the image in pixels.

## B.10 JAVASCRIPT KEYWORDS

| | | | |
|---|---|---|---|
| abstract | extends | int | super |
| boolean | false | interface | switch |
| break | final | long | synchronized |
| byte | finally | native | this |
| case | float | new | throw |
| catch | for | null | throws |
| char | function | package | transient |
| class | goto | private | true |
| const | if | protected | try |
| continue | implements | public | var |
| default | import | return | void |
| do | in | short | while |
| double | instanceof | static | with |
| else | | | |

# *Appendix C*
# *HTML Entities*

HTML supports several sets of character entities. These are often used inside Web pages to produce characters which are not part of the ANSII character set. The following table lists these entities. I've shown the text string which most people use in their pages, a numerical string which is equivalent to the text one and which can be used interchangeably. I've also included a short description taken from the HTML 4 recommendation document. Where possible I've given an example of the character which the entity produces. Because this is a book not a Web page the set of characters I can show is restricted by my typesetting software.

## ISO 8859-1 Characters

| Textual Name | Numeric Name | Description | Example |
|---|---|---|---|
|   |   | non-breaking space | |
| &iexcl; | &#161; | inverted exclamation mark | ¡ |
| &cent; | &#162; | US cent | |
| &pound; | &#163; | British currency pound | £ |
| &curren; | &#164; | currency | |
| &yen; | &#165; | yen | ¥ |
| &brvbar; | &#166; | broken vertical bar | ¦ |
| &sect; | &#167; | section sign | § |
| &uml; | &#168; | diaresis | ö |

| Textual Name | Numeric Name | Description | Example |
|---|---|---|---|
| &copy; | &#169; | copyright | © |
| &ordf; | &#170; | feminine ordinal indicator | |
| &laquo; | &#171; | left double angle quotation | |
| &not; | &#172; | not sign | ¬ |
| &shy; | &#173; | soft hyphen | |
| &reg; | &#174; | registered trademark | ® |
| &macr; | &#175; | spacing macron | |
| &deg; | &#176; | degree sign | deg |
| &plusmn; | &#177; | plus or minus | ± |
| &sup2; | &#178; | superscripted 2 | $x^2$ |
| &sup3; | &#179; | superscripted 3 | $x^3$ |
| &acute; | &#180; | acute accent | |
| &micro; | &#181; | micro | $\mu$ |
| &para; | &#182; | paragraph | ¶ |
| &middot; | &#183; | middle dot | · |
| &cedil; | &#184; | cedilla | |
| &sup1; | &#185; | superscripted 1 | $x^1$ |
| &ordm; | &#186; | male ordinal indicator | |
| &raquo; | &#187; | right double angle quotation | |
| &frac14; | &#188; | fraction one quarter | $\frac{1}{4}$ |
| &frac12; | &#189; | fraction one half | $\frac{1}{2}$ |
| &frac34; | &#190; | fraction three quarters | $\frac{3}{4}$ |
| &iquest; | &#191; | inverted question mark | ¿ |
| &Agrave; | &#192; | A with grave accent | À |
| &Aacute; | &#193; | A with acute accent | Á |
| &Acirc; | &#194; | A with circumflex | Â |
| &Atilde; | &#195; | A with tilde | Ã |
| &Auml; | &#196; | A with diaresis | Ä |
| &Aring; | &#197; | A with ring | Å |
| &AElig; | &#198; | Latin capital AE | Æ |
| &Ccedil; | &#199; | C with cedilla | Ç |
| &Egrave; | &#200; | E with grave accent | È |
| &Eacute; | &#201; | E with acute accent | É |
| &Ecirc; | &#202; | E with circumflex | Ê |
| &Euml; | &#203; | E with diaresis | Ë |
| &Igrave; | &#204; | I with grave accent | Ì |
| &Iacute; | &#205; | I with acute accent | Í |
| &Icirc; | &#206; | I with circumflex | Î |

| Textual Name | Numeric Name | Description | Example |
|---|---|---|---|
| &Iuml; | &#207; | I with diaresis | Ï |
| &ETH; | &#208; | Latin capital ETH | Đ |
| &Ntilde; | &#209; | N with tilde | Ñ |
| &Ograve; | &#210; | O with grave accent | Ò |
| &Oacute; | &#211; | O with acute accent | Ó |
| &Ocirc; | &#212; | O with circumflex | Ô |
| &Otilde; | &#213; | O with tilde | Õ |
| &Ouml; | &#214; | O with diaresis | Ö |
| &times; | &#215; | multiplication sign | × |
| &Oslash; | &#216; | O with a stroke | Ø |
| &Ugrave; | &#217; | U with grave accent | Ù |
| &Uacute; | &#218; | U with acute accent | Ú |
| &Ucirc; | &#219; | U with circumflex | Û |
| &Uuml; | &#220; | U with diaresis | Ü |
| &Yacute; | &#221; | Y with acute accent | Ý |
| &THORN; | &#222; | capital THORN | Þ |
| &szlig; | &#223; | sharp s | ß |
| &agrave; | &#224; | a with grave accent | à |
| &aacute; | &#225; | a with acute accent | á |
| &acirc; | &#226; | a with circumflex | â |
| &atilde; | &#227; | a with tilde | ã |
| &auml; | &#228; | a with diaresis | ä |
| &aring; | &#229; | a with ring | å |
| &aelig; | &#230; | Latin ae | æ |
| &ccedil; | &#231; | c with cedilla | ç |
| &egrave; | &#232; | e with grave accent | è |
| &eacute; | &#233; | e with acute accent | é |
| &ecirc; | &#234; | e with circumflex | ê |
| &euml; | &#235; | e with diaresis | ë |
| &igrave; | &#236; | i with grave accent | ì |
| &iacute; | &#237; | i with acute accent | í |
| &icirc; | &#238; | i with circumflex | î |
| &iuml; | &#239; | i with diaresis | ï |
| &eth; | &#240; | Latin eth | ð |
| &ntilde; | &#241; | n with tilde | ñ |
| &ograve; | &#242; | o with grave accent | ò |
| &oacute; | &#243; | o with acute accent | ó |
| &ocirc; | &#244; | o with circumflex | ô |

| Textual Name | Numeric Name | Description | Example |
|---|---|---|---|
| &otilde; | &#245; | o with tilde | õ |
| &ouml; | &#246; | o with diaresis | ö |
| &divide; | &#247; | division sign | ÷ |
| &oslash; | &#248; | o with a stroke | ø |
| &ugrave; | &#249; | u with grave accent | ù |
| &uacute; | &#250; | u with acute accent | ú |
| &ucirc; | &#251; | u with circumflex | û |
| &uuml; | &#252; | u with diaresis | ü |
| &yacute; | &#253; | u with acute accent | ú |
| &thorn; | &#254; | lowercase thorn | þ |
| &yuml; | &#255; | y with diaresis | ÿ |

## Symbols, Mathematical Symbols and Greek Letters

| Textual Name | Numeric Name | Description | Example |
|---|---|---|---|
| &fnof; | &#402; | small Latin f | |
| &Alpha; | &#913; | capital alpha | |
| &Beta; | &#914; | capital beta | |
| &Gamma; | &#915; | capital gamma | Γ |
| &Delta; | &#916; | capital delta | Δ |
| &Epsilon; | &#917; | capital epsilon | |
| &Zeta; | &#918; | capital zeta | |
| &Eta; | &#919; | capital eta | |
| &Theta; | &#920; | capital theta | Θ |
| &Iota; | &#921; | capital iota | |
| &Kappa; | &#922; | capital kappa | |
| &Lambda; | &#923; | capital lambda | Λ |
| &Mu; | &#924; | capital mu | |
| &Nu; | &#925; | capital nu | |
| &Xi; | &#926; | capital xi | Ξ |
| &Omicron; | &#927; | capital omicron | |
| &Pi; | &#928; | capital pi | Π |
| &Rho; | &#929; | capital rho | |
| &Sigma; | &#931; | capital sigma | Σ |
| &Tau; | &#932; | capital tau | |
| &Upsilon; | &#933; | capital upsilon | Υ |
| &Phi; | &#934; | capital phi | Φ |

| Textual Name | Numeric Name | Description | Example |
|---|---|---|---|
| &Chi; | &#935; | capital chi | |
| &Psi; | &#936; | capital psi | Ψ |
| &Omega; | &#937; | capital omega | Ω |
| &alpha; | &#945; | small letter alpha | α |
| &beta; | &#946; | small letter beta | β |
| &gamma; | &#947; | small letter gamma | γ |
| &delta; | &#948; | small letter delta | δ |
| &epsilon; | &#949; | small letter epsilon | ε |
| &zeta; | &#950; | small letter zeta | ζ |
| &eta; | &#951; | small letter eta | η |
| &theta; | &#952; | small letter theta | θ |
| &iota; | &#953; | small letter iota | ι |
| &kappa; | &#954; | small letter kappa | κ |
| &lambda; | &#955; | small letter lambda | λ |
| &mu; | &#956; | small letter mu | μ |
| &nu; | &#957; | small letter nu | ν |
| &xi; | &#958; | small letter xi | ξ |
| &omicron; | &#959; | small letter omicron | |
| &pi; | &#960; | small letter pi | π |
| &rho; | &#961; | small letter rho | ρ |
| &sigmaf; | &#962; | small letter sigmaf | |
| &sigma; | &#963; | small letter sigma | σ |
| &tau; | &#964; | small letter tau | τ |
| &upsilon; | &#965; | small letter upsilon | υ |
| &phi; | &#966; | small letter phi | φ |
| &chi; | &#967; | small letter chi | χ |
| &psi; | &#968; | small letter psi | ψ |
| &omega; | &#969; | small letter omega | ω |
| &thetasym; | &#977; | small letter theta | θ |
| &upsih; | &#978; | greek upsilon with hook | |
| &piv; | &#982; | pi | π |
| &bull; | &#8226; | bullet | • |
| &hellip; | &#8230; | horizontal ellipses | … |
| &prime; | &#8242; | prime/minutes/feet symbol | ′ |
| &Prime; | &#8243; | double prime/seconds/inches symbol | ″ |
| &oline; | &#8254; | overline | |
| &frasl; | &#8260; | fraction slash | / |
| &weierp; | &#8472; | script capital p | ℘ |

| Textual Name | Numeric Name | Description | Example |
|---|---|---|---|
| &image; | &#8465; | blackletter I | ℑ |
| &real; | &#8476; | blackletter R | ℜ |
| &trade; | &#8482; | trademark symbol | |
| &alefsym; | &#8501; | alef symbol | ℵ |
| &larr; | &#8592; | leftwards arrow | ← |
| &uarr; | &#8593; | upwards arrow | ↑ |
| &rarr; | &#8594; | rightwards arrow | → |
| &darr; | &#8595; | downwards arrow | ↓ |
| &harr; | &#8596; | left right arrow | ↔ |
| &crarr; | &#8629; | down arror with corner left | |
| &lArr; | &#8656; | double left arrow | ⇐ |
| &uArr; | &#8557; | double upwards arrow | ⇑ |
| &rArr; | &#8558; | double rightwards arrow | ⇒ |
| &dArr; | &#8559; | double downwards arrow | ⇓ |
| &hArr; | &#8560; | double left right arrow | ⇔ |
| &forall; | &#8704; | for all | ∀ |
| &part; | &#8706; | partial differential | ∂ |
| &exists; | &#8707; | there exists | ∃ |
| &empty; | &#8709; | empty set | ∅ |
| &nabla; | &#8711; | backward difference | ∇ |
| &isin; | &#8712; | element of | ∈ |
| &notin; | &#8713; | not an element of | ∉ |
| &ni; | &#8715; | contains as member | ∋ |
| &prod; | &#8719; | n-ary product | |
| &sum; | &#8721; | n-ary summation | ∑ |
| &minus; | &#8722; | minus sign | − |
| &lowast; | &#8727; | asterix operator | ∗ |
| &radic; | &#8730; | square root | √ |
| &prop; | &#8733; | proportional to | ∝ |
| &infin; | &#8734; | infinity | ∞ |
| &ang; | &#8736; | angle | ∠ |
| &and; | &#8743; | logical and | |
| &or; | &#8744; | logical or | |
| &cap; | &#8745; | intersection | ∩ |
| &cup; | &#8746; | union | ∪ |
| &int; | &#8747; | integral | ∫ |
| &there4; | &#8756; | therefore | |
| &sim; | &#8764; | tilde operator | |

| Textual Name | Numeric Name | Description | Example |
|---|---|---|---|
| &cong; | &#8773; | approximately equal to | ≅ |
| &asymp; | &#8776; | almost equal to | ≈ |
| &ne; | &#8800; | not equal to | ≠ |
| &equiv; | &#8801; | idemtical to | ≡ |
| &le; | &#8804; | less than or equal to | ≤ |
| &ge; | &#8805; | greater than or equal to | ≥ |
| &sub; | &#8834; | subset of | ⊂ |
| &sup; | &#8835; | superset of | ⊃ |
| &nsub; | &#8836; | not a subset of | ⊄ |
| &sube; | &#8838; | subset of or equal to | ⊆ |
| &supe; | &#8839; | superset of or equal to | ⊇ |
| &oplus; | &#8853; | circled plus | ⊕ |
| &otimes; | &#8855; | circled times | ⊗ |
| &perp; | &#8869; | perpendicular to | ⊥ |
| &sdot; | &#8901; | dot operator | · |
| &lceil; | &#8968; | left ceiling | |
| &rceil; | &#8969; | right ceiling | |
| &lfloor; | &#8970; | left floor | |
| &rfloor; | &#8971; | right floor | |
| &lang; | &#9001; | left pointing angle bracket | |
| &rang; | &#9002; | right pointing angle bracket | |
| &loz; | &#9674; | lozenge shape | ◇ |
| &spades; | &#9824; | spade suit | ♠ |
| &clubs; | &#9827; | clubs suit | ♣ |
| &hearts; | &#9829; | heart suit | ♡ |
| &diamonds; | &#9830; | diamond suit | ◇ |

## Markup-significant Characters

| Entity Textual Name | Entity Numeric Name | Description | Example |
|---|---|---|---|
| &quot; | &#34; | Quotation mark | " |
| &amp; | &#38; | Ampersand | & |
| &lt; | &#60; | Less than sign | < |
| &gt; | &#62; | Greater than sign | > |
| &OElig; | &#338; | Latin capital ligature OE | Œ |
| &oelig; | &#339; | Latin small ligature oe | œ |
| &Scaron; | &#352; | Capital S with caron | Š |

| Entity Textual Name | Entity Numeric Name | Description | Example |
|---|---|---|---|
| &scaron; | &#353; | Small letter s with caron | š |
| &Yuml; | &#376; | Capital Y with diaresis | Ÿ |
| &circ; | &#710; | Modified cirumflex accent | |
| &tilde; | &#732; | Small tilde | |
|   |   | En space | |
|   |   | Em space | |
|   |   | Thin space | |
| &zwnj; | &#8204; | Zero width non-joiner | |
| &zwj; | &#8205; | Zero width joiner | |
| &lrm; | &#8206; | Left to right mark | |
| &rlm; | &#8207; | Right to left mark | |
| &ndash; | &#8211; | En dash | – |
| &mdash; | &#8212; | Em dash | — |
| &lsquo; | &#8216; | Left single quotation mark | ' |
| &rsquo; | &#8217; | Right single quotation mark | ' |
| &sbquo; | &#8218; | Single low-9 quotation mark | , |
| &ldquo; | &#8220; | Left double quotation mark | " |
| &rdquo; | &#8221; | Right double quotation mark | " |
| &bdquo; | &#8222; | Double low-9 quotation mark | „ |
| &dagger; | &#8224; | Dagger | † |
| &Dagger; | &#8225; | Double dagger | ‡ |
| &permil; | &#8240; | Per mille sign | |
| &lsaquo; | &#8249; | Left angle quotation mark | « |
| &rsaquo; | &#8250; | Right angle quotation mark | » |
| &euro; | &#8364; | Euro symbol | |

# Index